Sports for

Women

THIRD EDITION

Illustrated by VIRGINIA DIX STERLING

PHILADELPHIA · LONDON

W. B. SAUNDERS COMPANY

Reprinted, October, 1956

MADE IN U. S. A.
Press of W. B. Saunders Company, Philadelphia

LIBRARY OF CONGRESS CATALOG CARD NUMBER: 55-6335

• Foreword •

The first edition of Individual Sports for Women was published during World War II, in the year 1943. At that time strong emphasis was placed upon activities for physical fitness. But it is interesting to note that even in those days of training activities and obstacle courses, programs of individual sports were expanded rather than curtailed. The greatest difficulty faced by those engaged in organizing sports programs in schools and colleges during the war years was the shortage of supplies and equipment. The volume of production of racquets, balls, and other sports equipment was decreased, and the demand by the armed forces for these articles made it almost impossible to secure adequate supplies for civilian use. The armed forces, interestingly enough, organized broadly varied programs of sports activities for enlisted personnel and officers along with the grueling conditioning activities so necessary in time of war.

The second edition of this book was published in 1949, during the postwar period.

The third edition appears at a time when the strongest emphasis in education, physical education included, is upon education for social living in a democratic society. Physical education holds a strategic position at this time. There is growing recognition of the great values relating to social living which are inherent in the sports program, especially in the individual and dual sports. Social efficiency is considered essential to rich and full living, to growing into maturity. The young woman who has grown up as the sort of person who must make such excuses as "I'm sorry, I don't play tennis," or "No, I never did learn to swim," or "I don't dance well" becomes a social liability. To be socially efficient, one needs to develop certain recreational skills—the skills comprising sports activities. These are social as well as neuromuscular skills. Schools and colleges today provide the best possible opportunities for girls and young women to learn sports skills. Those in the field of physical education make great efforts to provide facilities and leadership for broad sports experience. Tennis courts, golf courses, swimming pools, and riding rings become more and more a part of the college plant.

This book is intended to serve teachers of girls and women in schools, colleges, and other agencies providing recreational programs. The writers are women of long and varied experience, each an expert in one or more specific areas of sport. The materials presented here should prove to be of tremendous value to all teachers of physical education, but especially to young teachers in the field.

RUTH EVANS
*Director of Physical Education for Women
and Counselor for Women,
Springfield College*

Springfield, Massachusetts

Preface to
• The Third Edition •

The third edition of Individual Sports for Women has two new authors. They are Miss Helen Russell and Miss Marjorie Harris, who have contributed the chapters on badminton and bowling, respectively. The change occurred because the former authors, Mrs. Goss and Mrs. Pitkin, have married and are no longer in the teaching field. The other authors have all rewritten their chapters, adding new and interesting material. The revisions and additions include current material and new ideas which will make the book more useful and valuable.

At the Washington Conference on Physical Education for College Men and Women, held in October of 1954, individual sports held a very favorable place in the discussion of the program. Their value for adults both during and after college was cited. Co-recreation was strongly recommended, and opinion indicated that dual and individual sports were particularly well adapted for this part of the program. The value of these games in community and family living was also noted, and it was argued that skills in individual sports acquired in school and college would increase the use and enjoyment of sports in adult life.

The ideas expressed at the Washington Conference strengthen the conviction of the authors of this book that individual sports hold a most important place in the physical education program for girls and women. This conviction stems not only from faculty ideas on the subject, but much more from the very real popularity of these games with school and college girls and boys. The girls want to learn more of something which they can continue to use in their free time. They wish to play *better* tennis, golf or badminton. They want to play (and play well) with boys as well as with girls. They also know that it is much easier to find a partner for an impromptu game for two than to collect a whole team, enjoyable as team sports are. A girl can even take a swim, ride, practice a golf swing, or shoot a round of archery without a special partner. Skill in and enjoyment of one of these sports in college may be a source of lifelong pleasure.

Because of their interest in individual sports, students should be given every opportunity to improve their play and should have not only adequate but good coaching. Their teachers should be well trained. The students' interest is such that they will work hard and really struggle to improve even as they are enjoying the game. The girls are so interested that the classes cannot hold them all and many have to be turned away. Even so, the girls come back again and again hoping for a chance to enter a class in their favorite game.

More teachers and more good teachers of individual sports are needed. This book is written for such teachers to give a clear description and useful methods of teaching individual sports. The book is also written for the sportswoman and other players who like to know more of their favorite games and who wish to improve their performance through a better understanding of the techniques and various plays.

To teachers, students, and all players, we wish continued pleasure in these great sports. We hope that the games and the teaching continue to improve and that this book will serve both teacher and player well.

DOROTHY S. AINSWORTH

Northampton, Massachusetts

• Contents •

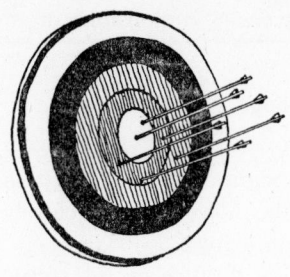

1 • ARCHERY • BY *Florence M. Ryder*

Archery has unusual charm and the actual ability acquired in the sport can be enjoyed for many years after school and college. In addition, it may correct standing posture and bearing of the archer so that there are related benefits as well as pleasure for the participant. For students with certain physical handicaps, archery is a sport which offers a safe field for competition and recreation.

Many books and articles have been written presenting the fascinating history of archery, describing the sport both as a means of self-preservation and as a means of recreation. Usually most novices are not interested in these historical facts until they have become somewhat proficient in the sport itself. However, something can be done to stimulate such an interest by presenting a summary of the place archery has taken in the sports history of the United States. References can be given and further interest thus aroused. If the instructor is well versed in the historical and romantic side of archery, she will easily influence her group to explore the past records as well as the present trends in this sport. An abbreviated list at the end of the chapter contains only a few of the many excellent references available for more detailed information on archery. All in all archery has had and will continue to have an established and deservedly popular place in physical education and recreation programs in schools and colleges.

RANGE AND EQUIPMENT

Before the actual teaching of archery can be discussed, we must turn to other important considerations. The question of *laying out of the range* must be studied. Included in this are matters of safety, correct

1

lighting, ground covering, dimensions of the field, and range equipment.

I. Laying Out of Range

(A) *Safety.*

1. THE BACKSTOP—BEHIND THE TARGETS (FOR SAFETY AND TIME SAVING).

(*a*) Most desirable: A well-turfed, closely cropped terrace or hill is the ideal backstop for arrows.

(*b*) Less desirable: 1. Bunkers of straw placed well back in the field. 2. Burlap curtains (at least two) hung one at a 10-yard interval behind the other, braced at either end by posts made of soft wood to prevent arrow breakage.

(*c*) Least desirable: An open, unused space, 25 to 30 yards behind the target line. (If no bunker or backstop is available, an additional 25 yards behind the targets is necessary. This area should be kept well mowed.)

2. PROTECTION AT SIDES OF RANGE TO PREVENT CROSSING.

(*a*) Barberry hedging is a desirable safety measure for the sides of the range. This may be planted from the shooting line to a point 10 yards behind the target line if an open space is behind the targets.

(*b*) This same area may be roped off to prevent people from strolling across the range.

(*c*) White lines can indicate the enclosure but are the least desirable as a safety measure.

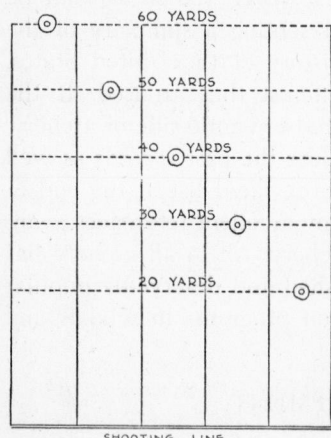

Fig. 1. Staggered ranges for safe method of shooting.

3. ONE SHOOTING LINE FOR ALL ARCHERS USING RANGE. Staggering of targets has been practiced in some situations where individual anchors for targets are used. With secure individual anchoring, targets may be moved up or down the field, allowing all archers to shoot from the same line, regardless of their distance from their individual targets. Figure 1 illustrates such an arrangement.

(B) *Correct Lighting.*

1. For morning shooting only, targets should be at the western end of the field.

2. For afternoon shooting only, targets should be at the eastern end of the field.

3. For all day shooting, targets should be at the northern end of the field.

(C) *Ground Covering.*

1. Good turf, well cropped and well raked to prevent loss of arrows. All stones removed.

2. Good drainage most essential.

(D) *Dimensions of Range for Girls and Women.*

1. LENGTH.

(*a*) The 60 yards of the National and American rounds and the 50 yards of the Columbia round necessitate having the range at least 65 yards long.

(*b*) If there is space and men are to use the range, there should be at least one lane of 100 yards in length.

2. WIDTH. Width of minimum range for one target is 6 yards; allow 3 yards between targets.

3. POSSIBLE SPACE FOR RANGES. The given dimensions are for actual length of range from farthest shooting line to the targets.

	Width	Length	No. of Targets	Yards for Each lane
Fair range	24 yds.	50 yds.	4	4
Good range	60 yds.	60 yds.	6	5
Excellent range	100 yds.	100 yds.	10	6

4. LAYING OUT OF INDOOR RANGE.

(*a*) Dimensions. At least 35 yards in length, 20 yards in width, and 9 feet in height, thus sufficient for Olympic round.

(*b*) Safety and prevention of arrow breakage.

1. A backstop, behind the targets, may be made of strips of loosely hung burlap, light carpets, or felt, or of bales of straw.

2. No approach to this end of the shooting area should be left unlocked.

(E) *Equipment for Range.*

1. Stationary quivers are placed directly opposite each target. These are placed on each shooting line (i.e., at 30, 40, and 50 yards from the target). These quivers should be set up just forward of the archer's stance at the shooting line.

2. Movable quivers may be used on either side of the stationary quiver.

3. Target and target stands, described under "Tackle" on page 7.

4. Bow stands and arrow racks for storage of tackle between classes, described on pages 5 and 6.

5. Bow racks, with a spiked end, are capable of accommodating at least four bows.

II. Archery Tackle

Archery equipment, technically called *archery tackle,* includes various types of bows, arrows, and accessories. A bow, 6 to 8 arrows adapted to the use of that particular bow and to the individual's specifications, an arm guard, shooting tab or glove and, if needed, a movable quiver, should be provided for each archer.

The initial expense of the tackle may seem large, but if considered on a basis of the number of archers using it, it is relatively inexpensive. If the instructor insists that the equipment receive good care, if she teaches correct form, and if she requires immediate minor repairs, the upkeep of the equipment is relatively small. The tackle provided should serve a class of from ten to fifteen. It is well to remember that good tackle, though not cheap, will outlast the poorer, less expensive equipment. Also it is wise to find a dependable tackle maker and continue to work in cooperation with him.

BOWS

There should be *at least* one bow on hand for each student in a class. As an adequate number for an average class of fifteen students, it is wise to provide twenty bows from which to choose. If financially practical, thirty bows will give a more accurate choice.

Material. Most authorities agree that lemonwood bows are best for class use. Osage, popular in the West, is somewhat more expensive, but otherwise similar to lemonwood. Recently Fiberglas bows have been introduced successfully in some situations. For school, camp or club use, they may remain too expensive except for private ownership. The same appears to be true of reflex and semi-reflex bows, which are becoming more popular at present. However, the trend is away from yew bows and toward composite bows with Fiberglas or plastic for backing.

Lengths. Select a very few 5-foot bows, a few 5-foot 3-inch bows, and a majority of 5-foot 6-inch bows. It is becoming increasingly common among manufacturers to make all bows of the same length and suitable for a 27-inch arrow. This eliminates breakage by overdrawing. Also a bow which draws 24 pounds at 27 inches will draw considerably less at 24 inches, thus giving a wider variation in drawing weight. Shorter bows are certainly more desirable for younger girls. The bows for such a group may be ordered on the basis of the average height of the group. Individually, of course, it is wise to own a bow approximately equal in length to one's own height.

Weights. Depending on the average strength of the students in the group, 18–28 pounds pull is a good average range in weight, with the majority around 22 pounds. 18 to 22 pounds should be provided for beginners; 20 to 24 for intermediates; 24 to 28 for advanced archers. It may be well to allow beginners to use lighter bows until good form is achieved.

Handles. Those affording long wear and good grips are of cordovan leather. Cord or cork are also acceptable.

Other requisites. A new bow should be examined for even and equal bend in both limbs from nocks to handle; return to nearly straight outline when unstrung; equal division of the entire length of the belly when the bow is strung; smoothly grooved nocks.

BOW-STRINGS

Extra strings, equaling in number at least the bows used, should be ordered and kept in a tin box. It is occasionally difficult and expensive to obtain good linen strings, but synthetic strings of Fortisan or Dacron stand up very well under hard use. These should be light in weight, well waxed and have good servings. They may be ordered either in lengths to fit bows purchased or in 6-foot strings adjustable at the lower nock to the various bow lengths. Strings should be strong enough to prevent constant breakage, which slows up shooting time. A small knot of thread should be placed on the serving to mark the spot at which the archer nocks his arrow. The knot should be placed so that the arrow is at right angles to the string as its nock rests against this knot.

KEEPERS

For keeping the upper loop of the bow-string from dropping down the bow too far and from getting tangled up with other strings in carrying bows to and from the range, we have found broad elastic bands to be best. These are strong and easily replaced if broken or mislaid. The least expensive way to buy the rubber bands is in 1-pound boxes. Strong but light-weight tape may be substituted, but is not so satisfactory.

BOW STANDS

Stands or racks can be purchased or made locally and will vary widely in price. Each should accommodate 12 bows on either side. The number of bows used daily will determine the number of racks needed for class use. These stands are similar in appearance to a portable coat rack. They can be made easily and according to specific directions by the school or local carpenter. They should be light enough to be moved comfortably and supplied with canvas bands or other supports at the top so the bows will not be blown off between classes. Hooks at each end are useful for arm guards, gloves, and tabs. These racks are for daily class use. The storage of bows is discussed on page 9.

Where transportation of equipment requires time and energy, an archery cart on small wheels may assist in the facility of handling tackle. It can be made to hold all equipment needed on the range with the exception of the targets. Such a cart is adequately described in an article in the Journal of the American Association for Health, Physical Education and Recreation, March 1954.

ARROWS
Required number

Fair	Good	Excellent
72 (6 doz.)	144 (12 doz.)	240 (20 doz.)

Material. Most authorities agree that for the hard usage that school or club equipment receives, Port Orford cedar or Norwegian pine is the most acceptable and satisfactory wood for self arrows. They are usually 5/16 of an inch in diameter. If the price is a consideration, divide the amount allotted to arrows between good cedar arrows of the dowel variety and run of the mill quality. Matched arrows should have a footing, either of two or four point variety, which increases greatly the life of the arrows. Aluminum arrows have become increasingly popular. Wood and metal arrows are both sold in matched sets with great variation in price. Matched sets are preferable but in many situations are probably best for personal rather than school or club purchase. There is no doubt that matched sets improve scoring and thus reduce discouragement, so it may be wise progressively to increase the number of matching sets for a given situation. They should be guaranteed to be range or flight tested, or to have accurate technical specifications as to spine and weight in grains, and balance point of the completed arrow.

Economy of purchase. The best method of purchasing arrows is to buy them in lots of 2, 4, or 6 dozens in sets of 8.

Lengths. 22- to 24-inch arrows are necessary for short-armed girls who use shorter bows. 25-inch arrows are a good average. 26-inch arrows are much in demand. 27-inch arrows are for taller, longer armed girls who use longer bows.

Markings. If practical, arrows may be labeled as to length with India ink and the mark then covered with lacquer. This facilitates correct choice and also accurate replacement after use.

Other requisites. Samples of arrows presented for approval or rejection should be examined closely, but more important to the instructor is the fulfillment of her order by the tackle-maker according to given specifications. A new order should be examined for:

FINISH AND CREST. A lacquered, well-polished arrow withstands use and weather well. Lacquer is preferable to varnish because it stays cleaner. A brightly colored crest helps to locate lost arrows and thus decreases scoring and retrieving time. The crest also establishes the identity of ownership.

STRAIGHT, ROUND SHAFT. The shaft must be completely round and straight as one looks down its length.

NOCKS. The material used for nocks varies with the tackle-maker, but replaceable nocks are commonly used. Some form of reinforcing at the nock increases the length of life of the arrow.

FEATHERS. Feathers should be checked from the nock end to see if the feathers are placed symmetrically, if the cock feather is at right angles to the nock, and if all three feathers are perpendicular to the shaft. The type of vane varies with the fletcher but has little effect on accuracy. The feathers are commonly slightly spiraled on the shaft.

PILE. The pile or tip is the covered point of the arrow and is important on two counts. It should be of the parallel type and must be strongly attached.

ARROW RACKS

A rack, approximately 40 by 28 inches, holding at least 12 individual sets of 8 arrows each, may be made by the local carpenter and seems the best way of storing arrows. The rack is also an easy means of transporting the arrows to the shooting range from the equipment room. There should be twelve lines of holes, ½ inch in diameter, bored at 3-inch intervals, eight in a line across the width of the rack. This is duplicated by a second level, 10 inches below the first and 6 inches above the base, with identical holes bored directly below those on the upper surface. Below the two levels is the base upon which are rows of matching cups placed directly below the holes to receive the arrow tips. Such an arrangement keeps the arrows neatly in place in their own sets. To have end handles on such racks makes carrying easier and these handles can be marked at 6-inch intervals so that string-to-handle distance can be measured by them. Each arrow set should be marked at the end of its row by a bit of adhesive tape on which is written with indelible pencil the length of that arrow set.

QUIVERS

There are four usable types. On the range a *stationary quiver* is placed opposite to each target at each shooting line. Wooden stakes painted green are sunk in the earth far enough for good support. A wire ring for arrows and a wire hook for the bow are attached to the stake. Iron *movable ground quivers* are also practical and may be bought reasonably. These should have tight fitting rubber tubing around the bow hook or other means of holding the bow without damage. This type can be made easily and inexpensively from wire coat hangers, with the aid of a pair of pliers, and bound with friction tape. *Movable indoor quivers* are often made of cardboard tubing or bamboo mounted on a square of wood so that they may stand alone for indoor shooting. *Leather wearable quivers* can be worn on the belt for roving, clout shooting, archery golf, and rabbit hunts. Such quivers may be bought at varying costs.

Other suggestions. Cardboard mailing tubes sealed with large corks, mounted squares of synthetic fiber or large open-mouthed jars may be used as substitutes if budget curtailment is necessary.

TARGETS AND TARGET STANDS

Regulation 4-foot targets approximately 50 inches in diameter are required. They should be about 4 to 5 inches thick of roped straw well bound and sewed spirally. Cheap targets are not economical. When targets have been shot thin, they may be reinforced with a backing of 4 or 5 layers of ordinary corrugated paper from large packing cartons. A stiff backing, such as heavy cardboard or building board, supports the target when placed behind it. This prevents the typical sagging of the target on the stand.

Stands can be made locally also and thus vary widely in price. The regulation standard consists of 3 soft pine boards, 3 inches wide by 1 inch thick and 6 feet long. The lower end of each of the 3 boards should be cut at a slight angle to act as a ground spike. A 4-inch bolt through holes bored at the upper ends of the uprights holds them together. Lengths of rope to keep the tripod from spreading apart are valuable aids in setting out the targets. Three hooks are generally used on the tripod, 1 at the top to receive the target above, and 1 for each of the 2 front legs, about 3 feet 9 inches from the top, on which to rest the target. *The center of the gold should measure 48 to 54 inches from the ground.* The legs of the tripod should be covered with discarded bicycle tires painted green. This removes some of the necessity of withdrawing arrows from the legs of the standard, as most arrows will rebound from the rubber. It also increases the length of life of the tripod itself. As substitutes for rubber, lengths of burlap or of corrugated paper painted green may be used. It is wise to tie the target stand securely to the ground by the use of rope and ground hooks. This prevents its tipping over accidentally or from wind and thus prevents arrow breakage.

TARGET FACES

Faces should be preferably of light canvas or sized muslin painted with a gold or yellow center 9.6 inches in diameter surrounded by 4 concentric circles each 4.8 inches wide. The outside edge beyond the white outer ring should be at least 1 inch in width and is known as the "petticoat."

FINGER PROTECTION

Finger protection varies with the individual archer, but protection must be provided for any amount of shooting. A shooting *glove* is efficient but relatively expensive for class use. Light, smooth Cordovan *leather finger tabs* may be purchased or inexpensively made. Such tabs may also be cut from a discarded inner tube. *Tips* cut to fit individual shooting fingers are usually made of light smooth leather and are cooler to wear than a glove or tab. A glove's 3 middle fingers may be reinforced by stitching on durable but pliable leather tips. Shooting gloves should be marked with the athletic association's mark or some other form of identification to prevent inadvertent removal from the range.

ARM GUARDS

Arm guards or bracers should be of thick pliable leather, 7 to 8 inches long and either laced to encircle the forearm or made strip-like and buckled on. These also should be marked for identification purposes. One should be provided for each archer.

REPAIR KIT

A compact repair kit should contain pliers for pulling out embedded arrows from trees; beeswax; box for extra bow-strings; Duco cement and wax; scissors; jack-knife; heavy linen thread for servings; pen and indelible ink; ½-inch wide adhesive tape; glass headed pins if sights are to be used; 6-inch ruler; bits of leather for rubbing bows and strings after waxing.

FIRST AID KIT

This part of the equipment is very seldom needed but occasionally it is very necessary. The box should include Band-aids, adhesive of all widths, iodine, rubbing alcohol, aromatic spirits of ammonia, gauze swabs, tweezers for removing splinters, tincture of benzoin for finger blisters, scissors.

SCORE CARDS

Two types of cards, daily tally cards and tournament record cards, are used. If there are many enrolled, the score cards can be multigraphed and pasted on cardboard for each target for each section. This is not so satisfactory to the individual archer, however, and should be avoided if possible. To keep the individual score cards from blowing away, the students usually hook them on the bow hooks of their stance quivers. The cardboard group record may be kept in possession of one named scorer for each target or tied to the back of the targets by the instructor before class. Unused score cards may be left in a box, while labeled and used ones for each section may be clipped or bound together.

BOX FOR MISCELLANEOUS EQUIPMENT

A neat compartment box can be made, approximately 20 by 18 inches, which can accommodate all the necessary "extras." This should eliminate the forgetting of some bit of equipment needed on the range. The arrangement of the compartments would be based on the size of the things to be stored therein: points of aim, extra bow-strings, keepers, pencils, pliers, and score cards.

QUIVER RACKS

If many movable metal quivers are used, a rack to support them is worth having for neatness in the equipment room. Such a rack can be made of two endboards connected at the base and top. The base should have a deep curb to prevent the points from slipping out and the top should have two 1-inch slots to catch and hold the rings of the quivers.

III. Archery Tackle Room

The room known as the Tackle Room should be the meeting place of advanced archers and beginners as well. The dimensions of an adequate room are 6 feet in width by 12 feet in length by 9 feet in height. Three wide shelves may occupy the full length of one side, leaving wall space for the hanging of the bows on two of the other walls. The bottom shelf should be high enough so the arrow racks may stand below it. The shelves may hold boxes for "extras," a box for arrows in need of repair, special equipment, such as box targets for archery golf, and quivers. In order that an archer may exit with both hands full, the door should be equipped with an automatic closing, so a door stop is also necessary. There should be sufficient space for a bulletin board and the daily "scoring" target at the end of the row of stored bows. The temperature should be kept as nearly at 65 degrees as possible, and a humidifier should be used to keep the bows from drying out. No radiator is needed within the room itself although it should be well ventilated. In summer the arrows should be covered and kept in a dry room with moth balls to protect the feathers. The wall bow rack may be constructed by using a series of rubber-covered pegs consecutively placed and about 6 feet from the floor. The distance between pegs is 8 inches. Above each peg should be a bit of adhesive tape with its number lettered on with indelible pencil. Each bow should be marked in a similar manner with the identical number of its peg. The bows should be classified from the lightest to the heaviest and a bow may be reclassified whenever it loses cast. If there is no provision made for hanging the shooting gloves and tabs and arm guards on the field bow racks, there should be boxes for them placed within easy reach. The repair kit does not have to be taken to the range each day, but it should be kept adequately filled during the shooting season. The miscellaneous equipment box should be on the shelf ready for the instructor of the first class of the day. If such is not used, the "extras" should be taken out individually by the first instructor of the day and returned by the last one.

CLASSES

I. Size and Caliber of Classes

In planning the actual teaching of archery, one must determine the number of students in one class somewhat by the number of targets, bows, and arrows available. But from the point of view of the number who will learn most in one hour from one instructor, it is obvious that a small group is preferable. Ten girls for a like number of targets is ideal and it is wise to provide not fewer than 5 targets for 15 archers. Interest should not be discouraged, however, as a larger number can be handled. The course can be greatly aided by the assistance of the advanced archers in the student body. In both schools and colleges, these student coaches can help in instructing and increase their own interest in the sport by so doing.

As in the other sports the classes should be arranged according to the varying ability and experience of the students. The novice or *beginners* classes should be separate from those for intermediates, if possible. *Intermediate* archers are those who have had the ground work in elementary form and enough shooting experience to be placed beyond the novice group. Usually the classes have to be of mixed caliber, of necessity, but the instructor should have beginners as well as intermediates cover material planned for a given week. Instructions also for the *advanced* archers, those with superior ability and previous experience in the sport, follow on pages 33-37.

II. Other Considerations for Instructors in Arranging Classes

(A) The allotment of free time on the range for practice and competition.

(B) The arrangement for class meetings indoors on rainy days when lectures, movies, and demonstrations of use and care of equipment can be given, if no indoor range is provided.

(C) The stressing of safe conduct of all the class—i.e., all shooting at once, the recovery of arrows at one time, proper use of equipment, and so forth.

(D) The checking of the equipment by the instructor after each class and the replacing of this in good order and condition—i.e., seeing that the bows are unstrung, the arrows are clean, the keeper on each bow is replaced, and that no frayed strings are used.

(E) The reporting of any breakage or loss of equipment and the putting aside of anything which needs repairs.

Having considered these preliminary steps, we may now turn to the actual teaching of archery. Outlines for a suggested 8 weeks' course of 16 lessons for beginners, intermediates, and advanced archers are presented. The lesson period is planned for 50-minute duration. The schedule is elastic and should be adapted to varying conditions according to the ability and progress within the group. Detailed explanations may be found directly after the outlines.

SUGGESTED OUTLINES FOR CLASS PROCEDURES DURING CLEAR WEATHER

I. Beginners

(A) *First Week.*

1. Bows already braced for number of beginners in each class.
2. Instructor's choice of tackle for each student.
3. Teaching of parts of bow and arrow, names of miscellaneous equipment.
4. Elementary care of all equipment.
5. Stressing of safety.
6. Practice in fundamental positions without tackle and with tackle.
7. Shooting at 20-yard range, or possibly at 15 yards.

(B) *Second Week.*

1. Checking by instructor of tackle chosen.
2. Reviewing of parts.
3. Practice in stringing and unstringing bow.
4. Explanation of point of aim, the range finder and adjustment nec-essary to correct point of aim.
5. Shooting at 20-yard range; at 30 yards if ready.
6. Demonstration of retrieving arrows, from target; from grass.
7. Corrections of individuals' points of aim.
8. Lesson in scoring.

(C) *Third Week.*

1. Review of point of aim method and use of range finder.
2. Explanation of use of bow sight (optional).
3. Shooting at 30-yard range in unison and remaining ends under observation. (Shooting time divided between 20- and 30-yard ranges.)
4. Correction of off-center groupings.

(D) *Fourth Week.*

1. Taking and discussion of photographs in groups of three.
2. Working in pairs with correction of partner's form while shooting trial end at 40 yards.
3. Explanation of individual faults by instructor. See page 30.

(E) *Fifth Week.*

1. Starting of the daily ladder tournament.
2. Shooting of at least two ends at 50 yards.

(F) *Sixth Week.*

1. Beginning of the first Columbia round.
2. Individual coaching of those needing more attention.

(G) *Seventh Week.*

1. Recording of the first Columbia round in two days.
2. Continuation of ladder tournament.

(H) *Eighth Week.*

1. Challenge tournament for those below the finalists.
2. Announcement of class winners in various sections.

The eight weeks' plan presented above will be considered in detail.

(A) *First Week.*

1. Two wise procedures are to have the bows braced beforehand by the instructor and to use arrows longer than necessary to draw to anchor point. Those extra bows not used by the class should be quickly unstrung by the instructor.

2. As the class lines up according to height, the instructor can readily pick out the length and weight of the bow and length of arrow

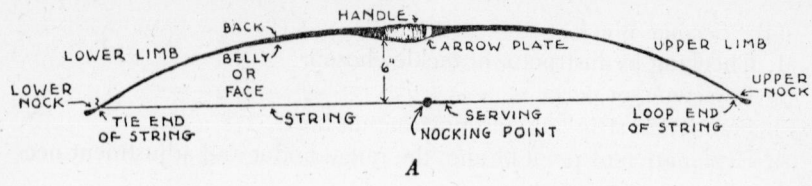

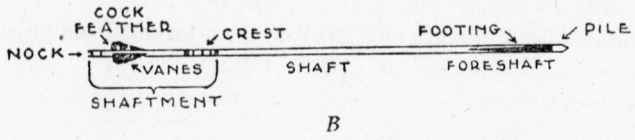

Fig. 2. *A*, parts of the bow. *B*, parts of the arrow.

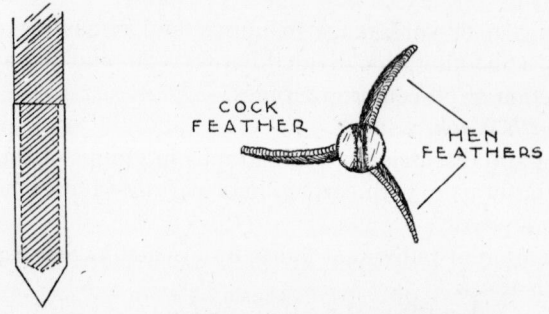

Fig. 3. *A*, parallel pile. *B*, spacing of feathers.

adaptable to each. This is accomplished by judging the girl's strength so that she may not be "over-bowed." The length of arrow is measured from the center of the chin, with the head turned to the left, to her left fist, raised to the side at shoulder level with the left elbow almost extended. An arm guard and finger protection of some sort should be fitted also. As the equipment is given out, the instructor can quickly state the reasons for the weight and length of bow and length of arrows for each student and the meaning of the weight of bow.

3. Teaching the parts of the bow and arrow (upper and lower limbs, back, belly, nocks, arrow plate; pile, shaft, foreshaft, shaftment, crest) as well as the adjustment of finger and forearm protection, comes next. (Figs. 2 and 3.)

4. Instruction in the correct handling and care of tackle should include emphasis on its beauty and its cost. Besides the admonitions about the bow, stressed in the safety rules, students should be taught to:

(*a*) Avoid dropping or leaning on the bow, as well as shooting with the bow over- or under-strung, or with the string twisted.

(*b*) Rest the bow rather than the string on the bow hook, with the bow at right angles to the shooting line.

(*c*) Prevent breakage by turning in any bow which has a frayed serving or string.

(*d*) Request directions for adjusting the bow-string if it is over- or under-drawn.

(*e*) Check always that an arrow of the correct length is used.

(*f*) Place the cock feather at right angles to the string when nocking arrow.

(*g*) Place the arrows loosely in the arrow ring of the quiver between shots.

(*h*) Carry arrows at their tip ends, preferably between the fingers with the feathers separated.

(*i*) Wipe the arrows clean for shooting as well as for return to arrow rack at the end of class.

(*j*) Return accessory equipment (gloves, tabs, arm guards) at the end of period to the storage box or hook provided for them. The file number of the bow, according to the weight, should be attached to the bow below the handle by means of a small bit of adhesive tape on which the number has been written with indelible pencil or ink. This number should be memorized so that that particular bow may be used repeatedly if it proves satisfactory, or may be avoided if not desirable.

5. The next step is to stress safety. The necessary rules should be as few as possible, direct and positive.

(*a*) Leave the shooting line *only* on signal from the instructor.

(*b*) Draw the bow *only* after being shown how.

(*c*) Draw the bow *only* with an arrow on the string.

(*d*) Draw the bow *only* when no one is in front of the shooting line.

(*e*) Draw the arrow up to the tip but *not* within the bow.

(*f*) Use arrows of the correct length for the given bow. These safety rules should be quickly reviewed at the beginning of each lesson with a beginning group.

6. When the instructor is confident that the students understand the safety rules and know the parts of the bow and arrow by name, then she may proceed with teaching the fundamental positions. The following description in method is specifically for a right-handed person. For a left-handed person the reverse of all described procedures would be necessarily followed. Place any who are left-handed at the left end of the shooting line with backs to the remainder of the class. It is best to have the students line up on the shooting line, place their equipment

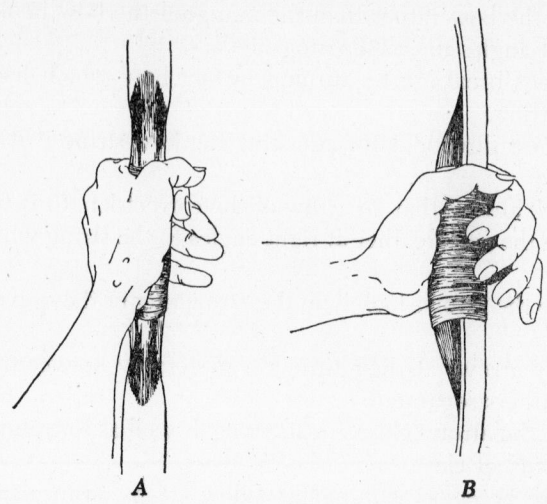

A   B

Fig. 4. *A*, archer's view of bow hand. *B*, side view of bow hand.

in the ground quivers, and await directions. The first instruction is given without bows.

(*a*) FUNDAMENTAL POSITIONS OF BODY AND FEET.

(*1*) The addressing of the target. An easy stance: feet about 10 inches or so apart; the weight evenly divided between the two feet; heels about opposite the center leg of the tripod, straddling the shooting line.

(*2*) The left shoulder pointing directly at the target but *not* elevated. A good test of whether or not the individual is in line with her target is to have her stretch out her left arm directly from her side toward the center of the target, then turn her head to check. If she is not in line, a slight adjustment in position, forward or backward, can correct it.

(*3*) Turning of the erect head to the left, the only change from the body's right angle position in relation to the target. No other part of the body turns toward it. Eyes should be level.

The class should rest a minute, moving their feet freely, and then repeat the correct stance with the bow arm extended toward the target to check each position. At this time the instructor should watch for uneven balance and incorrect placement of feet.

Instruction from here on should be with tackle.

(*b*) BOW HAND AND ARM.

(*1*) The *bow hand* should grasp the bow handle with the flat of the left fist at the top of the handle; the fingers and thumb firmly but not tightly holding the bow; the first thumb knuckle nearly to the center of the inside surface of the handle as shown in Fig. 4.

Watch for: (a) Separation of fingers. (b) Swinging outward of the palm.

(2) The *bow arm*. With the bow hand placed as directed above, the bow arm is elevated sideways toward the target to shoulder height with a very slight "give" in the elbow. This causes the elbow to point backward, and produces a decided lowering of the shoulder which relaxes tension throughout the arm.

Observe any: (a) Hunching of the left shoulder. (b) Pushing throughout the arm, which causes the left elbow to be straightened dangerously, bringing it within the string. (c) "Rolling" of the arm which tends to make the elbow point downward instead of backward. (d) Insufficient extension of the left elbow. The correct form should be practiced with a bent, but undrawn, bow several times until each student has attained an acceptable position in which to hold the bow at full draw.

(c) THE STRING HAND AND ARM.

(1) The bow is held horizontally at the side (upper limb forward, the string toward one's thigh) by the bow hand.

(2) Without an arrow, the right hand is brought toward the string, palm up, index finger slightly separated from the two central ones.

(3) The three fingers, quite straight, reach under and at right angles to the string, the last joints flexed over the string. The distal finger cushions should be pushed toward the finger tips by the "roll" of the string.

(4) The hand and wrist are flat, continuing a direct line to the elbow.

Under strict observation, the draw may be allowed for a few inches, but the admonition of never drawing a bow and never releasing the string without an arrow on it should be stressed. The repetition of the draw even for a few inches will give the novice the feeling for the direct pull which is important. Correct stance at full draw is illustrated in Fig. 5.

(d) NOCKING. This is the next step following training in fundamental positions. The nocking method described involves the minimum number of changes in hand positions. (Fig. 6.)

(1) The arrow is grasped at the nock end by the three shooting fingers and thumb.

(2) It is placed over the string and over the bow, resting on the arrow plate, that is, to the left of the bow when it is held upright.

(3) The arrow is drawn backward until the nock reaches the string.

Fig. 5. Correct stance at full draw.

(4) It is twirled until the cock feather is "up," that is, at right angles to the string, and the string slipped into the nock.

(5) The fingers automatically drop into shooting position with the index finger above arrow and second and third below. Then one is ready for the draw. This should be repeated until the fingers are accustomed to the new coordination.

The bow elevation and point of aim may change, but the nocking point is always constant.

(6) The fingers should just "feel" the arrow, but not grasp it. If the fingers hold the arrow instead, it will tend to roll away from the bow.

(e) THE CONTINUED MOVEMENT OF THE STRING AND BOW ARMS.

(1) With the arrow nocked and fingers of both hands in correct position, the draw is started from the side until the left hand is approximately at shoulder height and aiming directly at the target, shoulder low, elbow slightly bent as previously directed.

(2) The string hand pulls the string slowly back close to the left arm and up until the index finger of the right hand is directly under the jaw with the tip of the index finger touching under the chin.

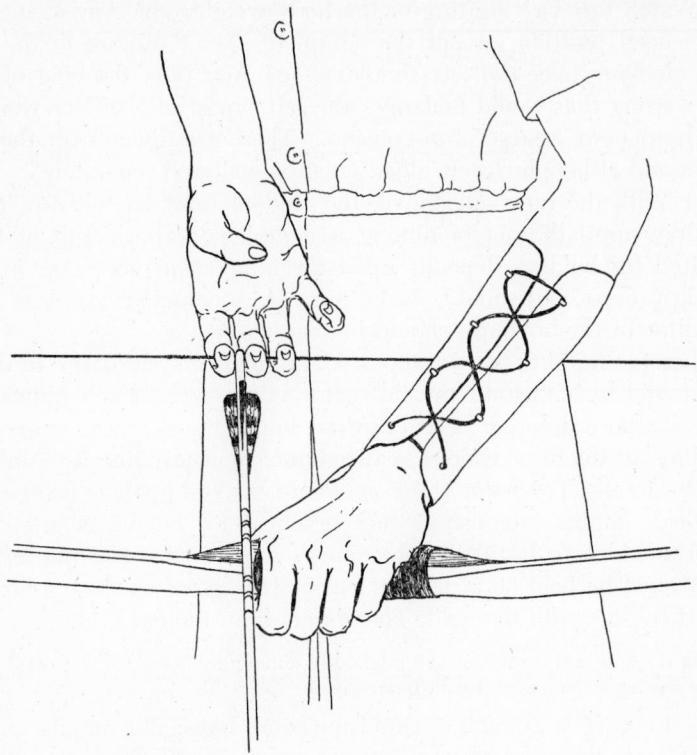

Fig. 6. Correct nocking position showing cock feather.

(3) The thumb is folded just parallel to the index finger and should lie close in against the archer's throat.

(4) The tip of the chin, not tilted upward, should be the definite spot which the index finger should touch on each and every draw. This point is known as the *anchor point* of the drawing process and must be drawn to always.

(5) The string should touch the center of the chin and the tip of the nose.

(6) The arrow is drawn its full length until the tip is just at the left side and forward edge of the bow. The length of the draw is identically the same for each range.

(7) The elbow, as it is pulled backward, should be at shoulder level so that a direct line of stress is applied.

NOTE: The draw has been analyzed by parts, but actually happens in a well-coordinated movement of the two arms started at the side and completed at shoulder level.

Watch for: (a) Shifting of the body weight. (b) Any change in head position, except the complete, direct turning to the left looking over the left shoulder. (c) Any poor drawing of the string that would endanger the left breast of a girl or woman.

(*e*) HOLDING, AIMING, AND LOOSING. These are difficult for the beginner and although closely allied must be analyzed separately.

(*1*) With the bow full-drawn, the student must be told to "hold" the draw until the act of aiming is completed. The length of time required for holding depends upon the adjustment necessary in the aiming process, but should not be hurried. A conscious check of lack of motion of the bow arm should be made.

When too rapid draws are repeated, the class may be asked to draw slowly and to hold until the instructor says "loose." Each individual releases after a different period of time, but at the start, this suggested "holding" of the draw is often realized only by controlling it in unison.

(*2*) Aiming: The *point of aim method* is agreed upon as being most practical. "Sights" are usually not practical for beginners' use. The important idea to instill in a beginner's mind is that the pile of the arrow must be held on a particular spot (the point of aim), which is in vertical line with the gold. This differs from range to range.

NOTE: Details in the point of aim method of aiming are discussed under the procedure during second week for beginners, page 23.

(*3*) Loosing is a much debated question, but again simplicity and directness in the releasing of the string at full draw is the best method. With the string hand at the anchor point, thumb against the throat, as soon as the aiming process is over, the fingers should release their pull by opening simultaneously in complete extension. This allows the string to roll off the fingers smoothly and evenly. They alone move on the releasing. Any sideward movement of the fingers on the release pulls the string away from its forward path.

Watch for: (a) Creeping (forward movement of string hand or backward swing of bow arm). (b) Relaxing (letting either arm and shoulder or both move).

NOTE: Some teach a loosing technique as a continuation of the movement of the two arms in the direction they were moving at the time of release. This provides a smooth loose with the fingers drawn across the throat from anchor point backward. This may be taught at the time of teaching the release or later when a more accurate anchoring has been acquired.

7. Shooting at 20-yard range:

Have the beginners, with their equipment, lined up on the 20-yard line. Directly in line with the center of each target and about 5 yards in front of it, a piece of wood (painted white and with a nail at one end) should be stuck in the ground. Under the observation of the instructor and the student assistant, have two students come to full draw position with the left eye closed. If each has the string hand and arm in correct alignment, with the anchor point at the chin held firmly, and the bow arm in easy position, she can give attention to focusing the tip of the arrow on the white bit of wood. This should show just above the arrow tip. Wherever the hits may be, the student should be kept concentrating on that spot, the "point of aim." She should get as good an arrow "grouping" as possible, that is, close proximity of the arrows when shot. Each one shooting, as well as those awaiting their turns for instruction, will learn a great deal in observing this "grouping."

The shooting of at least three arrows should be observed by the instructor, while the additional three may be shot independently. The instructor and assistant should proceed on down the shooting line, repeating the same method with each student. On a signal from the instructor, the class should rest their bows with the backs against the bow hooks while each retrieves her arrows. With the aid of the instructors, the piece of wood used as point of aim may be adjusted as necessary but always should be placed directly in vertical line with the gold. If the arrow grouping is low, the bit of white wood should be placed behind the center leg of the tripod. If not visible there, the student may use the center spot where the target meets the central leg of the tripod, or a central spot on the target. If the grouping spot is high, the learner should bring her point of aim out from the target toward the shooting line about 3 or 4 feet. The important result from the first shooting attempts is to have the arrows grouped closely. The fact should be stressed that grouping is much more important at the start than hitting the target at random, for it proves that the archer is using steady, consistent form. If the six arrows are found "all around the clock" and sometimes even on a neighbor's target, the archer is not remembering the fundamentals of form, or is not "holding" on her point of aim.

As the second "end" is shot, the instructor and the student assistant, starting from the center and moving outward on the line, should assist in the shooting of at least two arrows by each individual. Students should be allowed to shoot the remainder by themselves or wait for the instructor to return if they require help. It should be emphasized that the archer should never look up from her point of aim until she has heard the hit and should be analytical of others' shots as she waits. After the first end has been shot, the class should be grouped together and allowed to analyze mistakes and to tell what should be done to rectify the mistakes. They should understand that differences "up and down" the target may be due to incorrect points of aim or to other faults, but that differences right and left are due primarily to errors in form. These are listed on page 41.

The clock system of describing hits on the target is interesting and practicable in assisting correction of shooting. The target face can be considered the face of a clock. The hits are described as though they had been shot into a clock's face. For example, a twelve o'clock red would be a hit that had reached the target just directly above the center and in the red ring.

By having a shooting partner note the positions of certain hits, slight corrections may be made which will increase accuracy in shooting.

Each student should also unstring her bow, attach her keeper and place her bow on the bow rack. Arrows should be wiped clean and replaced in correct positions on the arrow stand. Auxiliary equipment (such as gloves, braces and points of aim) should be in their designated places also. Each day students should replace tackle in good condition and in an orderly manner so that it will become a natural habit.

(B) *Second Week.*

1. At the first meeting, the students should choose their own equipment, but their choice should be passed upon by the instructor. They should have all the required equipment which they used during the previous week, plus their white points of aim, and also a score card and pencil. Assistance should be offered in the putting on of their arm guards and finger protection. Their equipment, with the exception of the bows, should be placed up at their quivers.

2. Returning in a group, they should review parts of the bow and arrow as well as the student's responsibility for equipment and safety.

3. Then they are ready to learn how to string and unstring the bow. With the group in a shallow semicircle around the instructor, it may be demonstrated to them. This must be done slowly with explanation of each step.

(*a*) The bow grasped at the handle with the left hand, with the back of the bow toward the individual, the bow-string hanging down. The hand must not be moved from the handle until after the completion of the stringing or unstringing.

(*b*) With its keeper removed, the string not twisted around the bow and hanging directly down from the bow.

(*c*) The nock of the lower limb held against the instep of the left foot, not on the ground, with the bow held diagonally across the body from left to right. (See Fig. 7.)

Fig. 7. Position for bracing bow.

(*d*) The "heel" of right palm placed on the bow just below the eye of the string, the index finger and thumb reaching just lightly to the eye.

(*e*) The actual "bracing" of the bow is the result of a *pulling* by the *left* hand and a *pushing* by the *right*. With sufficient slack in the string, the eye is slipped into the nock by the finger tips.

NOTE: At first, the class should try just that: pulling and pushing simultaneously so that the strings hang loosely away from the bows. Some instructors teach the stringing in reverse of the directions just given, i.e., handle in right hand, and so on. If taught and practiced as described above, a change of hand is not necessary since the bow hand is used at the handle in the bracing process. Otherwise there seems no greater benefit from one method than from the other.

Observe: That the fingers are not pushing. That each arm is doing its share of the work.

When the students have the feeling for it, they should be taught to reach lightly to the eye of the string with the fingers and slip it ahead of the pushing "heel" of the hand and into the nock. The fingers should not be on the inside of the bow for, if they are, a painful pinch may result. Also the string should be centered. At this time it should be explained what a *fistmele* is—the approximate 6-inch measurement offered by the width of the palm with an extended thumb. This means is used to measure the distance between the bow at the handle and the string. However, this distance may vary with individuals and thus be inaccurate.

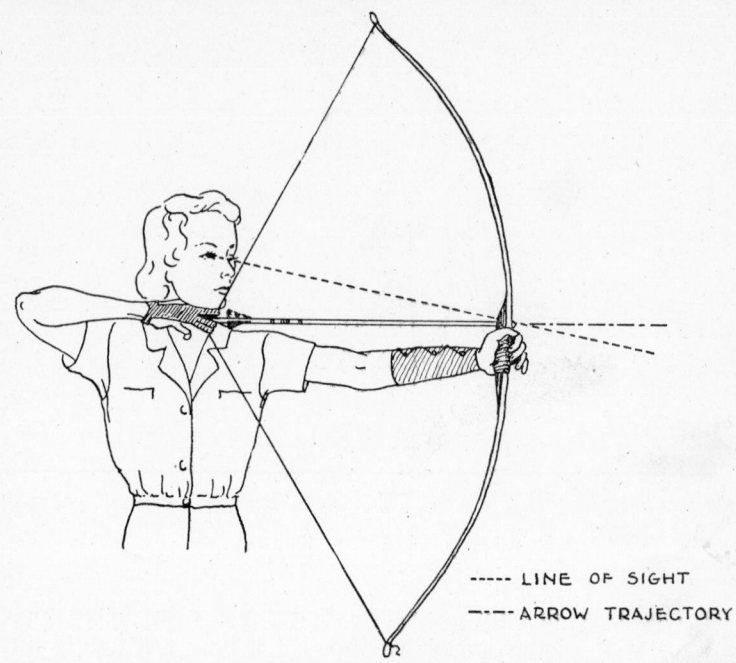

----- LINE OF SIGHT
----- ARROW TRAJECTORY

Fig. 8. Relation of string to nose, chin and anchor point.

If 6-inch bits of doweling or moulding have been provided, or if the handles of the bow rack have been marked in 6-inch lengths, each student may measure her own more satisfactorily. The unstringing (or unbending) is the reverse process of stringing. The bow should be held precisely the same as for stringing and the pushing-pulling process should continue until there is slack in the string. This time, however, the index finger actually "pulls" out the eye from the nock.

The class now should be ready for a review of the fundamental positions of bow and string arms and hands and of stance. They should return to the shooting line and take the correct standing position. The entire class should replace the equipment on the quivers, take the fundamental position for the beginning of the draw, and without the use of the bow and arrow continue into a full draw, observing all requirements of good form. They should then take the full draw position of the bow hand and arm, pointing the index finger of the bow hand at the point of aim.

Next the nocking of an arrow with the holding of it in correct shooting position with the right hand should be passed upon by the instructor or by the student coach. Those who have difficulties should

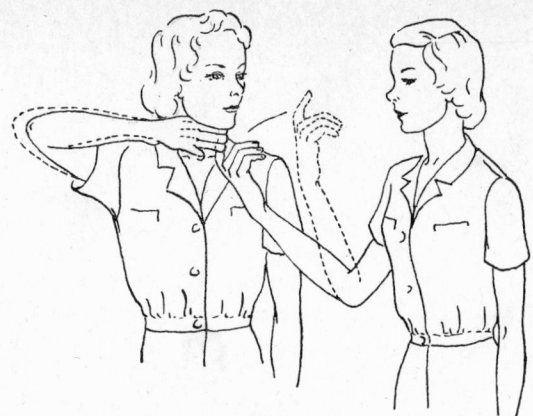

Fig. 9. Finger shooting.

be paired and should practice finger shooting with partners, criticizing each other's form as well as release. Finger shooting consists of the archer's partner facing her and offering her right index finger pointing upward as the "string." This should be placed about at the middle of the archer's elevated forearm. The archer reaches to the "string" with her three string fingers and pulls it up to anchor point. When at full draw and offering resistance, the "string" is allowed to roll off the archer's fingers. Figure 9 clearly illustrates finger shooting.

4. Point of Aim should be explained at this time. This use of an auxiliary spot at which to aim is essential to make the necessary adjustment between the straight line of vision and the trajectory of the arrow. (See Fig. 10.) This may be determined by use of the range finder discussed three paragraphs below. For each bow and its matching set of arrows, there is a *point blank range,* one spot from which an individual may hit the gold while aiming directly at its center. This may or may not be at the given range from which the individual is shooting. If the archer changes her shooting distance, as from range to range, she must also change her point of aim. For if she continues to aim at the center of the gold at different ranges, her arrow will fall short or fly behind the target, depending upon her distance from the target. Use of a point of aim at varying distances from the target is necessary because of the difference between the line of vision and the trajectory of the arrow. At close range the arrow flies in a less curved path. At a greater range it describes a greater arc in flight. At close range the eye sights the arrow tip well below the gold of the target. The difference in levels between the eye and the anchor point is several inches. These facts must be recognized in learning

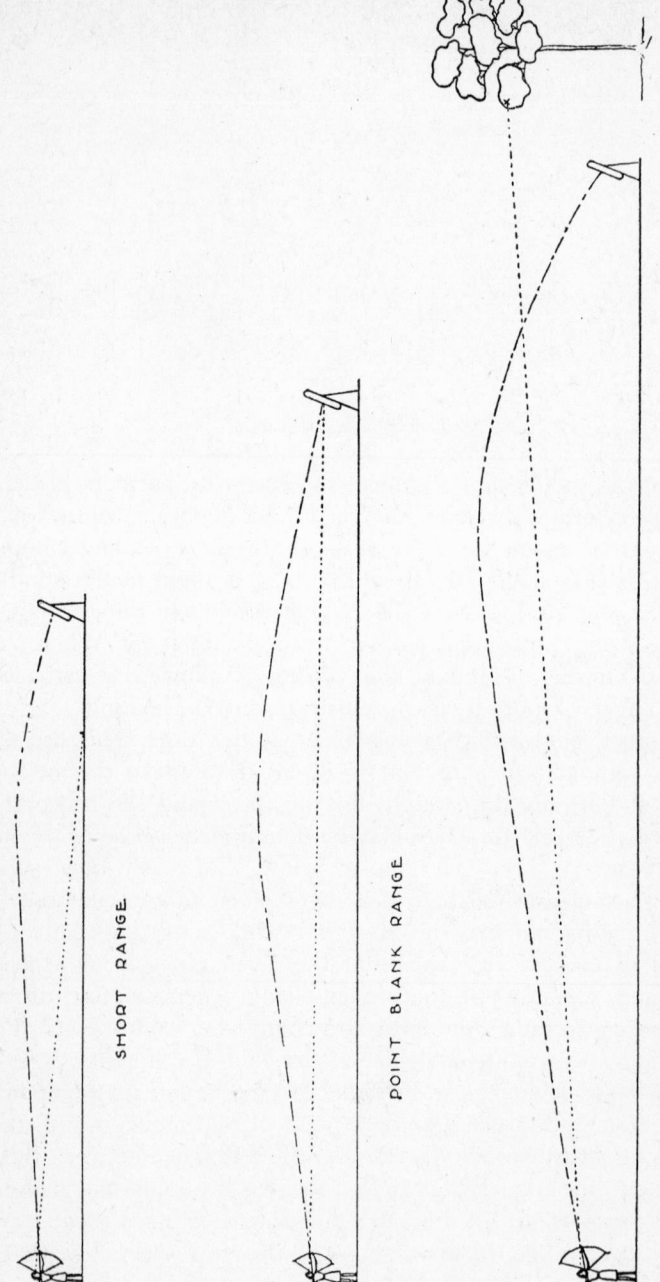

SHORT RANGE

POINT BLANK RANGE

LONG RANGE

Fig. 10. Diagrammatic explanation of point of aim.

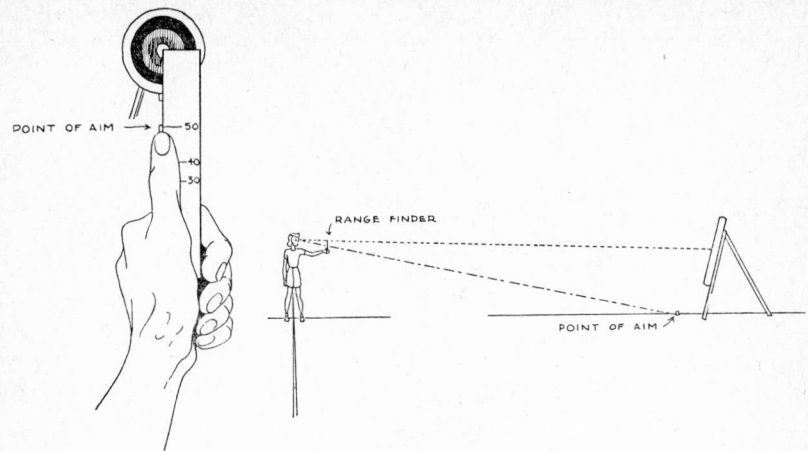

Fig. 11. Use of the range finder.

to aim. In sighting, the right eye focuses on the arrow tip by looking to the right of the string and to the left of the bow and holding the arrow tip directly on the point of aim.

The use of the perpendicular bow with the string bisecting the gold and aiming with the right eye, as in shooting, is the most accurate way of determining whether or not the spot used for the point of aim is in line with the center of the target. If there appears on the string the low point of aim for the nearer range and the higher points of aim for the farther ranges, then the particular spots chosen for points of aim are correctly centered. The arrow tip must be aligned directly on the point of aim at full draw and during the "holding" required in aiming.

If the arrows are landing high on the target, or consistently beyond, the point of aim must be lowered, i.e., brought nearer the shooting range. If the arrows are flying low or below the target, the point of aim must be raised. A definite object should be placed at the given auxiliary spot and is called the point of aim.

One method of consistently finding one's point of aim at different ranges is through the use of the *range finder*. On any convenient short stick, such as a tongue depressor, make, near one end, a mark which, when the stick is held perpendicularly at arrow's length in correct stance, will match the gold of the target. The holding hand should be adjusted so that the top edge of the thumb will coincide with the point of aim. At this point on the stick, make a mark indicating the given range. One to three arrows should be shot to prove the hold and aim. With the range finder or arrow, "measure" the distance from

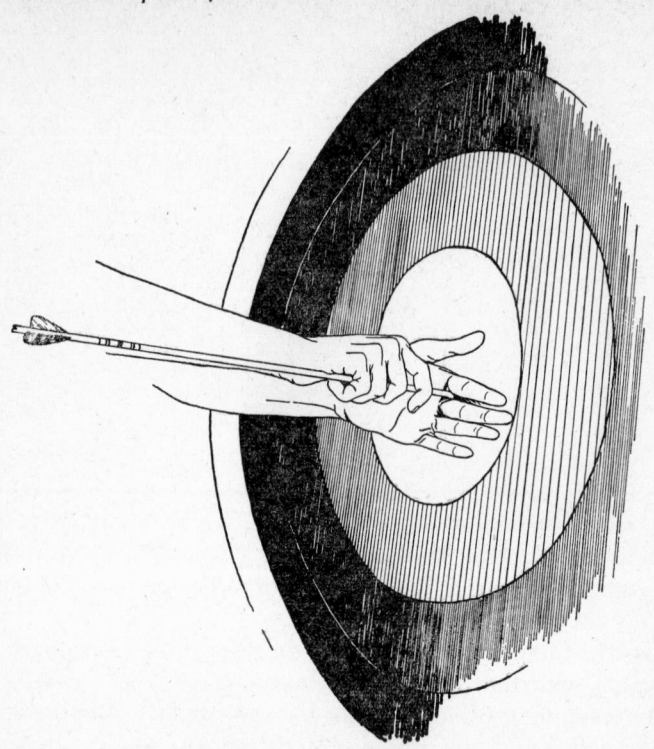

Fig. 12. Method of drawing arrows from target.

the hit on the target to the point of aim. Change the tip of the range finder from the hit to the gold. The new location of the point of aim should be checked. If necessary, the students may adjust the point of aim for their partners when first experiencing this method. Each student, after she has determined her points of aim, should keep her range finder with her name on it and use it with the same bow and arrows at each practice session. (Theoretically the point of aim method is difficult, but practically it is easy to apply. It can be worked out progressively in the class procedure.)

5. With their points of aim placed up, the entire group should shoot their first "end" at 20 yards. At a given signal the group goes up to retrieve the arrows. They should be warned about "shorts," arrows that fall short of the target, and those that may have "snaked" their way into the grass. If the group has progressed well, an end or two at 30 yards will be challenging.

6. Removal of arrows from the ground and target can be demonstrated by the instructor with the class grouped about one target. (See Fig. 12.)

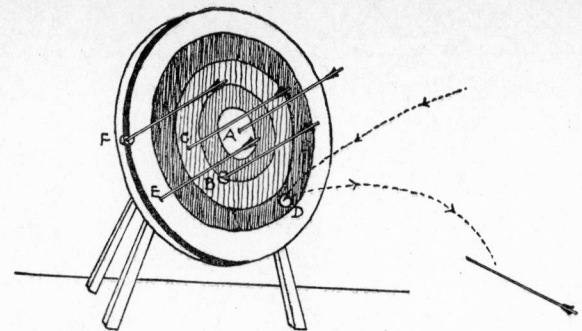

Fig. 13. Explanation of scoring of a given six arrows:

A. Gold   9 points
B. Split   7 "   —(higher valued ring always recorded)
C. Blue   5 "
D. Rebound   (7) "   —(from any part of scoring surface)
E. White   1 "
F. Petticoat   0 "

NOTE: During this particular end, no arrow hit the red ring, 7, nor the black, 3.

(*a*) Back of left hand flat against target with arrow between index and second fingers.

(*b*) Right hand grasp of arrow shaft close to target surface.

(*c*) Push with left hand against target and, with slight twisting motion, pull with right hand directly backward.

(*d*) Place tips of arrows under thumb, leaving feathers free. When an arrow has become embedded in the straw up to its crest, it should be continued on slowly through the straw and withdrawn from the back of the target.

(*e*) An arrow which has been forced deeply through the grass parallel to the ground so that it is almost hidden should be removed with a forward motion through the grass unless the feathers are free. If the feathers are not embedded, the arrow may be withdrawn backward, but never pulled straight up at right angles to the ground.

(*f*) Each member of the class should retrieve her own arrows, being reminded to carry them in the fingers at the tip ends, feathers, in fan formation, wide apart.

7. Advice at the targets also may be given on the necessary corrections of individual points of aim. On the return to the shooting line the second six arrows at 20 yards should be shot.

8. After this end, the class should bring up their pencils and score cards for the lesson in *scoring*. Again grouping them around one target, explanation in scoring in general should be given. By using the 6 arrows present (or placed) in the target, the recording of the score and the valuation of each ring should be taught. (See Fig. 13.) Scores

are always recorded with the highest score first, no matter which arrow scored which hit. If the first 2 shots are missed and then a gold, red, white, and black are made, in that order of shooting, on the score card it should be recorded as 9, 7, 3, 1, 0, 0. On the same line as the recording of that end, total hits and total score are written for that end: in this case, 4–20. A hit on the part outside the white, known as the petticoat, counts as neither score nor hit. A hit which cuts two colors is given the higher value. A rebound, that is, an arrow that hits and bounces off a scoring part of the target or an arrow that hits the scoring surface of the target and goes clean through the target, are both given a score of seven. The score for such a hit is indicated by a seven with a circle around it. An arrow dropped from the bow, beyond the bow reach of the archer, without moving her feet, counts as a shot.

After questions are answered, each student should record her own score, which should be kept continuously from then on. The instructor should also at this point observe how the arrows are retrieved and how carried back to the quivers, correcting those students who fail to conform. At this point it may be necessary to have a more open class discussion of point of aim and a more detailed explanation of it. Before the third end at 20 yards, the instructor should ask where the point of aim should be for a 30-yard range. Then the class should decide how each one should place up or find her point of aim. The third end should be shot off, and while retrieving the arrows and scoring up that end, the bits of wood should be placed up for a 30-yard shoot. One or two ends at 30 yards with any necessary corrections of point of aim should be shot off. Each member of the class should total the score for the day and hand in her score card. These should be checked by the instructor so she may modify any mistakes in scoring at the start. An easy check on the arithmetic is that the hits and score must both be either odd or even. An incorrect score would read 42 hits, 125 score; and a correct one, 42 hits, 128 score.

(C) *Third Week.* This week will go more smoothly and more enthusiastically if the instructor has faithfully required diligent effort on the part of the class in striving to perfect form. The choice of equipment and the stringing of the bows should still be observed by the instructor.

1. Before the class starts to shoot, point of aim theory should be reviewed with discussion about necessary correction of trial points of aim. If range finders have worked, they will be timesavers from now on.

2. The use of bow sights for beginners is questioned by some authorities. However, some archers improve their shooting by the use of a sight. A sight is a device used so that the aim may always be on the gold of the target. There are many mechanical bow sights but for school, college and camp use, adhesive strips attached to the back of the upper limb of the bow, plus a large headed pin, serve very well. This device is further discussed on page 35. If such a device is used, the location of the pin sight for various ranges should be marked on the tape. The archer should note that if the arrows are falling low, the sight should be lowered on the tape; if high, the sight should be placed higher.

3. The class may be started by helping, individually, one or two who may be having difficulties. The class should shoot the first end at 30 yards, preferably in unison. During the second end, the student assistant or the instructor should observe each student shoot at least two arrows, the second after the correction of the first. The second day's time should be divided between 20- and 30-yard ranges.

4. At the targets a discussion by the class of "groupings" of arrows and correction necessary if the groupings are "off-center" should prove stimulating. On completion, the instructor should check on retrieving, scoring, and carrying of arrows. During the third end, individual faults and explanation of how they may be overcome should be stressed.

(D) *Fourth Week.* Photographs, taken with an ordinary kodak while the small groups are shooting, should be planned for. As natural conditions as possible are desirable so it should be announced that some snapshots will be taken during the class, but that no attention should be given to the photographer.

1. It is well to have the student assistant take the pictures if possible. Not more than three girls in a group should be photographed at one time. Others may appear in the picture but the three should be in correct focus to facilitate analysis of any faults in shooting form. These photos should be developed immediately so that they may be shown at the next meeting of the class and discussed with each student. On the second day of the week, the class should become acquainted with the 40-yard range, shooting as many ends as possible with correction. At the end of the classes each day, the total score should be recorded, and the unstringing of the bows and replacing of the equipment should be observed.

2. On the first day of the fourth week, after checking on the choice of equipment and the stringing of the bows, the class should be divided in halves or individuals may choose partners. On a trial end at 40 yards

each group should take turns in correcting the other's shooting form. After the second end is shot off, and scored, the photographs should be shown. The three students whose pictures appear together should be grouped and should have pointed out their errors or excellence in form individually; meanwhile the remainder of the class, under the guidance of the student coach, should continue shooting. Such discussion of each photograph can prove very helpful, for the snapshot is a graphic description of certain peculiarities of form that often must be visualized to be appreciated.

3. As the students go to retrieve the arrows shot at 40 yards, the bows should be carried to the 30-yard quivers. On the first end at 30, each student should shoot two and hold four arrows, the latter to be shot under the observation of the instructor or the student coach. At this time, it is well for the two who are teaching the class to change halves of the shooting line so they may become familiar with each individual's progress. They should observe the shooting of two arrows, one without criticism and one with, first from behind the archer and then from the side. On the second day of the week, reference to the more common faults in technique should be made to the group and individually as needed. While the tackle is being put away on each day, and while scores are being tallied, more individual coaching, criticism, and encouragement and definite hints to be practiced during the next lesson or in open hour may be offered by both instructors. Better form and scoring should be noticed at this time.

(E) *Fifth Week.*

1. A ladder tournament for the class is stimulating, and very easily planned. Anyone on the ladder may challenge any other person on the ladder. With only ten to fourteen in the group, limiting it to a given number above is not necessary. Number four challenges number two for the total of the day's score. The one with the higher daily score has her name established in the higher place. Challenges must be accepted in the order received. In other words, number one can be challenged only by the first person who approaches her, not by two or three archers on the same day. The final day for completion of the tournament in class must be announced in advance. The concentration on scoring the best scores will be stimulation enough during class, but correction in details of form should be constantly offered. While observing the putting away of tackle, individual questions having specific bearing on some student's difficulties or misunderstanding should be answered.

2. Shooting time may be divided between 30- and 40-yard ranges, but at least two ends should be shot at 50.

(F) *Sixth Week.*

1. Begin the first recorded and completed *Columbia Round.* It is generally impossible to finish a Columbia in one class period, but as much as possible should be shot off the first day and the whole finished on the second. Practice arrows should be allowed at 50 yards only; and on the second day, no practice arrows should be allowed.

2. If there are in the group one or two students who seem to be unable to keep up to the "pace" of the class and who have difficulty at 50 yards in making hits, they should be kept working at 40 and 30 yards for form and accuracy. They should be placed at the right-hand end of the range as they face the target, while those shooting Columbias should take their stance toward the left-hand end. Striving to discover the real cause of each one's difficulties, either the student coach or the instructor should be responsible for the slower group. There are always some who are slower in progress than the average, but they should not be neglected.

(G) *Seventh Week.*

1. On the first day all those who have not completed their Columbia Rounds should do so. The ones in the slower group should start at least a "short" Columbia Round and finish it during the week. By a "short Columbia" we mean 12 arrows each, instead of the usual 24 at 50, 40, and 30 yards. This gives the students the feeling of having completed a modified Columbia Round without too much discouragement. The score cards should be marked "Short Columbia."

2. On the second day, the class may start a challenge tournament in pairs or have the semi-finals of the ladder tournament. The possessors of the two highest scores on the last day of the seventh week should shoot in the finals the last week.

(H) *Eighth and Final Week.* This week will be very full indeed with finishing off Columbias and with the finals in the ladder tournament. After the first day of this week, there should be a meeting of the instructors in the different sections and the highest Columbia Round score in each section and from all the sections determined from the score cards, with plans for announcing them to the classes on the last day. The individual winner of the ladder tournament in each class as well as the highest daily score from the recordings for the ladder tournament should also be determined. Prizes may be planned for but that is not necessary. The awarding of a pail of lollypops or a giant peppermint stick or a golden tassel easily made of wool often adds gaiety to the final roundup of the class. While the tackle is being put away, the group may be advised generally or specifically about buying their own equipment as well as shooting at home or on local ranges or at summer camps. For the most advanced, attendance at one of the archery camps may be proposed.

This is, of course, but a suggested procedure for novices for an eight-week term with clear weather. A greater variety can be introduced but the basic outline of procedure we believe to be sound in theory and practice.

II · Intermediate

A separate schedule for an intermediate group has not been prepared in detail, because the suggestions made for the beginners and for advanced groups can be modified in both extremes so that a happy balance of progress and interest may be obtained. Such repetition of material and methods as is found in the following clear weather schedule for intermediates is necessary in outline form so that, at a glance, the instructor can know whether or not each group has been planned for, and the material covered from week to week.

(A) *First Week.*

1. Review of safety laws.
2. Review of fundamental positions.
3. Summary of care of equipment.
4. Stringing and unstringing of bows and nocking under observation.
5. Start shooting at 40-yard range, standing between the beginning and the advanced groups or use targets adjusted as described on page 2.

(B) *Second Week.*

1. Review point of aim method and teach the use of pin sights.
2. Shooting at 50-yard and then at 40-yard range.
3. Recording of score from now on.

(C) *Third Week.*

1. Shooting of "short" Columbia Round.
2. Discussion of difficulty with point of aim as well as side groupings.
3. Individual correction of faults.

(D) *Fourth Week.*

1. Correction of form in pairs on trial end at 50 yards.
2. Continuance of Columbia Round.

(E) *Fifth Week.*

1. Rules for archery golf to be run in open hour given out.
2. Starting of first counting of Columbia Round.

(F) *Sixth Week.* Balloon or William Tell shooting at far end of range.

(G) *Seventh Week.*

1. Completion of Columbia Rounds for class team competition.

2. Suggestion to shoot Columbias for Intercollegiate Telegraphic Meet or Interscholastic Mail Match in open hour.

(H) *Eighth Week.* Challenge tournament for those not on class, school, or college teams.

III. Advanced

(A) *First Week.*

1. Review of safety laws, parts and choice of equipment.

2. Checking on tackle used and care of equipment.

3. Review of point of aim and bow sight methods of aiming; use of the range finder.

4. Start of shooting at 50 yards for a "short" Columbia Round.

(B) *Second Week.*

1. Discussion of point of aim method with necessary adjustments and use of pin sights.

2. Beginning of day's shooting at 50-yard range, recording of scores from now on.

(C) *Third Week.*

1. Posting of highest scores of Columbia Rounds.

2. Discussion of faults and methods of correction, first as a group and then individually.

3. Shooting of second Columbia Round.

(D) *Fourth Week.*

1. Choosing of class team material.

2. Shooting of first counting Columbia Round.

3. At one end of range, Popinjay Shoot.

(E) *Fifth Week.*

1. Giving out of multigraphed rules for archery golf to be run off in open hour during sixth and seventh weeks.

2. Continuation of Columbia Rounds.

(F) *Sixth Week.*

1. Archery golf contest in open hours.

2. Working on Columbia Rounds to be used for telegraphic or mail meet and class competition.

(G) *Seventh Week.*

1. By staying after class hour if possible, completion of Columbia Rounds.

2. Practice at the range most difficult for each individual.

(H) *Eighth Week.*

1. Final competitions.

2. Open challenge tournament.

3. Plans for archery picnic and rabbit hunt.

This eight weeks' plan, in detail, would be as follows:

(A) *First Week.* This is the time to get the advanced group off to a fast start.

1. and 2. As quickly as possible review *safety laws, parts, choice* and *elementary care* of the *equipment*. Although this may be covered during the two days in order to allow for more shooting time each day, details of such a review should not be neglected.

3. Before any shooting is done, however, point of aim method should be reviewed and pin sights discussed. To have point of aim clearly understood is most important especially if the advanced archers have received their fundamental training from some other institution. Despite differences in form, point of aim is basic and should be insisted upon for continuous efficient shooting. It is helpful with a new group of advanced archers, some of whose ability is unfamiliar to the instructor, to inquire as to types of rounds and tournaments entered previously. According to the findings, the students may be classified into two groups: *A,* the more experienced; and *B,* the less experienced. Divided into these classifications they may be placed at the shooting line quivers.

4. Shooting the first day should be at the 50-yard range with individual corrections given immediately. The form of an archer who has learned the "relaxed" method or any other particular variety of draw or release should not be changed. It is confusing and there is no real reason for changing if the archer is consistent. With those who have learned the method described for the beginners, assistance should be given in perfecting small details of form. Once form is consistent, the effort should be directed toward accuracy. On the second day the shooting should be divided among the 50-, 40-, and 30-yard ranges.

(B) *Second Week.* Set the goal for Columbia Round or Junior Columbia. The class should be acquainted with the highest score ever recorded at their institution for a Columbia and a National and be given the best score recorded in interclass competition and in any former telegraphic intercollegiate or interscholastic mail meet. This sets goals for the season.

1. On the first day a "short" Columbia should be shot off to get in training, especially as to adjustment of point of aim. This should include a practice end, then two ends each at 50-, 40-, and 30-yard ranges. This may be repeated if time allows.

2. On the second day there should be a recording made of a completed Columbia or the better part of one. Scores should be recorded regularly.

3. On either day, the use of sights should be explained and dis-

cussed. Sights are nearly as numerous in kind as the archers who use them. Perhaps half the tournament archers are sight shooters. Sights vary in price as well as in their acceptance by archers. A simple one which will adequately serve student purposes may be made by sticking a 6-inch strip of ½-inch adhesive tape marked with ¼-inch spacings upward from the handle of the bow, either on the face or the back, and thrusting a glass-headed pin crosswise through the tape. The head of the pin may remain as far out from the bow as may be found necessary.

To use the sight, find by trial the exact distance from the side of the bow at which the head of the pin must be so that, when shooting in consistent form, the head of the pin is held steadily "on the gold." After loosing, the arrow should strike there, other factors being equal.

The "average" location of the 50-, 40-, and 30-yard ranges should be marked prominently on the tape, with wider lines. The individual student must learn and memorize the exact location of the pin above or below the "average" lines for his own shooting with the use of that bow.

(C) *Third Week.*

1. The best scores of completed Columbias in each section should be posted on the bulletin board in the archery equipment room as well as announced in classes. A method of stimulating better scores which has worked well is the recording of individual scores, made either in class or during open hour practice on a large cardboard target posted in the tackle room. The method is described in greater detail under means of stimulating interest, page 42.

2. Discussion of faults and methods of correction. This should be done first as a group, then individually. Groupings give indications of errors in technique. In correcting an archer's performance, the instructor should not confuse her by suggesting too many things on which to work. She should rather see that one fault is eliminated before another is noticed.

(D) *Fourth Week.*

1. The instructor should be watching out for material for *class teams.* The names of these possible candidates, plus any who have proven to be worthy of consideration, even though in the beginners' or intermediates' groups, should be brought together by the instructors and with the aid of the student coaches placed on tentative class teams. After the second day of the week, the final judgment on the class members can be reached on an agreed-upon basis, either by majority agreement of all the instructors and the student manager or by the agreement of the head of archery and the student manager.

2. Each member of the class teams may shoot off her best Columbia Round within a given time, but the score must be recorded and certified by another person who also signs the score card.

3. A competition that is fun and calls for great accuracy is the Popinjay Shoot (see page 43), a modification of the traditional wand shoot, which can be shot off during the fourth week.

(E) *Fifth Week.*

1. Rules for Archery Golf competition, which have been simplified and multigraphed, should be distributed.

2. Any member of the advanced or intermediate group may enter and should be urged to practice shooting at short ranges in open hour The class teams should be announced in class as well as in the student paper and on the Archery bulletin board.

3. As much of a completed Columbia Round as possible should be shot off each day.

(F) *Sixth Week.*

1. Before the beginning of the sixth week the student coaches should be called together and they should plan to assist in running off the archery golf tournament. This may be arranged by challenging the best golf players in college or school to play off several holes of golf in competition with the shooting off of the same number of "holes" in archery during a designated open hour. The archer's "hole" consists of a wire ring 4½ inches in diameter (miniature golf, 2½ inches). The arrow must fly through the opening. Or, without so much planning. there may be the shooting at 9 or 18 small targets made of strong. 8- by 10-inch pasteboard boxes placed at intervals over a wide field, such as a hockey field. The shooting proceeds from one target to another as from hole to hole in golf. The object is to see who can score on each target with the least number of trials. An approach shot may be taken from a given distance toward the individual target and the following shot must be taken from wherever that arrow landed, with the target, of course, turned to face the archer. The boxes should be held down with a forked stick or croquet wicket, easily removed from the ground but strong enough to offer resistance to breezes. If a smaller target is desired to require greater accuracy, small circles of 3 inches in diameter may be painted on the center of the boxes. Many handicaps or changes in procedure can be managed from year to year to keep the interest in this type of archery alive.

In these two days, the three lowest scorers will be considered for the finals to be run off the following week. To each class also at this time, the rabbit hunt at the end of the season should be explained and signed up for in order that the "hunting courses" and the picnic may be planned. Details are described on page 43.

2. For the class time, Columbia Rounds or a National Round should proceed during the two days, so the scores may be used, if possible, for a telegraphic or mail meet or class competition.

(G) *Seventh Week.* A serious effort to complete a Columbia Round during class so that it may count for class competition, for intercollegiate or interscholastic competition should be encouraged, if it has not been accomplished previously. During open hour, the finals of the archery golf competition, with the three lowest scorers competing, should be supervised by the student manager of archery. It is well at this time to have each student practice shooting several ends at the range most difficult for her.

(H) *Final Week.*

1. Class competition as well as recorded scores for the annual Intercollegiate Telegraphic Meet or the annual Interscholastic Mail Match, which are organized by the National Archery Association, should be handed in, certified by official scorers.[1]

2. An open challenge tournament for each day is fun for those not competing otherwise.

3. Plans should be laid for the archery picnic to follow the rabbit hunt. The hunt can be one of the most anticipated events of the year and the climax of the season. Description of a rabbit hunt may be found on page 43.

At the end of the picnic supper and around the camp fire following the hunt is an excellent time and place to announce the winners of Columbia Rounds, class competition, and highest individual scores in the Intercollegiate Telegraphic Meet or the Interscholastic Archery Mail Match for High Schools. It is at such moments that the carry-over of interest is stirred. It is surely a high point at which to close the season.

SUGGESTED OUTLINES FOR CLASS PROCEDURES DURING INCLEMENT WEATHER

Inclement weather is the greatest handicap known to archers. It can play havoc even with the most advanced archer's form. In localities where rain is more than likely to force classes indoors, it is necessary to plan for such contingencies in advance so that as little time as possible is lost out of an all too short season. However, if the class is to meet indoors and no indoor range is available a combination of

---

[1] The secretary of this organization is Mr. Lawrence E. Briggs, 1157 No. Pleasant St., Amherst, Mass.

archery theory and exercise must be planned for. This will of necessity vary according to the situation, but the succeeding schedules may offer suggestions or tentative outlines of a plan for a term for those who have no indoor range.

I. Beginners

For *beginners* it really is no great hardship, even though a disappointment, to be indoors during the *first one or two weeks*, for much of the routine and fundamentals can be taught indoors as well as out. If a rainy day or two comes then, an excellent opportunity is afforded to teach or review parts of the bow and arrow, fundamental positions, care of the tackle both when not in use and in use, and to practice finger shooting in pairs.

If the weather closes in during the *third week*, practice in stringing and unstringing the bow under observation of the instructor is worth while. It may be practiced even for speed. One admonition that must be stressed is to be sure that the lower nock is against the instep and makes no contact with the floor. Nocking may also be practiced so that the co-ordination is mastered. On one of these two days a motion picture on archery may be shown to the class, stopping it wherever required to emphasize a point.

During the *fourth* or *fifth week* if it is necessary to meet the group inside, the photographs that were taken previously may be discussed. First, the most prevalent mistakes of that particular group should be analyzed; then the individual faults should be explained while the remainder of the class bowls, plays deck tennis, badminton, shuffleboard, or ping-pong—whatever is at hand to play. At some schools there may be a reflectoscope or delineoscope which will enlarge the picture of the group as well as show individual form. This is the most graphic means of visualizing for the students right and wrong methods.

A second motion picture on archery may save the day during the *sixth* or *seventh week*, if there is bad weather, or the one shown previously may be repeated. If repeated, comments by the class should be encouraged, for by now they should be keener in analysis of correct and incorrect form. Here, too, the instructor may offer reasons for learning the sport thoroughly and continuing it another term as well as outside both during and after school days. This showing and discussion only takes part of the period, the remainder of which should be given over to informal sports. Where there are those whose physical condition precludes their participation in the individual sports at hand, have a good book on archery from which to read to them.

By the *eighth week*, which is the most trying week of all to be forced indoors, there is much that the class can do to assist the instructor. The first day may be given over to adding, averaging, and recording class scores, individual and college or school competitions. On the second day there may be those who do not wish to exercise who will help in cleaning the arrows, wiping off the bows and who are eager to learn more in detail about the care of tackle when not in use.

II. Intermediate and Advanced Archers

For the *intermediate and advanced archers*, loss of shooting time is more disappointing than for the beginners, but if managed efficiently, much of the sport can be learned off, as well as on, the range. If rain comes during the *first two weeks*, parts of the bow and arrow and care of the tackle should be thoroughly reviewed as well as the fundamental positions of shooting. Before the informal sports are indulged in, finger shooting should be checked on by the instructor to insure the consistently perfect releasing, even of advanced archers. Emphasize the equal pull of all three fingers. The ring finger is often "lazy."

With bad weather coming during the *third week* it is an advantageous time of the term for the instructor to show a motion picture. She may use the film to stimulate suggestions from this better group of archers as to how the film may be improved upon another year and from what angles they believe the best "still" picture can be taken to show correct and incorrect form. This discussion and planning will consume the entire period for those sufficiently interested while the others play at their favorite informal sports. The location of privately owned films and kodachrome slides and projectors can be discovered by applying to local and state officers of archery associations. Such owners are almost invariably willing to lend them. If feasible from a financial standpoint, a teaching film can readily be produced which can be used for several years. Incidentally the taking of the film adds great interest and stimulates better form in those being photographed.

If the pictures have been taken previous to the *fourth* or *fifth week*, as they should have been, the individual's as well as the group's most common faults and difficulties may be analyzed here from the photographs.

If the local motion picture has already been shown on some other rainy day, plan during the *sixth* or *seventh week*, to have on hand another film on archery obtainable from the National Archery Association of from a neighboring school or college.

During the *eighth week*, tabulation of scores can be completed and checked, and the tackle cleaned. On one of these two days, a glossary "bee" is fun to spring on the group. Divide them as evenly as possible according to ability and run the competition much like an old-fashioned spelling bee. The one who misses goes to the end of the line, the two lines alternating in trials. At a given time, or when the glossary is exhausted, the ones at the heads of the lines are the winners. These might be "spelled" down by challenges from one of the opposite side until one or the other fails to know the answer. During the cleaning of tackle is a good time to discuss the type of equipment to buy for personal use.

There is not a sufficiently great difference between the rainy day material for beginners and for the *intermediate-advanced group* to make another schedule necessary for a mixed group. The instructor can best plan what to include and what to ignore according to the ability of the class and their tendencies toward progress. Those with physical handicaps may need special consideration, and the division of the class should result in as close competition as possible.

COMMON FAULTS IN ARCHERY FORM

Certain faults in form which occur commonly in archery have been recognized individually and in groups. If classified by the location of the hits, some errors are clearly understood. Unfortunately with beginners especially, more than one may be demonstrated at the same time. It is this combination of mistakes that requires keen analysis on the part of the instructor as well as an observant shooting partner. It must be pointed out that resultant errors in shooting may cancel each other and produce an acceptable hit. Others may be combined to increase the degree of difficulty, which results in a very poor hit or in a miss. In general, mistakes may be made which cause the arrow's flight to deviate in one of four directions, up, down, to the right or to the left. Agreement as to the recognition of all such influential errors in form has never been made, but at least a partial listing of the most outstanding ones follows.

Factors which cause the released arrow to ride *high*.

1. Riding the bow (extension of bow arm on the release).
2. Increasing slightly the pull on the string just before release.
3. Lifting the bow arm.
4. Lifting the index finger of bow hand.
5. Nocking the arrow low on the string.
6. Allowing the third finger to "slip" on string.
7. Dropping of elbow or string hand just before release.
8. "Peeking" at short ranges.

9. Poorly determined point of aim (too far) or lifting from point of aim.

Factors which cause the released arrow to ride *low*.

1. A "creeping" release.
2. Not reaching or not holding at anchor point.
3. Dropping bow arm.
4. Reaching forward with chin to string.
5. Nocking the arrow high on the string.
6. Using understrung bow which causes string to hit wrist.
7. Holding low on bow handle.
8. "Peeking" at longer ranges.
9. Poorly determined point of aim (too near) or lowering from it.
10. Too high an anchor.
11. Holding too long so that fatigued muscles "give" too quickly.

Factors which cause the released arrow to veer to the *right*.

1. Throwing bow arm to the right.
2. Plucking the string on release.
3. Tilting the bow to the right.
4. Failing to align the point of aim with the center of the target—too far to right.
5. Failing to allow for wind from the left.
6. Head tilt to the right.
7. Pulling fingers off string too quickly, whether from lack of protection or soreness.
8. Weight on the toes or toward the forepart of the foot.
9. Gripping the bow string too high on the fingers.

Factors which cause the released arrow to veer to the *left*.

1. Throwing bow arm to the left.
2. Fingers too tightly gripping the arrow.
3. Tilting the bow to the left.
4. Anchoring out from the cheek.
5. Failure to align point of aim with center of target—too far to left
6. Failure to allow for wind from the right.
7. String touching hunched left shoulder.
8. Using left eye to sight.
9. Weight on heels or swaying slightly toward heels.
10. Head dropped backward rather than rotated to left.
11. Too tight a grip on bow.
12. Sighting to left of string.

Recognition of these difficulties in form and correction of one at a time as they appear make for improvement in form and thus better scoring. It is wiser not to note many mistakes at once as the correction is confusing for the archer. Eliminate one before beginning to work on another. Be alert to their presence and if two or more are complementary, of course call attention to them only as one relates to the other.

MEANS OF STIMULATING INTEREST IN ARCHERY

Variety in the type of shooting is a means of stimulating continued interest in the sport. Any ingenious instructor who really loves the activity can arrange the seasonal schedule so that the various occasions well spaced throughout the year will catch the interest and effort of many an archer. Indoor shooting during the winter is an excellent stimulus toward maintenance of good form and the ability to maintain accuracy even under changes of range and size of target. During the season, clout shooting, flight shooting, archery golf, balloon shoots, wand shoots, field archery, roving, play days, exhibition shoot, recreational archery with mixed doubles in competition, William Tell or Popinjay shoots, ending the term perhaps with a challenge mail or telegraphic meet or a rabbit hunt in the woods, all add gaiety and variety to weeks of straight target work. Suggesting the purchase of tackle for personal ownership, wherever possible, is a stimulus to maintaining keenness for the sport. Visual aids besides the use of motion pictures are often more useful in stimulating interest and building background than in the study of technique. A full length mirror is helpful in producing an awareness of stance and form. A smaller mirror held close by the instructor makes it possible for the student to see and correct head position, anchor point, and finger position at throat. For the rest the teacher of archery is thrown on her own initiative in the making of diagrams and charts which will supplement instruction. These can readily give analytical, detailed demonstration of the steps in shooting.

A *weekly check* on *individual scoring* can be made by use of a target posted in the archery room. With a thumb tack in the tip, a cardboard arrow with the individual's name and pencilled score is attached. This target, 30 inches in diameter, painted with five regulation colored rings, has each of the five rings labeled in the hundreds. The white equals 100; the black, 200; the blue, 300; the red, 400; and the gold, 500. The majority of arrows perhaps remain in the blue, but great enthusiasm is demonstrated when an arrow can be moved up into the red. With the short season that is necessary in many eastern schools, the 500 gold ring is still but a goal which has not as yet been realized. If working with younger girls, the same system with modified scoring can be established.

The *Popinjay Shoot* is a colorful adaptation of the *Wand Shoot*. Onto a flat lath, 2 inches wide and 10 feet above the ground, at 1-foot intervals are tacked into place six birds jigsawed out of lathing, three on each side, with the seventh bird perched on the top, the Popinjay. The pattern for these can be a 6- to 8-inch long garden bird decoy. The "side" birds may be painted various colors that show up well in the light—yellow, blue, white, red. The Popinjay should be an inch longer preferably with a crest on his head and painted a variety of colors. Shooting at the birds in competition, in alternation, at 30 yards, each using two consecutive arrows, the score of seven goes to anyone who hits a bird, nine to the Popinjay hitter, and one to those who hit the upright. This may be shot off by sides, chosen as one chooses sides by counting off as in children's games or by dividing the class as equally as possible according to their Columbia Round scores, one high and one low on each side until all are placed. This livens up the class or group a bit and calls for accurate aim. It is often so popular that there is a demand for it during open hour, individually or in groups.

An outstanding feature on the semester program can be a *Rabbit Hunt*. According to the number who sign up to go, papier-mâché rabbits are purchased at a five-and-ten-cent store. These should stand at least 12 inches high. With the student manager and a few willing volunteers, the trails are laid. For safety it should be planned so that six archers are accompanied by one of the trail setters and that the trails never cross. In advance, permission to pass through farm land, cross fences, follow brooks, and such should be obtained from the farmers concerned. The trails can be laid the morning of the hunt. Each trail is laid in the following manner. From a given starting point, directional arrows of light pasteboard are thumbtacked onto the trees and fence posts at intervals wide enough to be interesting, but not confusing. At an unexpected spot a rabbit is placed, preferably protected against being blown over by the wind. The last arrow before the rabbit should read "shoot." If time is a consideration, the arrows at least could be placed the day before, but the bunnies should be spotted on the same day or they may disappear by other means than the arrows for which they were planned! Never set them on rocks or directly against a tree, however, for that offers too great a danger of arrow breakage.

The shooting range should vary both as to distance and terrain.

Sometimes shooting downhill at 40 yards, sometimes uphill at 15 yards and again on the level, half hidden in the grass at 20 yards, all make for variety and fun. The same number of rabbits as there are students on each trail and more if the cost is not too great, six to ten at least, should be spotted. The trail-following should be planned to consume about forty minutes of hiking, so, with adding shooting time of forty-five minutes or an hour, the entire time allowed would not be more than two hours of an afternoon, even with time out to look for lost arrows. The poorest arrow sets should be used so that loss or breakage will not be too expensive. Each archer must shoot at each rabbit, but the quarry belongs to the first one who hits the animal. If on the first trial no one makes a hit, after retrieving arrows, all must return to the original shooting spot and repeat until someone is successful. If transportation to the starting point for all the trails is obtainable and two hours are allowed for completion of the hunt, the cooking committee can have the picnic supper in readiness at a given time and at a spot within hailing distance of the final "rabbit spot" for each of the trails. Even "Hasenpfeffer" (German rabbit stew) might be served! With a little effort and ingenuity the rabbit hunt can be a memorable event. Other events can be added and modified from year to year for continuation of interest in archery.

Those of us who have both taught and enjoyed the intriguing sport of archery can only hope that increased ability in the sport will keep abreast of the enlarging interest and enthusiasm which are current today.

ARCHERY TERMS

In larger volumes will be found more inclusive glossaries. This one intends only to define the terms used in this treatise.

Addressing the Target. Standing ready for target shooting with the body at right angles to the target, feet straddling the shooting line.

American Round. For women, 30 arrows at 60, 50, and 40 yards each.

Anchor Point. A definite spot on the face to which the index finger of the string hand must come consistently in drawing.

Archery Golf. An adapted roving game, played on a real or simulated golf course, using the bow and arrow.

Arm Guard. Usually a leather protection worn on the lower bow arm to prevent string abrasions.

Arrowplate. An insert of hard material designed to prevent injury to the bow, set into the bow where the arrow crosses it on release.

Back. The flat of the bow; the side away from the string.

Backed Bow. A bow which is strengthened by a thin strip of wood, rawhide, or other strong material glued on the length of the back.

Belly. The surface of the bow which faces the string; also called "face."

Bow Arm. The arm, the hand of which holds the bow during shooting.

Bow Sight. A device on the bow used for aiming.

Bow-stave. A piece of wood from which a bow can be made.

Bowyer. A maker of bows.

Brace. To string a bow; to put the string's eye into the bow's upper nock.

Bracer. An arm guard.

Cast. The distance a bow can shoot; the release of the drawn string which sends the arrow outward.

Chrysal. A pinched spot or crack which has been caused by repeated compressions that develops in the belly of the bow.

Clout. A mark placed on the ground for long distance shooting.

Clout Shooting. A definite round, usually 36 arrows, 180 yards for men, 140 and 120 yards for women, shot at a 48-foot target laid on the ground.

Cock Feather. The feather set at right angles to the arrow nock, generally of a different color from the hen feathers.

Columbia Round. A round, usually shot by women or girls, consisting of 24 arrows shot at each of 50-, 40-, and 30-yard ranges.

Composite Bow. A bow which consists of various layers of material.

Creeping. A "give" forward with the string hand at the moment of release.

Crest. The identifying marks on the arrow at the feathered end.

Double Round. A round shot twice in succession.

Draw. The pulling back of the bowstring; also the distance to which the bow is drawn.

Drift. A deviation of an arrow in flight due to wind.

Elevation. The required height of the bow hand while aiming.

End: American. Six arrows which are shot in succession or in two groups of three; *English:* three arrows shot consecutively.

Eye. A loop woven into one end of the string which is fitted into the nock of the upper horn when the bow is strung.

Face. Of the bow. See "Belly."

Field Captain. Individual in charge of a tournament.

Finger Shooting. Method of practicing release of the string by using partner's index finger as the "string."

Finger Tip or Stall. Protection from the string, usually of leather, worn on the string fingers.

Fistmele. An old English term describing the approximate height of the fist with the thumb raised, used in measuring the distance from string to braced bow. Inaccurately, 6 inches.

Fletch. To secure feathers to an arrow.

Fletcher. One who secures feathers to an arrow; a device for securing feathers to an arrow.

Flight Shooting. The effort to shoot an arrow the farthest possible distance.

Follow the String. The tendency of a bow to retain the same curves unstrung that it holds when strung.

Footed Arrow. An arrow reinforced with a splicing of hard wood at the pile end, giving added strength and weight.

Foot Marker. A pair of flat markers which may be inserted in the ground to mark stance and against which the toes are placed on the shooting line.

Grouping. The clustering in close proximity of arrows that have been shot.

Handle. The mid-section of the bow which the bow hand grips.

Head. Point, tip, or pile of an arrow.

Hen Feathers. The other two feathers on the shaftment that are not at right angles to the nock and are similar in color.

Hereford Round. For women, 72 arrows at 80 yards, 48 at 60 yards, 24 at 50 yards.

Hit. To strike the target on its scoring surface.

Holding. Steadily keeping an arrow at full draw before its release.

Horns. The reinforcements of horn on ends of upper and lower limbs.

Jig. A device for securing feathers to the arrow shaft.

Junior American Round. For boys and girls, 30 arrows each at 60-, 50-, and 40-yard ranges.

Junior Columbia Round. A beginner's round, shot by both boys and girls, consisting of 24 arrows shot at each of 40-, 30-, and 20-yard ranges.

Keeper. A "leader," a bit of string or tape used to secure the upper eye of the string onto the upper limb, when unstrung.

Lady Paramount. The lady in charge of a women's tournament.

Leader. See "Keeper."

Let Fly. To release an arrow for flight.

Limbs. Upper and lower parts of the bow, divided by the handle.

Loose. To release the fully drawn bowstring.

National Round. For women: 48 arrows shot at 60 yards and 24 arrows at 50 yards.

Nock. The groove in the end of the arrow for the reception of the string; the groove at each end of the bow for the reception of the string; the reinforcements, usually of horn, attached to each end of the bow; the act of placing the arrow on the string.

Nocking Point. The point on the string at which the nock of the arrow should be placed.

Over-bowed. Using too strong a bow.

Over-drawn. For the arrow, to draw it so that the pile is within the belly; for the bow, to draw beyond the required length of the arrow.

Perfect End. Six consecutive arrows shot into the gold. If witnessed and attested to, official recognition is offered by the N.A.A. The goal of every archer!

Petticoat. The edge of the target face beyond the white ring.

Pile. The pointed metal tip of the arrow.

Pinsight. A device adjustable on the bow, used for acquiring and holding proper aim.

Point Blank Range. The distance, for any given bow, at which the point of aim is the center of the gold.

Point of Aim. A mark, used when sighting, upon which the tip of the arrow is aimed, not more than 1½ inches square or in diameter and not more than 6 inches above ground level according to N.A.A. ruling.

Quiver. A holder for arrows; three types: stationary at given ranges; ground, which is movable; and one worn on the belt of the archer.

Range. Shooting distance; an archery ground, indoors or out.

Range Finder. A device by which varying points of aim may be easily determined.

Reflexed Bow. A bow having an unusual outline when unstrung. This outline describes an obtuse angle where the backs of the upper and lower limbs meet.

Round. The name used to describe shooting a definite number of arrows at specific distances. All rounds recognized by the N.A.A. are described in its Official Tournament Rules, drawn up in August 1953.

Roving or *Rovers.* An archery game consisting of shooting a certain number of shots at given distances over an outdoor course.

Self-arrow. An arrow made from a single piece of wood without the reinforcement of a footing.

Self-bow. A bow made of one kind of wood.

Serving. The "whipping" or wrapping of thread around the bow-string in the center of the string which receives wear from nocking and drawing.

Shaft. The main part of an arrow.

Shaftment. The part of the arrow holding the crest and the feathers.

Shooting Line. The line which marks a specific distance on the range.

Sight. An aiming device on string or bow used so that the aim may be directly on the gold, without the use of point of aim.

Spine. A characteristic of an arrow's strength and resiliency.

Stave. A length of wood from which a bow is made.

Stringing. Bracing the bow; securing string correctly in nocks.

Tab. A protection for the string fingers, usually made of leather.

Tackle. An inclusive term for archery equipment.

Target Face. The front cover of a target, painted with the regulation colored rings.

Tassel. A bunch of yarn for wiping off of arrows, usually worn on an archer's belt.

Timber-hitch. The knot used in securing the bow-string to the lower limb.

Toxophilite. One who has studied the history as well as mastered the art of shooting with bow and arrow.

Trajectory. The path the arrow describes in flight.

Under Bowed. Using too light a bow.

Vane. A feather of an arrow.

Wand Shoot. Shooting at a narrow upright stick. The distances and dimensions vary. N.A.A. ruling calls for stick two inches wide with six-foot height above ground for both men and women archers.

Weight. The total pull, measured in pounds, required to draw a bow the length of its arrow; of an arrow, actual weight in grains.

Wide. Term to describe the flight of an arrow to either side of the target.

Windage. The possible influence of wind upon an arrow in flight.

REFERENCES

Books:

Craft, Dave and Cia: *The Teaching of Archery*. New York, A. S. Barnes and Co., 1936.

Duff, James: *Bows and Arrows*. New York, The Macmillan Co., 1927.

Elmer, Robert P.: *Archery*. New York, A. S. Barnes and Co., 1929.

Elmer, Robert P.: *Target Archery*. New York, Alfred A. Knopf Company, 1936.

Elmer, Robert P., and Faris, Nabih A.: *Arab Archery*. Princeton, N. J., Princeton University Press, 1945.

Lambert, Arthur W., Jr.: *Modern Archery*. New York, A. S. Barnes and Co., 1929.

Reichert, Natalie, and Keasey, Gilman: *Modern Methods in Archery*. New York, A. S. Barnes and Co., 1940.

Rounsevelle, Philip: *Archery Simplified*. New York, A. S. Barnes and Co., 1931.

Schmidt, Marvin: *Introduction to Archery*. Chicago, Ziff-Davis Publishing Co., 1946.

Stemmler, L. E.: *Essentials of Archery*. Queens Village, N. Y., L. E. Stemmler Co., 1937.

Sumption, Dorothy: *Archery for Beginners*. Philadelphia, W. B. Saunders Co., 1932.

Thompson, Maurice: *The Witchery of Archery*. Pinehurst, N. C., The Archers Co., 1928.

Yocum, Rachael B., and Hunsaker, H. B.: *Individual Sports for Men and Women*. New York, A. S. Barnes and Co., 1947.

Articles, Magazines and Pamphlets:

Archery Handbook of the Boy Scouts of America, Merit Badge Series, new edition edited by Lawrence E. Briggs, Amherst, Mass.

Archery Handbooks, by Eloise Jaeger of the Department of Physical Education at the University of Minnesota, published by The Athletic Institute, 209 So. State St., Chicago 4, Illinois.

Archery Activities to Stimulate Interest in Camps, Schools and Clubs, compiled by the Archery Staff of Teela-Wooket Archery Camp, Roxbury, Vermont.

Archery Enhances a Camp Program, by Lawrence E. Briggs, University of Massachusetts, Amherst, Mass. Originally published in *Archers' Magazine.* Available in mimeographed form.

Archery Magazine, a monthly on hunting and field archery, Palm Desert, California.

Technique Chart on Archery, published by the National Section on Women's Athletics of the American Association for Health, Physical Education and Recreation, 1201 Sixteenth St., N.W., Washington 6, D. C.

The American Bowman, a monthly for target archers, Albany, Oregon.

The Archers' Magazine, a monthly on sport, crafts and hobbies of target archers, field and target shooters and bow hunters.

The Bow Hunter Magazine, a monthly for bow hunters everywhere, 539 No. 99th St., Milwaukee 13, Wisconsin.

Ye Sylvan Archer, published in Corvallis, Oregon.

Associations:

National Archery Association: Sec.-Treas., Mr. Lawrence E. Briggs, 1157 No. Pleasant St., Amherst, Mass.

National Field Archery Association: Sec., John L. Yount, Box 388, Redlands, California.

Camp Archery Association: Sec., Fred D. Stern, 170 West 81st St., New York, N. Y.

2 • BADMINTON • BY *Helen L. Russell*

The game of "Poona," ancestor of badminton, originated in India about the middle 1800's. The English army officers adopted the game and transported it to England around 1873. The name of badminton came into being that year when the game was introduced at the Duke of Beaufort's country estate, "Badminton," in Gloucestershire, England. On that day, badminton became the official name for the game.

The first rules were printed in India in 1877 and these governed the game until 1887 when the Bath Badminton Association of England was formed. This group standardized the equipment and playing rules. In 1895, the English Badminton Association was established and took over the printing of the official rules.

From England, badminton spread to the United States and Canada. The Canadian Badminton Association was founded in 1922 and the American Badminton Association in 1937. However, badminton was being played in these countries long before those dates. The New York Badminton Club was formed in 1879 and has the distinction of being the oldest club of its kind in continuous existence in the world.

Few sports have enjoyed the rapid growth that badminton has had throughout the United States. It has shown its growth by the number of clubs formed, by the many sectional tournaments, by the increasing numbers of schools and colleges which are offering badminton as a curricular and extracurricular activity in their physical education programs.

The reasons for its growth are apparent to all who are familiar with the game. It can be played indoors or outdoors. The area required is relatively small for court games (44 by 20 feet), and no special court surface is necessary. One of its major values is that sufficient skill to enjoy playing the game can be acquired fairly quickly. This does not mean that the game of badminton is one of simple techniques and strategy. On the contrary, it is perhaps one of the fastest and most skillful racquet games when played by experts. However, persons of all levels of ability can participate and get desired activity.

In badminton, as in any sport, skill increases the pleasure and the satisfaction derived, and these encourage further participation. The aims of the badminton instructor should include: the clear presentation of the skills to be used in the game, the opportunity for intelligent and organized practice of these skills, and opportunity for their use in a game situation with competition among those of similar ability.

This chapter is organized on the following basis: Selection and care of equipment is discussed first; then specific techniques are analyzed; etiquette and strategy are described for the doubles and singles game; general suggestions, practice formations and sample lesson plans for all levels are given in the section termed Class Organization; finally, tournaments and testing are discussed in relation to badminton classes.

EQUIPMENT

I. Racquets

Badminton racquets are not guaranteed; therefore, it is important to purchase them from a reliable manufacturer in order to insure good construction. It is a mistake to invest in the cheapest racquets on the market or in the most expensive tournament racquets for general class use. A little better than average price should buy a good, serviceable racquet which can be restrung many times.

The instructor should consider certain specific factors when purchasing racquets for class use or in advising students in regard to buying their own racquets. The *weight* range of racquets varies from four to six ounces, light to heavy. A racquet weight of five ounces (strung) is considered best for the majority of players. The *size of the handle* is also a variable, ranging from three to four inches. Again, the median size, 3½ to 3¾ inches, seems best for general class use. The length of the individual's fingers can make a difference in the personal purchase of a racquet, shorter fingers requiring a smaller handle. The handle of the racquet should be encased in a *grip*, preferably a perforated leather one. This grip is included in the measurement of handle size. The *balance* of the racquet is a matter of opinion. Most racquets have an even balance and are a safe investment; however, some players prefer the weight in the head of the racquet, and therefore a number of racquets with this type of balance should be purchased for classes.

The *stringing* of the racquets is an important consideration because of expense and desired resiliency. There are three types of stringing— lamb's gut, silk, and nylon. Skilled players always prefer racquets that are gut-strung, which is the most expensive type of stringing. The recommended thickness of gut for standard play is 20-gauge; for top tournament play, 21-gauge. Silk stringing does not afford the resiliency or "touch" which is characteristic of tightly strung gut; however, it is considerably cheaper. Nylon may provide the answer to school racquet stringing. It is as low in price as the best silk and cheapest gut, while it rarely breaks in the center of the racquet where gut and silk fray. However, there is danger of the racquet stringing grooves cutting the nylon unless they are smoothed and filed before stringing. Regardless of the type of stringing used, these holes should be kept smooth.

The badminton racquet is the most fragile of all sports racquets and consequently good *care* of it must be taken. When not in use, it should be kept in a press of even tension and hung between pegs in a dry place. If the racquets are used throughout the day, fairly continuously, they should not be placed in presses until the end of the day. Students must be shown the correct way to apply pressure to the presses so as not to produce warping in the racquets. Students should also be trained to examine the racquet before playing with it and to do so at frequent intervals during play in order to discover a broken string as soon as it occurs. If the student puts aside the racquet immediately upon breaking a string, it is possible to replace the one string without the necessity of completely restringing the racquet.

II. Shuttles

In general, there are two types of shuttlecocks which can be used in classes. The first is the official tournament bird with cork base and 16 evenly matched feathers. These birds weigh 73 and 85 grains, the lighter weight being for indoor doubles play and the heavier for outdoor singles.

The expense of these shuttles makes the *care* of them an extremely important factor. The feathers must be straightened after evry rally; the bird should be put in play by hitting it underhand rather than tossing it up and hitting it overhead; and the bird should be picked up by hand from the floor—never hit or kicked along the floor. Before the feathered shuttles are used, they should be well humidified by placing them in a container with a temperature of 60 to 65 degrees Fahrenheit and a relative humidity of 70 to 75 per cent for at least one hour. This treatment prevents the feathers from becoming brittle and then breaking.

The second type of bird is the synthetic one made of a rubberized material. These birds are less expensive than the good quality feathered shuttles and they remain in good condition for a much longer time than the official bird. The only concern in the care of these birds is to avoid stepping on them. They are excellent for practice either on the courts or against the wall. The cost of birds will be cut in half if these are used for practice of strokes in beginning and intermediate classes.

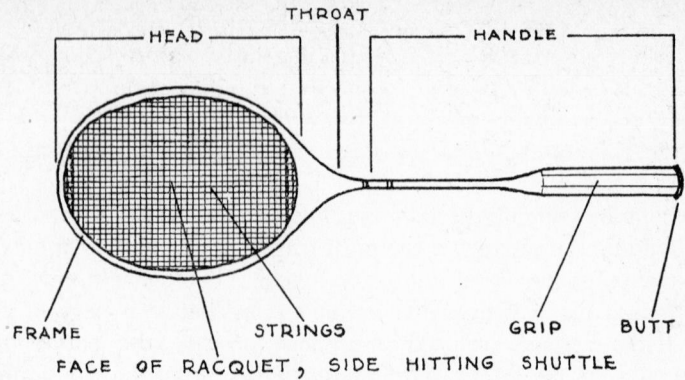

Fig. 14. The parts of the racquet.

III. Court and Nets

The rules specify the width and color of the lines which make up a badminton court. Ideally, the floor surface and walls should be dark, forest green being the favored color. The ceiling height should have a minimum clearance of 30 feet and 40 is preferable. Artificial lighting is more satisfactory than sunlight since nonglare lamps can be used in the former type.

Nets are standard in size but vary in price. The better quality will wear longer. Students should be instructed *not* to lean on the net or pull it down.

Well-kept equipment is essential for good play. Much can be done to insure cooperation in the care of equipment by presenting this as a part of the class work early in the course.

TECHNIQUES

The techniques are presented in this section under four headings: (1) use, (2) analysis, (3) presentation and practice suggestions for beginning class, and (4) common faults. The analysis is always given in relation to a right-handed player.

I. Grips

(A) *Forehand.*

1. USE.
(a) For all strokes taken on the right-hand side of the body.
(b) For all serves.
(c) For round-the-head shots.

2. ANALYSIS. This grip is very similar to the Eastern forehand grip in tennis. The "V" of the thumb and forefinger is very pronounced and is on the top plate of the handle (see Fig. 15). The forefinger is

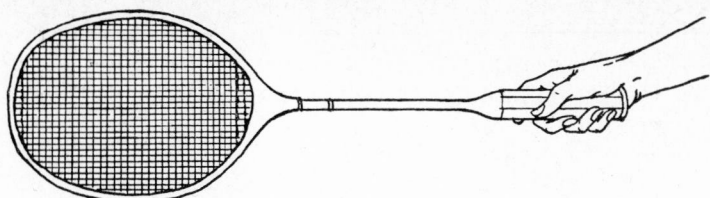

Fig. 15. The forehand grip.

diagonally across the back of the handle and hooked under it and ahead of the thumb. The racquet is held in the fingers with the butt of the racquet pressed against the heel of the hand; the racquet handle does not rest against the palm of the hand.

3. PRESENTATION TO BEGINNERS. The students stand in a semicircle around the instructor, holding the racquets by the throats in their left hands. The instructor demonstrates the grip and then has the students place their right hands on the racquet handles in the forehand grip position. Instructor checks the grip of every girl, then has the students put racquets back in left hands. Class repeats practice of assuming correct forehand grip several times—teacher checks grips each time. Importance of proper grip should be stressed by instructor because wrist action is most important single element in all badminton strokes and wrist action depends upon the proper grip.

4. COMMON FAULTS. The following faults all tend to limit wrist action:

(a) Fist grip—fingers not diagonally up racquet handle and racquet gripped in palm of the hand.

(b) Western grip—the "V" of thumb and forefinger is on the back plate of handle rather than on the top one.

(c) Forefinger is extended straight up handle rather than wrapped under handle.

(d) Thumb is extended along the top plate of handle.

(B) *Backhand.*

1. USE. For all strokes executed on the left side of the body.

2. ANALYSIS. This grip is almost identical to the Eastern backhand tennis grip. When the racquet face is perpendicular to the floor, the right hand is placed on the top plate of the handle (heel of hand) and the fingers are spread diagonally up and around the handle. The first knuckle of the forefinger is on the top plate. The thumb extends along the back plate of the handle, slightly diagonally across it. The "V" of the thumb and forefinger is somewhat more "closed" than is the case in the forehand grip.

3. PRESENTATION TO BEGINNERS. This grip is presented to the class in the same way as was the forehand. After the students have learned

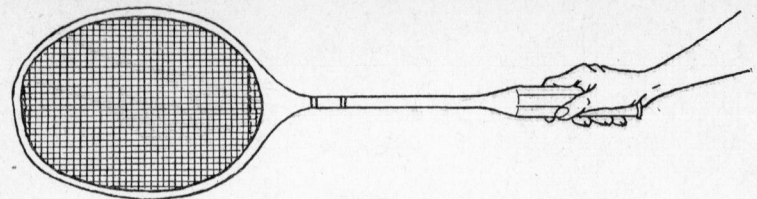

Fig. 16. The backhand grip.

the backhand grip, they then should practice the change in grip—from the forehand to backhand and again to forehand. At first the racquet is held at the throat by the left hand between changes; but as the practice continues the students should learn to make the change without the use of the left hand—by merely shifting the racquet within the right hand.

4. COMMON FAULTS. The following faults limit wrist action and weaken the resultant strokes:

(a) Fist grip—knuckles of fingers are lined up along the top plate of the handle; thumb is at right angles to fingers and straight along back plate of the handle.

(b) Hand is not shifted on racquet and forehand grip is used for backhand strokes.

(c) Hand is shifted too far behind racquet handle and forefinger is extended up back plate of the handle.

II. Wrist Action

(A) USE. The importance of the wrist action in badminton cannot be overstressed. The wrist is involved to some extent in every stroke. The racquet is light in weight and the handle is small (when compared with tennis and squash racquets) in order to let the wrist perform the whip action necessary to hit with any force such a light object as the shuttlecock.

(B) ANALYSIS. Wrist action is the term which describes the movement of the wrist from the backward, cocked position (extension) to the flexed position. The speed with which this action is performed will determine the speed of the bird. The correct forehand and backhand grips are absolutely essential for free wrist action.

(C) PRESENTATION TO BEGINNERS. On the first day of class, after the forehand grip has been taught to the students, the instructor demonstrates full wrist action by hitting the bird straight up in the air, starting with little taps and continuing to hit it higher and higher until the full underhand arm and wrist actions are used. She then stations the students far apart and has them practice it. (One bird to a pair of students.) This technique is more difficult than it may sound and is an excellent one for warm-up practice for any player.

If students during the first part of the season tend to have stiff wrists and lack of flexibility, practice in hitting the bird with the racquet in the left hand may help. The finer wrist coordination is absent in the left arm and a stiff, awkward motion usually results. When the change is made back to hitting with the racquet held in the right hand, the relief of having wrist control and action may increase wrist use.

(D) COMMON FAULTS.

1. Incorrect forehand grip which does not permit necessary wrist action.

2. Too tight a grip which tenses muscles of wrist and therefore locks wrist.

3. Inadequate acceleration of arm and wrist movement. Underhand swing is not an even, smooth stroke but is an upward whiplike hit which is gaining momentum as the bird is contacted.

III. Footwork

(A) USE. The game of badminton can be a terrifically fast one and it is through the work of the feet that a player covers the court. Footwork patterns must be learned and become habits—no time may be taken to think "how" to move.

(B) ANALYSIS. Each stroke necessitates a specific stance or position of the feet. In general, the footwork involved in badminton is similar to that in tennis. The principle of opposition is applied to all strokes with two exceptions (the serve and the return of drop shots from right front corner of the court). The weight is carried on the balls of the feet. Small steps are taken and to cover short distances, the slide or hop step is used.

For the forehand strokes, the left foot is toward the net, the right foot back and the body turned toward the right sideline. The body weight shifts from the rear (right) foot to the forward foot (left) as the stroke is made.

For the backhand strokes, the body faces the left sideline and the right foot is toward the net and the left foot back. The body weight shifts from the rear foot (left) to the front foot (right) as the backhand strokes are made.

The *"ready" position* (that which the player assumes when receiving the serve and during the rally between strokes) is the starting point from which footwork is taught. This position is an alert one with left foot slightly ahead of the right, weight evenly balanced on toes; the racquet is held up in front of the body with head pointing toward opponent. This "up" position of the racquet makes possible quick over-

Fig. 17. The ready-to-play position.

head returns of the bird; and every effort should be made to hit birds with an overhead stroke rather than with an underhand one.

(C) PRESENTATION TO BEGINNERS. Stance and body position are taught as a part of each stroke. Footwork drills can be practiced separately but always with the racquet in hand and in conjunction with a stroke. For example, after the forehand drive has been introduced, active footwork practice ending with a forehand drive in various parts of the court can be presented and practiced. Two elementary footwork practice formations are:

1. Change from forehand to backhand body position. With the right foot forward: (a) move the left foot ahead; (b) to step back, pivot on the left foot and place the right foot back (Fig. 18).

2. Change from backhand body position to forehand. With the left foot forward: (a) step forward with the right (pivoting on the left) or (b) back with the left (now pivoting on the right).

IV. The Serves

There are three types of serve which can be used to put the shuttle into play at the beginning of each rally: the long high, the short low and the drive. According to the official rules, only the server may score a point; therefore, these three strokes are very important and

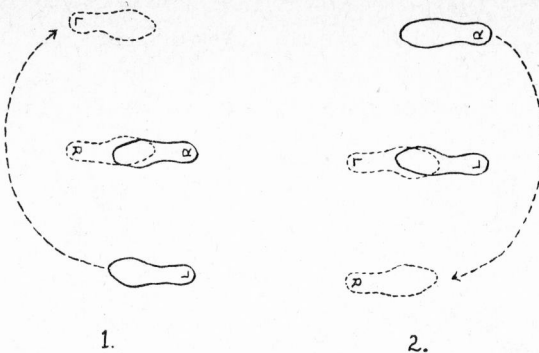

1. **2.**

Fig. 18. Pivot from stance for backhand to stance for forehand stroke. 1, moving the left foot forward. 2, moving the right foot back.

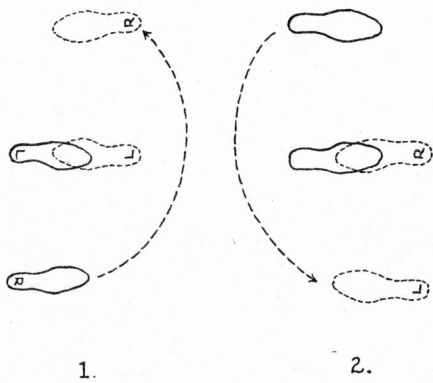

1. **2.**

Fig. 19. Pivot from position for forehand, to position for backhand. 1, pivot on left foot. 2, pivot on right foot.

considerable time must be devoted to their mastery. The serves are defensive strokes because they must be executed underhand. The rule states that in the serve, at the moment of impact with the bird, the top edge of the racquet head must be below the level of the wrist and contact with the bird must be below waist level.

The backswing is the same for all three serves. The only difference lies in the movement of the wrist at the time of impact with the bird. There should be as much similarity in the execution of all serves as possible so that the receiver will not be able to anticipate.

(A) *Long High Serve.*

1. DESCRIPTION AND USE. The bird as it passes the net is rising and reaches maximum height near the rear of court where it lands. This serve is the basic serve for singles play and is used only occasionally in doubles. The long narrow singles service court allows for the long

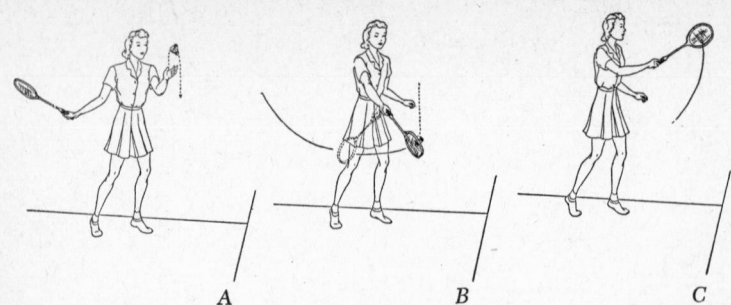

Fig. 20. The toss service. *A*, backswing. *B*, point of contact. *C*, follow-through.

high serve and forces the opponent into the rear part of the court.

2. ANALYSIS.

(a) Grip. The forehand grip is used almost exclusively for the serve.

(b) Stance. (1) For the beginner, the left foot is forward and pointing toward the net. The right foot is back with the toe at about a 45 degree angle with the net. The body is bent forward slightly. This position allows for weight transfer if necessary; however, the student should attempt to execute the serve without use of the body. (2) For the experienced player, the right foot is forward and pointing directly toward the receiver. The body weight is on this forward foot, the left leg is back with the knee flexed and the toe resting on the floor. The body is bent forward slightly.

(c) Arm and Wrist Action. (1) The arm is swung straight back from the shoulder, hip-height, the wrist cocked. The face of the racquet is parallel to the floor. (2) The racquet is swung downward and slightly outward and just before impact with the bird, the wrist is uncocked and whipped into the stroke. The racquet follows through above the head on the left side of the body with the wrist completely uncocked. (3) The bird is held in the left hand by the feathers between thumb and forefinger and is dropped ahead and to the side of the forward foot. The timing of the serve is, "Drop, swing."

3. PRESENTATION TO BEGINNERS. Students are on one side of the badminton court in several lines with space for swinging racquets; the instructor stands in front of them. This formation is the one used throughout this section for introducing all new strokes to beginners and will not be described under each stroke. The instructor explains the rules governing serves (execution and court lines) and describes the three types. She analyzes and demonstrates the long high serve. Students practice timing and swing mimetically (without bird) in unison. Two suggested practice formations are:

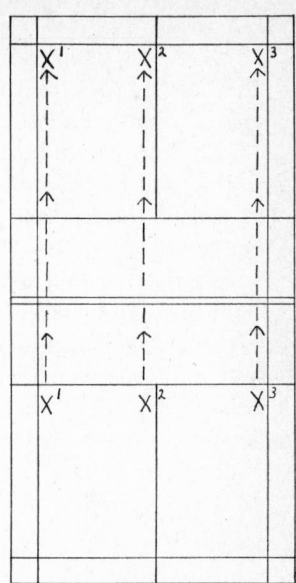

Fig. 21. Long serve practice
formation.

(a) One Bird per Pair of Students. Players on one side of the net stand about one yard behind the short service line and serve straight across to opponent, attempting to make bird land in the rear alley. Opponent lets bird drop, then picks it up, moves to serving position and serves back; no rallying during this practice. Three pairs can practice on one court. One pair of players can practice between courts.

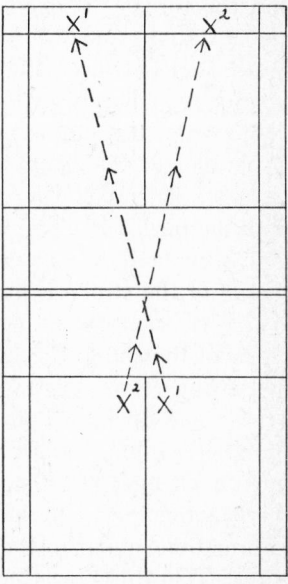

Fig. 22. Long serve practice
formation.

(b) Two Birds per Court. One player serves from right court and at same time another player serves from left court (both serve into diagonally opposite courts). Server attempts to hit back alley. Receiving players let bird drop, then serve back. There should be no rallying. Rear court players change with front after five serves and go through practice. The next practice is for players in right court to change with those in left and repeat long service practice from opposite court.

4. COMMON FAULTS.

(a) No wrist whip, resulting in weak hit.

(b) Wrist uncocks but arm does not continue through with stroke—bird goes high and short.

(c) Position where bird is dropped. (1) If too far ahead of forward foot serve will be short and high. (2) If too far behind forward foot, serve will be too low and can be returned with a smash.

(B) *Short Serve.*

1. DESCRIPTION AND USE. The bird barely clears the net in a flat line of flight and lands within the proper service court on or close to the short service line. This serve is the basic serve for doubles play and is used only occasionally in singles. The wider and shorter doubles service court lends itself to the short serve whereas the narrower and longer singles court lends itself to the long, high serve.

2. ANALYSIS.

(a) Grip. Same as for the long high serve—forehand.

(b) Stance. Same as for the long high serve.

(c) Arm and Wrist Action. (1) The racquet position at the beginning of the stroke is the same as for the long high serve. (Deception is important.) (2) The start of the downswing is similar to that of the long serve; but before impact with the bird, the racquet is checked and the bird is "stroked" gently. The wrist uncocks only enough to give a straight line of forearm and racquet and proper angle to racquet head. There is very little follow-through after contact. A second type of execution has been found successful with some students. On the downswing, the elbow is flexed to a 90 degree angle (the forearm is parallel to the floor) and the wrist *never* uncocks. This position insures a flat racquet face and not an open one at moment of contact with the bird. (3) The bird is held in the same manner as for the long high serve and is contacted in approximately the same position. The timing of the stroke is also the same.

3. PRESENTATION TO BEGINNERS. The instructor explains the principles of the short serve and demonstrates it. Students practice timing and swing. Two suggested practice formations:

(a) One Bird per Pair of Students. Players stand one yard behind short service line and serve straight across to opponents who allow the bird to hit on court. Then opponents serve back. No rallying during this practice. Serve should be directed into front part of service court. (Formation similar to Fig. 21.)

(b) Two Birds per Court. Players serve diagonally into opponents' courts (same formation as Fig. 22). Receiving players let bird hit court, pick it up and serve back. There should be no rallying. After five serves rear court players change with forecourt players and become servers. After five serves, right court players change with left court ones and practice serves.

4. COMMON FAULTS.

(a) In checking swing, wrist uncocks too much and bird goes high and short.

(b) No deception in stroke and opponent can anticipate where bird is going.

C. *The Drive Serve.*

1. DESCRIPTION AND USE. The bird is fast and low, combining the power of the long high serve with the low height of the short serve. The bird, if not returned by receiver, passes her at shoulder height and lands deep in service court. This serve is used occasionally as a surprise in doubles play and for the same purpose but more infrequently in singles play. This serve should be executed by experienced players only. The purpose of this serve is to get the bird past opponent before she can react or make a planned return.

2. ANALYSIS.

(a) Grip. Same as for other serves—forehand.

(b) Stance. Same as for other serves.

(c) Arm and Wrist Action. (1) The racquet position at the beginning of the stroke is the same as for the other two serves. (Again, deception is vital.) (2) The start of the downswing is similar to that of the other serves. Just before impact with bird, the wrist uncocks and whips through with force. The follow-through is toward the net in a flat "drive" position about chest height (not over the left shoulder as in the high serve nor in low position of short serve). (3) The bird is held between thumb and forefinger by the feathers and is contacted in the same relative position as for the other two serves. The timing of this serve is also the same.

3. PRESENTATION TO BEGINNERS. This serve should be taught to students who have completely mastered the other two types of serves and who have had considerable experience in playing the game. The stroke is presented to the students in the same manner as are the other two serves. The same two practice formations can be employed.

4. COMMON FAULTS.

(a) In an effort to keep the bird low over the net, a fault may be committed by hitting the bird with the racquet head above the wrist.

(b) Hitting the bird too gently and thus setting it up. Arm and wrist must be snapped into the stroke.

(c) Hitting opponent's racquet with the bird which results in such a fast return that server cannot recover in time.

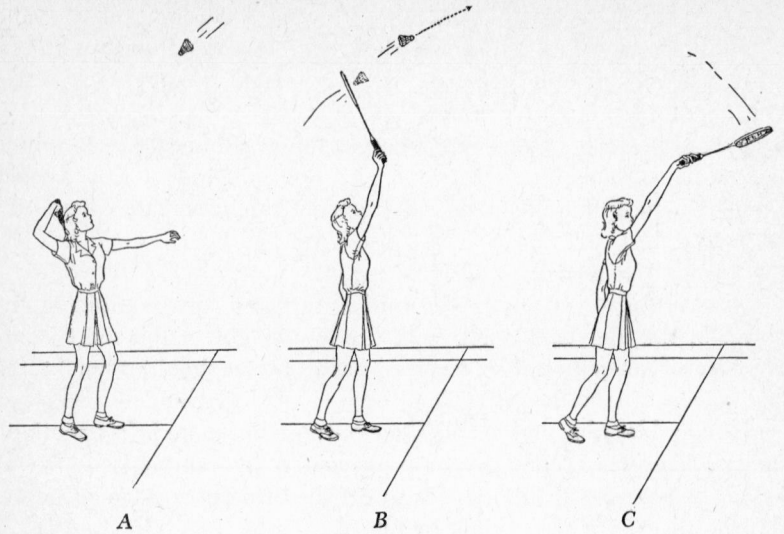

Fig. 23. The overhead clear. *A,* backswing. *B,* point of contact. *C,* beginning of follow-through.

V. Overhead Strokes

(A) *Overhead Clear (Forehand).*

1. DESCRIPTION AND USE. The bird rises high over net, continues in an upward flight and drops almost vertically near the baseline. This stroke is the most important one in singles play and a basic stroke in women's doubles. It can be used as an offensive stroke by putting the bird over opponent's head with a fast, low clear or as a defensive stroke by sending the bird to the baseline with tremendous height, which gives the player who made the clear time to recover court position.

2. ANALYSIS.

(a) Grip. Forehand.

(b) Stance. The left foot is forward at about a 45 degree angle with the net; the right foot is in a comfortable position behind forward foot. Weight transfers to the rear foot with the racquet backswing and then to the front foot with the bird contact and follow-through.

(c) Arm and Wrist Action. (1) The preparatory part of the stroke includes a full straight arm backswing which ends in a stationary position of the racquet behind the head with the right shoulder dropped and rotated back, right elbow bent and pointing toward floor behind body, wrist fully cocked. (2) Racquet is swung up and slightly to the right of the body, contacting the bird at a point ahead and to the right of the forward foot (left) with full arm stretch and full wrist whip. (3) The follow-through is up and forward and racquet finishes across the left side of the body.

3. PRESENTATION TO BEGINNERS. Instructor gives explanation of stroke's use and execution and demonstrates it. Class practices swing. Emphasis should be placed on acceleration of stroke through wrist whip so that racquet "whistles" through the air. Elementary practice formations are:

(a) One Bird per Pair of Students. Players stand in rear third of court, start bird with long high serve and rally with overhead clears. Each student directs bird straight across net. Three pairs per court can rally at one time and a pair between courts can also be practicing.

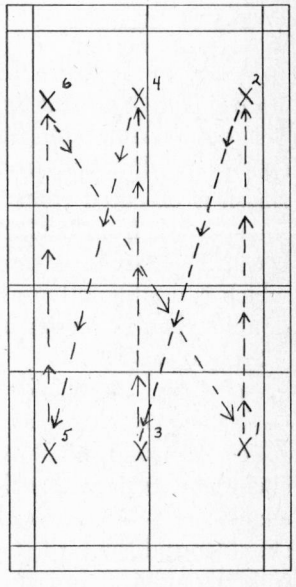

(b) Rally in Rotation. One bird per court in same formation as (a). Player 1 starts bird with long serve to player 2 who clears to player 3 who clears to player 4, etc. Player 6 clears to player 1 and the rally continues in rotation. Competition may be set up among courts by having each court count the number of times the bird is hit consecutively without a miss.

Fig. 24. Rally in rotation.

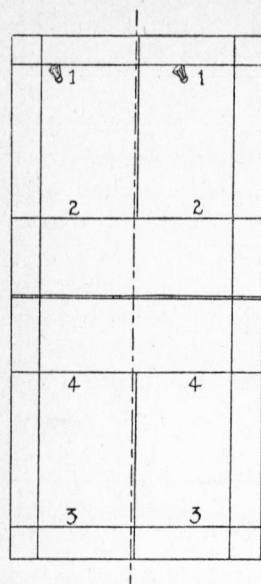

Fig. 25. High clear practice formation.

(c) Two Birds per Court. Rear court players hit overhead clears to each other. Forecourt players stand with toes on short service line and attempt to intercept birds with racquet. (Forecourt players cannot take more than one step backward.) Players reverse court positions after five or six minutes so that forecourt players have opportunity to practice clears.

4. COMMON FAULTS. A short high shot rather than the deep high clear may be caused by one or more of several faults:

(a) Improper grip which locks wrist.

(b) Contacting the bird behind head rather than in front of body.

(c) Contacting bird with flexed arm rather than at highest possible reach.

(d) Lack of acceleration and wrist snap.

(B) *The Overhead Smash.*

1. DESCRIPTION AND USE. The bird travels with great speed in a downward direction from the racquet, just clearing the net. If the smash is executed from the forecourt the bird will hit in opponent's forecourt; if from backcourt the bird will land deeper in opponent's court. This stroke is the number one offensive stroke in badminton which is used as often as possible to finish a rally. It is used more in doubles than in singles and is a very important stroke to master.

2. ANALYSIS.

(a) Grip. Forehand.

(b) Stance. Same as for overhead clear—left foot ahead.

(c) Arm and Wrist Action. (1) The preparatory part of stroke should be exactly like that phase of the overhead clear. Deception should be practiced. (2) The racquet is swung up over the right shoulder and the bird is contacted ahead of the left foot opposite the right shoulder at full arm's extension. The weight is transferred onto the forward foot and all the power of the wrist is brought into the stroke in a downward hit. (3) The follow-through is down past the left foot.

3. PRESENTATION TO BEGINNERS. This stroke is introduced to the class in the same fashion as the preceding strokes. The differences in

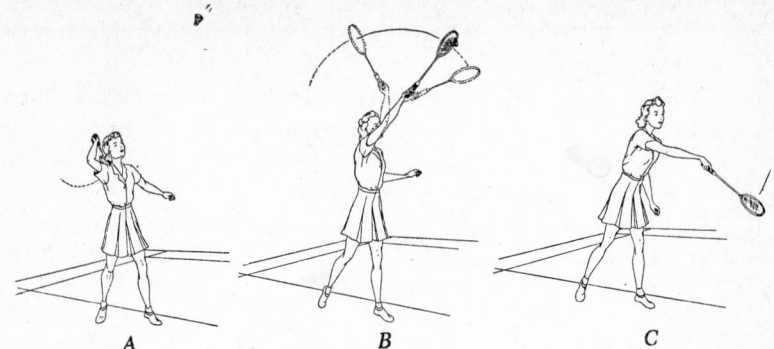

Fig. 26. The smash. *A*, start of swing. *B*, point of contact. *C*, beginning of follow-through.

the execution of the overhead clear and smash (position of bird at point of contact in relation to the body and the follow-through) are explained and demonstrated by the instructor. The stroke is practiced mimetically by the class with emphasis upon the fast wrist action and "swish" of the racquet. It is wise to have only two students practice the smash on one court. Suggested formations:

(a) Two Birds per Court. Players on one side hit bird high to players standing in center of opposite court. Receivers return birds with smash. No rallying during this initial practice. The players who set up the shots change with opponents and practice smash returns. On the second practice session the players should attempt to return smashes and the rally continues until one player is successful at finishing the point.

(b) Same Formation. Have students practice smash from position very close to net and then slightly farther back.

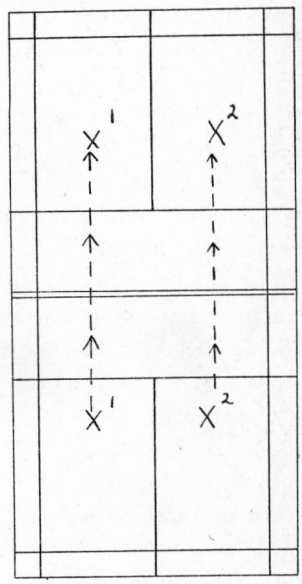

Fig. 27. Smash practice formation.

4. COMMON FAULTS.

(a) Improper grip which limits wrist flexion and therefore results in weak stroke.

(b) "Cutting" the bird by rolling wrist in a downward inward motion with the racquet following through past the right hip. This action usually causes the bird to be "carried" on the racquet and is a fault.

(c) Hitting the bird at a point straight overhead or behind rather than forward in front of the right shoulder. The strong flexion of the wrist has not had time to take effect and therefore the bird is sent up rather than directly down.

(d) Too little power in swing. Smash (similar to the overhead clear) is a strongly accelerated stroke.

(e) Failing to hit the bird at highest point of reach. Flight of bird will be too flat and not sufficiently downward.

(C) *The Overhead Drop (Forehand).*

1. DESCRIPTION AND USE. This stroke is used in place of the smash or clear for sudden change of pace when opponent is caught in rear court or when opponent anticipates a deep shot. It is a particularly effective offensive stroke in singles play but also has its uses in doubles play. The bird floats from the racquet, skimming the top of the net and lands in the very foremost part of court. A perfect drop shot is one which teeters on top of the net, then falls gently down the net into opponent's court. Such a shot is almost impossible to return.

2. ANALYSIS.

(a) Grip. Forehand.

(b) Stance. Same as for overhead clear and smash—left foot forward, right foot back.

(c) Arm and Wrist Action. (1) The preliminary swing (backswing) is identical to that of the overhead clear and smash. Opponent must not be able to anticipate what stroke is being used. (2) As the racquet is brought up from behind the head to contact the bird at point ahead of the body, the speed of the swing is checked and the bird is gently stroked. There is no powerful acceleration as in the other two overhead strokes. The wrist is used to direct and control the flight of the bird and not for power. Wrist is gently uncocked just before impact of the racquet and bird. (3) The follow-through is full but slow and the racquet generally finishes past the left side of the body.

3. PRESENTATION TO BEGINNERS. Using the same type of organization as with the previous strokes, the instructor introduces the overhead drop with explanation of its use, similarity to other overhead strokes

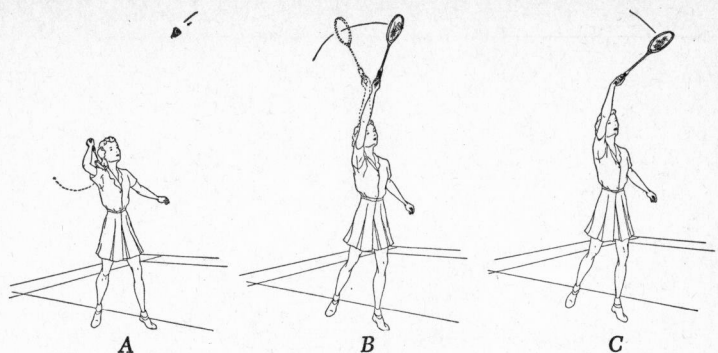

Fig. 28. The overhead drop shot. *A*, start of stroke. *B*, point of contact. *C*, follow-through.

and demonstrates it. Students practice swing and attempt to disguise stroke.

Suggested formation: More students at a time can practice this stroke on one court since the bird and racquet travel slowly and there is little danger to the students. The players on one side of the net stand fairly close to it and set up high shots to opponents who are standing in the first third of the court (same as formation in Fig. 21). Opponents return birds with overhead drop. After 10 practice shots, reverse pattern and have players who were executing drop shots now set up to opponents. As students become proficient in executing the drop, they should practice this stroke from deeper in the court.

4. COMMON FAULTS.

(a) Using too much wrist so that bird is netted.

(b) Hitting bird behind the body so that it is set up for opponent.

(c) Not disguising stroke so that opponent can anticipate it.

(D) *The Round-the-Head Stroke.*

1. DESCRIPTION AND USE.   This is an overhead shot in which the bird is hit above the left shoulder with a forehand stroke. The round-the-head stroke is used in place of the backhand whenever possible— whenever the player can move into position quickly enough to use it. Otherwise she will have to take the bird on her backhand. The stroke can be a drop, smash, or clear depending upon the desire of the player. This is definitely a stroke for advanced players to master, not for beginners.

2. ANALYSIS.

(a) Grip.   Forehand.

(b) Stance.   Left side to net and left foot forward.

(c) Arm and Wrist Action.   (1) The preliminary swing is simi'

Fig. 29. Round-the-head stroke at point of contact.

to that of any orthodox overhead (racquet dropped behind head, right elbow well away from the body, etc.). (2) The point of contact of racquet and bird is over the left shoulder (as high as possible) and somewhat behind the head. The body is arched back and the racquet swung up to meet the bird. The body weight moves with the racquet from the rear to the forward foot. Until the moment of impact, opponent should not know what the return will be. (3) At impact: *clear*—full arm and wrist moves into the shot and the racquet continues up and out to the right; *smash*—full arm and wrist moves into the shot in a downward direction, racquet finishing past the right leg; *drop*—arm stops at impact and wrist controls the direction with very little follow-through.

3. PRESENTATION. This stroke is a difficult one and should not be presented until the class has mastered all other strokes. Each of the three types of return (clear, smash, drop) can be practiced in the same formations as suggested for the orthodox overheads.

4. COMMON FAULTS.

(a) Letting bird drop too low which makes the round-the-head stroke almost impossible to execute.

(b) Getting into position for stroke too slowly.

(E) *Backhand Overhead Strokes.*

1. DESCRIPTION AND USE. In the game of badminton, a player avoids deep backhand shots whenever possible. The forehand is always favored. However, there are times when a backhand stroke must be played, so the students should learn the fundamentals of these strokes.

There are two types of shots from the deep backhand corner—a *clear* to opponent's deep court or a *flip* or *drop* just over the net. It is virtually impossible to smash with a backhand stroke from the rear of the court. Both strokes are defensive ones and used when there is no other choice.

2. ANALYSIS.

(a) Grip. Backhand.

(b) Stance. The back is turned toward the net, the rear foot (left) is parallel to the baseline and as the stroke is made, the weight passes from the rear foot to the forward (right) foot.

(c) Arm and Wrist Action. (1) For both strokes, the right arm is held high across the face and back with the racquet head pointing directly down; the wrist is cocked. (2) *Clear:* As the arm and weight move toward the net the stroke is accelerated and the wrist whips the racquet head through. The bird is contacted in front of the body at full extension of the arm with the weight on the forward foot at the time of impact.

> *Flick* or *drop:* The acceleration is less and the wrist is used to direct the shot just over the net. With the flick a stronger wrist motion is used than with the drop but the flight of the bird as it passes over the net is the same for both strokes. The flick lands a little farther beyond the net than does the drop but it is still in the forecourt and usually directed down the sidelines. (3) The follow-through differs for the two strokes. *Clear:* the arm and racquet follow up and out before coming down to the right of the body.

> *Flick* or *drop:* The arm and racquet do not follow through as far as in the clear. The swing is checked just before impact with the bird and the follow-through is a downward motion—in the flick, an abrupt, sharp downward arc and in the drop, a slow, gentle arc.

3. PRESENTATION TO BEGINNERS. The two strokes can be introduced to the class in the same manner as the forehand overhead strokes. Practice in the backhand clear and drop or flick can be organized in formations similar to those used for the corresponding forehand strokes.

4. COMMON FAULTS. The same faulty technique as described under forehand clear and drop will result in weak set-ups to opponents.

VI. The Drives

(A) *The Forehand Drive.*

1. DESCRIPTION AND USE. The bird skims just over the top of the net with great speed. This stroke is used more in doubles than in singles and can be either a defensive or an offensive stroke, depending upon the situation. It can be used offensively to pass an opponent for a placement; defensively, as a return of a smash. It should be used sparingly and as a surprise; it is usually directed down a sideline. The game of badminton is never based on drives as is the game of tennis.

A   B   C

Fig. 30. The forehand drive. A, backswing. B, point of contact. C, follow-through.

2. ANALYSIS.

(a) Grip. Forehand.

(b) Stance. Left side to the net with the right foot back and the left foot forward. Weight is transferred with the racquet swing, and just before the bird is contacted the player transfers all of her weight to her forward foot (left).

(c) Arm and Wrist Action. (1) The arm and racquet are swung well back at chest height with the wrist cocked and elbow slightly bent in an easy position; weight is on rear foot. (2) Weight is transferred forward as racquet is swung out and forward, parallel to the floor; arm straightens and wrist whips into the stroke. The bird is hit opposite the forward foot with power. (3) Arm and racquet follow through toward net at shoulder height.

3. PRESENTATION. Stroke should be practiced mimetically, emphasizing wrist whip and "swishing" sound of the racquet. The same formations as described for smash practice can be used for practicing this stroke (two birds per court). Each pair attempts to rally bird with drive strokes.

4. COMMON FAULTS.

(a) Hitting the bird with downward tilted (closed) racquet face which will either net bird or cause racquet to hit feathers of the bird.

(b) Not accelerating motion of the racquet by use of wrist whip.

(c) Letting the bird drop to waist or knees before hitting. This makes stroke totally defensive, and the bird must be hit somewhat more softly since it is likely to go over the baseline.

(B) *The Backhand Drive.*

The use, presentation and faults are the same for the backhand drive as for the forehand drive. The backhand grip is used and the stance is reversed—right side of the body to the net and right foot forward toward net. The execution of the stroke is similar to that of the forehand drive.

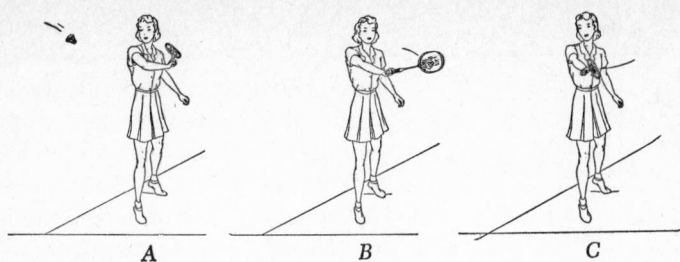

Fig. 31. The backhand drive. *A*, beginning of stroke. *B*, point of contact. *C*, follow-through.

VII. Net Shots

These strokes are executed at the net and are returns of drop shots which cannot be hit overhead because either the defender does not reach the bird in time or the drop shot is a very excellent one and the bird just skims the net tape. There are two types: (a) the drop shot returns—straight over the net and crosscourt which land as close to the net as possible and (b) underhand clears—in same two directions which land deep in court.

(A) *Straight (or hair pin) and Crosscourt Net Strokes.*

1. DESCRIPTION AND USE. These are defensive strokes generally, but can be used effectively when well placed and well timed.

2. ANALYSIS.

(a) Grip. Forehand or backhand, depending upon which side of the body the stroke is being made.

(b) Stance. On all forehand net shots the right foot is forward and also on all backhand net shots the right root is forward. Since very little body action is required in this shot, weight transfer is unimportant. The main concern is "reach" and by stepping with the right foot toward the bird just before making the shot the racquet side of the body is brought closer to the bird.

(c) Arm and Wrist Action. (1) There is practically no backswing of arm and only slight wrist cock since time does not allow for it and a delicate touch is required. (2) The bird is met near the top of the net (is returned as quickly as possible) with the racquet face turned up and at arm's length. It is gently stroked with wrist motion only, so the bird topples over the net band, the wrist determining the direction the bird takes (straight or crosscourt). (3) There is no follow-through but the racquet face is directed toward the spot where the bird was sent.

Fig. 32. The hairpin net flight.

3. PRESENTATION. The instructor should introduce these strokes through demonstration and then students should practice them on the court in pairs. Very little will be gained by having students practice the stroke mimetically. The "touch" of bird on racquet must be experienced. The footwork, however, can be practiced with racquet in hand (see preceding section on footwork drills). Practice formations:

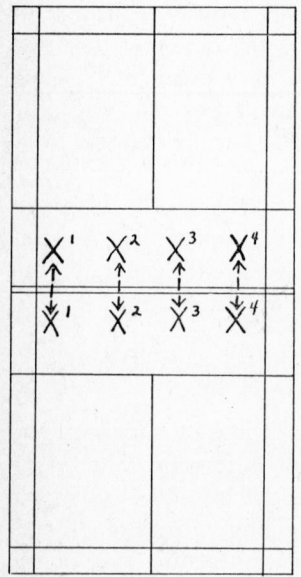

Fig. 33. Net shot practice formation.

(a) One Bird per Pair and Several Pairs per Court. Players stand fairly close to net (about two feet back) and hit straight-across drop shots to each other.

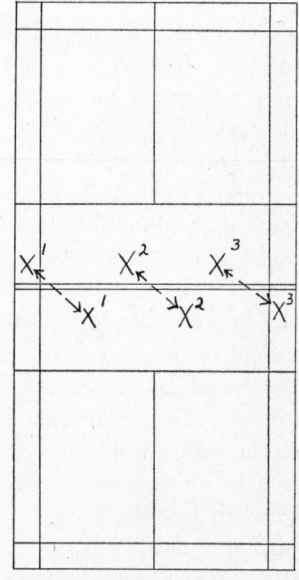

Fig. 34. Diagonal net shot practice formation.

(b) One Bird per Pair and No More Than Three Pairs per Court. Players stand close to net and hit diagonal or crosscourt drop shots to each other.

4. COMMON FAULTS.

(a) Too much arm action will lift bird more than desired "inch" over the net.

(b) Hitting net with racquet (a foul).

(c) Letting bird drop below net height before returning it.

(B) *Underhand Clears from Net Position.*

These strokes are variations of the drop shot return and can be either forehand or backhand shots. If the opponent is near the net, a quick clear over his head will be effective. However, a really good drop shot (one which barely clears the top of the net and clings to the side of net as it falls into opponent's court) cannot be cleared but must be returned by a drop shot.

The net clear is executed with the same technique as the drop shot. The only difference is that the wrist whips into the shot at the last moment. Little arm action is needed because the shot is executed in the forecourt and the bird has only half the distance to travel to reach the opponent's baseline as compared to the clear hit from rearcourt.

These strokes can be practiced in the same formations as given for the drop shots from net position, with one player starting the practice with a drop shot from close to the net and the other attempting to clear it. However, the bird should not be rallied when there are more than two pairs of students per court.

THE GAME

The actual game of badminton can be profitably introduced early in a season. This is in contrast to that of tennis in which a beginner should spend almost the entire season working on techniques rather than playing the game.

The terms and rules[1] of badminton should be learned early. Only a few of the terms are included here:

"In" Side. The side which is serving.

"Out" Side. The side which is receiving the serve.

"One Down" or *"One Hand."* One player has finished her turn of serving.

"Inning." The turn of serving for one side.

A *Fault.* An error by the player in which the shuttle fails to fall in the proper court or the shuttle is hit illegally.

Point. Only the serving side may score points (similar to volleyball). A fault by the serving side does not give the receiving side a point but causes the server to lose her turn of service.

Game. The required number of points to win; in ladies' singles—11 points; ladies', mixed, and men's doubles and men's singles—15 or 21 points. Generally, any doubles game involving women is 15 points and men's games are 21 points. However, the number of points to be played is determined before the game begins.

[1] See *Official Tennis-Badminton Guide, June 1952-June 1954.*

I. Etiquette

Etiquette in badminton is the same as in tennis or squash. It consists of good "court manners" and courteous, sportsmanlike behavior. Certain points of etiquette should be taught to the students:

Always "warm-up" with high deep clears, never with smashes or drops. This practice is a matter of etiquette but also one of common sense as far as muscular conditioning is concerned.

If there is no official, call wood shots and "carries" on yourself, but not on your opponent unless they are perfectly obvious. Also call any other faults on yourself such as hitting the net or serving faults.

Acknowledge your opponent's good shots but do not overdo this point. For example, if you set up a shot which means that because of your poor play your opponent wins the rally, do not congratulate her.

Learn to smile on the court. Even if you are losing, the game should be fun for all.

II. The Doubles Game

There are four players on the court, two on a side. The first thing players need to be taught is how to score a game. This can be intro-

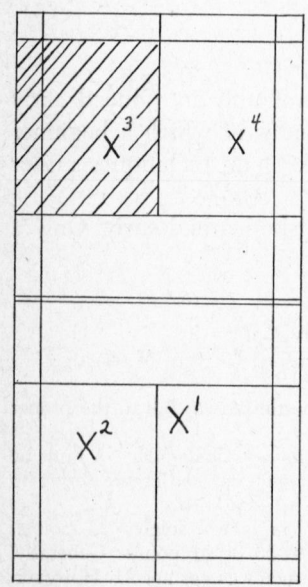

X^1 the server
X^1 and X^2: the "in" side at start of the game
X^3 and X^4: the "out" side
Shaded area: the service court in doubles

Fig. 35. The doubles court.

duced on a blackboard or on one court with four students playing. The rest of the class observes while the instructor scores the play.

(A) *Scoring*. The player in the right court always serves first, when her side is "in." She continues to serve, alternately from the right and the left court, until her side makes a fault. If she is the first server in the game, the shuttle then goes to the other side. Thereafter, both players serve before the side is "out." For example, X^1 serves from the right court and makes a point (Fig. 35). She then serves from the left court; she or her partner makes a fault and she loses her turn of service. X^2 then continues to play from the right court although it is not her original court. In this way the serve is delivered from alternate courts. When the serving side next makes a fault the shuttle is given to the opponents and so on. In the next inning the player in the right court serves first.

(B) *Team Play*. There are four systems of team play which may be used in doubles—parallel or side-by-side; forward and back or one-up-and-one-back; diagonal; and rotation.

1. PARALLEL. Each player is responsible for her own half of the court, dividing it lengthwise from the center of net to the center of the back boundary line. All shots down the center should be taken by the left court player since she can make the return on her forehand. Partners should call to each other in regard to the return of the bird— "mine," "yours," etc.—so that doubtful shots will be covered with minimum confusion.

The parallel system is the simplest for beginners to understand and the actual game and scoring should be introduced to a class of beginners with this type of team play. This system also requires speedy footwork in moving forward and backward and such should be developed in beginners.

A major problem with beginners is getting them to hit the bird "away from" their opponents. Their tendency is to return the bird to midcourt, the very spot where the opponent is standing. A suggestion for helping the students to vary their shots is to have each student, when side-by-side team play is first tried, hit alternately a clear and a drop shot. The next step is to mix these two shots and then, of course, add the smash when such is an appropriate return. Shots directed down the center are sometimes more effective than sideline shots against parallel team play. However, any weakness of opponents that is apparent should be attacked.

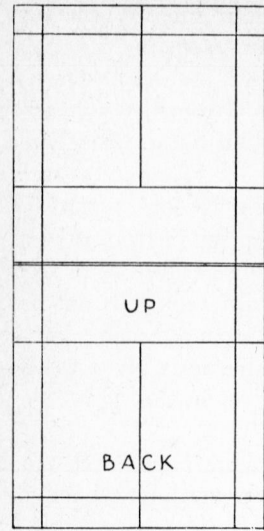

Fig. 36. Position of players in the up-and-back system.

2. UP-AND-BACK. The partners cover the court from side to side, with one standing in the center of the forecourt with her heels on the short service line and the other in the center of the rearcourt about a yard in front of the long service line. The forecourt player covers the first third of the entire court (all net shots and weak returns). Her partner covers the remainder of the court (two-thirds). In order to get into the up-and-back positions, three plans can be followed.

(a) Elementary. The player serving always moves into the front position and her partner into the rear. For the receiving team, the player served to always plays up and her partner back. With beginners, it is wise to introduce this type of team play which requires as few decisions as possible.

(b) Intermediate. After the elementary system has been experienced successfully, then the intermediate one should be presented. This consists of the same court coverage for the serving team (server up and partner back), but the type of serve determines the court positions of the receivers; i.e., if the serve is a short one, the player receiving returns it and covers the front court, her partner moving to cover the rear. If the serve is long, she moves to rearcourt, returns it and then takes up her position in rear center, her partner moving into forecourt position.

(c) Advanced. After players have experienced all types of team play systems, it may be that certain combinations of partners should play fixed positions in the up-and-back system. A combination of a strong and weak player should always play with the strong player in the rearcourt and the weak player in front. The rearcourt player must have a strong clear and a smash. The forecourt player should be adept at drop shotting and returning net shots. This type of play is used most frequently in mixed doubles with the lady playing the front position. The majority of shots should be directed down the sidelines. Medium length drives are sometimes difficult to handle in this system because the rearcourt player is pulled up or the forecourt player is forced back.

3. DIAGONAL SYSTEM. This type of team play is a combination of parallel and up-and-back. It should be taught to good intermediate and advanced players. The right-court player covers the forecourt and the left-court player, the rearcourt. The court positions are on a slight diagonal with the right-court player a couple of yards ahead of the left-court player but each stands in her own halfcourt. Each player returns to her court position after taking the shot in her own territory.

X^1 covers lined area
X^2 covers dotted area

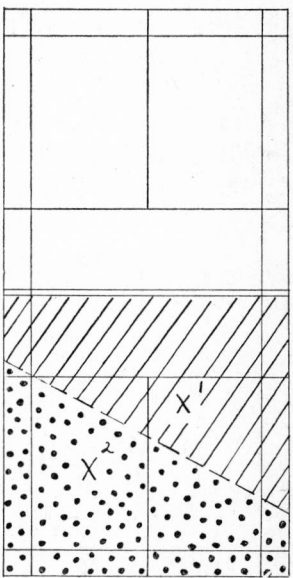

Fig. 37. Positions for diagonal system.

This type of play may be used in two different ways:

(a) With Partners of Equal Ability. If the partners are of equal ability and have the same strengths and weaknesses in their play, whichever player is in the right court will cover the forecourt, etc. Then when the team wins a point and the partners change courts, they cover the area indicated by the positions in which they are. With each point that is won, the partners reverse the part of the court for which they are responsible.

(b) With Partners of Unequal Ability. If one player is stronger than her partner, this player should station herself in the left court as soon as possible and cover the backcourt. The weaker partner moves into the right court and returns the short shots. This arrangement necessitates fast action on the part of the partners when they must start a rally from opposite half courts. As soon as the bird is served or returned, they exchange positions. This type of team play allows for combinations of weak and strong players and yet does not leave the entire sidelines open for opponents' shots as does the up-and-back system. Also, the deep backhand is avoided more than in up-and-back since the player in the left court can run around the backhand or use a round-the-head shot. Students should initially learn this system by the first method. They should gain experience in playing both positions.

If two left-handed players are teamed together, the diagonal of the court is reversed—the right-court player will cover the rearcourt and the left-court player the forecourt. This is to avoid moving into a deep backhand shot which would be required if a left-handed player covered the rearcourt from the right halfcourt.

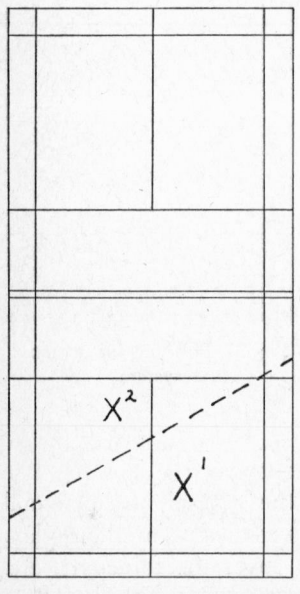

This type of team play is particularly well adapted to the combination of a right- and left-handed partner, each always being responsible for one particular area. The left-handed player always moves to the right court. If she is responsible for the short shots (the weaker player) the orthodox diagonal is used with the right-handed player in the left court covering the deep shots. If the left-handed player is to cover rearcourt shots, the opposite diagonal is used and she covers her area from right court.

X^1 is stronger left-handed player who covers area behind diagonal line.
X^2 is weaker right-handed player who covers area in front of diagonal line.

Fig. 38. Diagonal system for two left-handed players or for strong left-handed and weak right-handed partners.

4. ROTATION SYSTEM. This is the most advanced of the systems of team play and is a combination of all the others. In rotation play the right-court player (similar to diagonal) covers the forecourt and the left-court player, the rear court. The difference between the rotation and diagonal systems is that when a player crosses the halfcourt line (center) to return a shot she continues on and changes places

with her partner. Thus, they rotate positions and each becomes responsible for the area opposite to that which she had held. Obviously, this necessitates quick movement, interchange, and complete cooperation. Rotation for right-handed players is in counterclockwise direction and for left-handed players is in clockwise direction.

This system should be taught to advanced players only. It will not function unless a variety of shots is used—diagonal drops and crosscourt clears. Since beginners and low intermediate players do not always make such distinctive shots, the rotation system will not be needed and the parallel type will be the result. Until the strokes are well learned this type of play is too difficult for the players because they spend more energy and effort on thinking of where they should be than in actually hitting the bird.

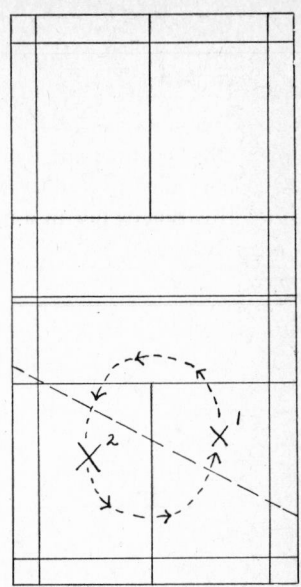

Fig. 39. The rotation system.

The players should be of equal ability; otherwise the diagonal system should be used. The strengths of the rotation system lie in the fact that players "move into" shots (not away from them) and openings are continually being closed.

There are certain vulnerable spots on the court and these are shown in Fig. 40. The four corners are the problems but this is true for all types of team play.

Shots to points x and y do not cause partners to rotate; but shots to 1 and 2 do make partners rotate.

The success of this system depends upon the alertness of the players—not moving until the exact right moment, not rotating unless pulled into the diagonal, then moving quickly into position. This system takes considerable practice and very often is not popular with the students when first tried. However, with practice and experience, it can become exciting and fun.

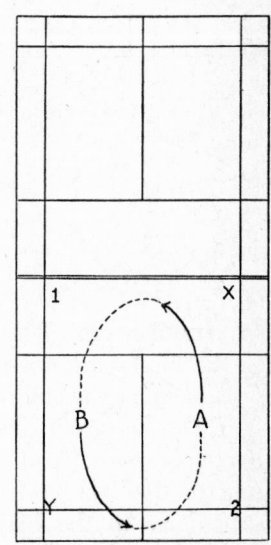

Fig. 40. Vulnerable spots in the rotation system.

(C) *Serving Position and Placements.*

1. POSITION. In doubles the position depends upon the system of team play which the partners are using and the court from which the serve is made. In parallel play, the server can afford to stand nearer the sidelines since she has only half the court to cover but in forward-back she may prefer to serve from a position nearer the center line since this places her in a midcourt position ready to make returns from either sideline.

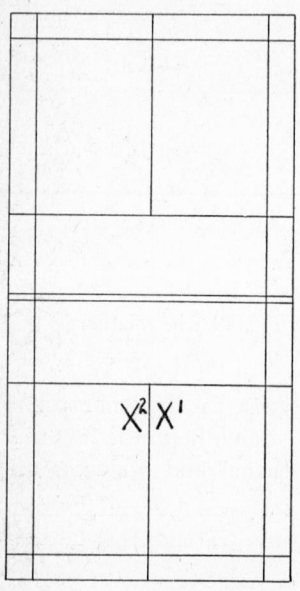

Beginners, however, must be instructed where to stand when they practice the serve and a consistent position is less confusing to them and also permits a "grooving" of the stroke. A position about one yard from the center line and a couple of feet back of the short service line is recommended for the beginner. This position should be the same in the right and left courts.

Fig. 41. Serving position in doubles play.

2. PLACEMENTS. The short serve is used for the most part since the doubles service court includes the side alley but not the rear alley. The two front corners of the court are effective targets. Also an occasional placement to the rear corners is recommended, particularly to the backhand corner when serving from the right service court.

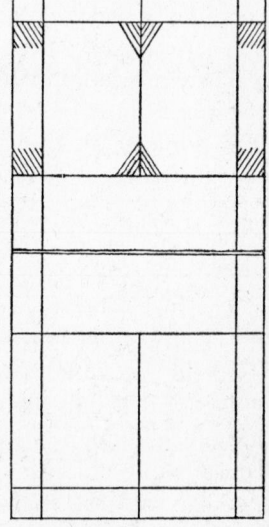

Fig. 42. Placement of the serve in doubles.

(D) *Receiving Position and Return of Serve.*

1. RECEIVING POSITION. In doubles, the receiver stands a couple of yards back from the short service line. She is closer to the front of the court than to the rear since the short service is the one most often served. However, she must be alert and ready to move back under a long serve. The backhand is protected and the receiver stands in the left side of the court so as to take the majority of serves on her forehand.

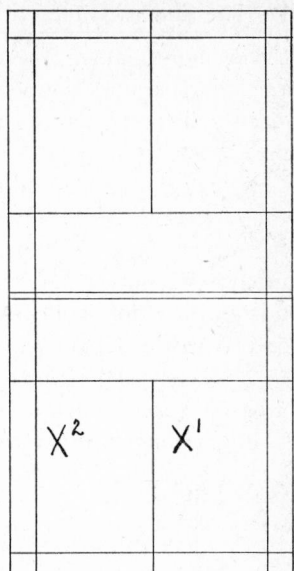

Fig. 43. Receiving position in doubles.

2. RETURN OF SERVE. If possible the short serve is rushed and returned quickly before the server can get set. However, if the serve is well placed, the receiver cannot smash or drive the return but must either use an underhand clear or an underhand drop. Generally, these returns should be directed to one of the four corners of the doubles court. If a high, long serve is received, the return should be an overhead stroke—a clear, a drop, or a smash—again to one of the four corners. Whenever in doubt, a clear to the backhand corner is a safe and intelligent return.

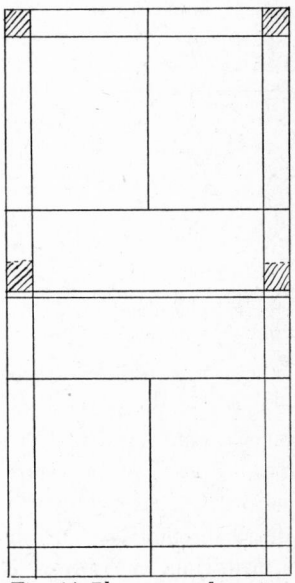

Fig. 44. Placement of service returns in doubles.

III. The Singles Game

The singles game, played by two opponents, can be extremely strenuous, more so than doubles. In certain respects it is not as complicated because there is not the team work involved nor two opponents to consider.

(A) *Scoring*. The ladies' game consists of 11 points. At the beginning of the game the server delivers her serve from the right court. As long as she wins the rallies, she continues to serve, alternating courts, and scores points. When the server commits a fault, her term of service ends and her opponent becomes the server. The court from which the serve is made depends upon the server's own score; when it is even (0, 2, 4, etc.) she serves from the right court; when the score is odd (1, 3, 5, etc.), from the left.

(B) *Serving Position and Placement of Serve.*

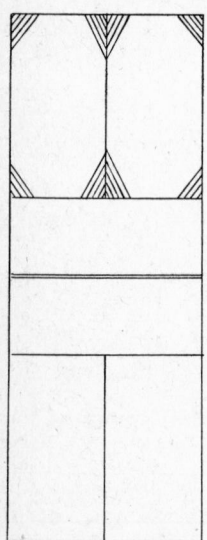

1. SERVING POSITION. In singles, the server stands somewhat farther back in court than in doubles—about a yard and a half behind the short service line. The position is close to the center halfcourt line for either right or left courts.

2. PLACEMENT OF SERVE. The long, high serve is used predominantly since the singles service court is long and narrow. The two rear corners of the singles court are vulnerable, the backhand corner the more so. Occasionally the short serve should be used for variety and then either of the two front corners should be the target.

Fig. 45. Placement of the serve in singles.

(C) *Receiving Position and Return of Serve.*

1. RECEIVING POSITION. The receiver stands halfway back in the service court and in the left side so as to take the serve on the forehand. She must be ready to move forward for a short serve but the majority of her returns will be from the deep court, so she cannot afford to stand in the same position as in doubles.

2. RETURN OF SERVE. The return of serve will undoubtedly be an overhead shot except on the rare occasions when a short service is

received. The return may be a smash, clear, or drop. If the serve is somewhat short, a smash should be the answering shot; otherwise a clear and, for variety, occasionally a drop. When receiving in the right court, a clear to the deep backhand is an extremely good response. The four corners of the singles court should furnish the targets for the returns. The purpose of the receiver is to put the server on the defense and force her out of position.

IV. General Court Strategy for Singles and Doubles Play

(A) *Coaching Points.*
1. Be alert with racquet held in ready position and weight on toes.
2. Recover court position quickly between shots.
3. Hit every bird with overhead stroke if possible.
4. Use smash whenever possible.
5. Avoid deep backhand shots by running around them or using round-the-head strokes.
6. Use deception in all strokes—do not telegraph your shot.
7. Analyze opponents' weaknesses and play them.
8. If opponent telegraphs shots, anticipate placement and move in that direction. However, this practice is dangerous against expert players because the stroke can be changed at the last moment.
9. Use variety of shots and keep opponent on the move.

(B) *Examples of Singles Strategy* (the same principles are effective in doubles).

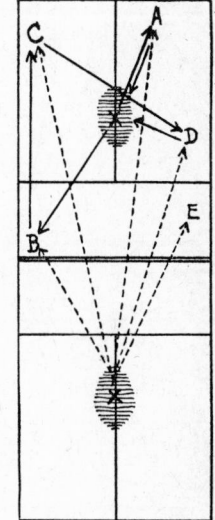

Shaded areas, X, indicate the best waiting positions.

- - - - Flight of shuttle.
——— Course of player.

1. TO CHANGE THE PACE (SPEED) OF THE BIRD AS WELL AS THE DIRECTION (Fig. 46).
   A: High Clear, to force opponent back.
   B: Drop shot.
   C: High Clear.
   or
   D: Smash or Drive.
   or
   E: Cross-court net flight.

Fig. 46. Strategy 1.

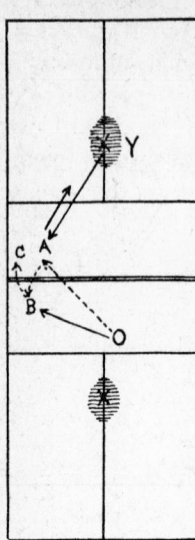

Fig. 47. Strategy 2-I.

2. TO CATCH THE OPPONENT RUNNING IN THE WRONG DIRECTION (Figs. 47, 48, 49).

I. 3 net flights.
   Y returns net flight A with net flight B and starts to move back to position since whole court is open.
   O immediately sends the third net flight C to the same spot.

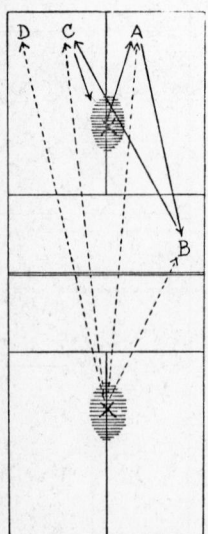

Fig. 48. Strategy 2-II.

II. Long—short—long—long: to catch opponent running forward.
   Opponent runs from A to B to C and starts back to center expecting another short shot.

III. Long—short—short: to catch opponent running back.

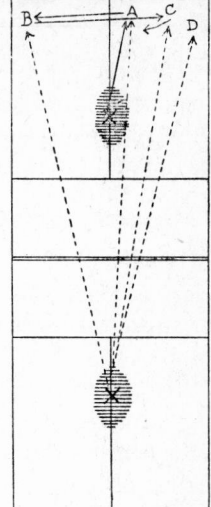

IV. Side to side.
 Opponent runs from A to B to C and starts back to center before D is hit.

Fig. 49. Strategy 2-IV.

3. TO MAKE OPPONENT RETURN ALTERNATE FOREHAND AND BACKHAND STROKES, PARTICULARLY WHEN NEAR THE NET (Fig. 50).

Various net flights
or
Drop shots
or
Drives

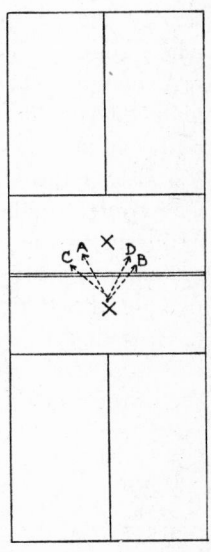

NOTE: In these examples the opponent conveniently returns the shuttle to your ideal spot. In actual play this is unlikely and accuracy is difficult to attain. One must think quickly while moving and executing each shot.

Fig. 50. Strategy 3.

CLASS ORGANIZATION

This section is organized under three main divisions: I. General suggestions for class organization; II. Practice formations for combinations of strokes and for game skills; and III. Sample lesson plans for beginning, intermediate, and advanced classes.

I. General Suggestions

Ideally, there should be four students per court in the badminton classes. Since this arrangement is rarely possible, the instructor must organize the class so that all have equal opportunities to practice and to play.

The practice formations which have been suggested for use in teaching strokes to beginners provide for six and sometimes eight students to a court. Additional space for practice can be made by stretching pieces of old net between courts from net post of one court to the net post of the next court. The short service line, long service line and baseline can be drawn with chalk on these "in between" courts.

Another practice area is furnished by a smooth wall on which the net height is marked. Rallying against a wall is very difficult for beginners but is excellent practice in timing and wrist action for intermediate and advanced players. There may be one or two students in a beginning class who have difficulty in coordinating and contacting the bird when attempting to serve. These individuals can practice the service against the wall. They will progress faster if working alone where they are not conspicuously poorer than the others on the court.

Although a class supposedly consists of one level of ability—beginning, intermediate, or advanced—there are always gradations in skill represented. It is helpful to both instructor and students if the instructor assigns the students to particular courts on the basis of ability. The students when they arrive at each class meeting then practice and play on the courts to which they have been assigned. A rotation system can be used for each court so that the students take turns playing or practicing on their particular court.

With this organization according to levels of ability, the instructor can have each court of students practicing different fundamentals if such procedure is deemed advantageous.

II. Practice Formations for Stroke Combinations and Game Skills

The formations for specific stroke practice were given with the analyses of the strokes. The formations presented here are for use in *reviewing* the strokes and not for *introducing* them.

(A) *Service Practice.*

FORMATION 1.

(a) Mark shaded areas A and C on the court.

(1) Serve to areas A or C in the doubles court. Allow the shuttle to drop into the court. 1 serves to 3's court, 2 to 4's, and 3 and 4 serve back: five serves to each; a's then do the same.

(2) Score successful serves, for accuracy. Allow shuttle to drop into court. Using above procedure (1), each player serves in turn from the right court and from the left. Five serves to A: 5 points each. Five serves to C: 5 points each. Possible score: 50 points in each court, or a total of 100 points.

(3) Serve and return of service diagonally. 1 plays with 3, and 2 plays with 4. Example: 1 serves to 3, who returns it successfully. They rally until there is a fault. 3 then serves to 1 and they rally. Then 1a and 3a proceed as above.

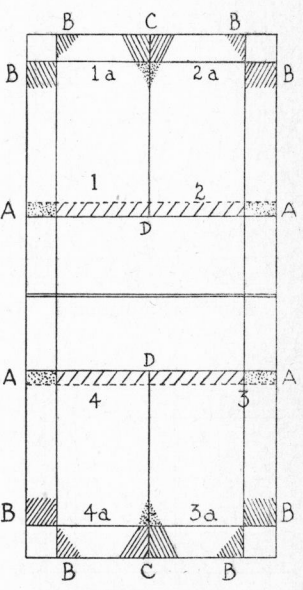

Fig. 51. Formation 1.

(Although 2 and 4 are playing at the same time as 1 and 3, there is not undue confusion if concentration and placement are stressed. While not participating, the other four watch for illegal serves and help coach their partners.)

(b) Mark shaded areas B and C and draw line, ADA, 1 foot within short service line. Score successful serves to these areas as in (2) above.

(c) Mark shaded areas B and C in singles service court. Score successful serves to these areas as in (2) above.

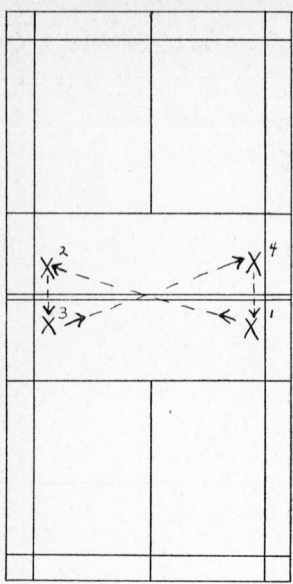

Fig. 52. Formation 2.

(B) *Net Shots.*

FORMATION 2. Four players to a court. Players stand in positions near sidelines and close to net. Player 1 hits diagonal net shot to 2 who hits straight across to 3 who hits diagonal drop to 4 who returns bird with drop to 1. After adequate practice, reverse order of hitting so 2 and 4 hit diagonal net shots and 1 and 3 straight across. Four extra players on court can practice same in rear of court without net.

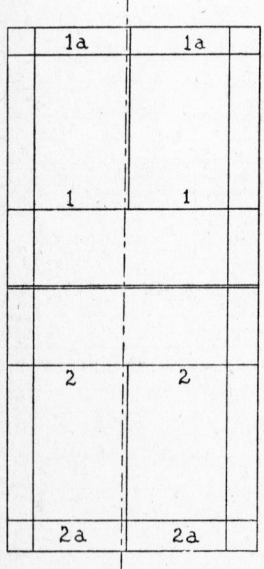

Fig. 53. Formation 3.

(C) *Smash and Clear.*

FORMATION 3. Two birds per court.

(a) 1a's and 2a's practice clears to each other.

(b) 1's and 2's attempt to intercept and smash. They can take only one step back.

(c) 1 point is scored for each successful smash by a net player.

(D) *Drop Shots and Clears.*

FORMATION 4. Four birds per court (same court formation as 3 above).

(a) Players 1 and 2 practice net shots while

(b) players 1a and 2a practice clears.

(c) Forecourt players change places with rearcourt and practice is repeated.

FORMATION 5. Two birds per court, four players per bird (same court formation as 3 above).

(a) Player 1 hits underhand clear to player 2a.

(b) Player 2a hits overhead clear to player 1a.

(c) Player 1a hits overhead drop to player 2.

(d) Player 2 hits drop shot to player 1.

This sequential rally continues until each player has hit successful shots from her position; then players 2 and 2a change positions with 1 and 1a. Eventually each player should have practice from each of the four positions.

(E) *Practice in Game Form.*

1. HALF-COURT GAME. Two birds per court—each half court plays independently of other half. Game is similar to table tennis in order of service and scoring; 21 points constitute a game. Forecourt player on serving side steps out of court until serve is made. Each player serves 5 times and a point is scored at the end of every rally. After 5 serves of first player, forecourt player on other team serves, then when second player on first team becomes server, she changes positions with partner, etc. Players may use any stroke and must keep bird in half of court bounded by outside alley line and extension of midcourt line of regulation court.

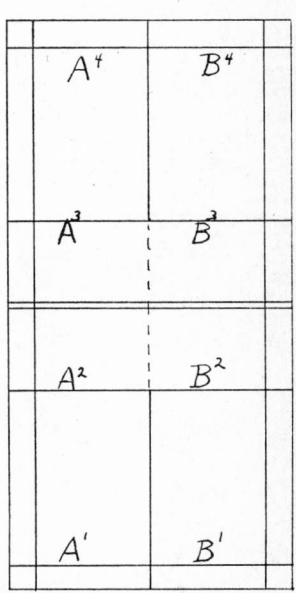

Fig. 54. Half-court game.

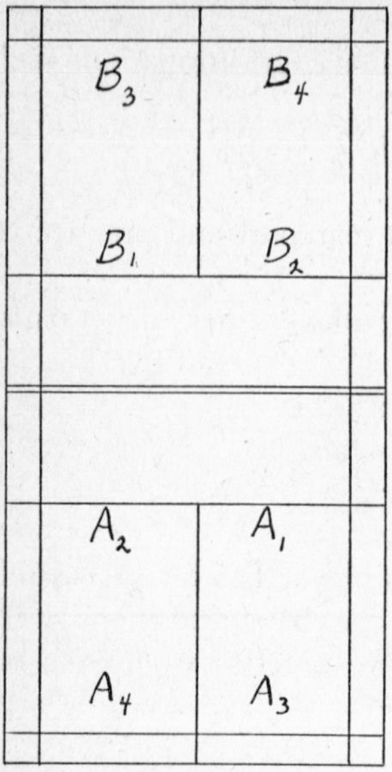

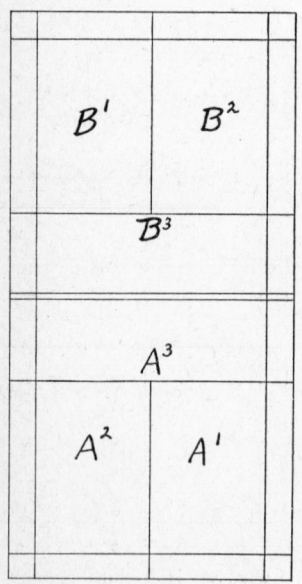

Fig. 55. Eight-player game.

2. EIGHT-PLAYER BADMINTON. One bird per court. A regulation badminton game is played with these exceptions: Forecourt players are restricted to the space between the net and short service line. The backcourt players receive the serve and the forecourt players serve. Net players may not touch the bird during service. They should stand near the sideline to be out of the way. Net players exchange places with those in the backcourt upon receipt of service (when their inning starts).

Fig. 56. Six-player game.

3. SIX-PLAYER BADMINTON. Rearcourt players are servers and receivers of the serves. Player at net exchanges position with one person in rearcourt when serving inning starts. The order of playing net is established before the game (one player is first, another always second, and the third last). The game is scored and played according to the regulation doubles rules.

4. PROGRESSIVE BADMINTON. Divide the number of players in half, and line them up as indicated (Fig. 57). One player with a racquet stands on each side of the net. One player starts the shuttle by hitting it across the net. As soon as a person has hit the shuttle she gives the racquet to the next player, who must hit the returning shuttle, hand on the racquet to the next in line, and go to the end of the other line. Anyone who fails to hit the bird starts it for the next one and then drops out of the game. When only two are left, instead of running around, they rally until one makes a fault. No smashes are allowed.

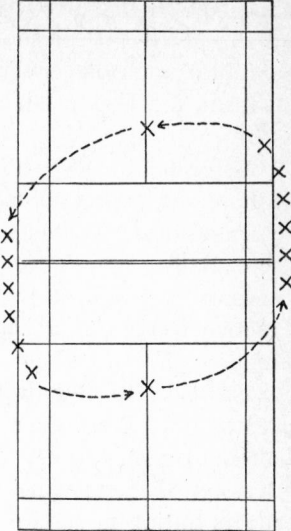

Fig. 57. Progressive badminton.

III. Sample Lesson Plans

The following lesson plans for each level (beginning, intermediate and advanced) are offered as suggestions. The amount which will be covered in each lesson will depend upon the progress of the particular class. Also the formation used will be determined by the numbers of students in the class and their abilities.

(A) *An Outline of 18 Lessons for Beginning Players (35 to 40 minute periods).*

All formations used are those included under the section on techniques. The order in which the strokes are presented to a beginning class in these lesson plans is: (1) long high serve, (2) overhead clear, (3) short serve, (4) drop shot, and (5) smash. Parallel and up-and-back systems are the types of team play taught.

LESSON 1. Discuss care and use of equipment. Describe game and terms used in badminton. Present: forehand grip, wrist action, mimetics of hitting to self, how to hold bird and drop it. Practice hitting bird to self. Present long high serve. Teach ready position. Rally with one bird per court.

LESSON 2. Review hitting birds to self. Review high serve. Present backhand grip, forehand and backhand overhead clears. On court—

one practices high serve, opponent returns it with overhead clear, no rallying. Next, one person serves, bird is returned with clear and rally continues; each player takes turn at serving for 5 times.

LESSON 3. Present short serve. Practice. Rally with one bird to a court.

LESSON 4. Review short serve. Practice deception—mix short and high serves, trying to take opponent by surprise (no rallying, just returning bird to server). Teach proper court position for receiving a serve. Rally.

LESSON 5. Present footwork for forehand and backhand strokes. Practice. Review overhead clears. Present underhand backhand clear. Practice.

LESSON 6. Review overhead clears. Present half-court game.

LESSON 7. Present net shots (drop shots). Practice. Rally and play half-court game.

LESSON 8. Review net shots. Rally in rotation (one bird to a court), players hitting in certain succession. Have competition among courts.

LESSON 9. Present doubles game—explain scoring, terms and essential rules. Present parallel team play. Play game.

LESSON 10. Rally. Play game, using parallel system.

LESSON 11. Present smash. Practice. Rally and play game with parallel system.

LESSON 12. Practice drop shots from center of court. Practice mixing drop shots and smashes from center of court (try to deceive opponent)—two birds per court, one sets up to midcourt, other practices shots—continue rally. Present up-and-back system of team play.

LESSON 13. Review both long and short serves (announcing that they will be tested at the next class meeting). Rally and play doubles game using up-and-back system.

LESSON 14. Test short and long serves subjectively (each player serving 5 birds after practice). Rally and play game using up-and-back system.

LESSON 15. Rally. Discuss important rules in singles. Present singles game. Play.

LESSON 16. Rally. Play singles.

LESSON 17. Rally. Discuss tactics for two types of doubles systems. Have each pair of partners decide on type of team play they will use and then play.

LESSON 18. Progressive bridge tournament—give out tallies at beginning of period. Play periods of 7 minutes; winners then advance and change partners. Winner of tournament is person winning the most times.

(B) *An Outline of 18 Lessons for Intermediate Players (35 to 40 minute periods).*

The intermediate level usually contains the widest range of abilities and because of this fact any set of lesson plans can only be tentative. The rate at which the lessons are covered will depend upon the girls' ability to master the fundamental techniques. With some intermediate groups, the lesson plans for beginners can be followed. Others may achieve the status of advanced players early in the season.

The strokes and order of presentation are the same as for the beginning group. The drive serve and forehand and backhand drives are the new strokes introduced. In addition to the parallel and up-and-back systems of doubles, the diagonal is taught to the intermediate class.

LESSON 1. Discuss care and use of equipment. Review forehand and backhand grips. Rally on courts (one bird per pair) and then play doubles while instructor rates each student's ability.

LESSON 2. Assign students to courts. Review high and short serves, stressing deception. Rally and play doubles. Check on court assignments and make any desired changes.

LESSON 3. Review short serve. Practice both serves, stressing deception—Formation 1 (a), (b), and (c). Rally and play doubles using parallel system.

LESSON 4. Review footwork, using elementary formations. Review and practice overhead clears, using elementary formations. Rally and play parallel system.

LESSON 5. Review and practice drop shots at net, using elementary formations. Rally and play doubles with parallel system.

LESSON 6. Review etiquette and rules for doubles. Review up-and-back system, using intermediate method of determining position. Play doubles using this system.

LESSON 7. Review and practice drop shots from rear court. Mix returns of drops and clears (practice deception). Play doubles using up-and-back system.

LESSON 8. Present drive serve. Practice. Play doubles using up-and-back system.

LESSON 9. Review smash using elementary formation. Practice smash, drops and clear from rearcourt, stressing deception. Play doubles using up-and-back team play.

LESSON 10. Review rules and strategy for singles game. Play abbreviated game of 7 points so that each student has opportunity to play.

LESSON 11. Present forehand and backhand drives. Practice. Play singles game.

LESSON 12. Present diagonal team play. Play doubles using this system.

LESSON 13. Review diagonal system on blackboard. Play doubles using it.

LESSON 14. Test serves, either subjectively or objectively. Play doubles, using diagonal system.

LESSON 15. Discuss strategy of doubles play and uses for different systems of team play. Play game using diagonal.

LESSONS 16 THROUGH 18. Informal doubles tournaments. Different partners each class meeting. Each pair should use system of team play best suited to own strengths and weaknesses.

(C) *An Outline of 18 Lessons for Advanced Players (35 to 40 minute periods).*

Four students per court should be registered in advanced classes since more time is devoted to playing than to stroke practice.

All strokes are reviewed and practiced with emphasis upon placement and deception. The truly advanced class can cover the basic techniques rapidly and class time can be devoted to singles and doubles strategy and tournament experience. The round-the-head stroke and rotation team play are added to preceding techniques.

LESSON 1. Discuss care and use of equipment. Rally and play doubles while instructor rates students for court assignments.

LESSON 2. Assign students to courts. Review three types of serves, practicing deception and placement (Formation 1). Play doubles with parallel system.

LESSON 3. Review footwork. Review returns of serves. Play doubles using parallel system.

LESSON 4. Review overhead strokes (clear, drop and smash). Practice deception and placement. Practice using Formation 5. Play doubles with up-and-back system.

LESSON 5. Present round-the-head strokes. Practice. Play doubles with up-and-back system.

LESSON 6. Review drop shots from net (Formation 2). Review diagonal system, No. 1. Play doubles using it.

LESSON 7. Present rotation team play. Play doubles using it.

LESSON 8. Discuss doubles tactics. Review drives. Play doubles using rotation system.

LESSON 9. Discuss singles tactics. Play short game of 7 points so that all have opportunity to play.

LESSON 10. Practice strokes which are weakest. Play singles.

LESSON 11. Same as Lesson 10. Play doubles instead of singles, using rotation system.

LESSONS 12 THROUGH 18. Play a round-robin tournament followed by singles elimination-consolation tournament. Instructor makes up doubles team. Partners decide what system of team play to use throughout tournament.

TOURNAMENTS FOR CLASS USE

I. Rotation (team)

(A) *Use.* An informal tournament for a single class period. It is particularly well adapted to intermediate and advanced classes.

(B) *Conduct.* The class time is divided into five 7-minute periods or four 8-minute periods or any convenient length of time. Players choose their partners, challenge another team and start playing a game. At the end of the first 7-minute period, the instructor blows her whistle and all teams move one court to their left. The team on the end court moves to the opposite side of the same court and plays the team from the next court. If there is an uneven number of teams and too few courts, the team on the end court can rotate off and umpire for one period, then step into the opposite side of the court, which they had vacated, for the next period.

If there is an odd number of teams and a sufficient number of courts, a singles game can be played on the end court. The couple moving to the end court plays singles, then moves as a team to the next court. Teams keep the same partners throughout the hour. The winning team will be the one which has won the greatest number of times at the end of the class period, or the team which has totaled the most points, or the team which has won the most games. Any one of these three methods for determining the winners can be used.

II. Rotation (individual)

This tournament is operated in the same way as that just described, except that partners change after every move and individual players keep score of their own wins and losses. Unless the class is small and there is ample supervision, this type of tournament is likely to be confusing.

III. Bridge

(A) *Use.* For the last class of the season when something different is desired, this type of tournament is popular.

(B) *Conduct.* Tallies, prepared before the class meeting, are marked Court 1, Couple 1; Court 1, Couple 2; etc. The courts are numbered 1 through 3 or for as many courts as there are available.

Students draw tallies and then go to the proper courts to find their partners. At the end of a given period of time (the class period is divided the same as for the rotation tournament), the winning pairs advance toward the head court (No. 1), the losing pairs staying on the same courts. The losing pair at the head court moves to the foot court. The teams change partners after every move, and each player records the wins and losses on her tally or the number of points won. The winner is declared at the end of the class period.

A less formal team bridge tournament can be organized without tallies. The players are allowed to choose their partners and play against any team for the first period. Then the tournament proceeds as described above. Another variation is to allow players to choose their partners and keep the same partners throughout the entire tournament.

IV. Two-Way Elimination or Elimination-Consolation

(A) *Use.* This tournament can be planned for the last part of the season after the strokes are learned and tournament experience is desirable. Play covers several periods and can be either singles or doubles, depending upon the size of the class.

(B) *Conduct.* The players may choose their own partners or the instructor can pair off the teams. The draw is made before the class meeting and with a consideration to seeded players, so that the better teams will not meet until the semi-finals and finals. The elimination and consolation brackets are arranged according to the usual method. As soon as a team loses, it moves into the consolation bracket. Each team should play one match every class period. Each team will play at least two matches before being eliminated completely and then the losing teams can play each other outside the tournament. Matches should consist of two out of three games of 15 points if the class period is 35 to 40 minutes long. If the period is shorter, one game of 21 points can be played.

V. Ladder

(A) *Use.* This tournament can follow an elimination tournament if the season permits the time. It gives an opportunity for the teams that lost to challenge the teams that defeated them.

(B) *Conduct.* The order of the ladder is determined by the results of the elimination tournament. The winners are placed at the top, runners-up are second, etc. Any team can challenge the team directly above or two above, but no higher. If the lower team wins, it changes places on the ladder with the losing team.

VI. Round-Robin

(A) *Use.* This tournament is particularly useful in a class which contains more than one level of ability. If there are two levels represented (intermediate and advanced), the class can be divided into two groups and two round-robin tournaments can be in progress at the same time. This tournament can be planned for the last part of a season to cover several periods.

(B) *Conduct.* The players may choose their own partners or the instructor can pair off the teams. The tournament schedule is arranged so that each team plays every other team. This is a single round-robin tournament. If each team plays every other team twice it is a double round-robin tournament. The schedule can be posted on the bulletin board so that teams know who their opponents are for each class meeting. Matches should consist of two out of three games of 15 points.

TESTING IN BADMINTON

The instructor consciously or unconsciously evaluates the students' progress during each class period. Generally, such ratings are informal and subjective in nature, and they do have an important bearing upon grades and future lesson planning.

Occasionally, a class period should be devoted to testing of specific strokes, the students having been informed of this fact several days in advance. The tests used may be of a subjective nature or objective. The choice of types will depend upon the strokes to be tested, number of students in class, and time allowance. For some strokes, there are no acceptable objective tests available. An experienced teacher can often rate students subjectively faster than they can be tested objectively.

The Miller Badminton Wall Volley Test[2] is one of the two standardized objective tests for badminton. It consists of three trials of volleying a bird against a wall for 30 seconds and has a reliability coefficient of .94 ± .008 and a validity of .83 ± .047. This test measures general badminton playing ability and not particular strokes; therefore, it can be used for classification, motivation, and general achievement but not for diagnosis of specific stroke weaknesses.

The second objective test is the battery reported by Scott and French.[3] Tests for the short serve, long serve, clear, volley and footwork are given with directions, coefficients of reliability and validity,

[2] Miller, Frances A.: "A Badminton Wall Volley Test." *Research Quarterly of the AAHPER*, XXII (208-13), May, 1951.

[3] Scott, M. Gladys, and French, Esther: *Evaluation in Physical Education.* St. Louis, C. V. Mosby Company, 1950, pp. 65-78.

and T-scales. These tests can be used individually to evaluate a specific stroke or as a battery for over-all playing ability.

One court can be set up for testing and the other courts used for stroke practice and game playing. In this way, more than testing can be accomplished in a single class period. Tests should be used if and when they will benefit the instructional program; they should be a part of that program and planned for carefully.

REFERENCES

Bourquardez, Virginia, and Heilman, Charles: *Sports Equipment*. New York, A. S. Barnes and Co., 1950, pp. 208-15.

Davidson, Kenneth R., and Gustavson, Lealand R.: *Winning Badminton*. New York, A. S. Barnes and Co., 1951.

Davidson, Kenneth, and Smith, Lenore C. (consultants): *Badminton, Instructor's Guide*. Chicago, The Athletic Institute, 1950.

Devlin, J. F.: *Badminton for All*. New York, Doubleday, Doran and Co., 1937.

Fisher, Herbert L.: *How to Play Badminton*. Minneapolis, Burgess Publishing Co., 1939.

Grant, Doug: *Badminton, the International Textbook of the Game*. Montreal, Graphic Publishing Co., 1950.

Jackson, Carl H., and Swan, Lester A.: *Better Badminton*. New York, A. S. Barnes and Co., 1950.

Official Tennis-Badminton Guide, June 1952-June 1954. Washington, D. C., AAHPER (NSWA), 1952.

Post, Julia H., and Shirley, Mabel J.: *Selected Recreational Sports for Girls and Women*. New York, A. S. Barnes and Co., 1936.

Thomas, Sir George: *The Art of Badminton*. London, Hutchinson and Co., Ltd., 1932.

Yocom, Rachael B., and Hunsaker, H. B.: *Individual Sports for Men and Women*. New York, A. S. Barnes and Co., 1947.

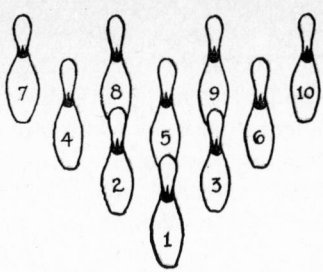

3 • BOWLING • BY *Marjorie M. Harris*

Bowling, in its most primitive form, is regarded by sport historians as one of the most ancient of all sports. The exact dates of origin for the various crude forms of bowling games discovered, however, have been disputed among historians. The game's origin in Europe is placed in northern Italy where the game resembled that of lawn bowling.

Bowling at pins originated in Germany during the third and fourth centuries A.D. as a religious ceremony. Later, when bowling at pins became a sport, only the more privileged people were participants since the alleys were privately owned. During the Middle Ages many variations of the game developed throughout Europe. The ninepin game was played in Holland, skittles was introduced in England and curling was started in Scotland.

The American Bowling Congress associates our modern game of tenpins with that of ninepins, which was introduced by the Dutch settlers of Manhattan Island in 1623. The ninepins were set in a diamond formation. The game increased in popularity until the sport was controlled by gamblers. Thenceforth it was prohibited by law. To evade the law which prohibited ninepins but not the sport of bowling, an ingenious person added a tenth pin with the pins set in a triangle formation. This was the introduction of our present game of American tenpins.

Variations of the American tenpin game have been introduced in the United States. These are the games of duck pins and candle pins which are more prevalent and popular in the East and the South. A general description of the balls and pins used in duck pin bowling, the more popular of the two games, is included in this chapter. The techniques are similar to those of tenpin bowling and will not be discussed separately.

The American Bowling Congress, organized in 1895, was instrumental in promoting the sport from a game infiltrated with organizers and participants of ill-repute to a highly organized game in wholesome surroundings with excellent supervision. Also through the efforts of the American Bowling Congress, uniformity in rules, regulations and equipment was established. Today bowling has become the greatest indoor sport for millions of men, women and children. Its popularity can be credited to the fact that it offers relaxation, entertainment, exercise and a challenge to bowlers of all ages and abilities.

The inclusion of bowling in a school or college physical education program is a valuable asset. It can be a team sport as well as an individual sport that has tremendous carry-over value for the students. It is one of the few sports in which many students with health or physical restrictions may participate.

EQUIPMENT

As in any sport, the proper equipment is important before the participant can hope to bowl proficiently. Since most bowling establishments abide by the rules and regulations of the American Bowling Congress, it is possible for every bowler to have access to the proper equipment for a small fee.

Costume

Regulation gymnasium costumes may be worn in school and college classes since the costumes are chosen for uniformity and freedom of movement. At public alleys, however, loose but neat sport clothing should be worn. Flared skirts or those of a too straight cut are a hindrance to good movement. Unless girls must do their own pin setting, shorts and slacks are not in good taste at public alleys.

The proper shoes are of prime importance for high scoring. They are necessary for efficient footwork on the slippery approach or runway to the alley. Bowling shoes are designed to allow for sliding as well as the maintenance of body control that is desired on the approach. For a right-handed bowler the left shoe is made with a pliable leather sole and a rubber heel for sliding, while the right shoe sole and heel are made of rubber for control. The soles of shoes for left-handed bowlers are reversed. At most public alleys bowling shoes are required because of the marks that street shoes will leave on the smooth approach surfaces. The shoes may be rented at very little cost. Where bowling shoes are not available in school or college situations, leather-soled shoes with rubber heels should be required. Rubber-soled shoes are extremely dangerous and unsatisfactory for efficient bowling.

Regulation Balls

1. *Tenpin Ball.* The weight of tenpin balls may range from 10 to 16 pounds. They are made of various compositions which withstand long and hard use. Either a two-holed or three-holed grip can be obtained. The thumb and middle finger are used for the two-holed grip; the three-holed grip is held with the ring finger in addition to the thumb and middle finger. The degree of pitch or slant of the holes varies on different balls. For girls, especially beginners, the three-holed grip is more satisfactory for control.

Great care should be taken in the selection of a ball. Its fit will affect the comfort and consistency of the bowler. In selecting the ball the thumb is inserted as deeply as possible into the largest hole. When the thumb is bent the joint should contact the edge of the hole to maintain friction. The other fingers should fit comfortably in their respective holes for a secure grip with the remaining fingers spread on the ball's surface. The distance between the holes affects the span over which the fingers and thumb must spread to fit into the holes. If the holes are too far apart for the size of the hand, the thumb and fingers cannot be inserted far enough into the holes and the edges will irritate the flesh. Holes that are too closely spaced will cause the hand and fingers to cramp and the finger tips to become sore from the amount of friction placed on them in using an incorrect grip. In order to check for a correct span insert the thumb in the large hole and extend the middle and ring fingers on the surface of the ball over the holes in which they are usually placed. The knuckles of the second joints should extend about a quarter of an inch past the inside edge of each hole. When a correct grip is secured it should also be possible to slide a pencil between the ball and the palm of the hand. Regardless of how well the ball was selected for comfort in grip, the proper selection is not complete until a ball is chosen that is comfortable in respect to weight at the time when it is swung and not when it is being supported by a ball rack or the other hand.

2. *Duck Pin Ball.* The maximum size of a regulation duck pin ball is five inches in diameter and three pounds in weight. A smaller ball in size and weight may be used but it is not recommended. The smaller balls are more difficult to control. There are no holes in duck pin balls. The ball is gripped with the fingers and thumb just as it would be picked up from a ball rack. The fingers control the ball; therefore, it should not rest in the palm of the hand. The game of duck pins allows three balls per frame. Each bowler should use three balls of the same size and weight to maintain consistency in her game.

Regulation Pins

1. *Tenpin.* The regulation tenpin is made of one piece of clear, hard, solid maple. Each pin must weigh within the range of three pounds to three pounds eight ounces.

2. *Duck Pin.* A duck pin is made of clear, hard maple and on its base it may have a fiber band. The pins in a set should be as near a uniform weight as possible.

Alley

The alley and its approach or runway must be constructed of wood. The alley consists of several parts of which the following are the more essential for the average bowler to know.

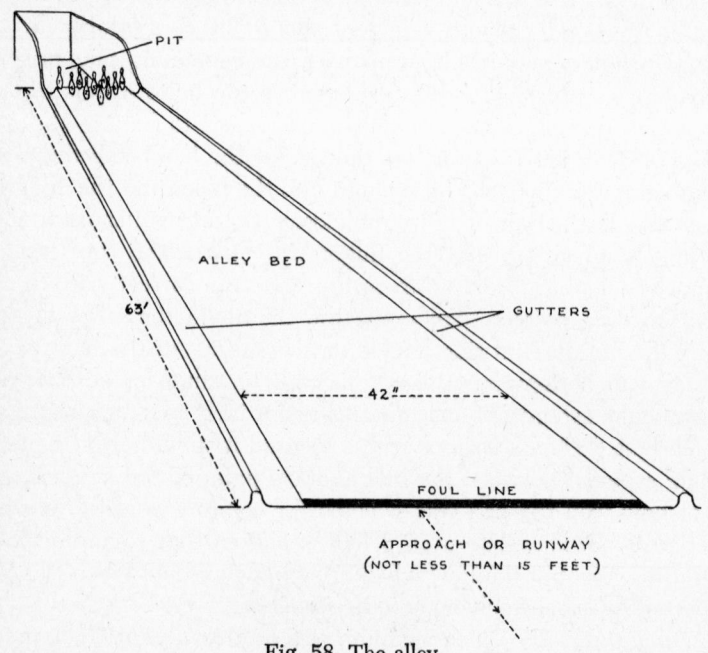

Fig. 58. The alley.

1. *Approach.* The approach is a level runway which extends back from the foul line's outer edge for not less than 15 feet. The approach has a clear finish which should be kept free from chalk. Steel wool should be available to remove any foreign substance from the alley surface.

2. *Foul Line.* A foul line of not less than ⅜ of an inch nor more than 1 inch in width must divide the end of the approach and the

beginning of the alley bed. This line must be clearly marked on the alley and extended on any adjacent wall or post which the bowler might touch near the foul line.

3. *Alley Bed.* The part of the alley upon which the ball is rolled is the alley bed. Its length from the foul line to the front edge of the pit is approximately 63 feet and its width must be between 41 and 42 inches.

4. *Gutters.* The gutters which run parallel to each side of the alley bed measure 9 to 9½ inches in width. They extend from the foul line to the pit.

5. *Pin Spots.* Ten spots upon which the pins are set are marked in a triangle formation at the end of the alley bed. The spots from center to center are 12 inches apart. The chapter heading and Fig. 58 show the numbering and the arrangement of the spots and pins.

6. *Pit.* At the far end of the alley bed is the pit, which is at least 9½ inches deep. A mat should cover the floor of the pit.

TECHNIQUES

Grip

The grip was previously discussed under the heading of Equipment. A basic principle for correct bowling is a comfortable, natural grip which permits a smooth release of the ball. The selection of a ball is made by finding one that is adaptable to the bowler's hand and fingers.

Holding the Ball

When the ball is taken from the rack it should be supported on the left hand or the left hip by a right-handed bowler and on the right hand or the right hip of a left-handed bowler. This prevents the fingers from accumulating perspiration before the bowler is in a position to assume her stance for bowling. The bowling fingers, hand and arm remain relaxed before the grip is taken and the stance assumed.

Stance

Various stances may be taken by the bowler. The experienced bowler should try the erect, crouch and semi-crouch positions and choose the one more comfortable and efficient for her style of bowling. The most common stance and the one recommended for beginning bowlers is the erect position. The ball is held slightly away from the body at waist or chest height. It should be supported with the left hand even though the grip has been taken. The right hand should grip the ball with the thumb pointing up and toward the pins. The bowler faces the pins squarely with the weight evenly distributed on both feet. The distance at which the stance is taken from the foul line will depend on each individual's approach.

Approach

A second basic principle for good bowling is efficient footwork. Each individual must practice and choose an approach which is natural and rhythmic. It should allow perfect coordination of the body for the timing necessary to release the ball for a smooth delivery. Ample room must be taken on the runway for executing the steps and slide used on any approach. To aid the beginner in deciding where she should start her approach have her stand with her back to the foul line and her heels at least three inches from it. From here all the movements of an approach can be made, and when the last step and slide are completed the beginner turns around and assumes the stance at the point where the forward foot stopped. This is recommended over the trial-and-error method of measuring while facing the foul line. Beginners will often note that the foul line is too close or too far for the number of steps they intended to take and they unconsciously lengthen or shorten their steps to such an extent that their coordination and timing are hindered.

Regardless of the number of steps, of which at least three must be taken, the weight of the ball begins the slow forward momentum of the body. As the ball is swung, momentum is increased so that the steps are taken in a straight line at a fast walk or slow run. The body, at the completion of the approach, is in a balanced semi-crouch with the left foot and right arm extended to the foul line.

Three-step Approach. It is frequently easier for the beginner to learn first a three-step approach. This approach, however, is not conducive to the greatest possible coordination between the arm swing and the footwork. Preceding the first step with the left foot the ball is started or pushed slightly away from the body.

STEP 1—LEFT FOOT. The ball starts the backswing. Balance is maintained with the left arm to the side.

STEP 2—RIGHT FOOT. The body leans forward into a slightly crouched position on this larger step. The right arm continues the backswing until the ball has reached its highest point between hip and shoulder level.

STEP 3 AND SLIDE—LEFT FOOT. Simultaneously with a large step and a slide the ball swings forward into position for the release. The body is now in a semi-crouch position with the shoulders facing the pins squarely.

Right
Count 1

Left
Count 2

Right
Count 3

Left
Count 4

Fig. 59. The four-step approach.

Four-step Approach. This is the most common and the most efficient approach. Each movement of the arm coincides with a movement of the feet, thereby providing the possibility for perfect body coordination and ball control.

STEP 1—RIGHT FOOT. As a short or half-step is taken the ball is pushed forward and down to begin the backswing.

STEP 2—LEFT FOOT. On this slightly larger second step the body leans forward into a slightly crouched position. The left arm maintains balance at the side as the ball swings back past the body.

STEP 3—RIGHT FOOT. This is the first full step as the body gains momentum. The ball reaches its highest point on the backswing.

STEP 4 AND SLIDE. The final step is long and combined with a short slide. Simultaneously with the foot action the ball swings forward to a point a few inches beyond the foul line. The body is in a semi-crouched position with the shoulders facing the pins squarely and the left arm out to the side to aid in the maintenance of balance.

Five-step Approach. Advanced bowlers will sometimes prefer the five-step approach. There is a tendency to gain greater momentum by using a fifth step; however, too much speed on the approach makes it more difficult to maintain control and balance.

STEP 1—LEFT FOOT. The initial step is short as the ball is pushed slightly away from the body.

STEP 2—RIGHT FOOT. The ball begins the backswing. The body begins its forward lean in a semi-crouched position.

STEP 3—LEFT FOOT. The step is larger as the ball swings past the body toward the completion of the backswing, which is high.

STEP 4—RIGHT FOOT. Momentum has increased on this step. The ball has completed the backswing.

STEP 5 AND SLIDE—LEFT FOOT. The forward swing takes place as the final step and slide are executed. The right hand is over the foul line as the left foot completes the slide.

Delivery

As the approach nears completion the bowler should not attempt to produce additional power for the release or delivery of the ball. Such an attempt can only throw the bowler off balance and result in a poorly delivered ball. Through slow motion film studies of balls released at various speeds it was found that deliveries made at slow or medium speeds were more effective than balls delivered at a greater speed. The pins hit with a fast ball were picked up and lifted in a nearly vertical position into the pit. They did not scatter other pins as they were lifted into the pit because they did not have time to fall into or nearly into a horizontal position.

As the ball is delivered, the hand should be a few inches over the foul line so that the hand is behind the ball when it is released.

It is not recommended that beginners progress beyond the straight ball delivery. Those students who have demonstrated average ability should be introduced to the hook ball. The other types of delivery should be taught only to those individuals who show a natural tendency to release the ball in a manner adapted to them.

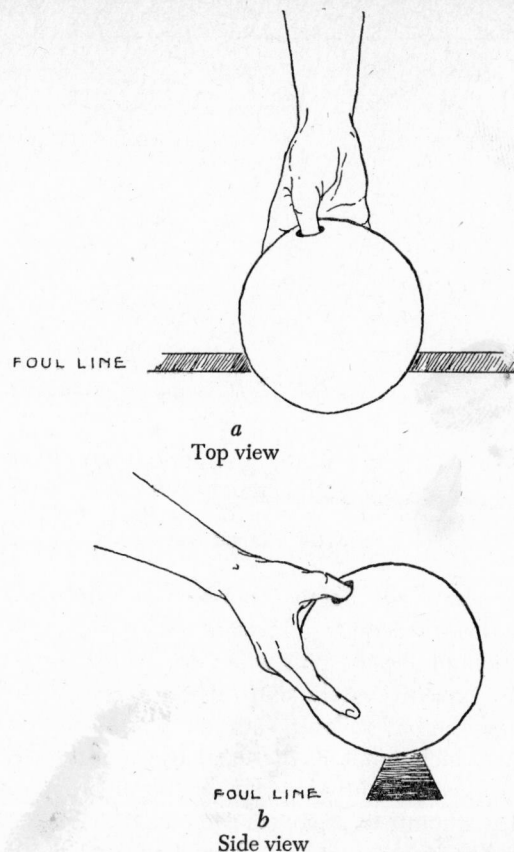

a
Top view

b
Side view

Fig. 60. The grip, just previous to point of release of straight ball.

Straight Ball. Beginners or those whose bowling is erratic should first master the straight ball, which revolves in a straight line from the point of release to the point of aim. The point of release is approximately six to eight inches in from the right side of the alley (Fig. 61). The hand is behind the ball with the thumb pointing toward the pins (Fig. 60). The thumb is released first. The forward follow-through of the hand with the thumb up must continue to permit the release of a smooth, straight ball.

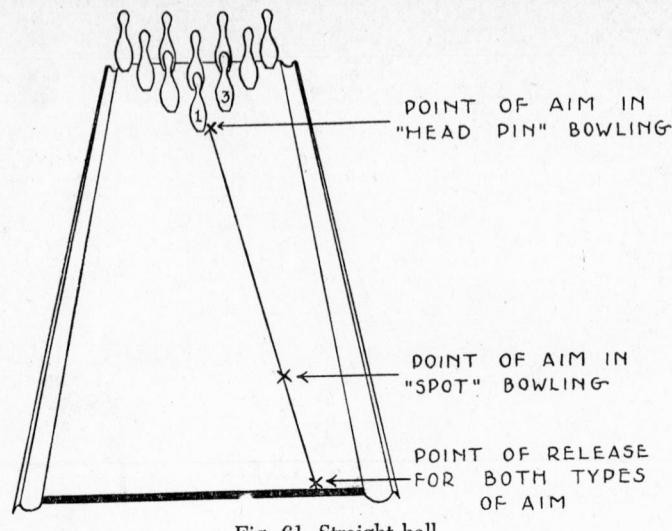

POINT OF AIM IN
"HEAD PIN" BOWLING

POINT OF AIM IN
"SPOT" BOWLING

POINT OF RELEASE
FOR BOTH TYPES
OF AIM

Fig. 61. Straight ball.

Hook Ball. The most effective, but a more difficult ball to roll is the hook. Its double action, a forward and side rotation, causes a greater deflection among the pins when it is aimed correctly. From its point of release, approximately six to fifteen inches in from the right side of the alley, the ball follows a straight path until the side rotation takes effect at which point it curves sharply to the left (Fig. 63). As the ball is released slightly beyond the foul line the hand is rotated to the left. The thumb is removed from its hole first and then the fingers as they lift slightly upward. The follow-through is with the arm forward and the hand is extended in a hand-shake position.

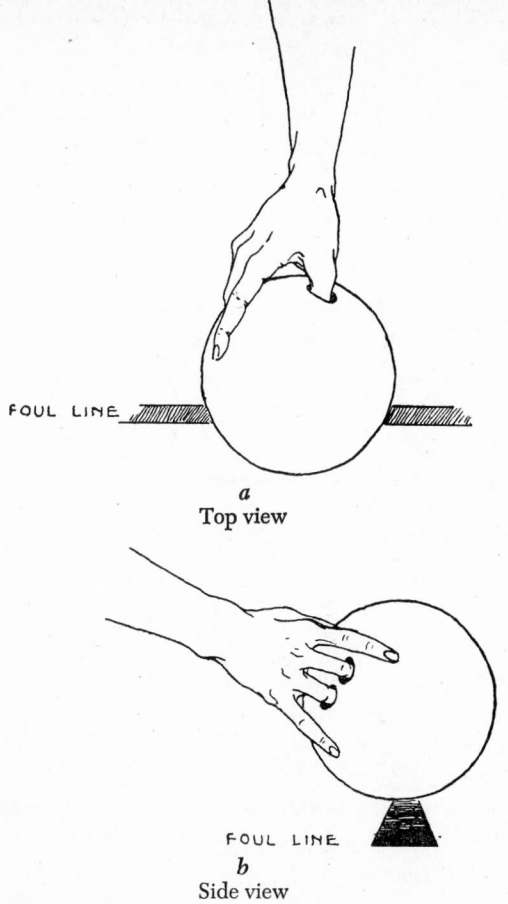

FOUL LINE

a
Top view

FOUL LINE
b
Side view

Fig. 62. The grip, just previous to point of release of hook ball.

Curve Ball. This effective but most difficult ball to control travels in a wide arc from its point of release to the point of aim (Fig. 63). It is released at a point near the center of the alley. Less wrist action is used than in the execution of the hook ball. The lift of the fingers also aids in imparting a degree of side action which is necessary for the ball to curve. The follow-through is forward with the hand maintaining its position from the point of release.

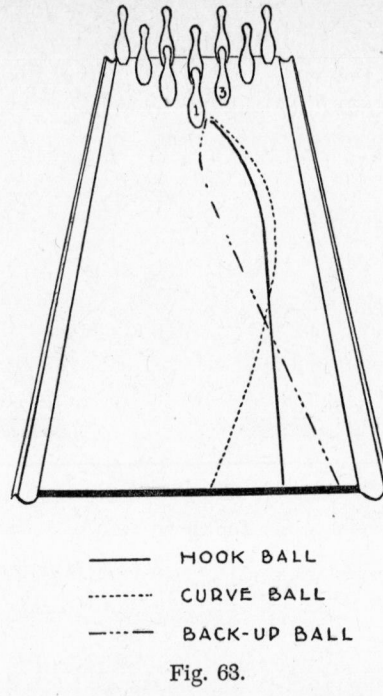

————	HOOK BALL
··········	CURVE BALL
—·—·—	BACK-UP BALL

Fig. 63.

Back-up Ball. The reverse action of a hook is the back-up with its double rotation forward as well as right to left. The ball is rolled onto the alley from the far right-hand corner (Fig. 63). As the ball is released the wrist rotates to the right with the fingers leaving the ball last. The follow-through of the arm is forward with the palm of the hand up and the thumb pointing slightly to the right.

Aim

The object at which one aims, for an effective ball, is a pocket or the space between two pins. The pocket for the right-handed bowler is the space between the number 1 and number 3 pins, whereas the left-handed bowler directs her ball to the space between the number 1 and number 2 pins. The popular concept is that the head pin should be contacted for a strike. Actually, the number 5 or king pin of the set must be contacted as well as the head pin.

There are two possibilities in selecting a point of aim. Pin bowling is recommended for beginners or the more inexperienced bowlers. The bowler keeps her eyes on the pin for which she is aiming throughout the approach, delivery and follow-through. The bowler who rolls the same type of ball consistently will find that spot bowling provides a more effective point of aim. In spot bowling the point of aim is shifted from the pins 60 feet away to a spot on the alley within a very few feet of the bowler. The eyes are not shifted from the spot on the alley until the delivery has been completed. The spot bowler will sometimes find it necessary to readjust her point of aim because of varying alley conditions.

Points of Aim.

STRAIGHT BALL. The 1-3 pocket is used for pin bowling. A point on the alley in line with the 1-3 pocket serves as a point of aim for the spot bowler. The spot is located six to eight inches in from the right side and a few feet from where the ball is released.

HOOK BALL. Pin number 6 is the point of aim for pin bowling. A point on line with the number 6 pin within a few feet of the foul line is used for spot bowling.

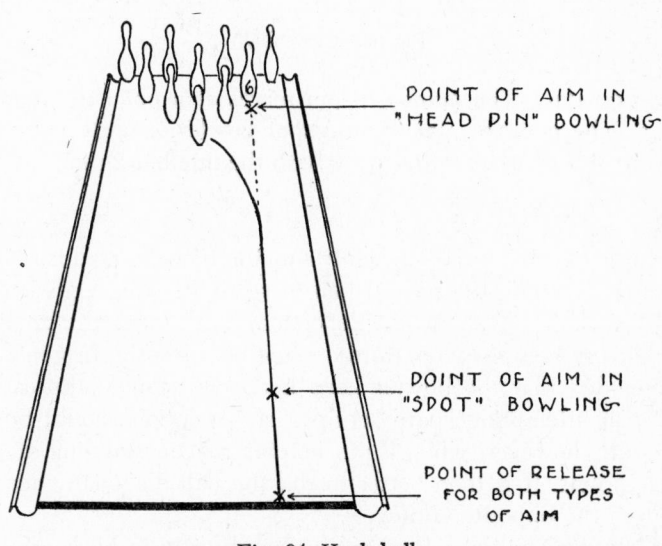

POINT OF AIM IN "HEAD PIN" BOWLING

POINT OF AIM IN "SPOT" BOWLING

POINT OF RELEASE FOR BOTH TYPES OF AIM

Fig. 64. Hook ball.

CURVE BALL. The pin bowler uses the far right-hand corner as her point of aim. The spot bowler aims at a point closer to the center of the alley and in direct line with the far right-hand corner.

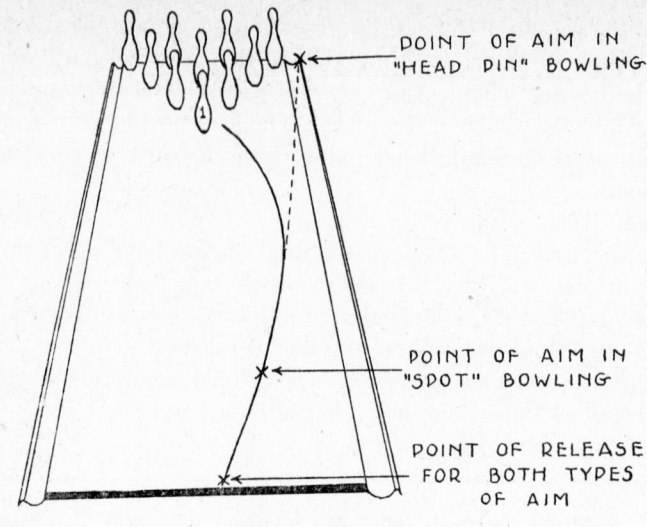

POINT OF AIM IN "HEAD PIN" BOWLING

POINT OF AIM IN "SPOT" BOWLING

POINT OF RELEASE FOR BOTH TYPES OF AIM

Fig. 65. Curve ball.

BACK-UP BALL. The number 2 pin serves as a point of aim for pin bowling. The point of aim for the spot bowler is fairly close to the right side of the alley in direct line with the number 2 pin.

Spares

Next to making a strike in each frame, the bowler's goal is to fell the remaining pins with the second ball to score a spare. A great deal of thought must be given to pin deflection, angles and the analysis of one's delivery before spares can be made consistently. In general it is recommended that the bowler keep her usual stance, approach and delivery in attempting spare set-ups. An exception should be made to this rule, however, when a pin or pins remain standing at one of the far corners. It is then better to roll the ball diagonally across the alley from the opposite corner.

The "sleeper" set-up, where one pin is directly in back of another, requires a full hit on the front pin. If the hit contacts the front pin on either side both the ball and the pin are deflected leaving the back pin standing.

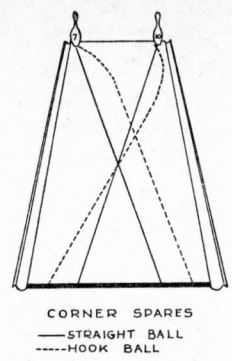

CORNER SPARES
——STRAIGHT BALL
-----HOOK BALL

Fig. 66. The corner spare.

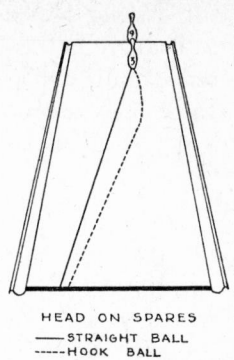

HEAD ON SPARES
——STRAIGHT BALL
-----HOOK BALL

Fig. 67. The head-on spare.

Scoring

The same method of scoring is used for tenpins and duck pins but higher scores are much more prevalent in the game of tenpins. One game or line consists of ten frames. Two balls per frame are rolled in

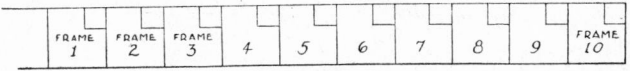

FRAME 1 | FRAME 2 | FRAME 3 | 4 | 5 | 6 | 7 | 8 | 9 | FRAME 10

Fig. 68.

tenpins, whereas in the game of duck pins three balls per frame are rolled. Each line or game on a score sheet is marked off into ten frames (Fig. 68). The recorded score is cumulative; the score marked

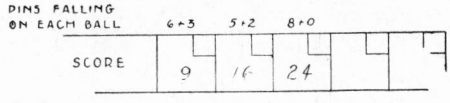

PINS FALLING
ON EACH BALL   6+3   5+2   8+0

SCORE   9   16   24

Fig. 69.

down in the space for the second frame is the score of the first frame plus the number of pins knocked down in the second frame. This continues, the score of one frame being added to the score marked down in the preceding frame (Fig. 69). If all ten pins fall with the first ball, a strike has been made and is indicated by a cross (X) in the small square in the corner of that frame. In this instance no score is recorded until two more balls have been rolled; then the sum of these three balls becomes the score for the strike frame (Fig. 70). A

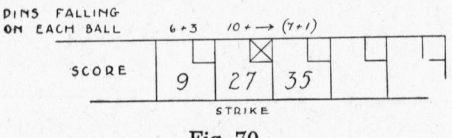

Fig. 70.

spare is made when all the pins fall with the second ball. This is marked with a single diagonal (\). In this case the score made on the first ball of the next frame is added to the ten points of the spare to give the final score for the spare frame (Fig. 71).

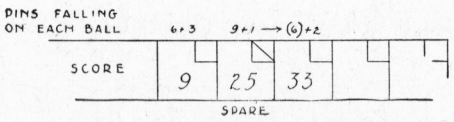

Fig. 71.

If, on the last frame, a strike is made, two extra balls are rolled; if a spare, the bowler is entitled to only one extra ball. The score for a perfect game is 300 points. Figure 72 is a diagram illustrating and explaining the scoring of a game.

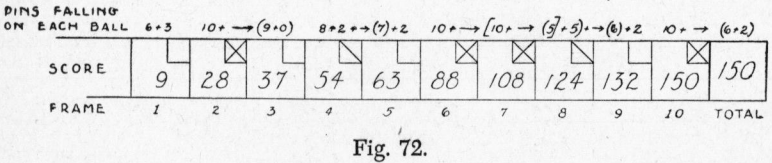

Fig. 72.

In addition to the strike (X) and spare (\) symbols, there are two more that are commonly used. A "split" or "railroad" occurs when there is more than a pin's width between the pins still standing. The symbol for a split is a small zero (o). The bowler makes an "error" or "blow" when she fails to bring down all the pins with her second ball if those remaining pins did not form a split. The symbol for this is a horizontal line (—). These symbols do not affect the actual scoring.

ETIQUETTE

Bowling, like other sports, has its unwritten code of etiquette with which all bowlers should be familiar. In classes, whenever the opportunity presents itself, the following rules of etiquette should be discussed and stressed:

1. Consideration should be given to the other bowler at all times.
2. Refrain from speaking to a bowler when she has assumed her stance.
3. The right of way is given to a bowler on the right.
4. Never take the approach simultaneously with a bowler in the next alley on either the right or the left.
5. The bowler, after noting her hit, should immediately walk away from the foul line on her own runway.
6. Another bowler's ball should not be used during class unless this arrangement is necessary or during a game unless the person whose ball it is has given permission.
7. Chalk should never be used on the soles of shoes. It ruins the approaches for those who follow.
8. The bowler should be ready for her turn.
9. Know the rules and learn to score.

SAFETY FACTORS

In addition to etiquette, safety factors should be introduced at the beginning of bowling instruction and emphasized throughout. Safety is all the more important in a class situation where the students do the pin setting. Carelessness, unfortunately, will always take its toll. The following safety rules, discussed and practiced, will aid in minimizing injuries:

1. Select a ball that will allow a comfortable grip so that the fingers can be easily released from the holes.
2. Wear bowling shoes or leather-soled and rubber-heeled shoes.
3. Refrain from using chalk on shoe soles. Steel wool is usually available to remove any substance from the sole or the floor that causes the shoes to stick.
4. In taking the ball from a rack, place the hands on the free sides of the ball. The fingers in this position will not be pinched or crushed by an unnoticed ball rolling on the rack.
5. It is the responsibility of the bowler to check and see that the pin setter is out of the pit before rolling the ball.
6. Pin setters should keep their legs out of the pit when the resetting is complete.

7. Before entering the pit the pin setter should make sure that the bowler is not in the act of bowling.

8. Follow the instructions given for the use of mechanical pin-setting devices.

SCHOOL ARRANGEMENTS AND CLASS ORGANIZATION

Schools which are not fortunate in having their own bowling facilities are in the majority. In all probability a suitable arrangement can be made with the proprietor of a local bowling establishment for the school classes to use public alleys. Morning and early afternoon hours are the more likely times for public alleys to be free or in little use. Most bowling proprietors are sufficiently foresighted to recognize the value of such an arrangement with the school. Not only will students frequent his establishment for extracurricular recreation, but they will often become such bowling enthusiasts that they promote the organization of school leagues. The fees for the school use of public alleys are generally quite reasonable, more so when the students do their own pin setting. Public alleys are able to accommodate larger classes than most school bowling facilities.

When public alleys are not available for regular class meetings or when school facilities are limited, the fundamentals of bowling may be introduced in the gymnasium. The alleys can be marked on the floor with chalk or masking tape. If regular balls and pins are available, matting should be placed on the area marked for the alley. Pin setters should be instructed to stop the balls with the feet unless side boards and a backstop are set up around the pit area. Softballs and Indian clubs can also be used for learning and practicing the fundamentals of bowling.

Ideally a class hour should allow time enough for each student to bowl a complete game. Forty-five minutes is ample for a class hour if the facilities permit only four bowlers to an alley. At least one hour is desirable for those classes which must allot time for getting to and from a public bowling establishment.

Both instructor and student can gain more when those of the same ability can be placed in one class. This situation is more likely to be possible in a college program than in a school program; however, it is the ideal class organization. The best alternative is that of organizing different abilities within a class into groups: beginners, intermediates and advanced grouped on different alleys. Those who have bowled very little or not at all are in the beginning group; those who have had some experience and have a fair knowledge of bowling fundamentals are in the intermediate group; while those who are the most consistent and experienced bowlers belong in the advanced group. With this type of class arrangement it is possible for the instructor to teach or to review a technique with the beginning group while the intermediate group practices spare set-ups and the advanced group practices rolling a hook ball. The instructor can then address her corrections and suggestions to aid those on the same level of ability.

Classes which are large and necessitate more than four or five students per alley make it difficult or impossible for games to be completed during a class hour. A rotation method can be used so that on some days two or more students observe and keep score or possibly set pins. In order to give a group larger than four or five per alley an element of competition with everyone participating in the bowling, various adaptations of a game can be devised. Each pin setter and group of bowlers are given a sheet of paper listing several spare set-ups numbered in the order in which they are to be used. The first set-up is placed and each bowler is allowed her two balls to knock over the complete set-up. If on the first ball the set-up is only partially hit, those pins are reset for her try with the second ball. As soon as the bowler is successful in knocking over the complete set-up she can progress to the next set-up on her second ball or on her next turn. The individual who knocks down the greatest number of spare set-ups is the winner. This game can also be used with groups competing against one another for team competition. As soon as one bowler on a team is successful in knocking down a complete set-up, the team may progress to the next. At the end of the class hour the team which has progressed through the greatest number of spare set-ups is the winner. In another adapted competitive team game for a large group, each person on a team bowls three or four frames. For example, the number of frames per game is increased to twenty-four and each of the six bowlers on each team bowls four frames. The team with the highest total score wins.

TEACHING PROGRESSION FOR BEGINNERS

The teaching progressions are presented in outline form since the variable factors of class time, size, organization and facilities will enable one instructor to cover more or less material than another. It is important with beginners that the teaching progression is slow and thorough to enable them to absorb and to learn a good sound basis of bowling fundamentals. Ample time should be devoted to a review on days following the presentation of a new technique.

1. Acquaint students with equipment and facilities.

(a) Discussion of proper costume.

(b) Selection of shoes.

(c) Selection of ball.

(d) Discussion of parts of alley and its care. If possible arrange for maintenance personnel in charge of the alleys to describe the care required for good alleys.

(e) Instruction in the use of automatic pin-setting machines or how pin setting should be done manually if it is to be done by the students.

(f) Introduce safety factors in the selection and use of the equipment.

(g) Introduce etiquette in regard to the use of the equipment.

2. Teach removal of ball from rack and how it is held.

3. Teach the stance.

4. Practice the arm swing with the ball. Stress the fact that the weight of the ball swings the arm.

5. Teach a one-step-and-slide approach, a straight ball delivery and the follow-through.

(a) Practice mimetically without a ball. Check each individual's body position.

(b) Show where the ball should be released and have students aim the ball for a point near the center of the far end of the alley.

(c) Practice with ball on the alley. Do not use pins.

6. Progress to a three-step approach. Use this as a stepping stone to the preferable four-step approach.

(a) Practice mimetically without a ball.

(b) Practice with a ball on the alley. Do not use pins.

(c) Teach a two-step approach to those who are having difficulty or have them return to the one-step-and-slide approach for more practice.

(d) Practice, using the 1-2-3 pins.

7. Introduce the elementary principles of deflection and angles used in bowling.

8. Teach the four-step approach.

(a) Practice mimetically without a ball.

(b) Practice with a ball. Do not use pins.

(c) Practice, using the 1-2-3 pins.

(d) Place those beginners who are progressing more rapidly on the same alleys. Have them use a full set of pins. Give the other bowlers a more thorough review of the one-, two- and three-step approaches.

9. Explain scoring, rules and etiquette of the game.

10. Bowl, keeping score.

11. Practice various spare set-ups.
12. Bowl games.
13. Start a tournament.

TEACHING PROGRESSION FOR INTERMEDIATES AND ADVANCED

Even though one might assume that an intermediate or advanced bowler would know how to select a ball and would have developed her own style of bowling with a fair knowledge of the fundamentals, it is best to spend time in review.

1. Discuss equipment.
 (a) Review selection of a ball.
 (b) Review safety and equipment.
2. Bowl so that the instructor can evaluate ability.
3. Review three- and four-step approach, delivery and follow-through for a straight ball. Have the students spend more time on the approach which feels more natural.
 (a) Check each individual's form.
 (b) Review point of aim for pin bowling.
 (c) Practice with ball using 1-2-3 pins.
 (d) Practice, using full set of pins.
4. Review scoring, rules and etiquette of game.
5. Bowl, using the straight delivery. Keep score.
6. Review principles of deflection and angles used in bowling.
7. Practice spare set-ups using a straight delivery.
8. Teach spot bowling; review it for those who have had it.
9. Bowl, using straight ball and spot point of aim. Keep score.
10. Teach hook ball, its release and point of aim.
 (a) Practice with 1-2-3 pins.
 (b) Practice with full set of pins.
 (c) Place those who are having difficulty in coordination and timing on the same alleys. Give them more review on straight and hook ball delivery.
 (d) Practice spare set-ups with a hook ball.
 (e) Bowl game, using the hook ball.
11. Teach a curve or back-up ball only to those individuals who show a natural tendency to roll that type of ball. Point out its advantages and disadvantages.
12. Bowl games, having each individual concentrate on the type of approach, delivery and point of aim most natural for her.
13. Start a tournament.

TOURNAMENTS

Students usually enjoy some form of competition during or, particularly, near the end of a sport season. There are various types of tournaments which can be played and enjoyed by those at all levels of ability.

Class Hour Tournaments

Toward the end of a season, after a class has had the opportunity to bowl practice games, their scores from these games can be used in dividing the class into teams. As evenly as possible, those with high, average and low scores are dispersed on the number of teams to be made. No team has an advantage over any other because all are composed of players of all abilities. Depending on the number of teams, the tournament can be of the round-robin or of the elimination type. If the class is small a ladder tournament is more successful.

School and College Class Tournaments

A method must be devised to choose class bowling teams. One suggestion is to require each girl who is interested in trying out for a class team to submit a specific number of game scores. These games should be bowled within a specified time on the alleys used by the school classes. At the designated time when all scores must be in, each individual's scores are totaled. If a team of four is to be chosen, those four with the highest totals will be selected for their class team. Depending on the number of teams chosen in each class, a round-robin or an elimination tournament can be arranged.

School and College Open Tournaments

The school or college open tournament can be offered in schools that offer a longer bowling season or where interest is greater in individual competition. Since it is open to any number from any class, this type of tournament is usually large. A straight elimination tournament is therefore recommended. When the matches are played off, the player having the highest score for two out of three games is the winner.

REFERENCES

Bowler's Manual. Milwaukee, Wisconsin, American Bowling Congress, 1950.

Falcaro, Joe, and Goodman, Murray: *Bowling for All.* New York, A. S. Barnes and Co., 1943.

History of Bowling. Milwaukee, Wisconsin, American Bowling Congress.

Keith, Harold: *Sports and Games.* New York, Thomas Y. Crowell Co., 1947, "Bowling," pp. 69-79.

Official Sports Library for Women: *Official Individual Sports Guide.* Washington, D. C., American Association for Health, Physical Education and Recreation, 1952-1954.

4 • FENCING • BY *Marion R. Broer*

Fencing is one of the oldest known sports and at present is enjoying a recurrence of popularity. This sport sprang from the duel and originally all swords were cutting and thrusting weapons used entirely for offense, the body being protected by armor.

Paradoxically enough, the development of the defense with the sword was a result of the invention of gunpowder. When it was possible to shoot through the armor the swordsman found he was better off to shed this type of protection and make his sword assume a defensive as well as an offensive role.

When the duel was banned in Spain in the fifteenth century fencing was born as a scientific art. The earliest teachers of swordplay were jugglers and sword dancers who traveled with fairs from town to town. Swordplay as something approaching a system seems to have begun in the early part of the sixteenth century, and about the middle of the seventeenth the style of fencing gradually began to shape along the present lines.

Three schools of fencing developed and have lasted through the ages—the French, Italian, and Spanish schools. Today these schools differ little except in so far as the peculiarities of the different types of weapon demand.

Fencing began to appear in this hemisphere in the late nineteenth century. It is now organized nationally by the Amateur Fencers' League of America which sponsors sectional tournaments classified for fencers of different degrees of skill. Through this organization, and through fencing clubs in many cities, anyone interested can continue fencing long after school and college years.

As a form of exercise fencing owes apologies to no sport. The muscles must be trained through continual, persistent practice to respond instantaneously to the rapid-fire commands of the brain. A fencer must be agile, nimble, and intelligent, and must have strength coupled with mental and nervous control. She must adapt herself to her opponent, have a constantly alert mind, and analyze with great speed. A fine correlation of mind and body is necessary for success. The hand develops a delicate sense of touch and controlled precision, the eyes acquire keenness, and the muscles are schooled to instantaneous reaction to the brain. The fencer develops stamina as a result of regular, methodical practice. Perseverance is another quality necessary in a fencer; hand in hand with it go patience and courage.

Fencing can provide a great deal of exercise in a short period of time. It can be carried on in any relatively small area, no especially constructed court or field being necessary.

There is much to recommend fencing, and its present popularity among students of high school and college age demands that it be given its well-deserved place in the physical education program. This means that the physical educator must know how to organize groups so that each individual will receive as much instruction and practice as possible during the short physical education periods.

EQUIPMENT

Foils, masks, and some type of protection for the body should be furnished by the school. Many beginners hesitate to buy their own equipment until they have learned something about the sport, even if they are financially able. If possible enough equipment for from 20 to 25 fencers should be provided. This will take care of a class which can be handled easily by one instructor.

A large gymnasium is not so desirable for fencing instruction as a smaller room but will serve the purpose. Very little space is needed for keeping the equipment. If there is no equipment room, it can be neatly arranged in one corner of the gymnasium.

I. Foils

(A) *Description.* French demountable foils with bell guards are recommended. The foil is made up of the blade and the handle. The blade is flexible at the point and strong near the handle. The tongue (tang) is that part of the blade which extends up into the handle. The handle consists of the guard, which protects the hand, the grip, and the pommel, which serves to hold the blade to the handle and also gives the foil weight and balance. The center of balance should be just outside the guard. A blade that is too flexible is not practical for teaching beginners. It is excellent, however, for trained fencers. Rubber tips can be purchased for five cents, but tipping the foil with adhesive tape takes very little time, is usually more satisfactory for class use, and is even less expensive. A few extra blades should always be kept on hand.

(B) *Method of Storing.*

1. A board about 12″ wide and long enough to take the required number of foils (figure 5″ for 3 foils and add 3″ to 4″ for the end of the rack) can easily be made into a rack. Inch wide slits should be cut approximately 10″ deep at intervals of 4″. This rack can be placed on the wall 4′ or more from the floor. Three foils can be placed in each slit so that the bell guard rests on the top of the board and the blade points toward the floor. A rack such as this would have to be 4′ long to hold 25-27 foils. (Fig. 73.)

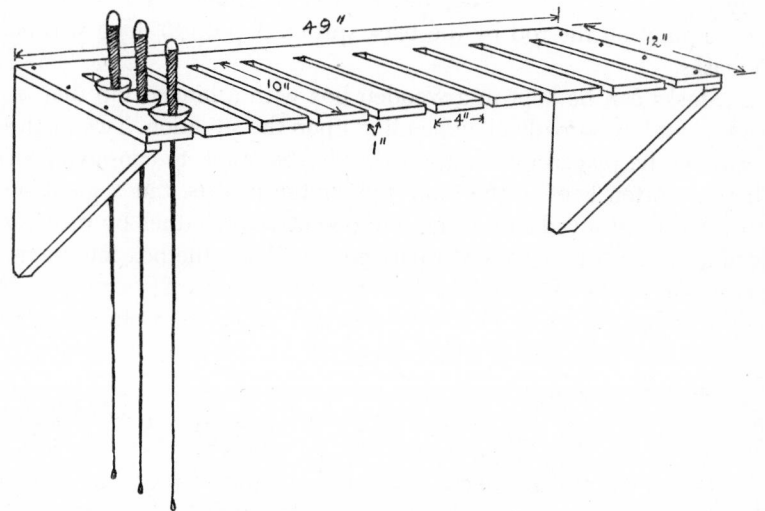

Fig. 73. Method of storing foils.

2. If it is desirable to lock up the equipment when it is not in use, a longer and narrower rack, holding only one foil in each slit, can be made. A second board with holes for the handles of the foils can be hinged to one end of the rack so that it will drop over the top of the bell guards and padlock at the other end. This type of rack would have to be 5″ wide and 11′ long to hold 25 foils. The inch wide slits would be cut about 4″ deep at intervals of 4″.

3. To keep the foils in the best condition, provide a rack as described above and at the proper distance down the wall build out a board on

which are clips to hold the tips of the foils in place. The long and shallow rack holding one foil in each slit would have to be used.

II. Masks

(A) *Description and Use.* Black masks of medium weight are the most practical. To avoid the development of a fear of being touched by the opponent's blade, start classes wearing masks at all times that two students practice together. Also, if masks are worn through preliminary technique practice, the students will become so accustomed to them that they will not feel hindered by the masks when they reach the more advanced bouting stage.

(B) *Methods of Storing.*

1. A mask rack, placed on the wall near the foil rack, can be made by bracing a rod about 1″ in diameter 2″ from the wall. The masks can be hung on the rod by the back spring. A pole 15′ long will hold 25 masks.

2. Masks can be kept in a wooden box with a hinged top that may or may not have a padlock depending upon the situation. Two or three masks can be placed together, one inside the other, to conserve space. They are often kept in the same box as the jackets, but a great deal of time can be saved in putting equipment away, either by providing separate boxes, or by having a partition to divide the box into definite spaces for masks and jackets. A box approximately $2' \times 2'$ and $2\frac{1}{2}'$ deep will hold 25 masks (figure a space $12'' \times 12'' \times 8''$ for 3 masks), and one 3′ long, 2½′ wide and 2½′ deep will take both masks and jackets. The partition should be about 15″ from one end.

III. Jackets or Plastrons

(A) *Types and Uses.* Some protection should always be worn on the body in fencing class. The fencing jacket, which covers the entire target and the arms, is desirable whenever the situation makes this purchase possible. However, because of the cost, many schools are able to afford only half jackets, which cover the front, back and right side of the body and the right arm, or plastrons which protect only the front of the body. The half jackets may be turned inside out for left-handed fencers, and are preferable to the plastrons.

(B) *Method of Storing.* A box or cabinet can be placed on the floor near the foil rack. A large wooden box with a hinged top, with or without a padlock, is satisfactory. A box $28'' \times 15''$ and 30″ deep will hold 25 to 30 jackets. If it is desirable to keep masks and jackets together, refer to the section on the storing of masks.

IV. Gloves

The glove is not absolutely necessary. It is the least important part of the fencing equipment and may be omitted if no funds are available. Students will often furnish their own gloves. Old pigskin gloves will serve the purpose.

V. Equipment for Practicing the Lunge

(A) *Mats.* The same mats that are used for tumbling, apparatus, or correctives can be hung on the wall for lunging practice. If there are no facilities for hanging them, students can work in pairs, and while one practices the other can stand beside the mat, which is stood on end on the floor, and support it by leaning against it with one shoulder. At the same time that she is supporting the mat, the student can watch her partner for corrections in form.

Some gymnasia are built with posts or with uneven walls with corners that are padded for safety in team games. These paddings can be used to good advantage in fencing practice.

(B) *Targets.* Targets on the wall may stimulate interest. Hearts cut out of thick sponge rubber mats with smaller hearts painted on them are attractive, are easily made, and are an incentive to practice. These should be at least 12″ × 10″.

VI. Costume

All fencers should be required to wear tennis shoes and a gymnasium suit or fencing costume as absolute freedom of movement is essential.

THE TARGET AND LINES OF ENGAGEMENT

I. Definitions

(A) *Target.* The target for men extends from the top of the collar to the groin lines (in back, down to a horizontal line passing through the top of the hip bones), exclusive of the arms. The seam of the jacket is judged as the line of attachment of arm and shoulder. For women the target extends only to a line passing horizontally around the body across the hip bones.

(B) *Lines of Engagement.* The target is divided into 4 parts for the different attacks and defenses. These sections of the target are named as follow:

A. high outside—that part of the target seen to the left of the opponent's blade, higher than the guard of the foil. This section of the target is guarded by the parries of 6th and 3rd.[1]

B. high inside—that part seen to the right of the opponent's blade, higher than the guard of the foil. This section is guarded by the parries of 4th or 1st.[1]

C. low outside—that part seen to the left of the opponent's blade, lower than the guard of the foil. This section is guarded by the parries of 2nd or 8th.[1]

D. low inside—that part seen to the right of the opponent's blade, lower than the guard of the foil. This section is guarded by the parries of 7th or 5th.[1]

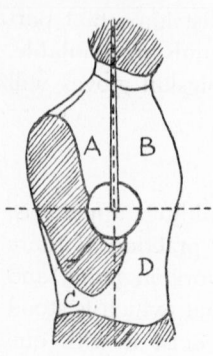

Fig. 74. The target.

(C) *Position of Engagement.* When two blades are crossed and are in contact, they are said to be engaged. When engaging for bouting, both fencers take the guard position (see page 131) with their heels on the same line. They should be close enough so that each can reach her opponent with a lunge when the right arm is extended. The foils should be crossed at the weak part of the blades, approximately 7 to 8 inches from the tips. If the foils are crossed on the right (or the inside), the fencers are said to be engaged in 4. This is simply an easy way of designating the crossing of the blades on the right. It has developed from the fact that the parry of 4[1] is the best defense against an attack high on this side. If the foils are crossed on the left (or outside), the fencers are said to be engaged in 6. It is the parry of 6[1] which best defends an attack high on the outside.

II. Teaching

(A) *Progression.*

1. Demonstrate by engaging with one of the students. Cross the blades on the right (in 4) and then on the left (in 6).

2. Divide the class into pairs and have them take the attention position (see p. 129) approximately 10 feet apart, holding their masks in

[1] The parries referred to are described on pages 148 to 152. To simplify the discussion of the different attacks, any attack made to the right (or inside) of the opponent's blade will be considered to be made in 4. If this attack is made high on the opponent's target, it will be designated as being made in high 4 (high inside), and if low, in low 4 (low inside). Any attack made to the left (or outside) of the opponent's blade will be considered to be made in 6—either high 6 (high outside) or low 6 (low outside).

their left arms. Have them take positions on lines marked on the gymnasium floor.

3. Have the students salute (see p. 129) their opponents.

4. Tell them to put on their masks.

5. Next have them go into the guard position with their blades crossed to the right, or in 4.

6. Tell them to change the engagement so that their blades cross to the left, or in 6.

(B) *Place in Progression.* The target and the lines and position of engagement should not be explained until the fundamental techniques such as grip, guard position, the advance and retreat, and the lunge have been learned. They must, however, be explained before any of the offensive or defensive tactics can be learned, since these necessitate practice with an opponent.

TECHNIQUES[2]

I. The Grip

(A) *Definition.* Method of holding the foil. The foil is held securely between the thumb and forefinger. The other three fingers are important in the control of the foil. They move it about the fulcrum formed by the secure grip of the thumb and forefinger. The thumb

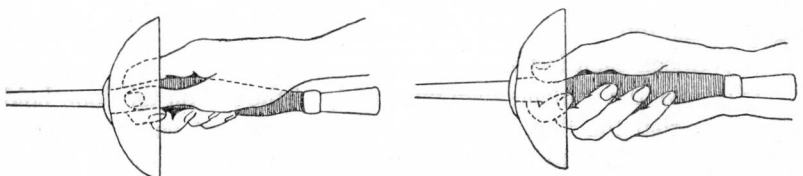

Fig. 75. The grip. Left, from above; right, from the side.

and forefinger can move the tip of the foil up and down, but the fingers control the movement of the foil tip from side to side.

(B) *Execution.*

1. The grip of the foil is curved slightly and should be grasped so that the convexity of the curve fits into the hand at the base of the thumb.

2. The grip of the foil should rest between the first and second joints of the index finger.

[2] The techniques are not discussed in the order in which they would be presented to a class. For this progression see page 157. All techniques are described for right-handed fencers.

3. The thumb should be extended on the top of the grip just back from the guard.

4. The thumb and forefinger should be on the broadest sides of the grip, which correspond to the broadest sides of the blade.

5. The other fingers curve around the grip naturally for control. The tips of the fingers should be on the concavity (inward curve) of the grip. This is extremely important, for if the fingers wrap farther around the grip, control of the foil will be lost.

6. The wrist should be straight.

7. The pommel rests against the center of the wrist.

8. If the foil is held correctly, there will be a straight line from the elbow to the tip of the foil.

(C) *Teaching.*

1. ORGANIZATION OF THE CLASS. Have the class in a semicircle around the instructor.

2. PROGRESSION.

(*a*) Have students hold the foil in the left hand and turn it until the convexity (outward curve) of the grip is toward the right.

(*b*) Tell them to place this outward curve against the heel of the thumb of the right hand.

(*c*) Have them extend the thumb along the top of the handle so that the tip of the thumb is just back from the guard of the foil.

(*d*) Then tell them to close the fingers of the right hand around the handle and put the tips against the concavity (inward curve) of the grip of the foil.

(*e*) Check each individual.

(*f*) Have the students then put the tip of the foil on the floor, holding it so that the thumb is forward, and exert just enough pressure to cause the blade to bend slightly. Point out the fact that if the foil is held correctly the bend in the blade will be forward. This means that with pressure on the tip of the foil when the foil is horizontal, the bend will be up. Demonstrate this by putting the tip of the foil against the wall.

(*g*) Have the class practice taking the grip several times, each time checking to see that the foil bends properly.

3. FAULTS.

(*a*) The foil may be held upside down. Point out the shape of the grip of the foil.

(*b*) The foil may be held sideways. Here again the shape of the grip must be emphasized. Also this can be checked by demonstrating that the blade will bend to the side instead of up when held in this manner.

(*c*) The foil is often held too tightly. Point out the necessity for slight movements of the fingers and thumb which are impossible if the grip is squeezed. The grip should be firm but not rigid. Have the students try to make little movements with the tip of the foil by the use of fingers and thumb, or even the thumb and forefinger alone. It may help to have them hold their right wrists with their left hands while practicing these movements.

(*d*) A tight grip may be caused by a student's wrapping the fingers too far around the handle. In this position the fingers cannot manipulate the foil tip. Have the student check to see that her finger tips are on the concavity of the curve of the grip.

4. PLACE IN THE GENERAL PROGRESSION. A correct grip is fundamental to the proper execution of all techniques and must be mastered before any other technique is presented.

II. The Salute

(A) *Definition.* The salute is the method of acknowledging the opponent and judges and is given before crossing blades in a lesson or bout and again at its completion.

(B) *Execution.*

1. POSITION OF ATTENTION OR INITIAL POSITION.

(*a*) The body is in profile with the right shoulder toward the opponent.

(*b*) The body should be erect but not stiff.

(*c*) The feet are at right angles, heels together, with the right foot in a straight line with the right foot of the opponent, and toes pointing toward the opponent. This right-angle position of the feet is important for all fencing techniques and therefore, should be emphasized from the first. The position of the left foot is important in maintaining stability by enlarging the base in the forward-backward plane. The right foot must be turned in the direction of the opponent since this is the direction of movement. If the toes are not toward the opponent, force will be exerted against the side of the ankle and knee on every lunge and injury will be likely to result.

(*d*) The left arm is extended slightly away from the left side of the body, or it may be holding the mask at the left hip.

(*e*) The right arm, holding the foil, is extended so that the foil and arm form a straight line which points diagonally to the floor. The thumb is upward and the tip of the foil is about 6 inches from the floor. (Fig. 76, no. 3.)

(*f*) The head is turned toward the opponent.

2. SALUTE.

(*a*) The foil is raised level with the shoulder and pointed directly

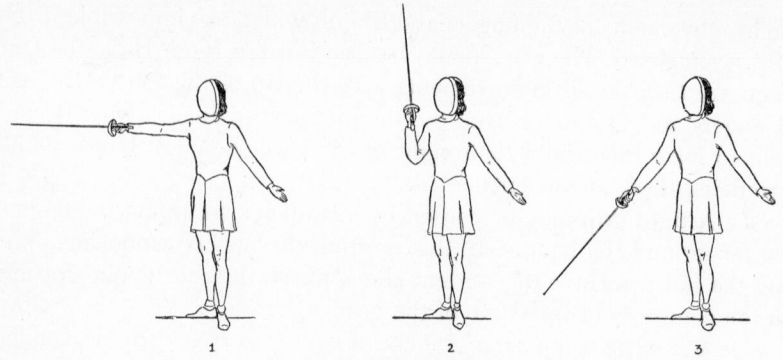

Fig. 76. The salute.

toward the opponent. The arm and foil form a straight horizontal line. The back of the wrist is toward the floor. (Fig. 76, no. 1.)

(*b*) The right arm is bent so that the foil is pointed up and the foil and forearm form a line perpendicular to the floor. The hand is level with the chin and the fingers are toward the face. (Fig. 76, no. 2.)

(*c*) The right hand is then snapped to the original position of attention. (Fig. 76, no. 3.)

(C) *Teaching*.

1. ORGANIZATION OF CLASS.

(*a*) Have the class in two or three lines facing the instructor.

(*b*) The students should be far enough apart so they will not touch each other when the right hand, holding the foil, is extended to the right, shoulder height.

(*c*) Make use of actual lines drawn on the gymnasium floor for various games, as it is much easier to learn the foot position if there is an actual line by which to guide.

2. PROGRESSION.

(*a*) Have the class take each of the following four positions on count (and hold while the instructor checks): (*1*) Attention. (*2*) Foil lifted to horizontal. (*3*) Foil lifted to chin. (*4*) Attention.

(*b*) Repeat with the counts speeded up.

(*c*) Give command for attention and one signal for the salute.

3. PLACE IN GENERAL PROGRESSION. The salute gives the position from which the fencers come on guard, and therefore should be taught immediately after the grip is learned.

III. On Guard

(A) *Definition*. The "on guard" position is that position from which all offensive and defensive tactics are started. (Fig. 77.)

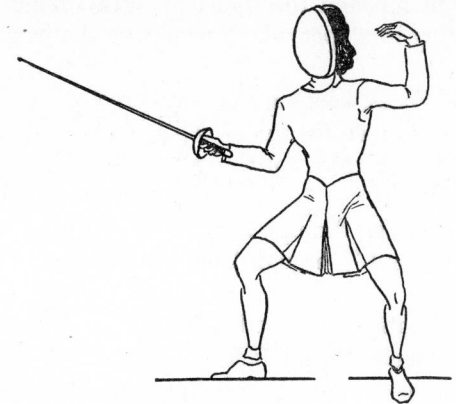

Fig. 77. On guard.

(B) *Execution.*

1. The feet are about 10 inches apart (or an easy distance for good balance).

2. The weight is evenly distributed.

3. The left toe points straight ahead, and the right is at right angles to the left foot and on a line with the left heel.

4. The knees are bent so that they are directly over the toes. This position is important to prevent strain of the knee joints.

5. The body remains upright.

6. The left arm is bent at the elbow so that the upper arm is horizontal and the forearm perpendicular to the floor. The hand is relaxed toward the head.

7. The right elbow is bent so that the foil and forearm, remaining in an unbroken line, point to the opponent's right eye. The elbow is about 6 inches from the hip.

(C) *Teaching.*

1. ORGANIZATION OF CLASS. The same organization as for teaching the Salute.

2. PROGRESSION. Teach from the position of Attention.

(*a*) Have the class go through the following steps on single commands so that the instructor can check at each stage:

(*1*) Swing the blade to the left across the body until it is horizontal to the floor, and put the left fingers under the tip of the blade. Both arms are straight but easy.

(*2*) Raise the foil above the head, keeping it horizontal to the floor.

(*3*) Keeping the left arm in this position, release the tip of the foil and relax the hand toward the head. Drop the right elbow until it is out from the right hip and the foil, making a straight line with the forearm, is pointing to a spot which would be the height of an opponent's eye.

(4) Bend the knees, keeping the body erect. If the weight is kept on the outside of the feet, the knees will bend over the toes.

(5) Move the right foot forward along the line of the left heel about 10 inches.

(*b*) Have the class go through the movements smoothly and quickly on the single command "On guard!"

3. FAULTS.

(*a*) Turning (rotating) the body toward the opponent is probably the most common fault. Explain and demonstrate that when the body is turned toward the opponent, it is more open to attack, but when in profile less target is presented to the opponent and it is much more easily guarded.

(*b*) A student may allow the right knee to drop in, which gives a very weak position both of the knee and foot. Have her check the position of this knee by running the foil down to the floor along the inside of the knee. If the knee is in a good position, with the foil vertical, the tip should be along the instep of the foot.

(*c*) A student may transfer most of the weight to the right foot. This means the body is off balance and makes advancing and retreating practically impossible. This can be checked by having the student pick up the right foot and stamp on command.

(*d*) The foil arm may be dropped too low. Demonstrate how much of the target is thus left unguarded.

(*e*) The body may be bent forward from the hips so that the hips are out instead of under. Give practice in bending the knees and moving the right foot without the arms, just concentrating on keeping the hips under.

4. PLACEMENT IN THE GENERAL PROGRESSION. A well-balanced, well-guarded position is absolutely essential to the proper execution of all offensive and defensive tactics and should be thoroughly taught before anything other than grip and salute are presented.

IV. The Call (Appel)

(A) *Definition.* The Call is the method of calling your adversary's attention to your desire to stop the bout.

(B) *Execution.* The right foot is quickly stamped twice.

(C) *Teaching.* Since this is a useful device for checking on the balance in the guard position, it can be presented at this time.

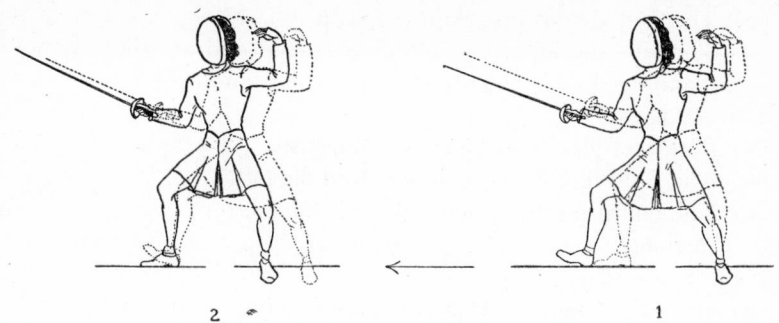

Fig. 78. The advance.

V. Advance and Retreat

(A) *Use.*

1. ADVANCE. The fencer advances to get, or to keep, within attacking distance of her opponent.

2. RETREAT. The retreat is used to get out of reach of the opponent or to adjust the distance before attacking an opponent who has got too close.

(B) *Execution.*

1. ADVANCE.

(a) This is done in the "on guard" position.

(b) The fencer steps forward with the right foot, lifting the toes first and landing on the heel. (Fig. 78, no. 1.)

(c) The left foot must follow immediately. (Fig. 78, no. 2.)

(d) At the end of each complete step, the distance between the feet should be the same as in the original guard position, and the body should remain in a perfect guard position.

(e) The feet barely leave the floor and the heels stay in line. However, there should be no sliding.

(f) The advance should be short and cautious because a counter attack is appropriate when an opponent is advancing.

2. RETREAT.

(a) It is the reverse of the advance.

(b) The left foot is placed back first.

(c) It is followed for the same distance by the right.

3. JUMP ADVANCE.

(a) The right foot leaves the strip first and is immediately followed by the left.

(b) Both feet land simultaneously, flat on their soles and in the correct guard position about 1 foot ahead on the strip.

(*c*) The feet should just skim the strip.

(*d*) The legs should at no time be extended and are slightly more bent on landing than in the original guard position.

4. JUMP BACK.

(*a*) Both feet leave the floor simultaneously.

(*b*) The right foot lands slightly before the left.

(*c*) The guard position should be maintained.

(C) *Teaching.*

1. ORGANIZATION OF CLASS.

(*a*) Have the class in two or three lines facing the instructor.

(*b*) Have them take positions on actual painted lines running lengthwise of the gymnasium.

(*c*) The student nearest the right should be at least 10 feet from the right wall to allow distance to advance.

(*d*) If the class is large or if there are no lengthwise lines other than the basketball court, it may be more satisfactory to have the class on the lines all around the gymnasium facing the instructor in the center of the floor.

2. PROGRESSION.

(*a*) Explain and demonstrate advancing.

(*b*) In the guard position have the class advance slowly on count Count for the moving of each foot separately. Have the class advance a long distance to get the feeling of the sequence of movement. Gradually speed up the commands.

(*c*) Have the class advance a complete step (move both feet) on a single command. Start the counting slowly and gradually speed it up.

(*d*) Explain and demonstrate retreating.

(*e*) Go through the same procedure as for advancing.

(*f*) Change from advance to retreat counting for each step. "Advance 1, 2, 3, Retreat 1, 2, Advance 1, 2, Retreat 1, 2, 3," and so forth. When this stage is reached, do not give more than three or four steps in one direction as more are seldom needed in an actual bout. Start counting slowly and gradually speed up the commands.

(*g*) Next give commands to advance or retreat without counting individual steps, and have the class continue in one direction until the reverse command is given.

(*h*) To develop speed in changing direction have the class advance one step and immediately retreat. The backward step should be executed by moving the left foot back immediately after it touches the floor on the advance. Next practice the reverse. That is, retreat one step and then advance.

(*i*) As soon as the position of engagement has been learned, give practice in advancing and retreating with an opponent. Tell No. 1's to advance on the instructor's command. No. 2's must retreat in response to the opponents' advance. The distance of the retreat is dependent upon the distance of each opponent's advance.

3. FAULTS.

(*a*) The feet may lose their right-angle relationship, thus throwing the body out of line and out of balance. Working on painted lines helps to avoid this.

(*b*) The outer border of the left foot may be allowed to leave the floor if too long a step is taken. This spoils body balance.

(*c*) The feet may not be advanced along the straight line. Stop often and check the foot position.

(*d*) Various parts of the body may lose the proper guard position. Again stop the footwork practice often to check the guard position.

(*e*) The feet may be dragged or scuffed on the floor. Go back to slow counting for the movement of each foot.

(*f*) Watch to see that the knees do not become straight during this practice.

4. PLACE IN PROGRESSION.

The advance and retreat should be taken up as soon as the guard position is mastered. They should be practiced carefully and persistently until they are performed smoothly, quickly, and automatically.

A short drill in footwork should be included as warm up at the beginning of each class hour. As the following offensive techniques are taken up, add advancing and retreating practice to each as soon as the execution in the static position is learned.

The jump is a more advanced technique and should not be taught until the class has become proficient in the fundamental positions.

VI. Lunge

(A) *Definition.* The lunge is the method used to reach an opponent with the tip of the foil to make a touch. It is always executed from the guard position.

(B) *Execution.*

1. The right arm is extended shoulder height without locking the elbow or hunching the shoulder. The tip of the foil should be slightly lower than the hand. This movement must precede the movement of the foot.

2. The left leg is snapped straight and the right foot is lifted and moved forward along the line of the left heel. The body is kept low.

3. The right-angle relationship of the feet in the guard position is maintained.

Fig. 79. The lunge

4. The right knee is perpendicularly above the instep.

5. The left foot remains flat on the floor.

6. The body remains erect. In this position some of the weight remains on the left foot. If most of the weight is transferred to the right foot during the lunge recovery will be slow.

7. The left arm is fully extended, and is dropped back parallel to the left leg. The palm of the left hand faces up and the hand is in line with the arm. This movement of the arm adds force to the lunge and balances the extension of the right arm. It puts the left arm into position to aid the recovery by helping to lift the weight of the body.

When perfected the lunge should be one smooth coordinated movement from the initial extension of the right arm until the blade bends on the target.

(C) *Recovery from the Lunge.*

1. The weight is thrown to the left foot, and the left knee is bent as the right knee is partially extended.

2. The left leg pulls and the right pushes the body back into position.

3. The right foot is lifted and placed, heel first, in its original guard position.

4. The lift of the left arm is very important in bringing the body back to position.

5. The knees are bent and both arms return to the original guard position.

(D) *Teaching.*

1. ORGANIZATION OF THE CLASS.

(a) For the first practice, to get the feeling of the position, the class can be lined up in two or three lines facing the instructor. It is well to have this preliminary practice on lines that are marked on the floor. The class may be all around the gymnasium, using the basketball court lines with the instructor in the center of the room.

(*b*) If the class is large and the instructor desires to have the students in one line, have them take their positions in profile to the instructor. In this organization it would not be possible to use the lines painted on the floor.

(*c*) If there are enough mats to hang on the wall so that there will be space for all to practice at once, have students spread out around the gymnasium, two or three in front of each mat depending on the size of the mats.

(*d*) If the mats are small and there is not enough mat space for all to practice at once, divide into pairs and have one watch and check her partner as she practices. Have them change on a signal from the instructor.

2. PROGRESSION.

(*a*) Explain and demonstrate the technique. It is well to explain here that the straightening of the arm gives the right of way to attack when bouting, and, therefore, the thrusting of the arm *preliminary to* the moving of the right foot is extremely important.

(*b*) Have the class practice thrusting and recovering. Count for each movement.

(*c*) Have the class practice thrust, lunge, recover. Count for each movement. Start counting slowly, have the students hold each position for checking before taking the next. Gradually increase the speed of the commands.

(*d*) Send the class to targets on the wall and have them take the guard position close enough to the mat so that the foil will be slightly bent when the right arm is extended. Have them practice the thrust on count to get the feeling of a touch. Check to see that the foil bends upward. If no mats are available, have one student stand facing her partner who can practice thrusting against her jacket. Students take turns practicing and acting as targets for their partners.

(*e*) Have the students move out from the wall to within easy lunging distance. Practice on count:

(1) thrust—(hold)—lunge—(hold)—recover. Check positions.

(2) thrust, lunge—(hold)—recover.

(3) thrust, lunge, recover.

Finally give simply the command to lunge and tell the students to recover immediately. Remind them that the hand should always have a fractional start on the foot even in the swiftest attack.

(*f*) Combine practice in advancing and lunging.

(1) Start the students about 10 to 12 feet from the wall and have them advance and lunge against the targets on the wall.

(2) During floor work drill give commands to advance and retreat, telling the class to continue in one direction until the reverse command is given, and occasionally call for a lunge when the students are advancing.

3. FAULTS.

(*a*) If students are not preceding the lunge with the thrust, go back to the practice of thrusting and lunging on command.

(*b*) If the right foot is lifted too high, the lunge will be slow and the body will be lifted and thus the tip of the foil carried out of line. If the right foot is dragged or slid along the floor the whole movement will be slow because of the friction of the foot against the floor. It may help to perfect the foot movements to give some practice in lunging without having the arms in the guard position. Have the students concentrate on the position of the feet and on barely lifting the right foot from the floor, carrying it forward quickly to a point where it can easily hold the weight.

(*c*) Often too much weight is taken on the right foot making the recovery slow. This can be detected easily because the left foot will be rolled over on the inner border. It may be due to taking too long a lunge step or bending the body in the direction of the target. Both of these faults are easily corrected by moving the student nearer the target. Have students concentrate on keeping their bodies erect.

(*d*) The right-angle position of the feet may be lost in performing the lunge. This means that the right foot is placed forward with the outside border instead of the toes toward the target, and since the weight is moving in that direction force will be exerted against the side of the ankle and knee and injury may result. Balance is also less stable. Mark a line for the student on the floor with chalk if there is no painted line where she is practicing.

(*e*) In concentrating on foot position and the thrust of the right arm, the extension of the left arm is often forgotten. Explain to the class the value of this movement because of the leverage action and balance. The lift of the left arm helps to make the recovery much easier. Have the class practice lunging, emphasizing the lift of the left arm when recovering.

(*f*) When attacking following an advance, the student often attempts to reach her opponent by bending her body instead of lunging with her foot. She simply stops the foot movement of advancing and reaches with arm and body. This places her in a very unstable position and makes recovery slow and precarious. Explain and demonstrate the lack of stability of this position of reaching so far beyond the base and have the class practice advancing and lunging on command with an immediate recovery.

4. PLACE IN PROGRESSION.

Since all attacks are made with a lunge, it is important that this be learned as soon as the guard position has been perfected.

VII. Attacks

(A) *Simple Attacks.* These are attacks made without any preceding feints, or threatening motions, against the opponent's blade. They consist of:

1. THE DIRECT THRUST.

(*a*) Execution. This attack is executed by extending the right arm in the line of engagement, with or without a lunge according to the distance between opponents. The hand is slightly higher than the shoulder, and when the point of the foil contacts the target, the hand should be lifted slightly to prevent the point from slipping. A direct thrust can be made from an engagement or with the blades not touching. This should be done with speed.

(*b*) Teaching.

    (*1*) Organization of Class:

        (a) Divide the class into pairs.

        (b) Have the pairs line up in two or three lines the length of the gymnasium and engage their opponents in 4.

        (c) Number all students facing one wall, No. 1, and all those facing the other wall, No. 2.

NOTE: This organization is used in teaching all the following techniques.

    (*2*) Progression:

        (a) Have No. 1's lunge on command three or four times, each time making a touch in high 4 (see p. 126). Have them hold the lunge position and check to see that the blade is bent up. This practice will show them in the beginning that a touch does not hurt the opponent and will help to prevent half-hearted attacks which might otherwise develop from a fear of hurting the opponent. Also this shows the students the need for defensive tactics.

        After they have made one or two good touches, have the class recover immediately without waiting for a command. If they establish the habit of holding the lunge position it will be difficult to teach a fast recovery.

(b) Have the No. 2's do the same.

(c) Repeat the above practice, attacking in low 4.

(d) Have them change their engagement to 6.

(e) Repeat the above practice in high 6.

(f) Repeat the above practice in low 6.

(g) Practice lunging in all 4 lines as the opponent practices the parries (see Parries, p. 148).

NOTE: Emphasize that when two students practice together, they must have the correctness of the form of the exercise as the objective. At first each movement should be executed on a separate command. As soon as the exercise is executed correctly the speed of the commands should be increased so that smoothness, precision, and the feeling for proper distance and timing will not be lost. The role of attacker and defender must be reversed after a few executions of any exercise. Emphasize the importance of maintaining a correct on guard position at all times.

(3) Faults: The same faults that are discussed under the Lunge (p. 138) will be made here. In addition, students may practice the attacks without making any real effort to land the tip of the foil on the opponent's target unless this is carefully emphasized. This is the reason for the preliminary lunging practice with no defensive action by the opponent.

(4) Place in the Progression: As soon as the guard position and lines of engagement have been learned, practice should be given in the direct thrust attack. This, of course, must go hand in hand with the practice of the parries (p. 148). This attack should be well executed before any other type of attack is presented.

2. THE DISENGAGE.

(a) Use. This is a method of engaging the foil in the opposite line from that in which it is engaged at the moment.

(b) Execution.

(1) It is done by passing the point of the foil under the opponent's blade to the opposite line of engagement, after extending the arm.

(2) It is followed immediately by the lunge.

(3) This attack, which is really a very small semicircle, is executed entirely by the wrist and fingers.

(4) The foil is kept close to the opponent's blade at all times.

(c) Teaching.

(1) Progression:

(a) Explain and demonstrate.

(b) Have No. 1 thrust in 4 and practice making small semicircles back and forth under her opponent's foil to get the feeling of executing the disengage with the fingers only. Emphasize the importance of keeping the tip of the foil close to the opponent's foil throughout. Since the on guard position is tiring and No. 2 is not practicing any technique but simply holding her foil for her opponent's practice, have her face her opponent and hold her foil with both hands at her chest still keeping the tip pointing at her opponent's eye. Change and have No. 2 practice while No. 1 holds her foil.

(c) With all students in the on guard position, have No. 1 thrust, in 4, disengage to 6, lunge and recover. Count for each movement except the recovery. Tell the students to recover immediately after making the lunge. Count slowly. No. 2 should parry 6 when No. 1 attacks with a lunge in high 6 (see parry of 6, p. 151). Change attacker and defender.

(d) Speed up to a count of one-two. The thrust and disengage should be executed on count one and the lunge on two. The parry of 6 and the recovery should be executed without a count.

(e) Tell No. 2 to start to parry 4 (see p. 150) when opponent thrusts in 4. No. 1 should wait for the start of the parry of 4, then disengage and attack in high 6; No. 2 then parries 6. Explain that this demonstrates the reason that the defense should wait for the lunge before parrying. If the thrust is parried, the defender's blade is pulled out of line making recovery to the opposite parry slower.

(f) Repeat the above progression from 6 to high 4.

(g) Repeat the above progression from 4 to low 6.

(h) Repeat the above progression from 6 to low 4.

(i) Have fencers engage in 4.

No. 1—thrust, disengage, and lunge either high or low 6.

No. 2—execute the correct parry depending on the attack (see Parries, p. 148).

Change attacker and defender.

(j) Have fencers engage in 6.

No. 1—thrust, disengage, and lunge either high or low 4.

No. 2—execute the correct parry depending on the attack.

Change attacker and defender.

(k) Have fencers engage in 4.

No. 1—attack in any of the 4 lines.

No. 2—execute the correct parry.

(l) The double and triple disengages can be taken up in the same manner.

(2) Faults:

(a) If the movement is made with the arm instead of the fingers, it will be large and the target will be left unguarded.

When the disengage becomes too wide, have the students go back to practicing the thrust and disengage back and forth under the opponent's blade without any lunge.

(b) If the disengage precedes the thrust, the attack loses its significance. The intended line of the attack is given away before the thrust and the opponent has all the time of the thrust to get ready for the proper parry. Have the students go back to practicing on count, thrust, disengage, lunge.

(c) Dropping the hand again leaves the target unguarded. Slow commands checking the position of the hand at each stage of the attack will help correct this fault.

(3) Place in Progression:

(a) The disengage in the high lines (from 4 to high 6 and 6 to high 4) should be taken up as soon as the parries of 4 and 6 and the direct thrust in these lines have been learned (see Parries, pp. 148-152).

(b) The disengage from 4 to low 6 follows naturally the learning of the parry of 2.

(c) The disengage from 6 to low 4 follows the learning of the parry of 7.

(d) After all four parries have been learned, practice all four disengages.

(e) Once the disengage into all lines has been perfected the double and triple disengages may be taken up at any time.

3. THE CUT-OVER.

(*a*) Use. This is another method of changing the line of engagement. This attack is used when the opponent's blade has dropped or when the opponent uses pressure with the weaker part (near the tip) of her blade against the strong part of one's blade, so that it is shorter to cut-over than to pass under with a disengage.

(*b*) Execution.

(*1*) The tip of the foil is sharply lifted over the opponent's foil by the fingers, wrist, and a slight use of the forearm.

(*2*) The arm extends as the point of the foil goes downward, and this is immediately followed by the lunge.

(*c*) Teaching.

(*1*) Progression:

(a) Practice the cut-over with a thrust only, to get practice in keeping the movement small. Have the partner of the fencer practicing the technique stand facing her holding the foil in both hands. Since this is used when the opponent's foil is low have the tip of the foil kept low during practice. Count slowly.

(b) With both fencers in the on guard position, No. 1 may practice the cut-over, thrust, lunge, while No. 2 parries. Count slowly, and gradually speed up the commands. Change roles of attacker and defender often.

Engaged in 4—cut-over, thrust and lunge in high 6.

Engaged in 4—cut-over, thrust high 6 and lunge in low 6.

Engaged in 6—cut-over, thrust and lunge in high 4.

Engaged in 6—cut-over, thrust high 4 and lunge in low 4.

(c) Practice the cut-over followed by the disengage. Be sure that the fencers get a good strong thrust after the cut-over, before the disengage.

1. Combined with the single disengage:

Engaged in 4—cut-over to 6—thrust—disengage and lunge in high 4.

Engaged in 4—cut-over to 6—thrust—disengage and lunge in low 4.

Engaged in 6—cut-over to 4—thrust—disengage and lunge in high 6.

Engaged in 6—cut-over to 4—thrust—disengage and lunge in low 6.

NOTE: The cut-over can be used *following* the disengage if the opponent drops her foil on the parry.

2. Combined with the double disengage:

Engage in 4—cut-over into 6—thrust—disengage to high 4—disengage to high 6—attack high or low 6.

Engage in 6—cut-over into 4—thrust—disengage to high 6—disengage to high 4—attack high or low 4.

(2) Faults:

(a) Over-use of the forearm takes the point of the foil too far out of line. To correct this go back to practicing the cut-over and thrust only.

(b) Using only the thumb and forefinger makes the grip so loose that control is almost entirely lost and a beat (see below) by the opponent may knock the foil from the fencer's hand. Slow practice emphasizing the use of fingers and wrist is necessary.

(3) Place in Progression:

The cut-over attack can be put into the progression after the beat has been learned. Since the students have already learned one method of changing the line of engagement (the disengage), it is better to teach the beat, which is an entirely different type of attack before the cut-over.

(B) *Compound Attacks.*

1. ATTACKS ON THE BLADE. This type of attack can be performed directly or with a change in the line of engagement. It should always start from a position very near or in contact with the opponent's blade to avoid the possibility of missing it.

(*a*) The Beat is a quick, sharp blow of the middle of the blade on the middle or weak part of the opponent's blade for the purpose of opening a way for the lunge attack which immediately follows. The beat has three objectives:

1. Opening the line.
2. As a feint before an attack.
3. As an invitation to the opponent's attack.

(*1*) Execution: It is executed entirely by the fingers. To beat when engaged in 4 (that is with the blades crossed on the inside), the blade is moved to the right by the thumb and forefinger. The grip of the last three fingers is relaxed but a light contact with the foil is maintained. The fingers are then snapped toward the palm and the foil moves sharply from right to left, and contacts the opponent's blade with a sharp blow. In executing a beat the foil should be stopped in line so that the hand is in its normal guard position ready to go through with an attack.

(*2*) Defense against the Beat: Let the fingers relax as the opponent's blade hits and then contract the fingers quickly, bringing the blade back into line or into the parry. If resistance is offered to the opponent's beat, the whole arm will be hit out of line and then recovery will be much slower.

(*3*) Teaching:

(a) Progression:

1. Explain and demonstrate the technique.
2. Have the students practice beating back and forth. This is good practice in using the fingers and also helps to strengthen the fingers and thumb. Have one beat and hold, then the opponent beat and hold, and so forth.
3. Continue the same practice adding a thrust immediately after the beat. Recover the arm to the guard position before the opponent does a return beat.
4. No. 1 beat, thrust, and lunge in high 4. No. 2 parry 4 (see p. 150). Change attacker and defender.
5. No. 1 beat, thrust, and lunge in low 4. No. 2 parry 7 (see p. 151). Change attacker and defender.

NOTE: The beat from the engagement of 6 is not strong and is used only as a surprise attack when the opponent is tiring.

6. Combine the beat with a disengage. Engaged in 4—beat, thrust high 4, and as the opponent recovers disengage to high 6 and attack either high or low 6.
7. Combine the beat with the double disengage. Engaged in 4—beat, thrust high 4, disengage to 6, disengage to 4, and attack high or low.

(b) Faults:
1. Making the movement with the whole arm carries the blade very wide and makes recovery very slow. Go back to the finger exercise of beating back and forth.
2. Following the opponent's blade out of line after the beat instead of stopping the tip of the foil at the mid line makes the attack slow. The tip must be stopped immediately on contacting the opponent's blade so that it remains in line for the attack. Again, use the beating exercise emphasizing the control of the blade after the opponent's blade has been hit.
3. Dropping the right arm leaves the target open for attack. Give slow practice on count.

(c) Place in the Progression:
The beat should be taught as soon as the four parries and disengage have been learned.

(b) The Press (or Pressure).

(1) Use: This tactic has the same purposes as the beat. It is particularly useful when the opponent's grip is weak or when she is tiring. It is not good from an engagement of 6 except as a surprise attack or if the opponent is very tired.

(2) Execution: The press is made by pressing on the opponent's blade with the arm in the normal guard position.

(3) Teaching:
(a) Possibilities for Practice:
Engage in 4—press, thrust, and lunge in high or low 4.
Engage in 6—press, thrust, and lunge in high or low 6 (not strong).
Engage in 4—press, thrust 4, disengage, and lunge in high or low 6.
Engage in 6—press, thrust 6, disengage, and lunge in high or low 4 (not strong).

(b) Possibilities of Combinations:
1. With single disengage.
2. With double or triple disengage.
3. With the cut-over occasionally if the opponent comes back with the foil low.

4. With the counter (see p. 153).

Example, counter 1-2-3-press-lunge.

(c) Place in Progression:

This is an advanced technique and should not be taken up until after the ripostes and counters have been learned.

(c) The Pressure Glide is a sudden forward and downward pressure on the blade of the opponent. It is carried through until the strong part of the opponent's blade is reached. For teaching possibilities see the discussion above on the Press. This also is an advanced technique and would not be taught to beginning or intermediate fencers.

(d) The Glide is an attack made by gliding the blade along the opponent's blade until the thrust is completed. It should be taught to advanced fencers only. The best defense is not to allow the opponent to glide. The minute a fencer feels her opponent's foil slipping down hers, she should either attack or counter immediately to do something to stop her.

2. TAKING THE BLADE. This is an action upon the opponent's blade in order to ward off the point and at the same time control it. It is preferably used against a straight arm. The strong part of the blade is against the opponent's weak part. It should be done with a controlled resistance to the opponent's blade, so that the point is not carried out of line. The fencer should complete the movement before delivering an attack. The blade is taken in three ways:

(a) The Opposition is a progressive opposition, without too much exaggeration, in the line of engagement, prolonged up to the attack.

(b) The Bind carries the opponent's blade from the high to the low line or vice versa, making a semicircle with the point and carrying the blade to the opposite line. The fencer contacts the weak part of her opponent's blade with the strong section of her own. The arm should be almost extended at the start and must extend completely straight forward during the bind. Contact of the blades must be maintained until the touch is made.

The bind is used against an opponent who holds her foil too tightly. When the opponent starts a bind, the best thing to do is to relax the foil and come through for an attack. The best procedure is to push hard against her foil, then suddenly relax and come through.

(c) The Envelopment is made up of two binds so that the blades end in the original line of engagement. The points make complete circles.

These attacks are all for the very advanced fencer and should not be taught to those in the intermediate stage.

3. COUNTER ATTACKS. These should be used: 1. When the opponent

attacks slowly or with a bent arm. In this case a precautionary beat may be necessary. 2. When the opponent attacks with a wide movement of her blade. The counter attack should be a fast straight thrust into the most exposed line of the opponent's target. If the wide movement accompanies a slow action a disengage attack may be necessary.

The action of a counter attack should always be simple—a straight thrust, a beat thrust, or a disengage thrust. The counter attacks are not preceded by parries and so must be very carefully timed, and should be taught only to very advanced fencers.

(*a*) The Time Thrust is a simple attack made so as to touch the opponent when she is making an attack and at the same time to close the line where she intends to come through. This is best used against an opponent who is advancing.

(*b*) The Stop Thrust is made upon the opponent's preparation to attack. It should be made at the moment that the opponent's right foot is lifted to make the lunge. Since it stops an offensive action at its inception, it is called a "stop thrust." It is best used against a fencer who feints wide, bringing the point out of line.

(C) *Secondary Attacks.*

1. DEFINITION. A secondary attack is one made immediately after the first, whether in the same line or not.

2. USE. Its object is to profit by the shock produced by the first attack on an opponent. It may be made up of any of the preceding simple attacks. Many combinations are possible. A secondary attack may be executed in two ways:

(*a*) Lunge and stay, and if the opponent does not riposte (follow her parry with an attack) make a secondary attack.

(*b*) Lunge and stay and when the opponent ripostes, parry and immediately make a secondary attack.

3. TYPES OF SECONDARY ATTACKS.

(*a*) The Redouble is a renewal of attack by changing the line of attack with a disengage, or cut-over if the opponent holds her parry.

(*b*) The Replacement (Remise) is a second attack made in the same line as the original attack. No attempt is made to find the opponent's blade after the preliminary attack.

(*c*) The Reprise is an attack made on the lunge in the same line as the preliminary attack after having found the opponent's blade by a parry.

4. PRACTICE POSSIBILITIES.

(*a*) Students engage in 4.

No. 1 lunge high 4 and stay in the lunge position.

No. 2 parry 4 without riposting (see Parries, p. 148, and Riposte, p. 155).

No. 1 disengage and attack high 6.

No. 2 parry 6.

(*b*) Students engage in 4.

No. 1 lunge high 4 and stay in the lunge position.

No. 2 parry 4 and riposte high 4.

No. 1 parry 4 and make a secondary attack in low 4.

No. 2 parry 7.

(*c*) The above practices can be done in all lines.

5. PLACE IN PROGRESSION. Since a secondary attack is made in the lunge position, the opponent is given an excellent opportunity to make a touch by simply extending her arm. This type of attack should be used with judgment and very sparingly, and should be taught only to advanced fencers.

VIII. Defense—Parries and Returns

(A) *Parries.* These are defensive movements of the blade by which the attacking blade is diverted from the target and a touch is avoided. It is possible to avoid a touch by retreating but this will not be included in this discussion of parries.

1. SIMPLE PARRIES. There are two types of simple parries both of which deviate the opponent's blade from the target without changing the line. In the *opposition parry* pressure is maintained against the opponent's blade until the return. The *beat parry* is a sharp light tap against the opponent's blade with an immediate return to position. All parries should be executed by the fingers and wrist with just enough movement of the foil to catch the opponent's blade and prevent her coming through on the target. In making a parry the middle part of the blade should contact the opponent's blade, never the weak tip.

(*a*) *First* defends the inside high line (high 4):

(*1*) Execution:

(a) The forearm is almost horizontal, with the elbow to the right.

(b) The hand is pronated so that the thumb is down and the fingers toward the opponent.

(c) The blade points to the adversary's toe.

(*2*) Teaching:

Since this parry moves the point of the foil so far out of line making recovery slow, and leaves too much of the target unprotected, it is seldom used and will not be included in the teaching progression.

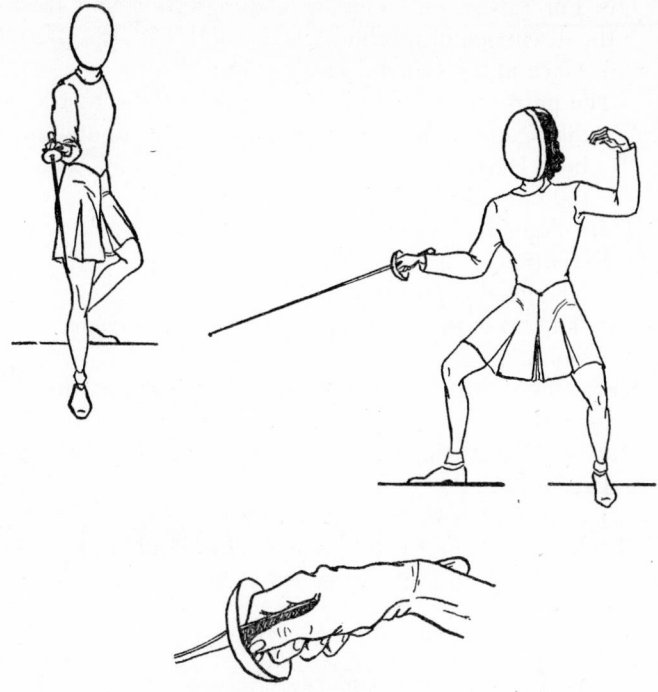

Fig. 80. The parry of second.

(*b*) *Second* defends the outside low line (low 6):
  (*1*) Execution:
    (a) The point of the foil describes a semicircle counterclock-
      wise.
    (b) At the end of the parry the hand is in pronation.
    (c) The foil points to the opponent's knee.
  (*2*) Teaching:
    (a) Method of Practice:
      Fencers engage in 6.
      No. 1 lunge in low 6.
      No. 2 parry 2.
      Change attacker and defender.
      1. Give a command for the thrust and lunge—hold—check the
        parry—give a command for recovery. Tell No. 2 to parry
        immediately on his opponent's lunge.
      2. Give a signal to start the action which then is carried
        through to the recovery of both the attacker and defender
        with no further commands.

(b) For further information on progression and practice, see the discussion of teaching the direct thrust (pp. 139-140).

(c) Place in the General Progression:

The parry of 2 should be taught after the direct attacks and disengages in high 4 and 6, and the parries of 4 and 6, have been learned. This parry is stronger than 8th which defends the same line.

(c) *Third* defends the outside high line (high 6):

(1) Execution:

(a) The hand is pronated and the foil is moved to the right.

(b) The tip of the foil is kept higher than the hand.

(2) Teaching:

Since this is more awkward, 6th, which defends the same line, is preferred.

(d) *Fourth* defends the inside high line (high 4):

(1) Execution:

(a) The hand is in "normal" position.

(b) The blade and hand are moved to the left at breast height just enough to protect the inside high line of the target.

Fig. 81. The parry of fourth.

(2) Teaching:
  (a) Method of Practice:
    Fencers engage in 4—No. 1 lunge in high 4.
    No. 2 parry 4.
    Change attacker and defender.
  (b) Progression: see parry of 2.
  (c) Place in General Progression:
    This is the simplest parry and should be taught as soon as the lunge has been perfected. It is the strongest parry covering this line.

(e) *Fifth* defends the inside low line (low 4):
  (1) Execution:
    (a) The hand, slightly in pronation, is moved to the left.
    (b) The hand is dropped lower than the elbow.
    (c) The point of the foil is kept higher than the hand.
  (2) Teaching:
    Since the hand is low, making recovery difficult and leaving more of the target exposed, 7th is recommended to cover this line.

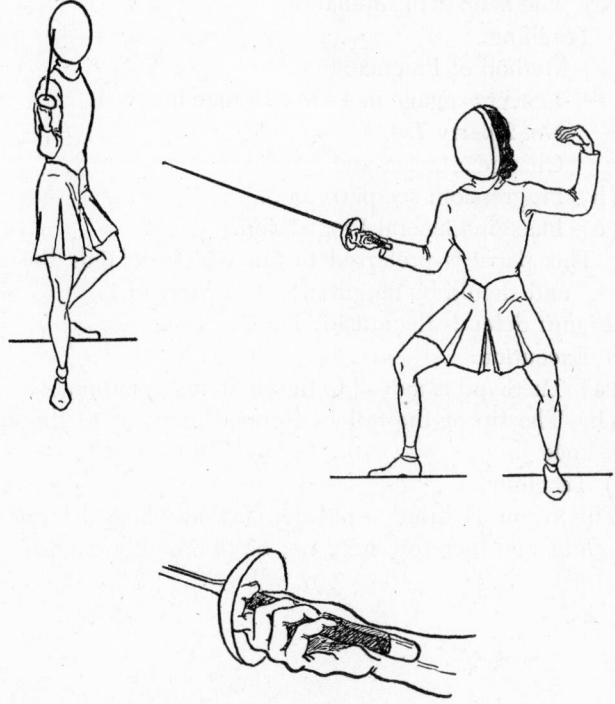

Fig. 82. The parry of sixth.

(*f*) *Sixth* defends the outside high line (high 6):

   (*1*) Execution:

      (a) The blade and the hand are moved to the right in supination. They are moved only far enough to protect the body and the arm.

      (b) The hand is higher than the elbow.

      (c) The point of the foil is higher than the hand.

   (*2*) Teaching:

      (a) Method of Practice:

         Fencers engage in 6—No. 1 lunge in high 6.

         No. 2 parry 6.

         Change attacker and defender.

      (b) Progression: see parry of 2.

      (c) Place in General Progression:

      This parry is preferred to 3rd which defends the same line and should be taught after the parry of 4 has been learned.

(*g*) *Seventh* defends the inside low line (low 4):

   (*1*) Execution:

      (a) The tip of the foil is dropped in a semicircle clockwise.

      (b) The foil points to the opponent's knee.

      (c) The hand is in supination.

   (*2*) Teaching:

      (a) Method of Practice:

         Fencers engage in 4—No. 1 lunge in low 4.

         No. 2 parry 7.

         Change attacker and defender.

      (b) Progression: see parry of 2.

      (c) Place in General Progression:

      This parry is preferred to 5th which defends the same line and should be taught after the parry of 2.

(*h*) *Eighth* defends the outside low line (low 6):

   (*1*) Execution:

      (a) The hand is moved to the right in supination.

      (b) The tip of the foil is dropped to point to the opponent's knee.

   (*2*) Teaching:

      This is not as strong a position as 2nd which defends the same line, and therefore need not be thoroughly taught.

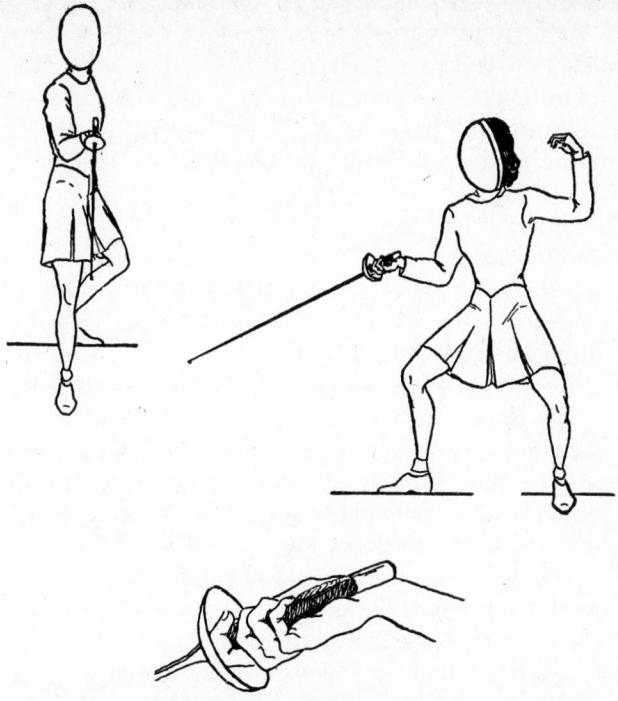

Fig. 83. The parry of seventh.

(*i*) Faults in Parries in General:

(*1*) If the parry is made by movement of the arm instead of just the wrist and fingers, recovery will be slow and too much of the target will be left unguarded. Have the students practice parrying a direct thrust so that judgment of the attack is not necessary and full attention can be given to the execution of the parry.

(*2*) Dropping the hand low leaves a great deal of the target unguarded and also makes recovery slow. Engage with the student and when she drops her hand into low 4 come up and lunge in high 6. Use this only to cure her of dropping her hand. It will demonstrate how it leaves the target open.

2. COUNTER PARRIES. These differ from simple parries in that not only is the blade deviated, but also the line of attack is changed.

(*a*) Execution: In making a counter the point of the foil describes a small circle around the opponent's foil. Only the fingers are used, the hand remaining in position. The counter parries are named in relation to the line in which they are executed. In the high line the circle is started under the opponent's blade, and in the low line, over the opponent's blade. The counter parries are not as fast as the opposition and the beat parries but they are more difficult to deceive.

Example: Two fencers are engaged in the line of 4. The attacker disengages to 6. The defender, to execute a counter parry, describes a small circle around the opponent's blade by going under and around, contacting the blade and deflecting it outside the limit of the target line of 4.

(b) Teaching:

(1) Progression:

(a) Teach the movement of the tip of the foil around the opponent's foil. With the fencers engaged in 4, have No. 1 disengage from 4 to 6.

No. 2 follows her foil around to complete the circle.

Repeat this several times in succession from the engagement of 4 and then from 6. Count for each counter. Start slowly and gradually speed up the commands. Have each student touch her opponent's foil on every counter to make sure she keeps her foil close to her opponent's.

(b) Combine the attack with this same practice.

1. Students engage in 4:

Count 1—No. 1 disengage to 6th.

No. 2 follows her blade around (end engaged in 4).

Count 2—repeat.

Count 3—repeat.

Count 4—repeat.

Count 5—repeat and after the counter have No. 1 lunge in high 4 and No. 2 parry. Change attacker and defender.

2. Engage in 6 and repeat the practice ending with an attack in high 6.

3. Engage in 4 and repeat the practice ending with an attack in low 4.

NOTE: The low 6 attack is not usually successful as the attacker does not often get free enough to attack in that line.

In counting for the practices it is well to change the number of counters preceding the attack each time. Always start the practices with slow counting which is gradually speeded up.

(2) Faults:

The main fault in the execution of the counter is the use of the arm instead of the wrist and fingers. This makes the foil movement large and leaves too much target exposed. It may help to have the instructor go around and hold each student's arm just above the wrist until she gets a feeling for making the movement with the wrist and fingers only.

(3) Place in the General Progression:

The counter is a fairly advanced tactic and should not be taken up until all the elementary attacks, the simple parries, and ripostes (see below) have been learned. It would probably come into the intermediate progression sometime after the middle of the season.

(B) *Returns.*

1. DEFINITION.   A riposte is the *return* thrust which is delivered after a parry. It is a reply to an unsuccessful attack. The more accurate the parry, the safer the riposte.

2. EXECUTION.   A riposte may be made with or without a lunge. The arm should be extended to reach the target.

3. TYPES OF RIPOSTES.

(a) A Direct or Simple Riposte is a straight attack, delivered immediately after the parry in the same line.

(b) A Compound Riposte is any return that consists of more than one movement; that is, a feint, one or more disengages, a cut-over, etc.

(c) A Delayed Riposte is so named because it does not immediately follow the parry, but allows sufficient delay to break the speed of the play. It deceives an initial counter parry, or waits for an opposing reaction in a line other than the direct line.

(d) Counter Riposte: When a *return* is parried and followed by a responding riposte, the latter is called a "counter riposte."

4. TEACHING.

(a) Simple practices: Start the practices by specifying the line for the riposte. Later allow the defender to choose any of the ripostes that are possible following the original attack.

(1) Students engage in 4.

No. 1 lunge high 4.

No. 2 parry 4 and riposte high 4, low 4, or disengage to low 6.

(2) Students engage in 6.

No. 1 lunge in high 6.

No. 2 parry 6 and riposte low 6. This is the only riposte that does not expose too much of the body from this position.

(3) Students engage in 4.

No. 1 lunge in low 4.

No. 2 parry 7 and riposte low 4, or disengage to high or low 6.

(4) Students engage in 6.

No. 1 lunge in low 6.

No. 2 parry 2 and riposte low 6, high 6, or high 4 coming up and over the opponent's foil.

(*b*) Combination practices (examples of counter ripostes):

(*1*) Students engage in 6.

No. 1 lunge high 6.

No. 2 parry 6 and riposte low 6.

No. 1 parry 2, disengage and riposte low 4.

No. 2 parry 7 and riposte low 4.

No. 1 parry 7.

(*2*) Students engage in 4.

No. 1 lunge high 4.

No. 2 parry 4 and riposte high 4.

No. 1 parry 4 and riposte low 4.

No. 2 parry 7 and disengage to riposte high 6.

No. 1 parry 6.

(*3*) Students engage in 6.

No. 1 lunge low 6.

No. 2 parry 2 and riposte high 6.

No. 1 parry 6 and riposte low 6.

No. 2 parry 2 and start to riposte high, but as the opponent comes up to parry drop to low 6.

No. 1 parry 2.

(*4*) Students engage in 6.

No. 1 lunge low 6.

No. 2 parry 2 and riposte high 6.

No. 1 parry 6 and disengage or a riposte in low 4.

No. 2 parry 7 and riposte low 4.

No. 1 parry 7.

NOTE: In all these practices the original attacker and defender should be shifted after 2 or 3 attacks.

(*c*) Faults:

(*1*) Using the riposte too often.

(*2*) Riposte before completing the parry.

(*d*) Place in the General Progression:

Ripostes should not be taught too early in the progression as the fencer must use judgment on when to use them. If beginners are taught ripostes too soon, they will use them after every attack. This is poor since many touches will be lost to a quick opponent. Also the surprise value of the attack is lost. Students should be taught to use the riposte when the opponent is slow in recovering from the lunge. Do not teach it until the four main parries (2, 7, 4, and 6) have become automatic.

SIZE OF CLASSES

Classes of 20 or less are ideal. However, it is possible for one instructor to handle fencing classes up to 40 if the situation demands larger classes. When this is necessary, money for equipment is likely to be limited. If so, a class of 40 can be taught with 25 foils and masks. This allows a foil and mask for each two students with a few extras in case of breakage. Since it is impossible to have a class practice continuously, the class can be divided into groups of 4 students with 2 working and the other 2 coaching. After a short practice period they can rotate so that the other two have equal practice time. The preliminary footwork drill can still be done by all regardless of whether each student has a foil and mask. Each student must have some type of body protection (jacket, half jacket or plastron) since a great deal of time would be lost in rotating if jackets had to be changed. However, masks and foils can be shared with little loss of time. While this situation is far from ideal, it has been found to be workable and while students have not progressed as far in a term as can be expected in smaller classes, the loss is not great. The 2 students who are coaching can learn a great deal if they work conscientiously with the others in their group. It is helpful if the instructor emphasizes specific points to be observed during each practice period.

If it is possible to have equipment for 30, the students can be divided into groups of 3 instead of four. This situation gives more practice time per student.

GENERAL PROGRESSION

1. Description of Equipment.
2. Grip of the Foil.
3. Salute.
4. On Guard Position.
5. Call (Appel).
6. Advance and Retreat.
7. Lunge.
8. Combine the advance and retreat with the lunge.
9. Explanation of:
    (*a*) the target and its divisions.
    (*b*) the lines of engagement.
    (*c*) the position of engagement.

10. Lunge for a touch (with no defense by opponent) in each of the four divisions of the target.
11. Direct attack in high 4 and the parry of 4.
12. Direct attack in high 6 and the parry of 6.
13. Disengage in the high line and parries of 4 and 6.
14. Direct attack in low 6 and the parry of 2.
15. Disengage from 4 to low 6 and parry of 2.
16. Direct attack in low 4 and parry of 7.
17. Disengage from 6 to low 4 and parry of 7.
18. All four direct attacks and parries.
19. All four disengages and parries.
20. Short period of bouting using direct and single disengage attacks only. The instructor signifies the original attacker and defender, and calls for their reversal after a couple of minutes of play.

    Score: 1 point for a successful attack.
          1 point for a successful parry.
21. Beat.
22. Beat combined with disengage.
23. Short period of bouting using all tactics learned to date as under 20.
24. Cut-over.
25. Cut-over combined with disengage.
26. Short period of bouting as above.
27. Riposte.
28. Short period of bouting as above.

    Score: 1 point for successful attack.
          1 point for successful parry.
          1 point for successful riposte.
          1 point for successful parry of the riposte.
29. Counter.
30. Short period of regular bouting. (From this time on a part of each period should be given to bouting.)
31. Press.
32. Press combined with other attacks.
33. Glide. ⎫
34. Bind. ⎪
35. Secondary Attacks. ⎬   **Very Advanced Fencers Only**
36. Stop Thrust. ⎪
37. Time Thrust. ⎭

SAMPLE LESSON PLANS[3]

1st Lesson Plan for Beginners

1. Explanation of Equipment.
2. Grip of the Foil.
3. Position of Attention: Students in three or four lines the length of the gymnasium, standing, facing the instructor, on lines painted on the floor.
4. Salute:
   - (*a*) on count.
   - (*b*) on a single command.
5. On Guard Position:
   - (*a*) on count.
   - (*b*) on a single command.
6. Advance: Advance 10–15 steps to get the sequence of movement.
   - (*a*) count for the movement of each foot (2 counts for a complete step).
   - (*b*) 1 count for a complete step:
     - (*1*) slowly.
     - (*2*) gradually speeded up.
7. Retreat (as above).
8. Advance and Retreat:
   - (*a*) 1 count for each step:
     - (*1*) slowly.
     - (*2*) gradually speeded up.
   - (*b*) Command to start the advance or retreat and students continue in that direction until given the command to change.

NOTE: Only three or four steps should be allowed in one direction before giving the command to change.

9. Lunge:
   - (*a*) Practice in lines.
   - (*b*) Practice against targets on the wall:
     - (*1*) thrust.
     - (*2*) thrust and lunge.
10. Advance and Lunge: Students in three or four lines as at the beginning of the lesson.

General Lesson Plan

1. Floor work on individual techniques. After the beginning stage

[3] Length of lesson—35 minutes.

is passed, this preliminary warm-up practice may be performed with the fencers in pairs engaged as for a bout. Number the fencers facing one direction "1" and those facing the opposite "2." Signify that the commands will apply to No. 1's and that if they are commanded to advance, No. 2's will retreat and vice versa.

2. Review of old material: (*a*) Questions and discussion. (*b*) Practice on instructor's commands.
3. Explanation and demonstration of new material.
4. Practice of new material on instructor's commands.
5. Short bout period using all techniques learned to date: (*a*) Beginners and Intermediates. Instructor designates attacker and defender changing after four or five attacks. Score: 1 point for a successful attack, 1 point for a successful parry. (*b*) Advanced: regular bout.
6. Floor work.

Outline of Lesson Plans for Beginners (twice a week for 8 weeks)

LESSON 1.   Equipment; grip; attention position; salute; on guard position; advance; retreat; lunge; advance and lunge.

LESSON 2.   Review—grip; salute; advance; retreat; lunge against mat. Take up—target; lines of engagement; position of engagement; lunge in all lines to make a touch against opponent's target (this is done with no defense by the opponent—to give the feeling for actually going through for a touch); direct attack in high 4 and the parry of 4th; direct attack in high 6 and the parry of 6th.

LESSON 3.   Review—salute; lunge against a mat; advance and lunge; retreat; direct attack in high lines and the parries of 4th and 6th. Take up—advance and retreat with the fencers in bout position, No. 1 attack in high 4 and No. 2 parry 4th and reverse; same with attack in high 6 and the parry of 6th.

LESSON 4.   Review—salute; lunge; attacks and parries in high lines. Take up—disengage in the high lines with the proper parries.

LESSON 5.   Review—salute; direct attack in high lines with the parries of 4th and 6th; disengage in the high lines with the parries of 4th and 6th. Take up—attack in low 6 and the parry of 2nd; attack in low 4 and the parry of 7th; advance and retreat with opponent, attack in line called by instructor, proper parry.

LESSON 6.   Review—all four direct attacks and parries (4th, 6th, 2nd, 7th); disengage in high lines. Take up—disengage in low lines with parries.

LESSON 7.   Review—4 parries; disengage in all lines. Take up—double disengage in high lines; advance and retreat with No. 1 attacking in stated line and No. 2 using the corresponding parry.

LESSON 8. Review—the four direct attacks and correct parries; single disengage; double disengage in the high lines. Take up—double disengage in the low lines. Short bout using all the techniques learned to date and scoring as suggested in General Progression 20 on page 158.

LESSON 9. Review—the four direct attacks and parries; disengage in all lines; double disengage in all lines. Take up—beat; beat combined with the disengage. Short bout scored as above.

LESSON 10. Review—parries; disengage; beat. Explain and demonstrate the other four parries (1st, 3rd, 5th, 8th) and explain why they are rarely used. Short bout as above.

LESSON 11. Review—disengage with all four parries (4th, 6th, 2nd, 7th); beat; advance and retreat with above attacks. Take up—cut-over. Short bout as above.

LESSON 12. Review—disengage with all four parries; beat; cut-over. Take up—riposte. Short bout giving additional points for successful ripostes. (See General Progression 28, p. 158.)

LESSON 13. Review—beat; cut-over; parries; ripostes. Take up—cut-over combined with disengage. Short bout as above.

LESSON 14. Review—beat; cut-over; riposte. Take up—beat combined with cut-over; beat and cut-over combined with ripostes. Explain the fencing strip and fundamental rules which have not been brought out as techniques were taken up. Short bout using rules.

LESSON 15. Review—combined attacks of beat and disengage; cut-over and disengage. Take up—counter. Bout.

LESSON 16. Review—all attacks taken up. Bout.

INTEREST MOTIVATION

I. Fencing Club

An organization for more advanced fencers will tend to stimulate interest in the sport. A student manager and an instructor of fencing usually collaborate on making plans for the club. To be a member a student should show interest and enthusiasm, and demonstrate fair ability, but she need not be a top notch performer. Some type of tryouts is necessary for the selection of the club's membership. It is well to hold tryouts at the beginning and again toward the close of the fencing season. The latter will take care of those who have become interested and more proficient during the season and will insure a nucleus for the club the following year.

Tryouts should be attended by the instructor who is advisor for the club, and a few of the more experienced members, and should in general consist of: 1. floor work for judging form and speed of reaction, 2. bouting with the experienced fencers.

If such an organization is to be successful, there should be a regularly scheduled weekly meeting in which attendance is required. Any student missing three such meetings should be automatically dropped. Floor work, practice exercises, and bouting constitute an evening's program. In a women's school an occasional tea following the practice period may add to the general interest and serve as a get-together for the planning of future meetings.

In some schools granting the privilege to club members to assist in regular fencing classes has proved very satisfactory. Opportunity to sign for coaching classes can be given during the club hour. Students should understand that if they wish to coach they must be responsible for reporting to the class early to allow time for the instructor to explain and demonstrate the day's order.

II. Exhibitions

By Visits of Noted Fencers. During the season the fencing club, if there is such an organization in the school, or the department of physical education, could stimulate a great deal of interest by sponsoring a demonstration by some outstanding fencers. This exhibition should be open to all interested.

By Fencing Club Members. If there is a fencing club it is well to have the members plan and put on an exhibition for any outsiders interested.

III. Class Teams

Four-fencer class teams will do much to add to the students' enthusiasm for fencing. These teams can be picked at regular tryouts scheduled near the end of the fencing season, or by ladder tournaments run in each class during the season. If the latter method is used, the top eight at the time for team trials would be the logical potentialities, and could fence in a round robin tournament. The best four would make the class team. The interclass round robin should be announced and posted in conspicuous places so that any student interested could attend.

IV. Additional Tournaments

1. *In Fencing Classes.* Ladder tournaments can be carried on in each class hour. The match between the first two on the ladder would make an excellent event for the final meeting of each class.

2. *College Open Championship.* The tournament for the selection of the champion of the school or college should preferably be a round robin. If there is not time for this, a double elimination (or elimination-consolation) tournament may be substituted.

3. *In Fencing Club.* A ladder tournament can be posted for the club early in the season. The last part of each weekly meeting could be given over to challenge bouts for this tournament. Each bout should have two judges for which the students themselves can arrange.

A round robin tournament among the club members might possibly be arranged depending on the size of the club.

OFFICIATING

Since fencing is a sport in which one cannot participate without the assistance of officials, a short discussion of officials' duties is included.[4]

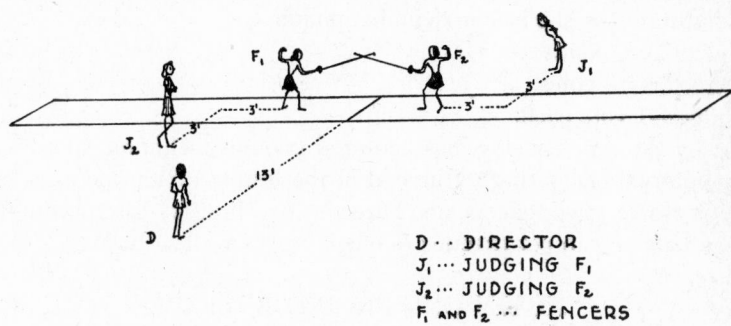

D ·· DIRECTOR
J₁ ··· JUDGING F₁
J₂ ··· JUDGING F₂
F₁ AND F₂ ··· FENCERS

Fig. 84. Diagram showing placement of officials for fencing bout.

The officials necessary to carry on a bout are a Director and two Judges. Four Judges are preferred for any match.

Placement of Officials on the Floor

Director. The Director stands between the two fencers approximately 13 feet from the strip.

Judges. The Judges stand at least 3 feet behind and to the side of the opponent of the fencer that each is watching.

Duties of the Officials

Director. The Director is in full charge of the conduct of the bout. Having ascertained that the fencers are ready, she starts the bout with the command "Play." She may halt the bout at any time with the

[4] For details of Officiating, see *Fencing Rules,* Amateur Fencers League of America, page 97.

command "Halt." The Director's attention is concentrated on the phrases[5] of the bout, but she may also decide upon the materiality of touches. When any Judge signifies that she has seen a foul or a touch, the Director stops the bout, confers with the Judges, and decides whether or not a touch should be awarded.

Judges. It is the duty of each Judge to engage the attention of the Director when she thinks she sees a touch or a foul. This may be done verbally or by some gesture of the hand. When questioned by the Director as to the materiality of the touch the Judge may reply:

"yes"—if she has a definite opinion that a touch landed on valid target.

"foul"—if she has a definite opinion that a touch landed on any parts other than the valid target.

"no"—if she has a definite opinion that there was no touch (foul or good).

"abstain"—if she has no definite opinion.

Value of Judgments.

Director—1½ votes.

Judges—1 vote each.

When the fencing class has acquired enough technique to enjoy a short interval of bouting at the end of the lesson, divide the class into groups of five (two fencers, one Director, two Judges). By rotating the individuals all can get practice in officiating as well as bouting.

NOTES ON FENCING RULES[6]

Target

The target for women is the body from the top of the collar to a horizontal line around the body through the hip bones, exclusive of the arms. The sleeve seam is usually used as the boundary between the body (fair territory) and the arm (foul territory).

Official Fencing Strip

The width of the official strip is between 1.8 m. (5'10⅞") and 2 m. (6'6¾") and its length is 12.2 m. (40'). This strip is marked with five lines drawn across the width of the strip:

(a) the center line.

---

[5] A phrase is a period in a bout during which there is no cessation of play. The term generally is used to describe a continuous sequence and alternation of play. It frequently includes an attack and one or more parries and ripostes. It comes to an end when the continuous action is interrupted even for a brief moment.

[6] *Fencing Rules,* Amateur Fencers League of America, 1951.

(b) two "on guard" lines drawn at a distance of 2 m. (6′6¾″) from the center line.

(c) two "warning" lines drawn at a distance of 1 m. (3′3⅜″) from either end of the official strip.

Bout

The number of touches for a women's bout is 4 and the time limit is 8 minutes. If at the end of this time neither contestant has scored 4 touches, the difference between 4 and the score of the contestant who is ahead is added to the score of each fencer.

Example: Actual score at end of 8 minutes is 3 (fencer A) to 1 (fencer B). Fencer A is declared the winner by a score of 4 to 2. If at the end of the time limit neither contestant has scored the number of touches for a bout and the fencers are tied, the score is brought to 3 all and the fencers compete for a single decisive touch without limit of time.

Hit in Foul Territory

A point-on hit in foul territory invalidates an immediately following hit in fair territory either by the fencer making the foul or by her opponent, but it does not invalidate a hit in the succeeding phrase.

NOTE: A foul in fencing is not like fouls in other sports, discreditable to the fencer making it, since it usually results from a bad parry by the opponent, and may often work out to the maker's advantage by invalidating a later hit in fair territory by her opponent.

Valid Hits

To be valid, a hit must be point-on and in fair territory. A point-on hit elsewhere is a foul (see preceding paragraph), and a hit with the side of the blade (a slap) counts nothing. A point-on hit is indicated by an upward bend of the blade or a bend away from the body of the fencer hit. A touch on the head, arms, hand, etc., may be judged valid whenever the fencer, either intentionally or as a result of an abnormal position (due to crouching, ducking, etc.) substitutes a normally invalid area for a part of the valid target.

Right of Way

The right of way is with the attack until the attack has been parried. If the lunge is made with a straight arm, the fencer attacked must meet the blade of the attacker with her parry before she may riposte. If she does not, and the attack lands, the point shall be awarded the attacker even though the two hits are simultaneous. Only if the time thrust is clearly ahead (an almost impossible occurrence) shall the hit be awarded the fencer attacked.

NOTE: An attack with the sword arm bent establishes no right of way. That is, it places the defender under no obligation to parry and the question becomes purely a matter of time. Many judges go even further and simply throw out a bent arm attack even if it lands ahead of the stop-thrust. This practice is probably preferable with beginners, but an advanced fencer should be able to defend herself by stop-thrusting without assistance from the rules. The presumption, however, should be against the bent-arm attack. That is, unless a bent-arm attack is clearly ahead, it should not be allowed.

Once an attack has been parried, the right of way shifts to the defender. When the defender's riposte has been parried, the right of way shifts back to the attacker, and so forth *ad infinitum*. That is, if the attack is parried and the defender ripostes immediately, her point shall be considered good as against that of the attacker, even though the hits are simultaneous, if the attacker does not parry her riposte.

NOTE: A parry does not establish a right of way unless it is immediately followed by a riposte. If the defender parries and does not immediately extend her arm, the attacker is under no obligation to withdraw or to await her counter attack, but may continue her own attack. The outcome of such a continuation depends solely on time. The fencer who lands first gets the point.

One cannot benefit from the right of way unless her attack or riposte lands point-on. If it lands point-on in fair territory, she shall be awarded the point. If it lands point-on in foul territory, it shall invalidate an immediately following hit by her opponent. If it is a slap or a pass (thrust which misses the opponent entirely) and her opponent lands, her opponent shall be awarded the point, since it is not necessary to parry an attack which is wide and will not land even if it is not parried.

Off the Strip End

In foil fencing, when the retreating fencer crosses the warning line the Director must stop the bout and warn the fencer. She is put back on guard at the warning line and if she then crosses the end of the strip with both feet, she is penalized one touch.

Off the Strip Sides

When a retreating fencer steps off the side of the strip with both feet she is put back on guard in the center of the width of the strip 3′3⅜″ closer to the end of the strip than the point where she stepped off. Only if this penalty puts the fencer beyond the end of the strip *after* she has been warned, is she penalized a touch.

VISUAL AIDS

A silent film, *Techniques of Foil Fencing*, was made in 1942. This film analyzes fencing techniques at various speeds of the camera with many close-ups. It has been rated "very good" by the National Section on Women's Athletics Committee. It takes fifteen minutes to run and can be purchased for $25.00 or rented for $1.00 from Bell and Howell Company, 1801–1815 Larchmont Ave., Chicago 13, Illinois (also New York City, Hollywood, Washington, D. C.).

For further information see Bernhard, Frederica and Flory, Elizabeth H.: *Educational Films in Sports*, American Film Center, Inc., 1946. (Write to: Elizabeth H. Flory, Educational Film Library Association, Inc., 45 Rockefeller Plaza, New York 20, N. Y.)

REFERENCES

Barbasetti, Luigi: *The Art of the Foil*. New York, E. P. Dutton and Co., Inc., 1932.

Breck, Dr. Edward: *Fencing*. Spalding "Red Cover" Series of Athletic Handbooks, No. 30 R. New York, American Sports Publishing Co., 1928.

Cass, Eleanor Baldwin: *The Book of Fencing*. Boston, Lothrop, Lee and Shepard Co., 1930.

Castello, Julio Martinez: *The Theory and Practice of Fencing*. New York, Charles Scribner's Sons, 1933.

Deladrier, Clovis: *Modern Fencing*. Annapolis, Maryland, United States Naval Institute, 1948.

Hett, G. V.: *Fencing*. London, Sir Isaac Pitman and Sons, Ltd., 1939.

Manrique, Ricardo E.: *Fencing Foil Class Work*. Spalding "Red Cover" Series of Athletic Handbooks, No. 11 R. New York, American Sports Publishing Co., 1912.

Michigan University Intramural Sports Department, James, A. A.; Johnstone, John; Mitchell, E. D.; Riskey, Earl N.; Webster, R. W.: *Sports for Recreation and How to Play Them*. New York, A. S. Barnes and Co., 1938.

Nadi, Aldo: *On Fencing*. New York, G. P. Putnam's Sons, 1943.

Sandoz, William: "Philosophy of a Fencing Master." *Journal of Health and Physical Education*, 6:3:20, March, 1935.

Schutz, Helen Joan: "Construction of an Achievement Scale in Fencing for Women." Master's Thesis, University of Washington, 1940.

Senac, Regis and Louis: *The Art of Fencing*. Spalding "Red Cover" Series of Athletic Handbooks, No. 30 R. New York, American Sports Publishing Co., 1928.

Vince, Joseph: *Fundamentals of Foil Fencing*. New York, Joseph Vince, 1937.

Vince, Joseph: *Fencing*. New York, A. S. Barnes and Co., 1940.

Fencing Rules. New York, Amateur Fencers League of America, 1951. Copies may be obtained from the Secretary of the League, Dernell Every, 3406 Chanin Bldg., New York 17. Price $1.00 per copy.

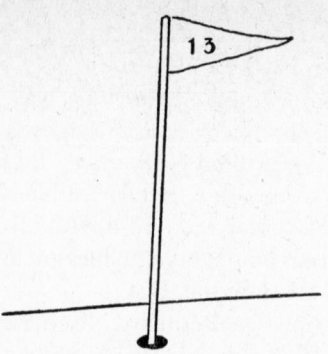

5 • GOLF • BY *Marion R. Broer*

The game of golf is one of the oldest of our modern sports. Historians do not agree on its origin and there seems to be a question as to whether it originated in Scotland or on the ice in Holland.

One story has it that a Scotch shepherd accidentally hit a round stone with his staff, knocking it into a hole. This gave him the idea for a game that would be interesting for one person to play alone and would help to pass the time while he was herding his sheep. Whatever its origin may have been, the game had become so popular in Scotland by 1457 that the king, becoming alarmed, put restrictions on its practice to force the youth of Scotland to archery.

The Dutch did play a game called "Kolf" on the ice and used clubs similar to those used later in Scotland. However, the game, as we know it today, undoubtedly came from Scotland where a much more advanced form was played than that originated on the ice in Holland.

Some claim that Robert Lockhart brought the equipment from Scotland and introduced John Reid to the game. Reid and four others formed the first golf club in the United States in 1888. Others claim that Alexander Findlay of Pennsylvania, having played in Scotland, brought the game to this country in 1887.

While golf can lay claim to most of the benefits derived from other sports, it has many merits that are unique. Few sports offer the long lasting carry-over value of golf, a game that can be enjoyed by an individual well past middle life. There is a great social value in the game for it enables one to make contacts with individuals of congenial interests. The leisurely pace of the game allows time to admire the beautiful natural surroundings and promotes a comradeship not possible in faster sports. Unlike many games in which real enjoyment of the players is dependent upon being well-matched in skill, a wide variation of skill does not spoil the enjoyment of either player, nor does it ruin the chances for keen competition. Golf provides a healthy form of exercise for all levels of physical ability, and it is enjoyed equally by all ages and both sexes.

For many years golf was considered a sport in which only the more privileged financially could participate and consequently only the wealthier private schools provided a place for it in their physical education programs. However, with the lower price of equipment, with many public courses opened for which the fee is no more than the price of a movie, and with many private clubs giving very low rates to students, the situation is greatly altered.

In short, golf is a game well within the means of most, played in beautiful surroundings and in the company of congenial friends, and can be enjoyed by *all* practically throughout life.

Recognizing the values of the game and in answer to the clamoring of students for instruction, most physical educators have now included golf in their programs. The teaching of golf is no longer primarily the teaching of individuals but has become largely a matter of group instruction.

COSTUME

Golf requires no special expensive costume. Flat heeled shoes are essential to avoid cutting up the fairways and greens as well as for the player's better balance. Cleats on these shoes will give the golfer a firmer base on which to swing. Any sport costume which gives freedom of the legs and even more particularly of the arms and shoulder girdle is acceptable.

EQUIPMENT

I. Clubs

(A) *Names and Uses.*

1. WOODS.
   #1—driver—150–180 yds.: tee-off.
   *#2—brassie—150–170 yds.: tee-off; long fairway shot, good lie.
   #3—spoon—145–160 yds.: tee-off on short holes; fairway—good lie.
   #4—140–155 yds.: takes place of #1 iron in newer sets.

2. IRONS.

(a) Distance	#1—driving iron—not practical for most women.
	*#2—mid-iron—140–150 yds.: fairway long shots—poor lie; fairway long iron shots; low rough.
	#3—mid-mashie—125–135 yds.
(b) Pitch and run; approach of medium distance	#4—mashie iron—115–125 yds.: often used by women for tee shots on very short holes; long approach club; short roll-up approaches; more distance and less loft than mashie.
	*#5—mashie—105–115 yds. and less: most popular approach club; rough and bad lies where distance is greater than can be obtained from lofted clubs; occasionally tee shots on very short holes.
	#6—spade mashie—100–110 yds.: bad rough—greater distance than niblick.
(c) Hazards; bad rough; short approaches; high pitch shots	*#7—mashie niblick —95–105 yds. Most often used in #8—pitching nib- sand traps and bad lick—85– rough and for short 95 yds. approach shots; high #9—niblick pitch shots.
(d) On green	*#10—putter

NOTE: * Clubs essential for minimum set. In many sets the putter is numbered 9 and the niblick 8.

(B) *Method of Supplying.*

1. Students usually supply their own clubs.

2. Many professionals will ransack their own stock of used clubs or campaign among members of the club to get rid of old used clubs and turn them over to schools.

II. Balls

(A) *Types of Balls.*

1. PRACTICE BALLS WHICH HAVE A SHORTER FLIGHT THAN REGULATION BALLS.

(a) Paper wadded into a ball is in no way dangerous and gives something at which to hit.

(b) Cotton or yarn balls may be secured at a sporting goods store, are inexpensive and more satisfying to hit.

(c) Plastic balls may be secured at any sporting goods store. These balls are also inexpensive, are more satisfying to hit than are the cotton balls, and tend to have a truer flight.

(d) Ensolite balls are also available at sporting goods stores. These balls look more like the regulation balls but are made of a spongy material. They sell for the same price as the plastic balls and at present are more popular with golfers.

2. REGULATION BALLS.

If a school furnishes the balls and wishes to buy large quantities at a low cost it is possible to purchase:

(*a*) Used balls from local professionals.

(*b*) Repaints from repainted-ball factories.

(B) *Method of Supplying.*

1. The school may supply buckets or baskets of balls. This method saves class time since the balls do not have to be sorted and returned to owners. However, it is an expense to the school.

2. The school may require each student taking golf to turn in two new balls. The total collection is then used by every class, the balls being divided among the members of each class for use during the period. This method has the same time saving advantage and is not expensive to anyone.

3. The school may ask each student to furnish as many balls marked with her own initials as possible. In this case the student uses her own balls. It is well to suggest that nail polish be used to mark the balls. This is one of the most successful methods of marking and almost every girl has some type of polish.

4. The school may require each student to furnish six balls well marked. The student uses her own balls.

III. Additional Equipment

(A) *Indoor Practice.* If possible have sufficient space to allow all members of the class to swing at once. If the room has to be used for other sports, the first consideration must be to have equipment that is movable.

1. GENERAL EQUIPMENT.

(*a*) Mats from Which to Play the Ball.

(*1*) Tumbling mats are not good because hitting the mat with the club wears out these expensive mats very quickly.

(*2*) Coco mats are excellent.

(*3*) Small door mats from the dime store will do.

(*4*) If possible to obtain, rubber mats made of hard rubber such as is used in car tires may be used. These do not wear out. They give a hard surface for hitting through on an iron shot, but as most students do not practice more than one-half hour at a time, their wrists can stand it.

(*b*) Some Kind of Platform to Stand On.

(*1*) A second coco mat may be used.

(*2*) A wooden platform may be built to the same height as the mat from which the ball is hit. Cover the platform with some material (rubber if possible) so the students won't slip. If the platform is not covered with rubber, have the students wear rubber-soled shoes.

2. SPECIAL EQUIPMENT, FOR PRACTICE OF DIFFERENT TYPES OF SHOTS.

(*a*) Distance Shots—Full Swing.

(*1*) Soft practice balls.

(*2*) Regulation balls.

(a) A canvas sheet or curtain can be suspended from the ceiling or held up by uprights. It should extend the entire width of the room to prevent the balls hitting any breakable fixtures. The canvas should be heavy and should be hung away from the wall. It should be long enough to allow an extra fold forward on the floor to keep the balls from bouncing when they fall to the floor. A curtain made of loose canvas strips is more satisfactory than one stretched in one piece, as it takes care of the rebound better. Cut the canvas into pieces about 3 yards wide. Join the strips together just at the top so that they overlap and string them on ropes so that they may be pulled into place or out of the way at the side of the room. Targets painted on the canvas stimulate the students' interest.[1] The Peoria Central High School made use of the canvas which was used around the football field during games.

(b) Driving cages have the advantage of being safer. If they

[1] Eastburn, Warrine: "Adaptation of Playing Fields and Gymnasium Equipment to the Teaching of Group Golf."

are in a place where they can be left permanently they can be used outside of class hours.

1. Safety Measures:
    (a) The side curtains should be deep enough to take all balls that are hit.
    (b) The backstop should be resilient and hang far enough from the wall to prevent rebounding.
    (c) All curtains must hang with sufficient looseness to absorb the force of the ball and prevent rebounding.
2. Suggestions:
    (a) Place the cages side by side to save in-between canvas.
    (b) If at all possible have at least one cage.
    (c) Try to have temporary cages if permanent ones are impossible.
    (d) High parallel bars or jumping standards may be used as braces over which felt or canvas is loosely draped to mark off individual cages against a canvas drop.
    (e) The manual training departments of many high schools will construct frames. Pad these, cover them with netting, and slide them into position in front of a canvas drop.

(*b*) Approach Shots.
  (*1*) Cotton balls or some other type of practice balls.
  (*2*) Hard sponge rubber balls. Use these with a commercial apparatus consisting of three recessed targets and a basket to catch the balls, called a "Pitch-it."[2] (Fig. 85.)
  (*3*) Regulation balls:
    (a) Hang a canvas drop with ample sized pockets into which the students can pitch the balls. Secure a sheet of medium weight canvas 8 to 10 feet square. Cut four or five holes in this canvas the desired sizes and sew pockets of any light material of a different color around these holes. Hang the curtain against the wall, with the bottom extended forward so the curtain slopes at about a 45° angle.[3]
    (b) Tumbling mats may be stood up against the wall if none of the above equipment is possible. The short chip shot is the only shot that is safe in this situation.
    (c) Waste baskets may be used for chip shot practice.

[2] May be secured from the Par Buster Manufacturing Company, 52 Vanderbilt Avenue, New York.
[3] Hall, Ray: "Suggestions for Equipment in School Golf Instruction," *Golf in Physical Education.*

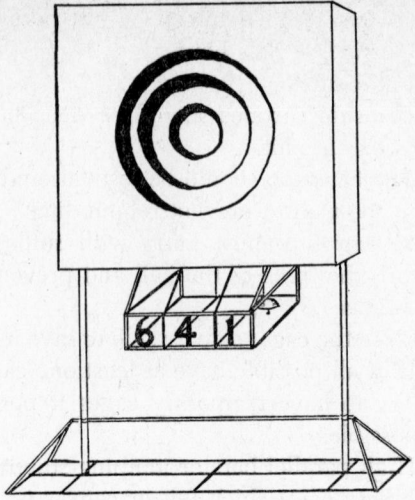

Fig. 85. Diagram of a "Pitch-it."

(*c*) Putting.
(*1*) Regulation balls.
(*2*) Putting surfaces:
    (a) There are many commercial devices that may be secured.
    (b) An inch thick padding of stiff, firmly made brown matted cloth can be used as a base and covered with a carpet ½ inch thick.
    (c) An inclined board covered with a thick carpet will give good practice.
    (d) It is always possible to secure a carpet or strip of rug. This should be 12 feet or longer to allow for the practice of various length putts. A beat board slipped under the end of the carpet will give some incline.
(*3*) Cups:
    (a) There are commercially made cups.
       1. Rubber cups.
       2. "Ringan Return" cups. When the ball enters this cup a bell rings and a spring returns the ball to the putter.
    (b) A regular cup may be built in the inclined board. The hole should be toward the high end.
    (c) Tin discs may be purchased or constructed. To construct a tin disc cut a hole 4 inches in diameter in the tin and round the sides of the tin so that they slant to the floor, sloping off

gradually. The edge of the cup should be 1 inch from the floor.

(d) A circle may be chalked on the rug or carpet. Have the students hole out by putting into or just beyond the chalked circle.

(B) *Outdoor Practice.* The area varies with the school. Usually the field is at least 100 yards long (the length of a regulation hockey or soccer field).

1. EQUIPMENT FOR THE PRACTICE OF DIFFERENT TYPES OF SHOTS.

(*a*) Distance Shots.

(*1*) If the field is too short for a full wood shot, use cotton or yarn balls.

(*2*) If there is ample length, use a regulation ball. Stake off tees far enough apart so that there is no danger of students hitting each other. Distance markers staked into the ground at various distances stimulate interest and help in grading.

(*b*) Approach Shots.

(*1*) Approach to the green (see below under Putting).

(*2*) Use markers at the edge of the field to judge approaches of various distances.

(*3*) Pitch into a sand pit (see below under Sand Trap Shots).

(*4*) Pitch over hockey goals or archery targets.

(*5*) Pitch regulation ball into "Pitch-its."

(*c*) Sand Trap Shots.

(*1*) Use a jumping pit filled with sand, dirt, or sawdust.

(*2*) Dig up a small plot of ground and play out of the overturned dirt.

(*d*) Putting.

(*1*) A regular practice green is expensive and difficult to keep up.

(*2*) Commercial imitation turf material is available but involves some expense.

(*3*) Oiled sand greens can be constructed at little expense. Waste drain oil from automobiles can be secured at little or no cost. If new oil is purchased, use a light oil as it mixes better.[4] A carpet drag will keep the green usable.

(*4*) Sawdust can be used but requires some treatment to make it pack firm as it is normally light and soft.

(*5*) A bit of smooth lawn, not necessarily level, outlined with lime lines can be used if nothing else is available.

2. EQUIPMENT FOR THE PRACTICE OF ALL SHOTS COMBINED. Two or three practice holes may be laid out if 200 yards or more of play space

[4] Hall: *op. cit.*

are available. Lay out the holes so that they do not cross each other. Each should be far enough from the other so that all holes can be used at once. Each hole should be long enough to warrant at least two or three good shots so that a variety of clubs can be used. It is well to mark the boundary lines of the fairways so as to keep each player on the hole she is playing. Lime lines may be used to mark the greens. A cup should either be marked or sunk on the green.[5] If the green is such as to allow holing out, always use a sunken cup.

TECHNIQUE[6]

I. Grip

(A) *Analysis*.

1. OVERLAP. This grip is advised by most authorities because the touch of the forefinger and thumb of both hands is more sensitive. This is important in sensing a feel of the club head.

(a) Left Hand.

(1) The club rests against the middle joint of the forefinger and lies diagonally across the palm of the left hand.

(2) Three knuckles of this hand should be visible.

(3) The thumb extends diagonally across the shaft and nestles snugly in the palm of the right hand.

(b) Right Hand.

(1) The club rests against the middle joint of the forefinger.

(2) The hand is placed on the club so that, if opened, the palm would face squarely toward the objective.

(3) The thumb extends diagonally across the shaft.

(4) The pad of the thumb rests on the left thumb.

(5) The little finger is placed on top of or between the first and second fingers of the left hand.

(c) In General.

(1) The grip should be secure but not squeezed.

(2) The club is held mainly by the fingers.

2. INTERLOCK. This grip is the same as the above except that the little finger of the right hand *interlocks* with the forefinger of the left. This grip is not highly recommended, for it eliminates the sensitive touch of the forefinger and thumb of the left hand and tends to overpower the left hand with the right.

---

[5] Eastburn: *op. cit.*

[6] Directions are given for right-handed golfers and should be reversed for left-handed persons.

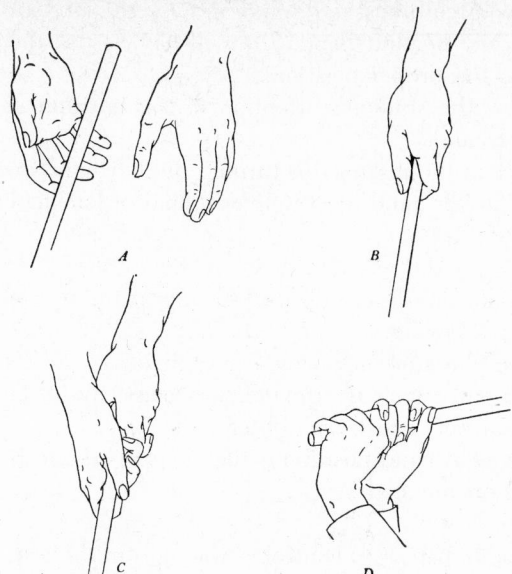

Fig. 86. The grip. *A*, right hand supporting the club; left ready to be placed on the club, palm down. *B*, left hand in place. *C*, the complete grip, front view. *D*, the complete grip showing the little finger of the right hand overlapping the first finger of the left hand.

(B) *Method of Presentation.*

1. EXPLANATION. ⎫ of both overlap and interlock to see which
2. DEMONSTRATION. ⎬ is best adapted to each pupil.
3. PRACTICE.

(*a*) Organization of Class. Have the class stand in a semicircle around the instructor so that the instructor's eye can quickly reach all in order to check every pupil at each step.

(*b*) Common Progression.

(*1*) Have the pupil hold the end of the shaft with the right hand and place the club on the ground so that it is soled.[7] Then ask her to place her left hand on the end of the shaft so that three knuckles are visible. The instructor should check to see that the knuckles are visible.

(*2*) Have the pupil place the right hand on the club. The instructor checks.

(*3*) Have the pupil take her hands completely off the club and then retake the grip several times. Each time the instructor checks.

(*c*) Suggested Simple Effective Way to Teach Beginners.[8]

[7] See Golf Terms, p. 211.
[8] Thompson, Ben: "A High School Golf Program." *Scholastic Coach*, December, 1939, p. 16. Also, Thompson, Ben: *How to Play Golf*, p. 2.

(1) Place a club on the ground and ask the student to pick it up using only her left hand. She will always put the hand on the club in the proper position.

(2) Draw the student's attention to the position of the back of the left hand.

(3) Explain the reasons for turning the left hand over:

(a) The left hand must deliver a kind of backhand blow to the ball.

(b) When the left thumb is on the right side of the shaft, it will not interfere with the cocking of the wrists at the top of the backswing.

(4) Help the student swing her club using the left hand only, until a full swing is attained. (In class, divide into two's and have partners assist each other.)

(5) The right-hand position is then explained and both hands are placed on the shaft.

(C) *Common Faults.*

1. An all-palm grip loses control of the club in the upper part of the swing.

2. An all-finger grip defeats the mobility of the wrists.

3. Squeezing tightens the muscles in the forearm. Tell the student to grip with the right hand no tighter than when holding a pen to write.

4. Right or left hand too far under or around shaft:

(a) If the left thumb is down the top of the shaft, it interferes with the cocking of the wrists.

(b) If the left hand is not far enough around, the face of club is not kept in position to hit the ball squarely and straight ahead.

(c) If the right knuckle is under the shaft instead of at the side, there is a loss of power and control.

(D) *Placement in Progress.* The only preliminary to the teaching of the grip would be a short explanation of the object of the game, the lay-out of the course, safety measures, minimum equipment necessary for an individual, the names of the parts of the club, and a feeling for the swinging action. The grip is the basis of the swing and must be mastered before proceeding.

II. Stance

(A) *Analysis.* "Stance" is the position the player takes to make a stroke.

1. GENERAL POSITION.

(a) The stance should be comfortable with the knees easy and the weight about evenly divided between the two feet.

(*b*) The weight should be back toward the heels rather than on the toes to counterbalance the tendency of the force of the swing in front of the body to pull the body off balance forward.

(*c*) If the toes are turned out slightly, balance is improved and the pivot in both directions is facilitated.

(*d*) The width of the stance depends upon the amount of force desired. The longer the desired shot, the wider (up to the width of the shoulders) the stance. The wider stance allows for freer transference of weight without imperiling balance. However, when the feet are placed farther apart than the width of the hips a horizontal component of force is introduced and as this becomes greater the counter pressure of the ground against the feet is lessened. Too wide a stance also limits body rotation. In general, the feet are placed about the width of the shoulders apart for distance shots, and the width of the stance becomes narrower for shorter shots.

(*e*) Always place the club behind the ball with the face pointing squarely toward the point of aim (club face perpendicular to the line of flight of the ball) and then take the stance.

(*f*) When the club is soled, the length of the club and arm will give the proper distance to stand from the ball.

2. TYPES OF STANCE.

(*a*) "Square" or "Parallel."

   (*1*) Explanation: The feet are placed evenly so that a line through the toes is parallel to the line of flight of the ball. (Fig. 87.)

   (*2*) Use: This is the most commonly used stance. It is always used for distance shots unless a curve in the line of flight of the ball is desired. It is the best stance to teach beginners for all shots because with this stance the path of the club head more naturally parallels the line of the intended flight of the ball.

(*b*) "Open."

   (*1*) Explanation: The left foot is withdrawn away from the line of flight of the ball. This turns the body slightly toward the direction of play. (Fig. 87.)

   (*2*) Use: This is often used in iron play, particularly the shorter iron shots for which less force and greater accuracy are desired. It restricts body rotation on the backswing but allows the club to follow through farther along the line of the intended flight of the ball. It tends to lead to hitting across the back of the ball from the outside in, thus resulting in a slice.

(*c*) "Closed."

   (*1*) Explanation: The right foot is withdrawn away from the line of flight of the ball. This closes the body from the direction of play. (Fig. 87.)

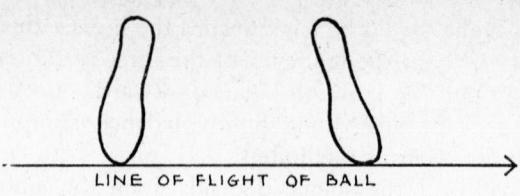

SQUARE STANCE

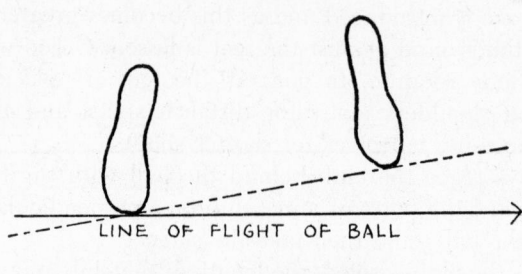

OPEN STANCE

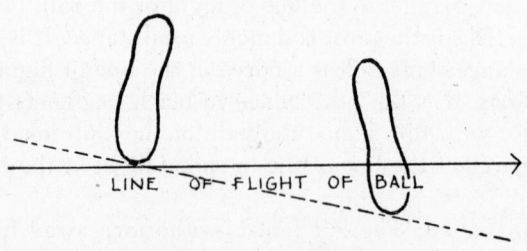

CLOSED STANCE

Fig. 87. Types of stance.

(2) Use: This stance allows for free rotation on the backswing but limits rotation on the follow-through. It tends to lead to hitting across the back of the ball from the inside out, thus resulting in a hook.

3. POSITION OF THE BALL.

(a) General Principles. The spin of the ball is of utmost importance in the control of a great many shots. Forward and backward spin

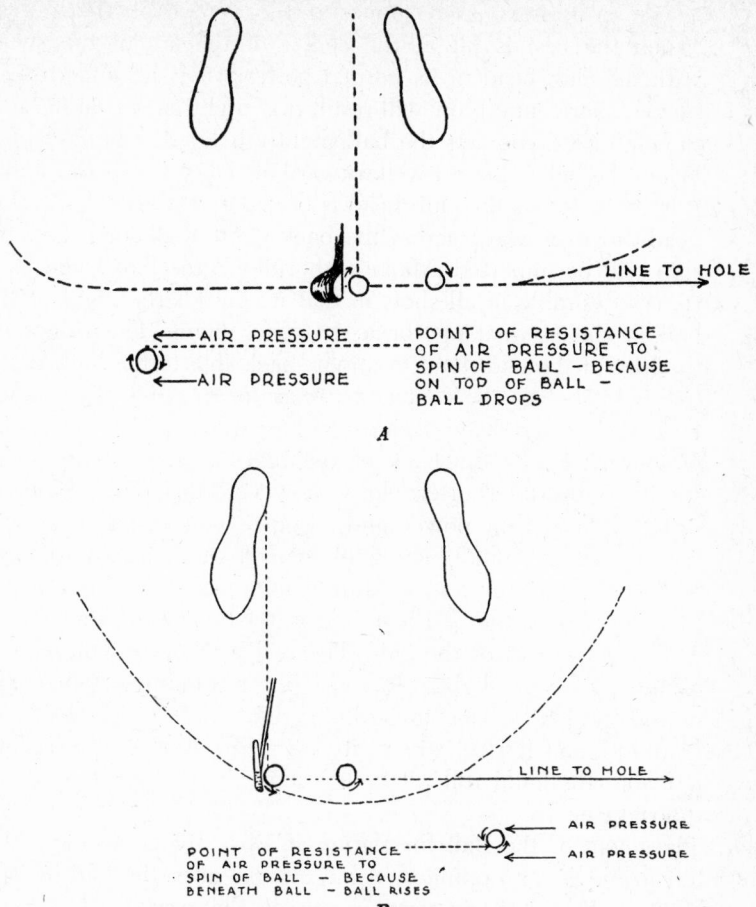

Fig. 88. The relation of the swing to the spin of the ball. *A,* full swing imparting forward spin to the ball. *B,* short iron imparting back spin to the ball.

are regulated by the point in the arc of the swing at which the club head contacts the ball, and therefore, by the placement of the ball in relation to the feet.

 (*1*) The relation of spin to the roll of the ball:
   (a) Forward spin will cause the arc of flight to be lower and will increase the forward roll of the ball upon landing.
   (b) A ball with back spin will rise and its roll will be restricted upon landing. The degree of the rise and the amount of roll will depend upon the amount of back spin.
 (*2*) The relation of the swing to spin: The center of the arc of the

swing is approximately opposite the center of the stance. When the ball is hit at the center of the arc of the swing with the club head in its normal position it is hit a horizontal blow. A horizontal blow will result in a slight back spin because the club head contacts the ball slightly below the ball's center. When the ball is placed well forward of the center of the stance it is contacted as the club head is traveling upward. If the club head moves upward across the back of the ball some forward spin will be imparted. Many authorities agree that some back spin is desirable in all shots in that it controls the flight of the ball in the air making for a straighter flight. The ridges on the face of the club tend to impart back spin to the ball. If the ball is hit before the center of the arc of the swing is reached (while the club head is hitting downward so that it passes downward across the back of the ball) more back spin will result. With the shorter clubs, however, the swing is more upright. Maximum power and distance will result when the ball is hit a horizontal blow while placed at, or slightly forward of, the center of the stance. More height and less roll will result the farther back the ball is placed in relation to the stance.

(3) The placement of the ball: The ball is placed at the center of the stance or slightly forward for maximum distance and moved gradually back toward the right foot as less distance, more loft, and less roll are desired, until in playing a maximum loft and minimum roll pitch shot it is placed almost opposite the right heel.

(b) Placement of the Ball for Various Clubs. There seems to be some shift in the general opinion on the placement of the ball for the long shots. In the last few years many of the professionals have changed from advocating placing the ball opposite the left heel when playing the long wood shots, to placing it about halfway between the left heel and the center of the stance. Some have gone so far as to advocate playing the ball off the center of the stance even with the driver.

(1) *Woods:*
#1—driver—about halfway between the left heel and the center of the stance.
#2—brassie—ball slightly back of above.
#3—spoon—ball slightly back of above.

(2) *Irons:*
#2 and 3—just ahead of the middle of the stance.

#4 and 5–approximately the middle of the stance.

#6 and 7–behind the middle of the stance.

#8 and 9–almost opposite the right heel.

(B) *Faults and Correction.*

1. Leaning too far forward causes the weight to be primarily on the toes. This may be caused by standing too far from the ball. To demonstrate the importance of weight placement to body balance during the swing, have the student stand upright with her feet together and weight back on the heels. Ask her to pivot her body fully. She will find that she is well-balanced throughout the pivot. Then tell her to place her weight on her toes and repeat. Body balance now will be very difficult if not impossible to maintain.[9] When the swing is added balance will become even more precarious if the weight is on the toes. The weight of the club and the force of the swing are in front of the body; therefore, the body weight must be kept back to counterbalance these forces.

2. Using a closed stance restricts the pivot and hinders a full backswing. When the backswing is restricted loss of force results as there is less time to work up momentum. It is often difficult for a student to tell whether or not her feet are parallel. To demonstrate this, place a club on the ground so that it touches the toes of both feet. It will then be easy for the student to see that this line is not parallel to the desired flight of the ball.

3. Placing the feet too far apart introduces a horizontal component in the force of the feet against the ground and may cause slipping of the feet. This also restricts the pivot.

4. Keeping the legs stiff also restricts the pivot.

(C) *Place in Progression.* The teaching of the stance should follow the teaching of a feeling for the swinging action. The relation of the ball to the feet for various strokes should be taken up after each swing is mastered without a ball.

III. The Full Swing

The action is that of centrifugal force, applied from a solidly grounded triangular foundation, the three points of which are the two feet and the head.[10]

(A) *Analysis.*

1. BACKSWING.

(*a*) The weight shifts onto the right foot and the hips rotate toward

---

[9] Thompson: "A High School Golf Program."

[10] *Golf Lessons.* The National Golf Foundation, Lesson 9.

the right around the spine as an axis. This puts the body into position to use the strong trunk muscles as well as the arm and shoulder girdle muscles in the swing.

(*b*) As the hips turn, the left knee relaxes and bends in. The right leg straightens since it becomes the support for the body weight. A relaxed left side and shoulder make proper turning possible.

(*c*) The club head is pushed straight back away from the ball and at the beginning of the backswing the club head is kept low. The farther the club head travels in line with the path of desired flight of the ball, the flatter the arc and the greater the chance for accuracy in contact and the more horizontal the blow.

(*d*) The cocking of the wrists adds to the length of the backswing.

(*e*) At the top of the backswing the club is:

wood—parallel to the ground.

iron—varies for different length clubs—#5 about 45° angle; #7 and #8 about 90° angle.

2. DOWNSWING.

(*a*) The downswing begins with a rhythmic shift of weight from the right to the left foot.

(*b*) The left leg straightens as it takes the weight, producing a solid wall (left side) against which to hit.

(*c*) The hips unwind and wind up to the left around the spine as an axis.

(*d*) The right side and shoulder are relaxed to allow them to follow the swing.

(*e*) The wrists uncock toward the end of the swing to add to the speed of the club head at the moment of impact. Since the club is long the distal end must move through a considerable distance while the hands move through a short distance and therefore, a great deal of speed is added to the club head. If the wrists are uncocked too soon the extra spurt of speed will be spent before the ball is contacted; if too late, the hands will be ahead of the club head at the moment of impact and the club will strike the ball with an open face (at an angle with the heel ahead of the toe). Most authorities agree that there is no uncocking of the wrists until the hands have come down to about waist height.

(*f*) The swing should sweep through smoothly without any sudden acceleration.

3. FOLLOW-THROUGH.

(*a*) The club head follows out behind the ball in the line of flight as far as the arms will permit before it is allowed to sweep around and complete the arc of the swing.

Fig. 89. *A*, wooden club, the full swing, side view. *B*, wooden club, the full swing, front view. *C*, #5 iron, the full swing. *D*, short iron, the full swing.

Fig. 90. Full wood swing showing a false pivot.
Fig. 91. Exercise for practicing the pivot.

(b) The body completes its pivot with the right side relaxed.

(c) The eyes are kept down on the spot behind the ball until *well after* the ball has been hit.

(B) *Faults.*

1. Making a "false pivot" or bending the knees straight forward over the feet instead of relaxing them toward the opposite knee causes the hips to stay square and makes any turning of the body impossible. (Fig. 90.) It also causes the weight to be on the left foot during the backswing and right foot during the forward swing, thus pulling the body weight out of the stroke instead of putting it into the shot. A suggested exercise for practicing the pivot follows (Fig. 91): (a) Hold a club across the back of the shoulders. (b) Shift the weight to the right heel. (c) With the eyes on the ball, or a spot on the ground out from the point halfway between the left heel and the center of the stance, twist the body to the right until the end of the club points to the ball. (d) Shift the weight to the left heel and twist the body to the left until the other end of the club points to the ball.

2. Allowing the head to move with the body is a very common fault. To teach students to move the body independent of the head, the same exercise as noted for pivot practice can be used. Divide the class so that each student has a partner. While one student practices the pivot, her partner immobilizes her head by placing a hand securely on each side of it. As the student gets a feeling for keeping the head still as

the body moves, her partner gradually lessens the pressure until she is able to withdraw her hands altogether, and the student practicing is able unaided to accomplish a full pivot with practically no movement of the head.

Have the students face their shadows and practice the above exercise keeping eyes on the shadows of their heads. They will find it easy to see any movement of the head. When the students are able to keep the heads motionless during this practice, have them try swinging the club while watching their shadows.

3. Starting the stroke by lifting the club head abruptly with the hands instead of bringing it back low along the ground does away with the pivot, and the result is a lifting of the body and head. Usually the right hand is at fault. Keep the grip of this hand as light as when gripping a pen in writing.

4. Rotating or pronating the left hand as the club is started back puts the face out of position for a square hit.

5. Hitting too soon or trying to hit too hard is caused by throwing the club with the hands from the top of the swing. This brings the club down too fast for the club head to keep pace. The head of the club does not strike the ball squarely. Have the student swing to music.

6. Omitting the weight shift or merely whirling the body around suddenly leaving most of the weight on the right foot changes the arc of the swing. Practice the pivot exercise emphasizing the shift of weight to the left heel *at the beginning* of the downswing.

7. Attempting sudden acceleration at the instant of the impact detracts from both accuracy and power. Have the student practice continual rhythmic swinging.

8. A tensing of the body from attempting to put too much force into impact causes inability of the right side to follow around. Usually this is accompanied by a bending of the arms, and therefore the ball is topped. To overcome general tenseness, have the students swing continuously in rhythm. Music may be a great aid.

9. Lifting the head before impact causes the ball to be hit above the center, or "topped." This is usually due to the golfer's desire to see where the ball is going. Have the student count 3 slowly, after impact, before looking up to see the results of her shot.

10. Playing the ball too far forward may cause a topped shot. Move the ball back toward the center of the stance.

11. Loosening the grip at the top of the backswing may mean an altered grip at the time of impact and any type of shot can result. Tell a student with this tendency to squeeze the club at the top of the backswing.

12. The tendency to push or pull against the club instead of swinging causes many different shots. To show the student the difference between leverage and a swinging action, the following is suggested:[11]

(*a*) Have the student swing something with a flexible shaft like a length of cord or a large handkerchief with a small weight attached to the end. Have her whirl it around her hand in a circle noting how little strength and movement of the hand it takes to produce this smooth whirling motion. Then have the student push or pull on the end of the cord and note how this interrupts the smooth swing of the weight. This will show the student the irregular path produced by leverage as opposed to the smooth path of a swinging motion.

(*b*) Have the student hold the handkerchief and the club together and swing so that their movements are synchronized.

(*c*) Omit the handkerchief.

(C) *Teaching.* The full swing should be taught as soon as the students have learned the grip. Give the students as *few* essential points to think about as possible. The most important single factor in a good golf stroke is relaxation. A swinging action of the club head is possible only in the absence of all tenseness. The golf stroke involves movements of many parts of the body, but these will be taken care of if the player controls a few essentials. Any attempt on the part of an individual learning golf to analyze every sequence of the swing and every movement of each segment of the body can result only in confusion, and confusion will cause tenseness. All the student need think about is to take the club head back easily and swing out *through* the ball on a line with the green.

1. PROGRESSION FOR TEACHING THE FULL SWING.

(*a*) Explain the swinging action. First demonstrate this with something heavy on the end of a piece of string or a large handkerchief. Betty Hicks suggests holding the club between the thumb and forefinger and letting it swing, emphasizing feeling the swing of the head at the end of the shaft. She then has her students turn the club over and hold it by the head to demonstrate the difference in the feeling of the weight, and the swing, with and without the club head. Next demonstrate an easy swing of the club. (The grip must be taken up at this point.)

(*b*) Give the students clubs and let them swing back and forth. Many will unconsciously transfer weight, pivot, and so forth correctly. Many teachers believe in starting beginners with a #5 iron, others with a #2 iron, and some with a #2 wood. The shorter shaft of the #5 makes

---

[11] Hicks, Betty: *Fundamentals of Golf*, pp. 5, 6. Morrison, Alex J.: *Better Golf Without Practice*, p. 32.

it easier to control and therefore it may be preferable. The important thing is to start with a full swing. Music is a great aid in developing an easy rhythmical swing. Either use a victrola, if one is available, or have the class sing a well known waltz.

(*c*) When the students have a feeling for the swinging action, the stance can be introduced.

(*d*) Give the group a few general suggestions:

(*1*) Avoid hurrying or trying to swing hard. (Emphasize relaxation.)

(*2*) Explain the head position. Tell the students either to keep their eyes on the balls or to point their chins at a spot behind the ball. Emphasize the importance of maintaining this position at all times throughout the swing. An accurate contact with the ball will result only if the body parts are in the same relative position at impact as when the stance was taken. Since the head is the most important *single* factor in assuring a return to this stance, control of its position is essential to a good hit.

(*3*) Let the club head follow down the fairway along the line of the flight of the ball as far as it is possible to reach before allowing it to come up and around.

(*e*) Have the group swing, and give individuals suggestions. The student who transfers her weight and pivots naturally need not be troubled with thinking about these things and can concentrate on the one or two principles which will help her. It may be a general aid to have the class swing several times with the left hands only and then place the right hands lightly on the clubs.

(*f*) When the group as a whole has developed an easy, relaxed, and rhythmical swing, give them soft balls. Explain that the ball is being added simply to check on accuracy of impact, not to see how hard they can hit. This is a good point at which to explain how important accuracy is. Since the ball is so small and the club head which must contact it is also small, the possible margin of error, if *any* contact is to result, is very slight. Unless the ball is hit in the center (in line with the center of gravity) most of the force of the club head will not be imparted to the ball.

(*g*) Finally have them hit regulation balls.

2. METHODS OF PRACTICE.

(*a*) Swinging—no ball. If the indoor space available is large enough so that the entire class can swing at once, and if there are two coco mats or one coco mat and a wooden platform (or even just one coco mat) to a student, the situation is ideal. With this situation have the class take their positions in two or three lines the length of the gymnasium. The number of lines will depend on the length of the room and the number in the class. Have them stand so that they are all facing one end of the gymnasium. This makes it easier for the instructor to talk to the class and to demonstrate general faults and corrections.

If the space is not large enough for all to swing at once or if the equipment is limited, divide the class into two's (or three's if necessary) and have them take turns. While one student swings, her partner can watch and criticize. Rotate on the instructor's signal.

(*b*) Swinging with a Cotton Ball. When not limited in space or equipment, divide the class into two lines the length of the gymnasium. Have the students stand about 10 feet from the wall and practice hitting balls toward the walls. Since there is no danger of injury from being hit by one of these balls, students may retrieve the balls at any time. Warn them to be careful not to get in the way of the club of any other student.

If the space or equipment is limited, divide the class into groups as for swinging. One student of each group may be given the responsibility of retrieving the balls.

Soft balls also may be used outdoors if the field is too short for a full wood shot with a regulation ball.

(*c*) Swinging with a Regulation Ball.

(*1*) *Indoors.* Practice with a hard ball indoors is only possible with a canvas back-drop or driving cage. If only one or two cages are available have the rest of the class practice with soft balls and then rotate so that each individual has an opportunity to hit several regulation balls in a cage.

(*2*) *Outdoors.*

(a) If the outdoor facilities include a field 150 yards long:
1. Line up the class across one end of the field and have them hit out all the balls the length of the field.
2. On a signal from the instructor, the class walks forward in a line extending the width of the field.
3. Every student is instructed to pick up all balls in her path and carry them to the far end of the field.
4. If the students are playing their own balls, have them pile all the balls that are not their own near the center and each student can sort out her own.
5. If the school furnishes the balls, any student with more balls than she hit out gives the extras to the instructor.
6. If she has less than she hit out, the student reports to the instructor who redistributes.

7. If balls are missing after redistribution, the entire class can go back on the field until the correct number are found.
8. The class then hits the balls back the length of the field.

(b) If the field is too short for a full wood, either a shorter club or a soft ball must be substituted. The club chosen will depend on the length of the field and the ability of the group.

IV. The Short Game

The short game consists of nothing more than a sound golf stroke the length of which is varied according to the distance required. Accuracy, not distance, is the essential of all iron play, and therefore, a shorter backswing is used. While authorities vary greatly as to the exact stance, they all agree that the stroke should be a smooth swing with no jabbing motion. In general the stance is slightly narrower and the ball is a little nearer because of the shorter shaft of the club. This causes the swing to be more upright and gives less distance but more accuracy. Many authorities teach an open stance which allows a freer follow-through for greater accuracy in making short approaches. There is a very common misconception that if a lofted shot is desired, the player must, by her swing, aid the club in elevating the ball. This misconception causes the player to try to strike the ball upward, and as a result the ball is not hit squarely; it is usually hit above its center of gravity, and it rises little if at all. The pupil must be made to understand that the ball will rebound perpendicular to the face of the club; in order to elevate the ball she must choose a club with an open face and then hit the ball squarely, allowing the club to do the work of lifting. If a sharp loft is desired, a club with a very open face is chosen and the ball is given back spin by being hit on the downward swing. This can be accomplished by playing the ball toward the right heel and playing the usual smooth stroke to hit through the ball. A ball hit with back spin will stop dead where it lands, or run only a few feet.

(A) *Approach Shots.*

1. TYPES OF APPROACH SHOTS.

(*a*) The chip shot is a low running shot played from the edge or immediate vicinity of the green where the ground between the ball and the green is fairly level. The ball should be played so that it will clear the fairway, land on the green and roll toward the cup. For best results the straightest faced club possible should be used which will permit landing on the putting green and stopping close to the hole. Up to about 5 feet off the green use a #4 or #5 iron, and if farther away a #6 or #7. The ball is placed about opposite the middle of the stance. The swinging action is the same as any swing except that both the backswing and the follow-through may be shortened depending on the distance the ball has to travel. The club points toward the hole at the end of the follow-through. This may be made easier by slightly opening the stance.

(*b*) The pitch shot is a high shot which lands with little or no roll. Since height and back spin are desired, a #6, 7, or 8 club is used and the ball is placed almost opposite the right heel. For this shot the arc of the swing should be more upright. The backswing and follow-through may be shortened if the distance is short.

2. GENERAL PRINCIPLES. If the ball lies a few feet off the green, play a run-up shot with an iron that has just enough loft to lift the ball over the fairway to the green. Play for a roll toward the pin. As the distance to the green becomes greater or as the hole approaches the edge of the putting surface, increase the loft of the club, move the ball toward the right foot, and continue to play the same stroke, lengthening the backswing and follow-through according to the distance. A little practice with the short lofted clubs, starting about 30 or 40 yards from the green and working back, will give the student her range for each club and the length of backswing and follow-through that is necessary for the various distances.

(B) *Sand Trap Shots*. It is infinitely better to get out of the sand trap in one shot even though the ball travels only a short distance, than to waste several swings in attempting a long shot. While there are several methods of playing from traps, there are two that are the most fundamental.

1. THE CHIP SHOT.

(*a*) This is used when the ball is resting on the top of the sand and the bank in front is not too steep.

(*b*) Choose a #6 or #7 iron.

(*c*) The swing is the same as for any short approach except that the club may not touch the sand in addressing the ball or during the backswing.

2. THE BLAST OR EXPLOSION SHOT.

(*a*) This must always be used when the ball is partly or wholly buried in the sand or when the bank in front is steep.

(*b*) Choose a #8 or #9 iron.

(*c*) Plant the feet firmly in the sand to avoid slipping.

(*d*) Since the sand should be hit behind the ball, the ball is played forward. The distance that the sand should be hit behind the ball depends on how far the trap is from the green. In a normal sand trap shot, aim to hit the sand about 2 inches back of the ball.

(*e*) The most important thing is to use a full iron swing *with a full follow-through.*

(C) *Shots from the Rough.* When playing a shot from the rough the main purpose is to get the ball out onto the fairway, and distance should be sacrificed to this end. If the club head contacts grass or weeds on the downswing before impact with the ball a very weak shot will result.

1. Choose a club with ample loft. In the average rough a #5 iron will be sufficient.

2. Take the usual stance.

3. Use an upright swing with a full follow-through.

(D) *Faults.*

1. Lifting the club too soon because of feeling a necessity to lift the ball by the swing instead of allowing the proper club to do the work will cause the bottom edge of the club head to contact the middle of the ball and the ball to be "topped." To demonstrate how the club lifts the ball, give the student who is attempting to "lift" the ball by her swing a lofted club and ask her to hit balls at a golf bag a few feet away. The loft of the club will cause the ball to go over the bag instead of against it.[12]

2. When the golfer tries to lift the ball into the air with body action or with a flick of the wrists, she usually fails to shift the weight to the left foot, keeping too much on the right, and the result is that the lowest point in the arc of the swing is moved back and the ball is hit above the center.

3. The tendency to take too long a swing on a short shot often leads to checking the follow-through. The student gets a feeling during the down stroke that the swing is too long and unconsciously cuts it off at impact. Have this student practice hitting balls with a very short back-swing to see how far they go with very little swing if the impact is clear.

(E) *Teaching.*

1. PROGRESSION. The short shots should not be taught until the student has developed a feeling for the full swing with the essential clubs. The sand trap shots, being the most difficult, should be taught at the end of the progression.

2. METHODS OF PRACTICE.

(*a*) Indoors: Students can get good practice by chipping balls into baskets, into pockets in a canvas drop, or into mats standing against the walls. The pitch shot can be practiced with soft balls, with hard rubber balls into "Pitch-it," or with regulation balls against a canvas drop.

[12] Jones, Robert T., Jr., and Lowe, Harold: *Group Instruction in Golf*, p. 37.

(*b*) Outdoors: Mark the field at various distances and have the students attempt to put the ball between two markers. This set-up can be used for practicing approaches of various distances. If the field is marked for hockey or soccer, the hockey striking circle or the soccer penalty area can serve as objectives for the students' approach practice. Lime lines can be used to enclose a space to serve as a green. Students can also practice pitching over stationary equipment such as hockey or soccer goals or archery targets, or into a jumping pit or sand trap. The chip and explosion sand trap shots can be practiced out of a jumping pit or overturned dirt if no sand trap is available.

V. Putting

In teaching putting one must include a discussion of factors that vary and therefore, must be considered on every green, as well as the method of lining up the putt, and the actual stroke itself.

(A) *Some of the Factors That Must Be Considered.*

1. The distance of the ball from the cup.
2. The speed of the green:

Fast Green	Slow Green
dry	wet
grass closely cropped	grass not closely cropped
hard	top dressing

3. The contour of the green and the effect it will have on both speed and accuracy: (*a*) When putting against the slope more force is necessary. (*b*) When putting with the slope less force is necessary. (*c*) When putting across the slope the aim must be above the cup.

(B) *Method of Lining Up the Ball for the Putt.* To line up a putt, crouch behind the ball and look over it toward the cup. Draw an imaginary line from the cup to the ball and pick out a spot on that line which is 8 to 10 inches in front of the ball. Concentrate on that spot while addressing the ball. Putt the ball to pass over that spot. If the green is not level, the player must judge the roll of the ball according to the slope, and when crouching behind the ball, line up the ball with a spot above the cup.

(C) *Technique of Putting.* There is probably no other phase of golf with the variation of style that is found in putting. Some golfers use a very narrow stance, some wider; some a square stance, and others point their feet toward the cup. Some players shift the grip to the reverse overlap in which the forefinger of the left hand overlaps the little finger of the right, others turn the hands on the club slightly so that the palms are facing each other, and still others putt with the same grip that is used for the full swing. Some players stand fairly upright and many use a low crouch. In spite of the wide variation, however, there are certain principles which hold:

1. The grip is fairly light. A tight grip prevents relaxation.
2. The left shoulder should be toward the cup.
3. The stance is easy and relaxed.
4. The ball is played close to the feet. This puts the head more nearly over the ball and the player can look more directly down on it and less at an angle.
5. In addressing the ball, the club head is placed behind the ball so that the face is perpendicular to the line of putt.
6. The left elbow is pointed toward the cup. This helps to keep the face of the club toward the cup throughout the stroke.
7. The stroke should be smooth with the backswing and follow-through equal in length. This length is dependent upon the distance to be traversed and the contour and condition of the green.
8. The club head is brought backward and forward close to the ground along the line of putt.
9. The follow-through is toward the cup.

As noted, there are many different styles of accomplishing the above principles. Only two will be suggested here: 1. With the arms free of the body and the elbows slightly bent, putt with a pendulum motion of the arms. 2. With the right forearm immobilized by resting it on the right thigh, putt with the wrists. This style necessitates a bent right knee and a low crouch.

(D) *Most Common Faults.*

1. A jabbing stroke with no follow-through makes it impossible to judge the force that is imparted to the ball. Also, stopping the club suddenly makes it difficult to keep the face of the club perpendicular to the line of putt, and thus the accuracy of the putt is affected. This same difficulty may arise from stopping the left arm or wrist, thus blocking the stroke at the start of the follow-through. Have the students putt on a carpet with no targets marked and concentrate on a smooth stroke.

2. Keeping the left elbow close to the side of the body causes the face of the club head to be pulled around to the left. Have the student check the left elbow before each putt. Tell her to feel that she is moving the club head itself into the hole.

3. Too often players think of accuracy only in terms of direction and lose their putts because they give little thought to force. Have the students putt for a certain distance marked by a line instead of for a target.

(E) *Teaching.*

1. PROGRESSION. Since beginners should always start putting on a level surface, it is an excellent rainy day exercise and it may be put into the golf progression at any time.

(a) Explain the factors to be considered, the method of lining up the ball for the putt, and the principles of putting.

(b) Demonstrate these principles bringing out the reasons for each. Then demonstrate a few different styles of putting.

(c) Have the class practice.

2. METHODS OF PRACTICE.

(a) Indoor: The first practice in stroking the ball can be done with a 7-inch sponge rubber ball or a tennis ball. These balls roll smoothly and noiselessly on a board floor and make it possible for the entire group to practice in safety. Divide the group into two's. One player places her club head on the floor in a position so that it can be used by her partner as a goal for her putt. Have the students practice parallel to the boards so that they may have a specific line to guide the club head.[13]

Next, divide the class and while part work on putting with regulation balls on a carpet, the rest can practice any swing that is being studied at that point in the progression. Rotate the groups. It is well to have the beginners start their putting on a carpet without any particular target, trying only for a smooth stroke. When this is accomplished, mark targets on the carpet and teach the students to attempt to have the ball stop just beyond the chalked targets so that they will work on judging force as well as direction. Have them start with very short putts and progress to longer distances. The next step indoors is to use an elevated board covered with carpet if one is available.

(b) Outdoor: Putting can be practiced out-of-doors on a green or, if none is available, on any very smooth, not necessarily level, plot of closely cut grass.

If the class has had preliminary work inside, they can begin immediate practice in putting for the cups or marked targets. Warn them that the grass will be slower than the carpet, and therefore, more force will have to be imparted to the ball for any given distance.

If the group has had no indoor experience in putting, the same general progression as stated above can be used; that is, putting first with no definite target, and then, when the target is added, working first on short putts and progressing to longer ones.

[13] Alway, Leonore K.: "Making Use of an Objective Record of Putting Progress," *Official Individual Sports Guide.*

CONSIDERATION OF OUTSIDE FORCES
AND GROUND CONTOUR

I. Wind

Since heavy gusts of wind make balance more difficult, the player must take a firm position. A slightly wider stance and less vigorous swing will increase the stability of the body.

(A) When playing the ball into a cross wind it is necessary to allow for the drift of the ball due to the wind. It is wise to keep the ball lower than usual as the wind close to the ground tends to have less velocity than that higher up. Therefore a club with less loft is chosen.

(B) In hitting into a head wind, again the ball should be played low so that it will not have to resist the force of the stronger wind higher up. Also in a low hit there is proportionately more horizontal force, which is needed to resist the force of the wind. Again a club with less loft than would be normally used is selected.

(C) When there is a strong wind at the player's back the ball should be played higher than it would normally be played in order to take advantage of the wind with higher velocity and to keep the ball in the air as long as possible so that the wind has more time to act on the ball before gravity pulls it to earth. A club with more loft than would normally be used for the distance is chosen.

II. Resistance of Various Surfaces

(A) Hard ground offers little resistance to the forward roll of the ball. Since there is little or no "give" as the ball hits, most of the force of the ball hitting the ground is transferred back to the ball and the ball bounces and rolls.

(B) Soft ground offers a great deal of resistance to forward roll because the ground gives with the weight of the rolling ball. When the ball lands on soft ground the ground "gives" and therefore, much of the force is absorbed and the ball bounces little if at all.

(C) The longer the grass the greater the resistance to a rolling ball. A ball with a given momentum will roll farther in short grass than in long.

(D) Wet grass offers more resistance to a rolling ball than does dry grass and therefore, a ball with a given momentum will roll farther on a dry surface.

III. Contour of the Ground

Allowance must be made for various contours of fairways and greens.

Since a ball will roll down-slope because of the pull of gravity, the shot should be aimed "uphill" of the green or of the cup.

FAULTS IN THE DIRECTION OF THE FLIGHT OF THE BALL

I. Slicing

(A) *Definition.* A "slice" is a curve in the flight of the ball to the right of the intended flight. A slice results from hitting the ball when the head of the club is facing to the right of the direction it is following, or from hitting from the outside in, or from drawing the club across the ball from the right to the left, thus imparting clockwise spin.

(B) *Causes.*

1. The player, trying to avoid a slice, attempts to yank the shot to the left thus pulling the club head across the ball and imparting the spin which causes the slice.

2. An incorrect grip makes it impossible for the club head to meet the ball squarely. The right hand may be too far under or the left hand not enough on top of the club. Dante and Elliott[14] advocate gripping the club so that only two knuckles of the left hand are visible from above. This places the back of the left hand toward the objective.

3. Too open a stance cuts down the pivot of the body during the backswing.

4. Too wide a stance may cause a player to slice.

5. The right hand lifting the club at too sharp an angle also retards the complete pivoting of the left side.

6. Uncocking the wrists too soon creates a tendency to throw the club head forward away from the body on the downswing. This causes the club to cut diagonally across the ball from the outside in. It also puts the right hand in control. Lack of proper control by the *left* hand causes the club to be drawn sharply in toward the left side at impact.

7. Pulling in the arms as the ball is struck gives a clockwise spin to the ball.

8. Lifting the head and not watching the ball because of anticipating the shot may result in any type of shot but is one of the main causes of slicing.

(C) *Suggestions for Correction.* First check the grip, stance, and placement of the ball. If everything is correct, ask the student to swing several times.

Determine whether the wrists are turning as the club head is taken back. If the wrists are "rolled" the face of the club will be angled and

[14] Dante, Joe, and Elliott, Len, *Stop That Slice,* p. 7.

the wrists will have to be "rolled back" exactly the same amount if the ball is to be hit squarely. It is the failure of the student to return to the square face position at impact that causes many slices. If the face is opened and closed during the swing the chances of it being square when it meets the ball are less than if it is kept square throughout the swing. Dante and Elliott[15] advocate teaching students to keep the club head face square throughout the swing by not allowing the wrists to roll.

If the student is pulling the club head back with the right hand, emphasize the use of the left arm in pushing the club back. Have the student take several easy swings with only the left hand on the club and then put the right hand on very lightly (have the right just "ride along").

If, on the downswing, the student is throwing the club head away from the body, have her place a handkerchief or piece of paper between the right upper arm and the thorax. Ask her to attempt to hold the handkerchief while swinging, until the ball has been struck. This will keep the right arm close on the downswing and prevent hitting from the outside. Another method of accomplishing the same thing is to place a piece of paper or cardboard on the ground behind the ball and have the student swing inside of this marker to hit the ball. Or, one can place a marker out from the right toe and tell the student to swing many times at this marker, following through as far out to the right as possible. Then have her swing with the ball placed properly, still concentrating on swinging down through this marker.

If the difficulty is in the follow-through, ask the student to try to throw the club down the fairway as far as possible before allowing it to come up to finish the arc of the swing. This often overcomes the tendency to pull the club in and up at impact. It is sometimes necessary to put a marker on the ground forward and to the right and tell the student to aim for this marker after impact.

Have the student attempt to hit the ball to the *right*.

II. Pushing—"Quick Slice"

(A) *Definition.* The ball goes off at a sharp angle to the right. This results not from spin but from the face of the club being open at impact.

(B) *Causes.*

1. The chief cause is the bending of the left arm allowing the elbow to go outward, thus opening the face of the club.

2. If the body is brought around too far ahead of the hands, the

[15] *Ibid.,* p. 4.

face of the club will be open at impact. This is usually caused by the player being overanxious to hit the ball.

(C) *Suggestion.* Coach a student to keep the left arm straight throughout backswing and downswing and to swing easily.

III. Hooking

(A) *Definition.* A "hook" is a curve in the flight of the ball to the left of the intended flight. A hook results from hitting when the club head is facing to the left of the direction of swing or from hitting from the inside out thus imparting counterclockwise spin to the ball.

(B) *Causes.*

1. Gripping the club with the right hand too far around the club.
2. Closing the stance and thus limiting the pivot on the follow-through and causing the backswing to be flatter than usual.
3. Overworking the right hand.
4. Punching at the ball.

(C) *Suggestions for Correction.* First check the grip, the stance, and the position of the ball and then check the swing. Coach the student to try for a slow, relaxed swing. Use the exercise of swinging with the left arm alone and then placing the right on lightly. Have the student attempt to hit the ball to the *left* of the fairway.

IV. Pulling

(A) *Definition.* The ball goes directly to the left. This again is not a matter of spin but results from the club head being closed at impact.

(B) *Causes.*

1. The face of the club may be closed too much at "address."
2. The wrists may roll at impact and close the face of the club.
3. If the right elbow is too far out from the body on the downswing, the club head may be thrown out and the face turned toward the left at impact.
4. The right shoulder may be higher than the left at impact.

NOTE: If the club hits the ball squarely as it is traveling from right to left, it will send it off sharply left. If the club head is pulled across the *back of the ball* from right to left, spin will be imparted and the result will be a slice.

(C) *Suggestions.* If the right elbow is out from the body, use a handkerchief or paper under the right arm as suggested to help cure a "slice." If the fault comes from rolling the wrists, have the student swing several times stopping the follow-through when the club is at its farthest point along the desired flight of the ball so that she can check the face of the club and work to have the face up at this point in the swing.

INTENTIONAL CHANGES IN THE FLIGHT OF THE BALL

I. Direction

Many times on the course it is desirable to hit a ball so that there will be a curve in its flight. Most golf courses have one or more dog leg holes, making a curve to the right or left distinctly advantageous.

(A) *Hitting an Intentional Slice.*[16]

1. Use an open stance.
2. Play the ball opposite the center of the stance.
3. Take the club head back outside the intended line of flight of the ball. Push away from the body on the downswing.
4. The hands and club should be quite high at the top of the backswing.
5. Pull down and across the ball (from the outside in) toward the left foot.
6. Keep the face of the club slightly open at all times. Be careful that the club head does not turn over at any time during the downswing or follow-through.
7. Use a good follow-through.

(B) *Hitting an Intentional Hook.*[17]

1. Use a closed stance.
2. Play the ball nearly opposite the right foot.
3. Pivot the right hip away from the ball, bringing the club head sharply around as it is brought back. This results in a flat swing.
4. Swing the club head away from the body allowing the wrists and club head to roll at the moment of impact.

It is possible to regulate the amount of the hook by the degree to which the stance is closed and the swing flattened.

II. Height

Just as it may at times be advantageous to curve the flight of the ball, it may be necessary to loft the ball more than normal or to play to keep it particularly low. Long distance may be desired, and therefore the usual pitch shot which gives very little distance and no roll is not desirable, and still there may be a tall tree directly in the path of the line of flight of the ball to the green. If the tree branches do not grow too low it may be more practical to play a low shot under the branches. A low flying ball is also good when there is a high wind.

(A) *Hitting the Ball High (without Backspin).*[18]

1. Play the ball approximately off the left heel.

[16] Nelson, Byron: *Winning Golf,* p. 180.
[17] *Ibid.,* p. 182.
[18] *Ibid.,* p. 172.

2. Keep the weight more on the right foot than on the left so that the ball will be caught on the upswing.

3. Hit with the hands slightly behind the club head. Uncock the wrists a little earlier than usual. This also causes the ball to be caught on the upswing.

(B) *Hitting the Ball Low (without Spin).*[18]

1. Play the ball opposite the right foot.

2. The hands should be unusually far ahead of the club head on impact. The effect is to pinch the ball between the club face and the turf, causing it to travel in a low trajectory.

3. The stance should be slightly open.

4. The weight should be kept firmly on the left foot throughout the swing.

5. Avoid any turning of the club head at the time of impact.

6. Shorten the swing.

HILL LIES

When a ball lies on a hill, study the slope of the ground and play for safe direction even at the sacrifice of distance. A good general rule is to allow the club head to follow the contour of the ground.

Three factors must be considered: the relation of the slope to the desired line of flight, the degree of slope, and the distance to be traversed.

I. Different Types of Hill Lies

(A) *Uphill Lie.* Use a slightly closed stance with the ball played from the center of the stance. The nature of the stance due to the lie of the ball is such that the player is hitting up on the ball and thus exaggerated height results. For this reason a longer club with a less open face than would be normally used for the same distance on level ground should be used. The weight will be more on the right foot as it is the downhill foot, and the left knee will be bent to compensate for the slope; therefore the arc of the backswing will be flattened. As the club head follows the slope it will be more on the inside, resulting in a "pull." Allow for this by aiming slightly to the right. After impact allow the club to follow-through up the slope of the hill. Allow the club to do the work. Do not attempt to "lift" the ball.

(B) *Downhill Lie.* Use a slightly open stance with the ball placed slightly nearer the right foot. The right knee will be bent and the weight will be on the left or downhill foot thus limiting the pivot of the left side. Since there is more weight than usual on the left foot at impact and the arc of the swing is downward, the ball will travel abnormally low. Therefore a club with a more lofted face than would normally be used for the same distance on level ground should be chosen. The backswing must be more upright because of the slope. There is a tendency to slice. Allow for this by playing a little to the left. Be careful to allow the club head to follow-through along the slope and not to try to lift the ball.

((C) *Sidehill Lies.*

1. BALL BELOW THE FEET. If the ball is below the feet, the weight is naturally forward on the toes. Therefore, take a stance that gives the best balance. Stand closer to the ball than usual and play the ball off the center of the stance. Grip the club as far up on the shaft as possible since the distance from the shoulder to the club head is longer than usual. It may help to use a longer club than would be chosen for the same distance on level ground. The tendency is to slice since the body pivot is cut down, so allow for this by aiming to the left.

2. BALL ABOVE THE FEET. If the ball is above the feet the distance from the shoulder to the club head is shorter than usual; therefore, a shorter club should be chosen or the club should be gripped well down the shaft. Play the ball nearer the right foot and slightly open the stance. Play a flat swing, shorter than usual, and keep the hands low. Since the tendency here is to pull, aim to the right.

ORGANIZATION OF GOLF CLASSES

I. Classification of Players

Players should be classified according to previous golf experience into beginning, intermediate, and advanced groups. If the teaching situation allows students with some experience to play a round or more before registration, it would be well to classify on the basis of scores for nine or eighteen holes on a given course. While one or two rounds is not a truly reliable criterion of a student's ability, it would, in most cases, tend to be more reliable than the student's own judgment of her ability. This would probably be possible only for fall registration in the greater part of the country, as most golf courses are not open for play at the season when schools register for spring physical education classes.

II. Number Registered in a Section

The number of students registered in a section depends on the facilities available indoors and outdoors and the degree of skill of the group. A beginning group should be kept smaller than a section of students who have had some previous golf experience. If only one instructor is available, fifteen to eighteen should be the absolute maximum number in any section. Ten to twelve beginners and twelve to fifteen intermediates is ideal, but in few situations can classes be kept as small as this. In many schools offering a major course in physical education, students who have previously had a theory course in the sport coach under an instructor. In this situation a few more students may be taught successfully.

CLASS SAFETY PRECAUTIONS

1. Never swing near another student. Always check to see that there is plenty of space before swinging a club.
2. Avoid walking close to anyone swinging a club.
3. All students stay behind the line until all have finished hitting the balls out and the instructor gives the signal to collect the balls.
4. Care of the hands: (*a*) Advise a glove for the left hand to avoid blisters. (*b*) Advise against rings. (*c*) Advise the student to stop swinging if the hands begin to become sore.

SAMPLE LESSON PLANS

I. *The First Golf Lesson with Beginners Should Be Indoors Where It Is Easy to Talk to the Students.*
(A) Announcements pertinent to a particular teaching situation such as place and time of meeting, and so forth.
(B) Costume for golf class.
(C) Short history.
(D) Object of the game.
(E) Layout of the course.
(F) Clubs and their uses, and clubs required for class work.
(G) The names of various parts of the club.
(H) Safety precautions.
II. *Sample Indoor Plan for a Class That Is Working on a Full Swing.*
(A) Have all students swing without any balls for a few minutes.
(B) Discuss and demonstrate putting.
(C) Practice: If cages are available divide the class and have one-third putt, one-third swing at cotton balls, and one-third hit hard balls in cages. If necessary, assign two or three students to a cage and have each hit six balls before changing. Have the groups rotate on signal. Rotate from putting to swinging at cotton balls, to hitting in cages, to putting.
If no cages are available, have one-third of the class putting, one-third swinging without a ball, one-third swinging with cotton balls, and rotate as above.
(D) Include a short discussion or lecture.

III. *Sample Indoor Plan for a Class Working on Approaching.*

(A) Short oral quiz on previous lecture material such as terms or etiquette. Occasionally a very short written quiz will help to stimulate interest.

(B) Practice:

1. All students practice swinging without balls.

2. Divide class for special practice: While one-third of the class putts, have a group work on approach shots at a canvas, "Pitch-its," or mats, and another group hit with a full swing in cages if they are available. If there are no cages one group can work on the full swing with cotton balls. Rotate from putting, to approaching, to the full swing, to putting. (Fig. 92.)

(C) New lecture material.

SUGGESTED PROGRESSION FOR A TERM OF ABOUT 6 WEEKS
Class Meeting 3 Times Per Week for 40 Minutes

I. Beginners	II. Intermediates	III. Advanced
(A) Object of game, layout of course		
(B) Clubs: names of parts and general uses		
(C) Grip		
(D) Stance		
(E) Full swing #5 iron (3 lessons)[19] #2 iron (3 lessons) wood (5 lessons)— preferable #2 or 3 With each club go through: 1. Specific uses for club 2. Swing without ball 3. Position of ball 4. Swing with soft ball 5. Swing with hard ball	Review (10 lessons)	Review (4-5 lessons)
		Intentional changes in the flight of the ball (2 lessons)
(F) Chip shot (2 lessons)		
(G) Putting (3 lessons)		
(H) Lecture and discussion of rules, etiquette, etc.		
	(I) #7 iron (2 lessons) (J) Short approach (2 lessons) (K) Sand trap shots (2 lessons)	
	(L) Play on course (2 lessons)	Play on course (11-12 lessons)

[19] The number of lessons is approximate and is given only as a general guide. The speed of progression necessarily depends on the size and ability of the group. Few lessons would be spent entirely on one club. A part of each would be allotted to the review of clubs previously studied. The object of the game, rules, etiquette, and so forth, would be worked into the lessons at convenient points in the progression.

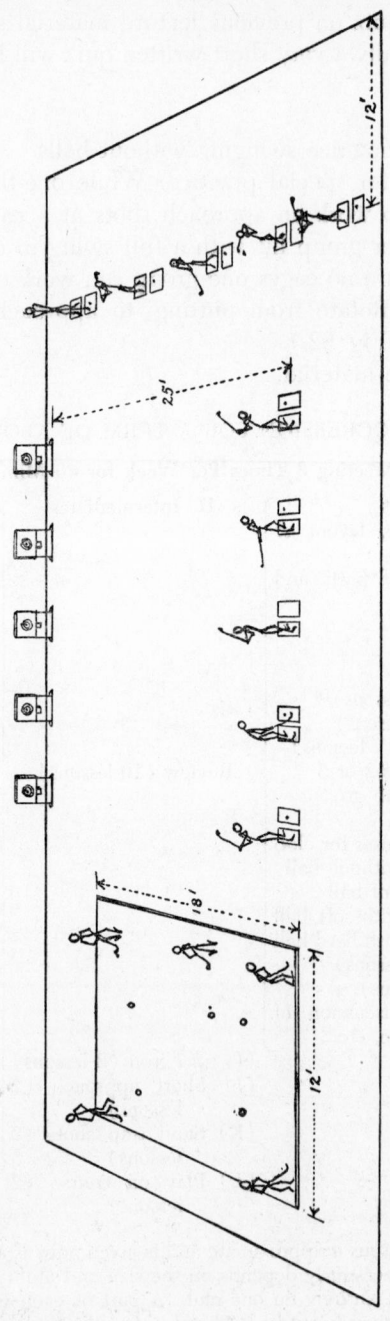

Fig. 92. Diagram of an indoor golf class.

RAINY DAY MATERIAL

Although an outdoor game, golf offers many possibilities for interesting indoor lessons both in lecture material and practice.

I. Lecture and Discussion Material

  (A) History of the Game
  (B) Golf Etiquette
  (C) Golf Terms
  (D) Fundamental Rules
  (E) Difficult and Unusual Lies
  (F) Competitive Play

II. Practice Material

  (A) *Full Swing.* This may be practiced by swinging without a ball, hitting cotton balls toward a wall, and hitting hard balls in golf cages or into properly constructed canvas drops.

  (B) *Approaching.* Practice swinging without a ball, hitting hard rubber balls into "Pitch-its," and hitting regulation balls into a canvas drop with pockets. The short chip shot can be practiced into tumbling mats stood against the wall.

  (C) *Putting.* Good practice may be obtained on a carpet or putting boards.

  (D) *Contests.*
   1. Putting.
   2. Approaching.
    (*a*) Pitch-its.
    (*b*) Baskets.

INTEREST MOTIVATION

Class teams, picked toward the end of the season, will do much to stimulate interest in golf. Also a tournament for the selection of the school champion creates enthusiasm for the sport. From the results of this tournament an honorary varsity can be chosen.

In co-educational schools mixed tournaments have been run very successfully. The two-ball foursome, in which the boy and girl hit the ball alternately, has proved very satisfactory.

GOLF ETIQUETTE

I. On the Tee

1. Observe the tee markers. Always tee the ball behind them. These are frequently moved to give the grass a chance to grow again.

2. The player with the "honor"[20] drives first.

3. Never talk or move around when another player is driving.

4. Never swing a club where you can be seen or heard by the player driving.

5. The best place to stand is diagonally in front and to the right of the player.

6. Wait until the players ahead have played their second shots *and* are out of your driving range before teeing off.

II. On the Fairway

1. The player who is "away"[21] plays first.

2. Never stand in the line of a player's shot.

3. Be still while a player is taking a shot.

4. If a ball is lost, or if you are playing more slowly than those behind you, signal the players behind to go through. Then wait until they are out of range before playing again.

5. Wait until the preceding players are *off* the green before making an approach shot.

6. Replace, and press down with your foot, all divots.

7. Call "Fore!" if your ball goes near or is likely to go near any other player.

III. In a Sand Trap

1. Leave your bag at the edge of the trap.

2. Enter and leave the trap at the point nearest your ball.

3. Smooth over foot marks and club marks with your club when you leave the trap.

IV. On the Green

1. Leave your bag at the edge of the green.

2. While holding the flag in the cup, stand quietly and to one side of the cup so that your shadow does not fall across the line of putt.

3. Place the flag at the edge of the green when it has been removed from the cup.

4. The player "away" putts first.

5. Keep your body and your shadow out of the line of any player's putt.

6. Do not move or talk while players are putting.

7. Avoid stepping on the turf at the edge of the cup.

8. Replace the flag in the cup immediately after holing out.

[20] See Golf Terms, p. 210.
[21] See Golf Terms, p. 209.

9. Leave the green immediately after holing out. Record the score after you have left the green.

V. In General

1. Only flat-heeled shoes should be worn on a course. These make possible a better stance. High heels damage the course.

2. If for any reason you are playing slowly, motion the players behind you to go through. Wait until they are out of your range before taking another shot.

GOLF TERMS[22]

Address the Ball. Get into position to play the ball.

Approach Shot. Any shot made with the intention of landing on the green.

Away. The ball farthest from the hole.

Bent. A grass commonly used in the United States on putting greens.

Birdie. One below par.

Bisque. A handicap consisting of strokes to be taken at the choice of the player.

Bulge. The convexity of the face of a golf club.

Bunker. An obstacle placed on the fairway—may be a hummock of soil planted with grass, or a sand trap.

Bye. The holes remaining to be played to determine the winner of the match.

Caddie. A person who carries the golfer's clubs and who can give her advice in regard to the course.

Casual Water. Water which accumulates on a course after a storm, not always present—not part of a hazard.

Cleek. A narrow iron-headed club of little loft.

Closed Stance. The left foot slightly in advance of the right—the player tends to face slightly away from the line of flight of the ball.

Club. The implement with which the ball is struck.

Course. The area within which play is permitted.

Cup. The hole sunk in the green into which the ball must be played in order to terminate play on that hole.

Dead. A ball is said to be "dead" when it lies so near the hole that the putt is a dead certainty. A ball is also said to "fall dead" when it does not run after alighting.

Divot. A piece of turf removed by the club in making a shot.

Dog Leg. A sharp bend in the fairway.

Dormie. One side is said to be "dormie" when it is as many holes ahead as there remain holes to play.

Down. The number of holes or strokes a player is behind an opponent.

Drop the Ball. The player stands facing the hole and drops the ball over her shoulder.

Eagle. Two below par.

Face. The striking surface of the club.

Fairway. The well-kept turf between the tee and the green—usually bounded by rough.

Flag. Marks the spot on the green where the cup is located.

Flight. Division of players according to ability for tournaments; also, the path of the ball in the air.

---

[22] For detailed terms see Herndon, Charles: *Golf Made Easy*, p. 185.

Fore. The warning cry on the golf course.

Four-ball Match. Two players play their better ball against the better ball of their opponents.

Foursome. Two players playing one ball on each side; partners alternate hitting the ball.

Green. The plot of closely cut grass which surrounds the cup—may be level or sloping.

Grip. That part of the club which is grasped and the grasp itself.

Half-shot. A stroke that is less than a full swing.

Halved. Each side makes the same score on a hole.

Hanging Lie. The ball lies on a downward slope.

Hazard. Any obstacle that interferes with the free flight or roll of the ball (natural: trees, natural water, rocks, and so forth; made hazards: bunkers, sand traps, and so forth).

Head of the Club. The heavy part of the club, used for striking the ball.

Heel of the Club. The part of the club head below the point where the shaft and the head meet.

Hole. One unit of the course including the playing tee, fairway, hazards, green, and cup.

Holing Out. Sinking the ball in the cup.

Honor. The privilege of playing first, acquired by winning the preceding hole.

Hook. The flight of the ball curves to the left.

Impact. The contact of the club with the ball.

Irons. A graded series of metal-headed clubs.

Lie. The position of the ball with reference to the ground.

Like. A player is playing "the like" when she makes an equal number of strokes to that just played by her opponent.

Links. The golf course.

Loft. To elevate the ball; also, the angle of pitch of the face of the club.

Loose Impediment. Any obstruction not fixed or growing.

Match. The game itself.

Match Play. Competition by holes; the player winning the most holes wins the match.

Medalist. The low score player in a medal tournament.

Medal Play. Competition by total scores for all holes; the player with the lowest total score wins the match.

Nassau. A system of scoring awarding one point for the winning of each "nine" and an additional point for the match.

Neck. The point at which the shaft joins the head of the club.

Odd. A player is playing "odd" when on a given hole she is making a stroke one more in number than that last played by her opponent.

Open Stance. The left foot is drawn back so the player tends to face somewhat in the direction of the flight of the ball.

Out-of-bounds. The area outside the proper course, from which balls may not be played.

Par. Perfect score for a hole; an arbitrary standard of excellence based on length of hole.

Penalty Stroke. A stroke added to the score of a hole under certain rules.

Playing Through. At the invitation of the group ahead, players behind may pass them and continue play.

Press. An error in stroke caused by trying to hit the ball too hard; an attempt to hit beyond one's normal power.

Pull. A shot which goes to the left without curving.

Push. A shot which goes to the right without curving.

Putt. A stroke taken with the putter in which the ball is rolled along the green.

Rough. The unkept territory surrounding the fairway or green.

Sand Trap. A patch of ground from which the top soil has been removed and sand substituted.

Set. A full complement of clubs.

Shaft. The handle of the club.

Single. One player plays against another.

Slice. The flight of the ball curves to the right.

Sole of the Club. The surface upon which the club rests when addressing the ball. The club is said to be "soled" when this surface is flat on the ground.

Square Stance. An imaginary line from the toe of one shoe to the toe of the other shoe is parallel to the line of flight of the ball.

Stance. The position of the player's feet when addressing the ball.

Stroke. The act of hitting the ball.

Stymie. One ball lies directly in the line of putt of another.

Tee. 1. A small wooden elevation for the ball.

2. The ground from which the ball is put in play—markers on the tee indicate the point behind which the ball is to be played off.

Three-ball Match. Three players each playing her own ball.

Threesome. A match of three players in which two partners play one ball against the ball of the other player.

Toe of the Club. The part of the head opposite the heel; front portion of the club head.

Top. To strike a ball above the center.

Upright. A club is said to be "upright" when the angle between its face and shaft is less than ordinarily obtuse.

Water Hole. A large water hazard which lies between the tee and the green.

Winter Rules. The privilege of improving the lie of the ball on the fairway; used seasonally under local rules.

Woods. A graded series of clubs with wooden heads.

A FEW OF THE MOST IMPORTANT RULES OF GOLF[23]

Honor: Rule 12

The option of taking the honor at the first teeing ground shall, if necessary, be decided by lot. The side which wins the hole shall take the honor at the next teeing ground. If a hole has been halved, the side which had the honor at the previous teeing ground shall retain it.

Lost and Unplayable Balls: Rule 29

1. If a ball is lost or deemed to be unplayable (except in water or casual water), the player shall play the next stroke as nearly as possible at the spot from which the ball that was lost or unplayable was played, adding a penalty stroke to the score for the hole. If the ball is deemed to be unplayable, the player may have the option of dropping and playing the ball under penalty of two strokes provided the ball is dropped as near as possible to the spot from which it was lifted but not nearer to the hole.

2. If the stroke was played from the teeing ground, a ball may be

[23] For the complete official wording see *The Rules of Golf,* United States Golf Association, 1954.

teed; if from the fairway, rough, or a hazard, it shall be dropped; and if on the putting green, it shall be placed.

Out of Bounds Balls: Rule 29

1. If a ball lies out of bounds, the player shall play her next stroke as nearly as possible at the spot from which the ball which is out of bounds was played.

2. If the stroke was played from the teeing ground, a ball may be teed; if from the fairway, rough, or a hazard, it shall be dropped; and if on the putting green, it shall be placed.

How to Drop a Ball: Rule 22

1. The player shall face the hole, stand erect, and drop the ball behind her over her shoulder.

2. If, in dropping, the ball touch the player, she shall incur no penalty; or, if it roll into a hazard or out of bounds, she may re-drop without penalty.

Moving or Bending Fixed or Growing Objects: Rule 17

Before playing a player shall not improve her lie by bending or breaking anything fixed or growing, except:

1. so far as is necessary to enable her fairly to take her stance in addressing the ball.

2. in making her backward and forward swing.

Removal of Loose Impediments: Rule 18

1. Except when the ball lies in or touches a hazard, any loose impediment may be removed without penalty.

2. If the ball move after any loose impediment has been touched, the penalty shall be one stroke.

Play in Hazards: Rule 33

1. When a ball lies in or touches a hazard, the club shall not touch the ground, nor shall anything be touched or moved before the player strikes the ball. (See exception in official rules.)

2. If a ball be completely covered by sand, only so much thereof may be removed as will enable the player to see the top of the ball.

Ball in Water Hazard

1. Rule 33—If a ball lies or is lost in a water hazard, the player may drop a ball, under penalty of one stroke, either behind the water hazard

or as near as possible to the spot from which the original ball was played.

2. Rule 32—If a ball lies or is lost in casual water, the player may drop a ball without penalty as near as possible to the spot where the ball lay but not nearer the hole.

Putting

1. Touching the Line of Putt—Rule 35—The line of putt must not be touched, except in placing the club immediately in front of the ball in addressing it.

2. Moving opponent's ball—Rule 35.

(*a*) If the player's ball knock the opponent's ball into the hole, the opponent shall be deemed to have holed out at her last stroke.

(*b*) If the player's ball move the opponent's ball

1. in match play, the opponent may, if she choose, place the ball as near as possible to the spot from which it was moved.

2. in stroke play, the player incurs a penalty of two strokes, and the ball that was struck shall be replaced.

REFERENCES

Alway, Leonore K.: "Indoor Group Golf Instruction." *Journal of Health and Physical Education,* 9:1, January, 1938.

Armour, Tommy: *How to Play Your Best Golf All the Time.* New York, Simon and Schuster, 1953.

Berg, Pattie, and Dypwich, Otis: *Golf.* New York, A. S. Barnes and Co., 1941.

Brown, Innis, and Rice, Grantland: *How to Play Golf,* and Jones, Bobby: *How I Play Golf.* Spalding's Athletic Library No. 224. New York, American Sports Publishing Co., 1940.

Dante, Joe, and Elliott, Len: *Stop That Slice.* New York, McGraw-Hill Book Co., 1953.

Eastburn, Warrine: "Adaptation of Playing Fields and Gymnasium Equipment to the Teaching of Group Golf." *Athletic Handbook,* Spalding's Athletic Library. New York, American Sports Publishing Co., 1936.

Forrest, James: *Golf Made Easy.* New York, E. P. Dutton and Co., 1934.

Guldahl, Ralph: *Groove Your Golf.* Indianapolis, Bookwalter-Ball-Greathouse Printing Co., 1939.

Harris, Mark G.: *New Angles on Putting and Approaching.* Chicago, Reilly and Lee Co., 1940.

Hartwig, Marie: "An Experimental Study of Fundamental Coaching Factors Influencing the Learning of a Golf Swing." Master's Thesis, University of Michigan, 1938.

Herndon, Charles: *Golf Made Easy.* Los Angeles, Parker, Stone and Baird Co., 1930.

Hicks, Betty: *Fundamentals of Golf.* Chicago, J. A. Dubow Mfg. Co., 1948.

Hogan, Ben: *Power Golf.* New York, A. S. Barnes and Co., 1953. New York, Pocket Books, Inc., 1953.

Jones, Ernest, and Brown, Innis: *Swinging Into Golf.* Revised ed., New York, Robert M. McBride and Co., 1946.

Jones, Robert T.: *How to Run a Golf Tournament.* The American Golf Institute, 19 Beekman St., New York.

Jones, Robert T., Jr.: *Rights and Wrongs of Golf.* A. G. Spalding and Bros., 1935.

Jones, Robert T., Jr., and Lowe, Howard E.: *Group Instruction in Golf.* New York, American Sports Publishing Co., 1939.

Kreatz, Reuben: *Golf in 10 Lessons, with the Rules of Golf and 200 Golf Tips.* San Bernardino, Calif., Golf Publications Co., 1938.

Lindblad, Virginia: "A Guide for Group Instruction in Golf." Master's Thesis, University of Wisconsin, 1943.

Mangrum, Lloyd: *Golf, a New Approach.* New York, McGraw-Hill Book Co., 1949.

Martin, Harry Brownlow: *What's Wrong with Your Golf.* New York, Dodd, Mead and Co., 1930.

Martin, H. B.: *Fifty Years of American Golf.* New York, Dodd, Mead and Co., 1936.

Metz, Dick: *The Secret to Par Golf.* New York, The Macmillan Co., 1940.

Morrison, Alex J.: *A New Way to Better Golf.* New York, Simon and Schuster, 1935.

Morrison, Alex J.: *Better Golf Without Practice.* New York, Simon and Schuster, 1940.

National Golf Foundation: *Golf in Physical Education.* Chicago, 1941.

National Golf Foundation: *Golf Lessons; The Fundamentals as Taught by the Foremost Professional Instructors.* Chicago, 1952.

National Section on Women's Athletics: *Official Individual Sports Guide.* New York, A. S. Barnes and Co.

Nelson, Byron: *Winning Golf.* New York, A. S. Barnes and Co., 1946.

Novak, Joe: *How to Put Power and Direction in Your Golf.* New York, Prentice-Hall, Inc., 1954.

Novak, Joe: *Par Golf in 8 Steps.* New York, Prentice-Hall, Inc., 1950.

Runyan, Paul: "Magic Eye Golf." *Golf,* National Golf Review, Inc., 4:22, Nov., 1940.

Schleman, Helen B., and Hayes, Virginia: *Group Golf Instruction.* New York, A. S. Barnes and Co., 1934.

Snead, Sam: *A Quick Way to Better Golf.* New York, The Sun Dial Press, 1938.

Snead, Sam: *How to Hit a Golf Ball from Any Sort of Lie.* Garden City, N. Y., Blue Ribbon Books, 1950.

Snead, Sam: *How to Play Golf and Professional Tips on Improving Your Score.* New York, Garden City Publishing Co., 1946.

Snead, Sam: *Natural Golf.* New York, A. S. Barnes and Co., 1953.

Stanley, Louis T.: *How to Be a Better Woman Golfer.* New York, Thomas Y. Crowell Co., 1952.

Stein, Jennette A., and Waterman, Emma F.: *Golf for Beginning Players.* Columbus, Ohio, Heer Printing Co., 1938.

Thompson, Ben: *How to Play Golf.* New York, Prentice-Hall, Inc., 1939.

Thompson, Ben: "A High School Golf Program." *Scholastic Coach,* 250 E. 43rd St., New York, 9:21, Nov., 1939; 9:16, Dec., 1939; 9:5, Jan., 1940; 9:18, Feb., 1940; 9:10, March, 1940.

Thompson, Ben: "Putting, Golf's Simplest Swing." *Scholastic Coach,* 9:22, April, 1940.

Thompson, Ben: "Slicing and Pulling." *Golf,* National Golf Review, Inc., 4:15, Nov., 1940.

Woodfin, Gene: "The Teaching of Motor Skill." Master's Thesis, University of Wisconsin, 1946.

Tests

Autrey, Elizabeth P.: "A Battery of Tests for Measuring Playing Ability in Golf." Master's Thesis, University of Wisconsin, 1937.

Coffey, Margaret: "Achievement Tests in Golf." Master's Thesis, University of Iowa, 1946.

Glassow, Ruth B., and Broer, Marion R.: *Measuring Achievement in Physical Education*. Philadelphia, W. B. Saunders Co., 1938.

Lumpkin, Margaret: "Evaluation of a Putting Test in Golf." Unpublished Study for Master's Degree, Wellesley College, 1940.

Waglow, I. F., and Rehling, C. H.: "A Golf Knowledge Test." *Research Quarterly*, 24:463-470, Dec. 1953.

Watts, Harriet: "The Construction and Evaluation of a Target for Testing the Approach Shot in Golf." Master's Thesis, University of Wisconsin, 1942.

Wright, Dorothy L.: "Measures for Evaluating Some of the Skills Used in Playing Golf." Master's Thesis, University of California, 1942.

Visual Aids

Bernhard, Frederica, and Flory, Elizabeth H.: *Educational Films in Sports*. The American Film Center, Inc., 1946. (Write to Elizabeth H. Flory, Educational Film Library Association, Inc., 45 Rockefeller Plaza, New York 20, N. Y.)

Sports, Physical Education and Recreation Film Guide, Business Screen Magazine in cooperation with the Athletic Institute, Vol. 1, No. 1, May, 1947. (Write to Film Guide Department, The Athletic Institute, 209 S. State St., Chicago 4, Illinois.)

Rules

The Rules of Golf. New York, United States Golf Association, 1954 Edition, Distributed by Wilson Sporting Goods Co.

6 · RIDING · BY *Evelyn Jennings*

When riding in an automobile, a person may be either a passenger or the driver, but when on a horse one should always be the driver and never merely a passenger on the animal's back. This means that the rider determines the speed and direction in which her horse moves. When all is left to the horse's discretion, the would-be rider is not safe. Moreover she will miss one of the supreme enjoyments of the true horsewoman which is the moving of the rider in harmony with a well-controlled horse. To establish this feeling of control and harmony, a firm seat and correct use of the aids, which are the hands, legs, weight, and voice, must be developed. Once a student feels the difference between the "driver" and the "passenger" attitudes, her interest increases, with the result that she puts forth more effort and improves faster.

This chapter is written for the experienced rider who is teaching or who intends to teach, not for the novice. For this reason elementary techniques, such as approaching the horse, leading the horse, adjustment of stirrups, mount, dismount, and so forth, are not described, since it is assumed that anyone qualified to teach riding would already know these things. Emphasis is placed throughout on methods of developing horsewomen capable of riding all types of horses, and a description of technique is used only as a means of clarifying the procedure of the exercises for learning how to ride and how properly to apply the aids.

Before the more specific ways and means of developing "drivers" and not "passengers" are discussed, a few general suggestions are given which are essential to the creation of this attitude. First it is necessary that an instructor spend time in developing the student's confidence. Great care should be taken in the selection of a horse for the rider who lacks confidence. She should be given a horse that is quiet, well-mannered, and "easy-gaited." The timid student is an individual problem and it is impossible to say whether she will acquire confidence in a week or a month. Some pupils need to be made to do a little more than they believe they are able to do in order to develop their confidence. Others should not be forced at all but permitted to do only as much as they wish. An instructor helps the timid rider by being patient and encouraging, and doing everything in her power to prevent anything happening that will destroy whatever confidence a pupil has gained.

Many accidents can be prevented if the instructor is alert and foresighted. Following are a few illustrations of alertness and foresightedness that contribute to the safety of the group and give the students confidence in the instructor, which is essential to the development of their own confidence. (1) Keep the speed of the class steady. Do not permit the trot or canter to get faster and faster. (2) Know thoroughly the dispositions of the horses used in classes so that one is aware of what a particular horse might do. Often if the instructor knows a horse's characteristics, she can see the animal getting ready to do something, and can prevent it from happening by bringing the group to a walk or stop. (3) Walk (do not trot or canter) by anything that *might* cause a horse to shy. (4) When crossing a road allow space for the entire class to cross. If necessary stop traffic, but never leave half the class on one side of the road and the rest on the other. (5) Never canter on the way toward the stable. (6) A general admonition to follow is: if there is a doubt in your mind whether to do a thing or not, *don't do it*, because there is a reason for that doubt being there.

It is better to be over-cautious than careless, not only because of the element of danger involved, but because of the necessity for developing a student's confidence in herself, the horse, and her instructor. As the confidence of the rider grows, her ability will improve.

A second general suggestion is that during a lesson, emphasis should be placed on whatever a particular class needs the most. Although there is always a general plan for the season, it is impossible to develop riders if the program is not elastic and consideration not given the progress each class has made. If an instructor plans her work in an inflexible way, she may be asking some classes to attempt more than they are capable of doing. For example, she may plan that in the sixth lesson every intermediate class shall learn to canter. If the class is slow to progress, better results are obtained in the end by working on whatever its greatest need is, rather than by pushing it beyond its ability.

To develop horsemanship a third necessity is to have various types of horses in the stable. When a student has confidence and can control a quiet, well-mannered, "easy-gaited" horse, she should be given a horse that requires a little more handling. She should also ride horses whose gaits are not so easy. As the rider's ability improves, she should be given horses that are more sensitive and require more horsemanship. The stubborn horse is needed in order to teach the rider to use her legs and hands correctly. A pupil can progress only so far on the good, quiet beginner's horse. When that point is reached, a different type of horse is essential to insure further progress. An instructor tells the rider how to do something, but it is the horse that gives the pupil the feeling of doing it. For this reason, it is necessary that the string of horses in the stable be varied as to gaits, mouths, "free-goingness," and playfulness.

One more point should be mentioned—the attire of the rider. Even though a rider cannot afford a complete riding habit, the instructor should insist that each student wear breeches or jodhpurs, a shirt, and tie. Blue jeans and slacks should be permitted on the day that a class is riding bareback.

Since an instructor should have some knowledge of the equipment—namely, the horse and the tack—a brief section on this is included before the more specific discussion of riding.

EQUIPMENT

Only the major points about the equipment are covered in this section. An instructor who is responsible for the care of the horses and the tack should acquire a greater knowledge of the subject than is presented here.

I. The Horse

(A) *The Parts of the Horse.* The parts of the horse are shown in Fig. 93.

(B) *The Care of the Horse.*

1. GROOMING.

Implements. Currycomb, dandy brush, body brush, grooming cloth, mane and tail comb, hoof pick.

Procedure. The horse should be groomed daily. Start at the neck

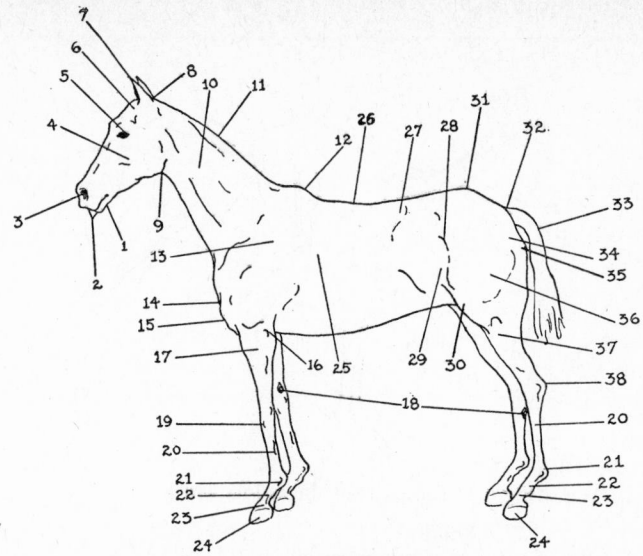

Fig. 93. The parts of the horse.

1. Chin	11. Crest	20. Cannon bone	29. Flank
2. Lips	12. Withers	21. Fetlock or	30. Stifle
3. Nostril	13. Shoulder	fetlock joint	31. Croup
4. Cheek	14. Point of	22. Pastern	32. Dock
5. Eye	shoulder	23. Coronet	33. Tail
6. Forehead	15. Chest	24. Hoof	34. Buttock
7. Ear	16. Elbow	25. Barrel	35. Point of rump
8. Poll	17. Forearm	26. Back	36. Thigh
9. Throat	18. Chestnut	27. Loins	37. Gaskin
10. Neck	19. Knee	28. Point of hip	38. Hock

on the left side of the horse. Use the currycomb, both in small circles and back and forth, over that entire side, working toward the hindquarters. On the legs do not use the currycomb below the knee and the hock. Also it is never used on the head or face. Now go to the right side and curry the horse.

Return to the left side of the horse and take the dandy brush. Brush first the horse's head and face and then continue over the animal's body in the order in which the currycomb was used, but brushing with the hair. With the brush, however, his legs should be brushed all the way to the hoof.

Next use the body brush on his entire body. Brush and comb his mane and tail. With the hoof pick clean out his feet. Wipe him off with the grooming cloth to remove any remaining dust.

2. FEEDING AND WATERING.

Daily Schedule. In the morning the horse should be fed and

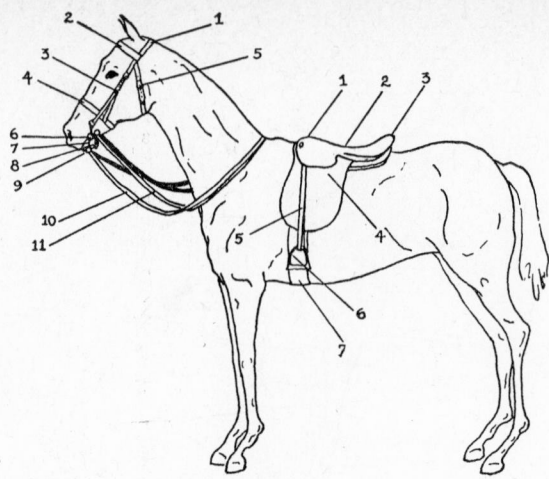

Fig. 94. The parts of the saddle and bridle.

The Bridle		The Saddle
1. Head stall	7. Curb bit or bit	1. Pommel
2. Brow band	8. Curb chain	2. Seat
3. Cheek straps	9. Lip strap	3. Cantle
4. Cavesson	10. Curb rein	4. Skirt
5. Throat latch	11. Snaffle rein	5. Stirrup leather
6. Snaffle bit or bridoon		6. Stirrup iron
		7. Girth

watered in this order: hay, grain, and *at least one hour later,* water. At noon and in the evening this order should be followed: water, hay, grain. In the late evening the horse should again be watered.

Amount of Feed.

A rule that should be followed is that a horse's daily ration should be increased when his work is heavier and decreased as his work becomes lighter.

The exact amount to be fed a horse cannot be given. Each horse will have to be watched to determine whether he is getting the proper amount of feed, since horses, just as people, vary in the amount of food required to maintain a good physical condition. As a basis to go on, the estimate of one large riding school of the amount of feed used when the horses are working is given. This stable figures 8 quarts of grain and 12 pounds of hay per day per horse. However, some of the horses need only 6 quarts of grain a day to remain in good condition, while others require 12.

Salt should be available to the horse at all times.

Amount of water. Under normal conditions a horse requires about

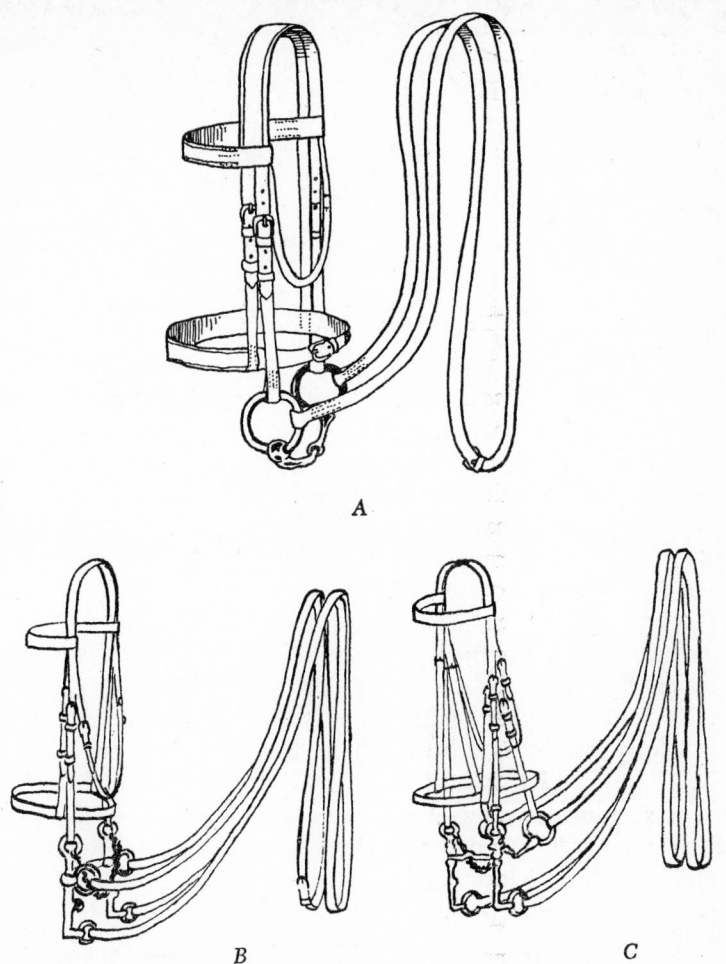

A

B   C

Fig. 95. Types of bridles. *A*, Snaffle bridle. *B*, Pelham bridle. *C*, Weymouth bridle.

8 gallons of water a day. If the weather is very warm or if the horse has worked hard, he will require more.

3. SHOEING. As soon as a horse's shoes are worn he should be shod. At the end of four weeks the horse should always have his shoes removed and his feet trimmed even if he has not been ridden enough to wear his shoes thin.

II. The Tack

(A) *Parts of the Saddle and Bridle.* The parts of the saddle and bridle are shown in Fig. 94.

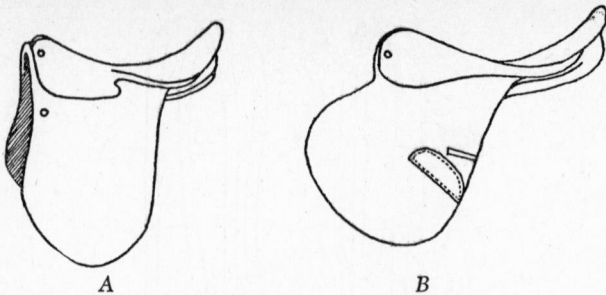

Fig. 96. Types of English saddles. *A*, Hacking. *B*, Forward seat.

(B) *Care of the Tack.* Each day the tack should be thoroughly cleaned with saddle soap and a damp sponge. All the leather should be treated with neat's-foot oil at least six times a year. Steel wool or scouring powder should be used to polish the metal parts.

(C) *The Most Commonly Used Bridles* (Fig. 95). Which bridle should be used is determined by the sensitiveness of the horse's mouth and the work he is required to do.

(D) *The Most Commonly Used English Saddles* (Fig. 96). The style of riding taught or the type of work the horse performs determines which saddle is used.

(E) *The Two Types of Martingales.* A martingale is used on a horse which carries his head too high, tosses it or throws it up suddenly. There are two kinds of martingales—the running and the standing. The standing martingale is a single strap that runs from the girth to the cavesson. The running martingale starts in a single leather at the girth and then divides into two leathers with a ring on each through which the snaffle reins pass.

DESCRIPTION OF THE FUNDAMENTAL POSITION (Fig. 97)

The fundamental position is described first because it is from this point that the rider varies her position and moves her body in accordance with the horse's movements and actions.

(A) The stirrup iron is straight across the widest part of the rider's boot.

(B) The inside of the foot is on the lowest point of the stirrup so that the sole of the boot and the stirrup are at an angle to the ground.

(C) The pressure is on the inner border of the foot.

(D) The heel is lower than any other part of the foot.

(E) The stirrup leather hangs perpendicular to the ground.

(F) The widest part of the horse's barrel is the point at which the

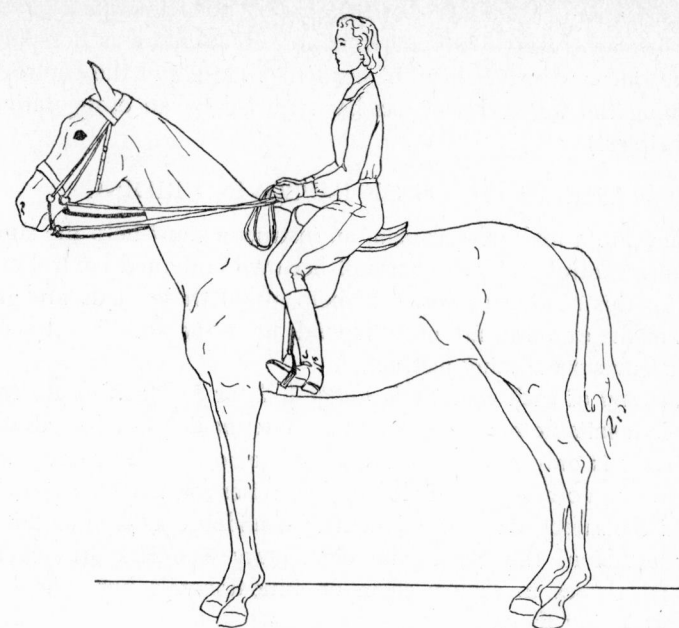

Fig. 97. Fundamental position.

rider's leg begins to have contact with the horse. From this point up, the lower leg, knee, and thigh are always in contact. Below this point the leg only makes contact when it is being applied as an aid in turning or urging the horse forward.

(G) The kneecap points straight ahead.

(H) The rider sits well forward in the saddle.

(I) The spine is erect but not stiff.

(J) The upper arm hangs naturally at the side with the elbow falling just in front of the hip joint.

(K) The thumb is higher than any other part of the hand and is on top of the reins.

(L) If a double bridle is used, the little finger separates the curb and snaffle reins.

(M) The wrist is slightly rounded.

(N) The hands are as far forward as the withers.

(O) The hands are separated and at a height that puts them as nearly as possible in a direct line with the horse's mouth.

(P) The rider looks straight ahead.

(Q) As the horse moves forward at a faster speed, the rider's weight moves forward with him and comes back with a decrease in pace.

Great care should be taken that the student does not exaggerate this principle of the weight moving forward. If attention is not paid to this, the rider is always ahead of her horse. (Much of the controversy concerning the forward seat has been caused by an exaggeration of its principles.)

THE METHODS OF IMPROVING RIDING

To develop a real horsewoman, an instructor must help the student to acquire control and proper use of her own body and control of her horse. In this section exercises to help attain these goals are given. Which of the exercises are used depends upon the ability and need of the particular class being instructed.

At the end of each exercise is found 1, 2, or 3, which means that 1 is safe and suitable for beginners, 2 for intermediates, 3 for advanced. This listing is only approximate because some classes progress faster or slower than others. When choosing exercises for a class, always bear in mind the safety and development of confidence as well as the particular needs of the class. The elementary exercises are given to advanced classes to review them on fundamentals but time is not spent practicing them.

When work without reins and stirrups is done, the instructor should be sure of the dependability of the horses used. When a class rides without reins, it is better to have the first rider in the line keep her reins and act as a leader. If the ring is not enclosed or the instructor feels that it is unsafe for the horses to be free without reins, such work may be safely done in the following manner: The riders work in pairs. One student takes the reins of her partner's horse and leads her while the other student rides without her reins. Unless otherwise stated, when the exercises are done at a jog, the rider sits. Many of these exercises greatly aid the development of the rider's confidence as well as improve her ability. Some of them serve more than one purpose. For example, drilling bareback is aiding the rider's control, firmness of seat, balance, and use of the legs.

I. Development of Better Use and Control of the Body

(A) *A Firm Seat.* A firm seat means that the rider is secure and able to remain with her horse when the mount moves in any direction or at any speed. A good seat is a combination of contact and balance. It is necessary to develop this contact and balance, otherwise the student will depend on her reins and stirrups for security. It will then be impossible ever to develop a good hand, correct use of the legs, a feeling of being in balance with the horse, or control, because the pupil

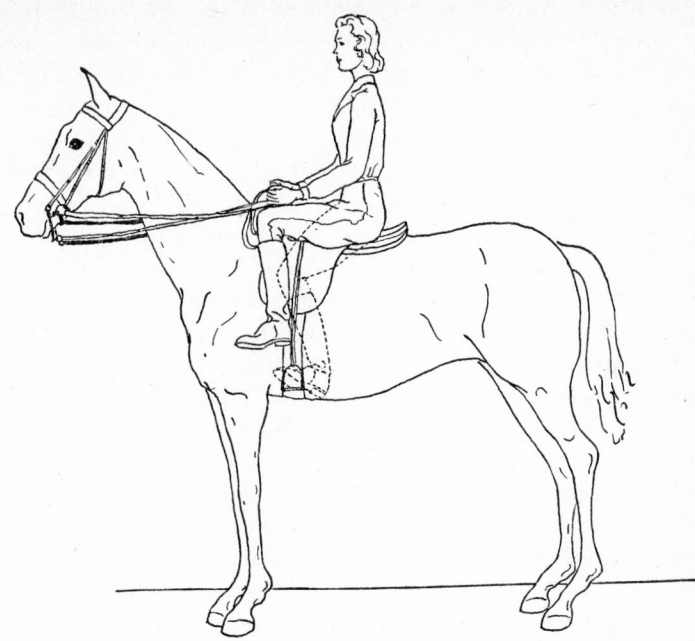

Fig. 98. Attainment of position of buttocks in the saddle.

will be stiff and tense from pushing on the stirrups and will, for the sake of security, be hanging on to the reins with unnecessary harshness. Also there are times when a horse becomes unruly and to control him the rider must "sit down." If this "sitting down" is not learned when the horse is moving quietly, the instructor cannot hope that the student will do it when the need arises merely because she has been told that it is the correct thing to do. The rider must learn the feeling of putting the weight on to the seat and upper thighs.

Following are the methods of developing this firmness of seat.

1. ATTAINMENT OF THE POSITION OF THE BUTTOCKS IN THE SADDLE. Take the feet out of the stirrups. Sit well forward in the saddle. Draw the legs up until the thighs are parallel with the horse's spine. Draw the hips under, and straighten but do not stiffen the spine. The upper body is erect. Drop the thighs until the legs and feet are in the correct position. (Refer to page 223 for correct position.) The position of the hips and upper body remains unchanged. There is a contact but no squeezing with the thighs, knees, and upper portion of the lower legs. *1, 2, 3.* (Fig. 98.)

2. WALK WITHOUT STIRRUPS. Weight is on the buttocks. There is only contact with the legs. There is no gripping or squeezing with the

thighs, knees, and upper portion of the lower leg. The upper body is erect. The waist is loose so that the seat can move with the motion of the horse. The class is stopped and the position corrected as often as necessary by doing exercise 1. *1, 2, 3*.

3. WALK WITH STIRRUPS. Everything is the same as in exercise 2, except that the feet are in the stirrups. Only the weight of the feet and lower legs is on the stirrups. A way of making clear what is meant by the weight of the feet and lower legs only in the stirrups is to have each member of the class lightly drop one hand on her thigh. Now only the weight of the hand and arm rests on the thigh. Next the student pushes down on her hands and feels the difference in the amount of weight that is thrown on the thigh. Now have the pupil lightly drop her feet on to the stirrups and then have her push down on the irons to feel the contrast of the correct and incorrect way. *1, 2, 3*.

4. SIT A SLOW TROT WITH THE STIRRUPS.

(*a*) With Stirrups the Correct Length: The position and emphasis are the same as in exercise 3, plus the fact that the jar received from the horse is now greater, so that it is more necessary to keep the weight on the buttocks and the ankles and spine flexible. The class is stopped as often as necessary so that it may correct its faults at a walk. At first the pupils are capable of jogging only a few steps without losing their positions because they become tense and increase the weight in their stirrups. As the class improves the length and speed of the trot are increased. *1, 2, 3*.

(*b*) With Very Short Stirrups: Take the stirrups up so short that the thighs are almost parallel with the horse's spine. The upper body is erect and the spine is flexible. With the stirrups this short the rider is forced to balance on her buttocks and is unable to push down on her stirrups. This is not given to a class until it can control the horses at a jog. *2, 3*.

5. SIT A SLOW TROT WITHOUT THE STIRRUPS. The position of the seat, thighs, and knees remains unchanged. There is no gripping to stay on— only a contact. The lower leg is either held in the position it would be in if the foot were in the stirrup or allowed to hang completely relaxed from the knee down. Whichever position of the lower leg is used, it does not drop under the horse's barrel, so the rider is holding on with her heels. The class is stopped as often as necessary to correct its position at a walk. The length and speed of the jog are increased as the class improves. *1, 2, 3*.

6. WALK AND TROT WITHOUT REINS. The reins are knotted on the horse's neck. Arms are folded on the chest. The class walks, sits a jog, and posts a trot. When posting a trot the rider must post forward and

up, not just straight up, to remain in balance with her horse. This exercise gives the rider the feeling of maintaining her balance without the aid of the reins. If the horses will respond to the instructor's voice, the speed is varied by her commands, and the riders do not touch the reins for a change of pace. *1, 2, 3.*

7. POSTING WITHOUT STIRRUPS. The feet, lower legs, and thighs are held as if they were in the stirrups. The rider's body is inclined slightly forward from the hips. She rises forward and up only as much as is absolutely necessary to be in rhythm with the horse. No aid or support should be received from the reins. As the rider rises it is necessary for her to grip slightly with her knees. This exercise is very tiring and should always be alternated with sitting at a jog. *2, 3.*

8. CANTERING WITHOUT STIRRUPS. Looseness through the waist and keeping of contact with the legs are essential. The class canters first with the upper body erect so that the buttocks slide back and forth on the saddle. Only when the students can "polish the saddle with the seats of their breeches," do they canter with the upper bodies inclined forward from the hips. Now the buttocks leave the saddle slightly. *2, 3.*

9. RIDING WITHOUT REINS OR STIRRUPS. This is done at a walk, jog, and trot. The reins are knotted on the horse's neck. Leg and body positions are the same as when the feet are in the stirrups. Arms are folded on the chest. The class varies its speed. If possible this should be controlled by the instructor's voice. *2, 3.*

10. RIDING BAREBACK. The rider pulls her hips well under her so that she sits on the fleshy part of the buttocks. The bend in the thighs is the same as when the feet are in the stirrups. The lower legs hang relaxed from the knees down and are in contact with the horse where they naturally fall against his sides. They do not drop under him. At first the class only walks and slow jogs bareback, but as its ability improves, all gaits are ridden. *1* (walk and very slow jog), *2, 3.*

(B) *Flexibility of the Rider.* Many of the exercises given under the other sections will also improve the rider's flexibility. She will also lose her stiffness as she gains confidence and courage.

When a horse moves there is a jar which must be absorbed by the rider's joints. If these joints are stiff and rigid, the rider is jolted and jostled.

Stiffness and its effect on the rider's ability and comfort can be shown very well by the instructor sitting a slow jog. First sit correctly with loose, flexible joints, and then stiffen, especially the ankles and spine. Point out how the whole body is affected by the lack of flexibility. The hands are bounced so they cannot keep contact with the horse's mouth; the rider is jarred up and down in the saddle, and the stirrup irons bounce back under the arches. Sit correctly again and emphasize the greater comfort and security when the rider is flexible.

Following are the methods of improving the rider's flexibility:

1. EXERCISES FOR THE ANKLES.

(*a*) Without Stirrups. The position of the rider from the calves of her legs upward is not altered. These exercises are done at a walk and jog.

(*1*) Make small circles with the feet. The movement is down, in, and up. *1, 2, 3.*

(*2*) Let the toes drop toward the ground and then pull them up as high as possible (the down motion is merely a relaxation of the muscles). The effort is on the up movement. *1, 2, 3.*

(*3*) The lower leg, without dropping under the horse, hangs as relaxed as possible from the knee down. *1, 2, 3.*

(*b*) With Stirrups.

(*1*) Keep the ankles as flexible as possible so that they can give up and down with the motion of the horse. If the ankles are flexible, the stirrup iron will remain under the ball of the foot. Practice at a jog. *1, 2, 3.*

(*2*) Lift the balls of the feet from the stirrups by pulling the toes up. This allows the stirrups to drop back under the arches. Then kick the stirrups forward again to the balls of the feet. Practice at a walk, jog, trot, and canter. *1* (at walk and jog), *2, 3* (at all gaits).

(*3*) Tap the balls of the feet quickly up and down on the stirrups. The motion comes from the ankle joint and the range of movement is small. Perform at a walk and jog. *1, 2, 3.*

(*c*) Ride in Jumping Position. With lower legs and thighs in correct position and reins shorter, place the hands on either side of the horse's neck just in front of the withers. Lift the buttocks out of the saddle and incline the trunk diagonally forward from the hip joint. Keep weight on the hands to avoid losing balance and jerking the horse's mouth while the buttocks are out of the saddle. If the joints of the legs are flexible, the stirrup leather perpendicular to the ground, and the weight forward, the rider will have no difficulty in staying up. Practice at a walk, jog, trot, and canter. *1* (at walk and jog), *2* (walk, jog, and trot), *3* (at all gaits).

2. EXERCISES FOR THE HIPS AND SPINE.

(*a*) The reins are in the left hand with no fingers between them, but are snug enough to control the horse. Bend down and touch the right toe with the hand. Come up to the correct position in the saddle. Change the reins quickly to the right hand. Bend down and touch the left toe with the left hand. Repeat. The feet do not move forward to meet the hand as the rider bends down. They remain in the correct position (refer to page 223) throughout the exercise. This is done at a stand, walk, jog, and trot. *1* (at stand and walk), *2* (at stand, walk, and jog), *3* (at walk, jog, and trot).

(*b*) Place the left hand, with the reins in it, on the crest of the neck. Put the right on the cantle of the saddle. Stand up. Twist the body as far as possible to the right. Remain in that position for seven or eight steps. Sit down. Rise again with the position of the hands and the body twist reversed. Practice at a stand, walk, trot, and canter. *1* (at stand and walk), *2* (at stand, walk, and trot), *3* (at all gaits).

(*c*) Knot the reins on the horse's neck. Remain seated in the saddle. Raise both arms to shoulder level. Twist the trunk slowly from one side to the other. Perform at a stand, walk, and jog. *1* (at stand and walk), *2, 3* (at stand, walk, and jog).

(*d*) With the reins in the left hand, bend forward and touch the poll with the right hand. Reach back and touch the croup. Change reins and repeat to the opposite side. This is done at a walk, jog, trot, and canter. *1, 2* (at walk, jog, and trot), *3* (at all gaits).

NOTE: This exercise may be made instructive by having the students touch various parts of the horse and tack as they are named.

(*e*) Knot the reins on the horse's neck. Lean back until the head rests on the horse. Remain there a few seconds. Come to the sitting position. Repeat. The legs remain as still as possible while doing this exercise. Practice at a stand and walk. *1, 2, 3*.

3. EXERCISES FOR SHOULDERS, ARMS, AND WRISTS.

(*a*) The reins are knotted on the horse's neck. Shrug the shoulders and arms, and shake the hands to get the shoulders, arms, and wrists as loose as possible. This is done at a stand, walk, and jog. *1, 2, 3*.

(*b*) Reins are the same as in (*a*). Hold hands as if reins were in them. Use the arms to draw the hands slowly toward the body and to move them slowly away. This movement is slow and soft. Practice at a stand. *1, 2, 3*.

(*c*) Reins are the same as in (*a*). Hold hands as if reins were in them. Bend the wrists slowly so the tips of the thumbs move toward each other. Then slowly straighten them. The movement is very soft and slow. The wrists should not bend so far that they become stiff. Practice at a stand. *2, 3*.

(*d*) Combine exercises (*a*) and (*b*). *2, 3*.

(C) *Control of the Lower Leg.* These exercises are for the purpose of aiding the rider to get the feeling of a correct and controlled leg position. The leg position is described on pages 222 and 223.

Fig. 99. Exercise (*C*) 2 for improvement of lower leg control.

1. With feet in the stirrups and the stirrup leathers hanging perpendicular to the ground, relax the thighs, lower legs, and feet, so that the feet and lower legs drop under the horse, and the thighs and knees fall away from the saddle. Next, move the feet directly to the side so that they are brought out from under the horse, the pressure coming on to the inner side of the feet and bringing the knees and thighs into contact with the saddle. Hold this position. Repeat. Practice at a stand, walk, and jog. *1, 2, 3.*

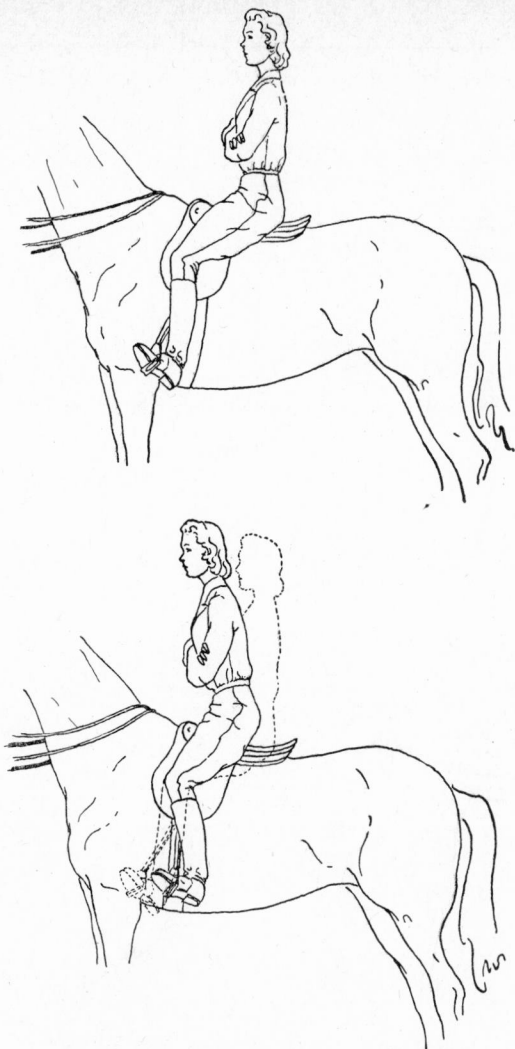

Fig. 100. Exercise (C) 4 for improvement of lower leg control.

2. The feet are in the stirrups correctly and reins in the hands. Place the hands on the withers of the horse. Rise in the stirrups and lean on the hands for support so the upper body is forward and buttocks are off the saddle. Put the weight that falls into the stirrups toward the toes of the feet. Now shift the weight so that it falls on the back edge of stirrup. Remaining out of the saddle, shift the weight back and forth from the front edge to the back edge of the stirrup. This shifting back and forth of the weight gives a contrast of the two weight lines.

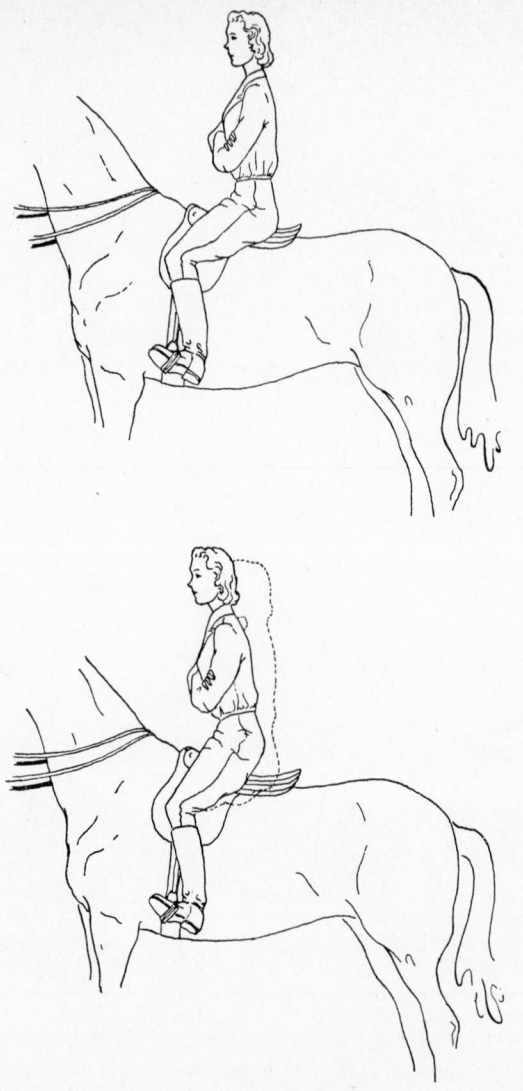

Fig. 101. Exercise (*C*) 4 for improvement of lower leg control.

When the weight comes down the legs on to the front edge of the stirrup, the heels come up and the rider is overbalanced forward. When it falls on to the back edge of the stirrup, the heels drop and the rider is balanced and more secure. Perform at a stand, walk, jog, and trot. *1* (at stand, walk, and jog), *2, 3* (at stand, walk, jog, and trot). (Fig. 99.)

3. (a) The feet are in the stirrups correctly and the reins are in the hands. Place the hands on the withers of the horse for support. Stand up in the stirrups, inclining upper body forward from the hip joints. While up, force the heels down and the pressure to the inner side of the feet. Sit down keeping the lower legs and feet the same. Consider the knee as a hinge that opens on the "up" and closes on the "down." At this hinge is the point where the motion of the rising and sitting takes place. Practice at a stand, walk, and trot. 1, 2, 3.

(b) The same as (a) except that the "up" and "down" is a continuous movement. The lower legs are held as still as possible throughout the exercise. Practice at a stand, walk, and trot. 1, 2, 3.

4. The feet are in the stirrups and the reins knotted on the horse's neck. Fold the arms on the chest. Move both feet forward so that the stirrup-leather is on a diagonal line in relation to the ground. Stand up. Note the amount of effort that it requires to rise and that the feet are under the body while "up." Sit down and allow the feet to go forward. Now bend the knee until the stirrup-leather is perpendicular to the ground. Rise, using the knee joint as a hinge. Note the difference in the expenditure of energy required to rise, and that the feet remain under the body whether up or down. Practice at a walk and trot. Do this a greater number of times in the correct rather than the incorrect position. 1, 2, 3. (Figs. 100, 101.)

5. Without the stirrups, hold the feet and lower legs in the correct position. Do this at a stand, walk, and jog. 1, 2, 3.

II. The Development of the Aids

The four aids which make it possible for the rider to control her horse are the hands, the legs, the weight, and the voice. In this section each one is discussed separately. The use of each is explained and various methods of developing them are described.

(A) *Use of the Hands.* The hands control the speed at which the horse moves forward and the direction in which his forequarters move. This control must be accomplished with the lightest possible pressure on the horse's mouth. In other words "good hands" must be developed to use the hands properly.

Ability to stay on an unruly horse does not mean that a person is a good horsewoman. The rider who is not only able to remain on, but who can quiet the horse, is the real horsewoman. A good hand is one that never applies any more pressure on the reins than is absolutely necessary. This means that a person with a good hand is firm when the mount requires firmness but never when he does not need it. A good hand is always in contact with the horse's mouth, is flexible, never stiff, slowly and determinedly pulls the horse to a slower speed, never snatches or jerks him to reduce his pace. The rider always rewards the animal by giving with her hands when the horse responds.

Because of the difference in the lightness of horses' mouths, it is necessary that a student ride both hard-mouthed and light-mouthed horses. If she is always on a hard-mouthed horse her hands will always be heavy, and if she is always on a light-mouthed horse she will never be able to hold a "puller." To learn the feeling of the amount of firmness required in the hand and how it varies with each horse must be acquired by riding horses with different kinds of mouths.

A person cannot have a truly good hand until she has a firm seat, but from the very first riding lesson as much as possible is done to develop good hands. The first steps in acquiring hands are learning to keep a light contact with the horse's mouth and to move the hands slowly and steadily. This is started in the very first lesson.

Classes are often helped to understand what is meant when commonplace comparisons are used as examples. The reins may be compared to telegraph or telephone wires over which messages are received. If the wire is not connected no message can be received until it has been connected. In a like manner the reins deliver messages to the rider from the horse. If the reins are not held snugly enough to keep a connection between the rider's hand and the horse's mouth, a message cannot be received until the slack in the reins has been taken up. If the rider maintains the necessary contact with the horse's mouth, all messages are received promptly.

Stopping or slowing a horse may be compared to reducing the speed of a car or bicycle. A good driver, except in cases of emergency, very gradually brings his car or bicycle to a slower speed by slowly and steadily applying pressure to the brakes. When the vehicle has reached the desired slower speed, he removes the pressure on the brakes. When stopping or slowing a horse, the reins are similar to the brakes. The pressure on them is gradually applied and then released when the desired response is gained.

Following are ways of developing good hands. The exercises are grouped under two headings: 1. contact with the horse's mouth; 2. flexibility and softness of movement. They are classified in this manner because it is impossible to have flexibility and softness of movement at any gait until the student has learned to maintain a "feeling" of the horse's mouth at that gait.

1. CONTACT WITH THE HORSE'S MOUTH.

(*a*) At a Stand. Move the hands forward so that the reins are slack. Draw the hands, without any tenseness, slowly toward the body until the reins are just snug. Release the contact by moving the hands forward and repeat. With each attempt to get the lightest possible "feeling" of the horse's mouth. *1, 2, 3.*

(*b*) At a Walk.

(*1*) Repeat exercise (*a*) holding the contact for ten or fifteen steps and then releasing it. With each attempt try to get the contact lighter and the hands more relaxed. *1, 2, 3.*

(*2*) Watch the motion of the horse's head as he walks. To maintain contact the rider's hands move with this motion. Walk around the ring following the motion of the horse's head with the hands maintaining the lightest possible contact and keeping the hands as relaxed as possible. *1, 2, 3.*

(*c*) At a Slow Jog: Before a rider is capable of keeping contact with the horse's mouth at this gait, she must be able to sit a jog correctly. Jog around the ring maintaining the lightest possible feeling of the horse's mouth to keep him at the desired speed. The hands are still. *1, 2, 3.*

(*d*) At a Trot: Post a trot keeping the pressure on the reins as light on the "up" as on the "down." *1, 2, 3.*

(*e*) At a Canter: Canter around the ring. The hands move backward and forward with the horse's head to maintain contact with his mouth. *1, 2, 3.*

(*f*) While Shortening the Reins: Use the right hand to shorten the left rein. Contact is kept on the left rein by the right thumb and index finger as the left hand slides down the left rein. On the right rein, while shortening the left, a feeling of the horse's mouth is maintained by tipping the little finger side of the right hand toward the body as much as necessary to keep the required snugness of the right rein. Repeat shortening the right rein with the left hand. Practice slowly at first. Gradually increase the speed with which it is performed as the ability of the class to maintain contact without jerking improves. Practice this at a stand, walk, trot, and canter. The pace of the horse should not increase while the reins are being shortened. *1* (at stand, walk, and trot), *2, 3* (at all gaits).

(*g*) While Turning or Keeping a Horse Moving in a Given Path:

(*1*) At a Stand: Maintain a very light contact on both reins. Gradually increase the pressure on the right rein until the horse's head is turned slightly to the right. As the horse's head turns to the right, the left hand releases the tension on the left rein. Maintain a light contact on the left rein. Change the position of the horse's head by applying pressure on the left rein and decreasing it on the right rein. *1, 2, 3.*

(*2*) At a Walk: Increase the pressure on the rein that is on the inside of the turn. The outside rein is brought against the horse's neck. The pressure on the outside rein is decreased as it is increased on the inside rein, but contact should not be lost. The horse is gently and gradually guided around the turn. His body is bent slightly in the direction of the turn, the hands bending his forequarters and the legs, which are considered next, bending his hindquarters. *1, 2, 3.*

(3) At a Jog, Trot, and Canter: The greater the speed, the larger the space that is needed to turn the horse correctly. At all gaits the hands gently guide the horse around the turn and there is an increased pressure only on the inside rein. *1* (at jog and trot), *2, 3* (at all gaits).

NOTE: The use of legs when turning a horse is described under Use of Legs on page 238.

2. FLEXIBILITY AND SOFTNESS OF MOVEMENT.

(*a*) Exercises for the Shoulders, Arms, and Wrists (see page 229).

(*b*) Walk and Stop.   The hands are drawn slowly toward the body to stop the horse. If a slight rounding of the wrists is sufficient, the arms are not used. If more pressure than the rounding of the wrists is needed, then the arms draw the hands closer to the body. As soon as the horse responds, the increased tension of the reins is released slightly and then applied again and released, and so forth. The movement is slow, smooth, and soft but determined enough to bring the desired response. The wrists should not be rounded so far that they become stiff. *1* (without rounding the wrists), *2, 3.*

(*c*) Jog and Walk.   The same as "walk and stop," always keeping the movement soft, smooth, and as light as possible. *1* (if capable of keeping contact), *2, 3.*

(*d*) Changes of Pace.   Vary the pace from a walk to a jog, to a walk, to a trot, and so forth. At all gaits the arms, shoulders, and wrists are flexible, only the necessary amount of pressure is applied, the hands give as soon as the horse responds, the movement is slow and smooth, and pressure is released slightly when increasing the pace. *1* (if capable of keeping contact), *2, 3.*

(B) *Use of the Legs.*   The legs are used to create the forward motion of the horse and to control the direction in which his hindquarters move. They, as the hands, are never used with any more force than is necessary to get the desired response.

Not using the legs may be compared to driving a car without any gas in the tank. If there is a hill the car will coast down it and may have enough momentum to reach a gas station. The driver is entirely dependent upon the momentum received from the hill for the distance his car will coast. Riding a horse and not using the legs makes the rider entirely dependent upon the horse's desire to move forward just as the driver of the car without any gas in the tank is dependent upon the hill for motion. A horse may move forward because he is free-going or because he is following the horse ahead of him. A person whose horse moves forward only because he wishes to is a passenger. A rider always has her legs in readiness to apply with whatever degree of severity is necessary to create the forward motion.

When turning or keeping a horse moving in a direction that he does not wish to go, it is essential that the legs be used both to keep him moving forward and to keep his hindquarters in line. Without leg pressure there may be a loss of forward movement, and only his head is pulled over toward where the rider desires to go.

To learn to apply the legs correctly, it is necessary to ride horses that range from those that require a severe application of the legs, to those that respond immediately to a very gentle leg pressure.

The rider must be able to maintain the position of her buttocks and upper body in the saddle, avoid throwing additional weight into the stirrups, and coordinate the correct use of the hands when applying the legs. A common fault is leaning forward from the hips and increasing the pressure or jerking on the reins when attempting to use the legs. Assuming this position makes it impossible for the lower leg to swing easily because of the added weight thrown into the stirrups. Also the horse's mouth is abused.

The application of the legs to drive a horse forward is rhythmical and persistent. A series of light rhythmical squeezes produces better results than an attempted hard kick and then a period of waiting and hoping that the horse will respond.

Following are exercises to develop the correct use of the legs:

1. AT A STAND, WALK, AND JOG. Feet are out of the stirrups. The toes are up and the inner side of the foot is nearer the ground. Swing the legs slowly backward and forward from the knee. The heels remain down. The swings are small and the lower legs do not touch the horse. The position of the thighs, buttocks, and upper body remains unchanged by the motion of the lower legs. *1, 2, 3.*

2. EXERCISE 1 IS REPEATED WITH THE FEET IN THE STIRRUPS. *1, 2, 3.*

3. EXERCISE (*b*) ON PAGE 228 IS USED TO OVERCOME PUSHING ON THE STIRRUPS.

4. RHYTHMICAL APPLICATION OF THE LEGS.

(*a*) At a Stand without and with Stirrups.

(*1*) The heels remain down. The position of the upper body, buttocks, and thighs is unaltered. Turn the toes slightly outward. From the knees, move the lower legs back and in until the calves of the legs are brought lightly against the horse's sides just behind the girth. Be sure the big toe side of the foot remains nearer the ground. Return to starting position and repeat. *1, 2, 3.*

(2) The movement of the lower legs is the same as in 1 to bring them in contact with the horse. The legs remain in contact with him while the very light pressure is alternated five or six times with a squeeze of the calves. Return to the starting position and repeat. The hands lessen the pressure on the reins while the legs squeeze and release. Vary the amount of force that is used in the squeeze from a very light one to a severe one. *2, 3.*

NOTE: This method of applying the legs is not taught to beginners because, as a general rule, the horses used in a beginners' class are not so responsive to leg pressure.

(*b*) At a Walk and Jog without and with Stirrups. At a command from the instructor, the class applies a rhythmical squeeze and release until the horses jog. The hands give but do not lose contact as the horse receives the signal to move forward. Bring the horses to a walk and repeat. *2, 3.*

(*c*) At a Trot with Stirrups. Movement of the legs and hands is the same as in (*b*). The pressure is applied when the rider is in the saddle. Then the legs immediately return to their original position for her to rise. To get this co-ordination of the legs coming in as the body falls, practice it first at a stand and then at a walk. Post a slow trot. At a command from the instructor increase the speed of the trot by rhythmical squeezes of the legs. The upper body moves more forward with the increase in speed. *2, 3.*

(*d*) Rhythmical Slaps with the Calves of the Legs. This method of applying the legs is next in severity and varies in force from light taps to hard slaps. The movement and rhythm are the same as when the legs squeeze, except that more of the lower leg is brought into contact with the horse. Practice at a stand, walk, jog, and trot. *1* (at stand, walk, and jog, possibly trot), *2, 3.*

(*e*) Rhythmical Application of the Heels. This is the most severe method of using the legs. The rhythm is the same. The toe is turned out slightly more and the entire lower leg and heel are brought into contact with the horse. Use quiet, slow horses and practice at a walk, jog, and trot. *1* (at stand, walk and jog, possibly trot), *2, 3.*

5. USE OF THE LEGS TO TURN OR TO KEEP A HORSE MOVING IN A GIVEN PATH. The way in which the hands must work with the legs has been described on pages 235 and 236. The horse is kept between the rider's hands and legs throughout all turns.

(*a*) Maintenance of the Forward Motion. Turn horses at a walk, jog, and trot using both legs with the necessary severity to maintain the same forward motion throughout the entire turn. Start to apply the legs a step or two before the hands start to turn the horse. This ability to keep the horse moving forward at the same rate of speed throughout a turn is one of the most essential elements of a correct turn and of keeping a horse straight when he wishes to turn. Both legs are used for all turns until the students have the ability to maintain forward motion and to use their hands correctly. *1, 2, 3.*

(*b*) Use of the Inside Leg Only. Each horse makes an individual circle on the command, "Single file circle to the left (or right)—Go!" To determine the size of the circle consider the horse as the radius. The rider returns to the track at the place where she started her circle. The leg that is on the inside of the circle is used with whatever severity is necessary to keep the hind legs of the horse in the same path as his front legs and to maintain the forward movement. The leg on the outside is not used and remains in the correct position. To reverse the direction in which the horses are moving a half circle is made. All turns are toward the center of the ring. Practice at a walk, jog, trot, and canter. *2, 3.*

(*c*) Use of the Outside Leg.

(*1*) Just before each corner of the ring, the student places the leg that is toward the center of the ring just behind the girth, and pushes steadily against the horse with the calf as the hands are used to move the forequarters deeper into the corner. If calf pressure does not produce the desired response, the rider should use the leg with greater severity. *2, 3.*

(*2*) In a line one behind the other, the first rider leads the class down the ring, straight across the ring, diagonally across the ring or in a serpentine down the ring. The riders in back of the leader keep their horses directly in her path. They prevent them from turning too soon by the proper use of the hands and by blocking with the leg on the side toward which the horse wishes to go. If the lead horse has made a right turn, the other horses will attempt to turn to the right before they reach the spot where the leader turned. To prevent this the rider increases the pressure on the left rein, decreases the tension on the right rein, and brings the latter to the horse's neck. At the same time the right leg is placed just behind the girth. Use both legs while executing the turns that the leader makes. Practice at a walk, jog, and trot. *2, 3.*

(*3*) Repeat exercise 2 with the addition of the following: Use only the outside leg while executing the turns the leader makes. Practice at a walk, jog, and trot. *2, 3.*

(*4*) The riders walk, jog, and trot anywhere they wish in the ring and make turns using the legs and hands correctly. *2, 3.*

6. "LIFTING" A HORSE WITH THE LEGS. This feeling of a lift with the legs is very essential to put a horse into a canter.

(*a*) At a Stand. Place the calves of the legs just behind the girth and squeeze in and up with them as if the horse were to be lifted up between them. Release the pressure and return the legs to their correct position. Repeat. *1, 2, 3.*

(*b*) From a Walk to a Canter. The desire of the horse to move forward is created by the proper application of the legs before he is told to canter. The use of the hands must co-ordinate with the use of the legs.

(*1*) When the horse is collected, use both legs to lift him into a canter. *1, 2, 3.*

(*2*) Use only the leg on the side away from the desired lead to lift the horse. *2, 3.*

(C) *Use of the Weight.* By weight is meant all of the rider's body above the hip joint. Generally speaking, to keep her center of gravity over the horse's, she moves forward from this joint with an increase of speed, and backward with a decrease of pace (Fig. 102).

Before describing the exercises which aid the correct use of the weight, a few examples of how the forward position must be varied according to the type of horse and what he is doing at the moment might prove helpful. First, a comparison of the hunter and saddle horse, as to center of gravity, shows that the hunter's is further forward than the saddle horse's because of the different way in which each moves. Because of this fact a person riding a hunter should be further forward than someone riding a saddle horse, and each should be over the center of gravity of her particular horse. Second, when riding a horse that is attempting to buck or move faster forward than the rider desires, the forward position is not maintained or increased, but the weight is brought back as pressure on the reins is increased, so that the rider may "sit down." To sum up, the amount one may and should be forward is dependent upon the horse's schooling, his gaits, and his behavior.

1. EXAGGERATION OF THE USE OF THE BODY WEIGHT. Performed by students at a walk, jog, and canter. Hold the reins so long that the hands are against the abdomen when feeling the horse's mouth. The rider does not pull with her arms at any time during this exercise but maintains her contact and increases the pressure on the reins by bringing her upper body backward with her hands remaining against her abdomen. The instructor gives various commands as: "Walk!," "Jog!,"

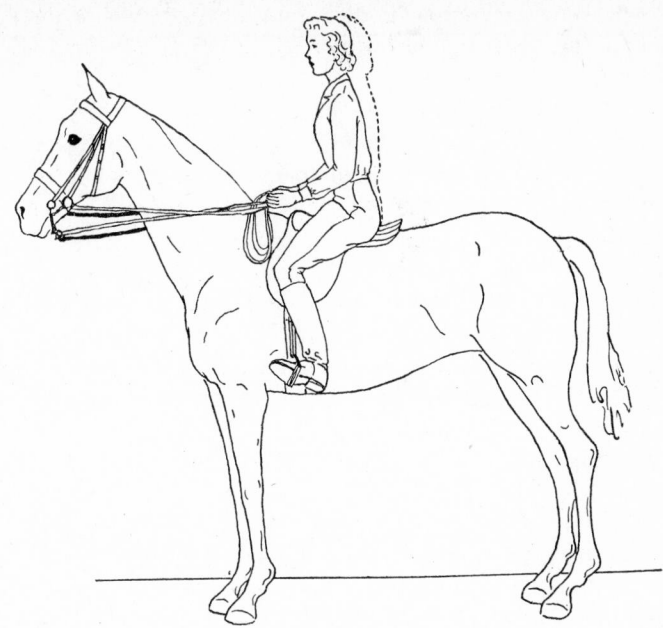

Fig. 102. Shifting of weight from hip joint.

"Walk!," "Canter!," and so forth. The upper body moves forward with the increase in speed and comes backward to slow or steady the horse. With the reins carried so long, a feeling of the use of the weight is established. *1, 2* (at walk and jog), *3* (at all gaits).

2. MOVEMENT OF THE BODY WEIGHT WITHOUT REINS. Practiced by the students at a walk, jog, and trot. The reins are knotted on the horse's neck. The commands are the same as in Exercise 1 except cantering is omitted. Without the reins, the rider must keep her weight in the correct relation to the speed of the horse in order to feel at all balanced or secure. *1, 2, 3.*

3. PROPER USE OF THE WEIGHT. Performed by the students at a walk, jog, trot, and canter. The reins are held the correct length. Commands are the same as in Exercises 2 and 3. The weight moves the correct amount forward and backward with the increase and decrease in speed.[1] *1* (at walk, jog, and trot), *2, 3* (at all gaits).

4. MAINTENANCE OF THE CORRECT BODY POSITION UNTIL THE PROPER MOMENT TO MOVE THE WEIGHT FORWARD. The instructor creates situations which make the riders' horses desire to move forward faster. The

[1] Beginners are never allowed to be the least bit forward at the hip joint in a canter so that they will learn to "sit down."

students prevent their upper bodies from moving forward and do not permit their horses to move on until the proper moment. Following are a few such situations.

(*a*) All the horses are in a line jogging around the ring. All but the last horse increase their speed to a fast trot. The rider on the last horse maintains the jog until she is told to move on. As soon as the last rider increases her speed, the others bring their horses back to a jog. The next time the last two riders remain jogging while the others trot out. Repeat until the whole line has done it. The instructor watches carefully to see that the students' upper bodies do not move the slightest degree forward until they are told to trot out. 2, 3.

(*b*) All the horses are cantering in a line and come to a walk starting with the last horse. The instructor watches to see that the weight does not go forward as the rider attempts to slow the horse and that it moves back as the horse responds. 2, 3.

(*c*) This is done only when the instructor is certain of the riders' ability and the temperament of the horses and there is no traffic danger. On the bridle path the class comes to a walk from the back of the line to the front. It goes from a walk to a trot or canter by having the first two horses move on, and then the next two, and so forth. This requires much greater control than all starting or stopping at the same time. 3.

(D) *Use of the Voice.* The voice as an aid is used to quiet, encourage, or scold a horse. One precaution that must be taken if the voice is used when riding with other horses is that it does not disturb anyone else's horse. For example: clucking to your horse to urge him forward might excite some other horse.

III. The Development of Control

The degree of a rider's control of a horse is determined by the rider's ability to coordinate the use of the aids and her ability to apply each one with the proper severity. If a rider is to improve her ability to control a horse, lessons should include work that requires the rider to use the aids and handle her own horse.

Drilling, working individually, and tandem are three effective means of improving the rider's control. Each of these is discussed separately in the next three sections.

(A) *Drilling.* Drilling brings into use the application of all the aids and requires that great effort and determination on the part of the rider be exerted. In a drill it is necessary for the rider to increase, decrease, maintain a steady pace, and turn the horse. These things must be done at a definite time or place which makes the rider react more

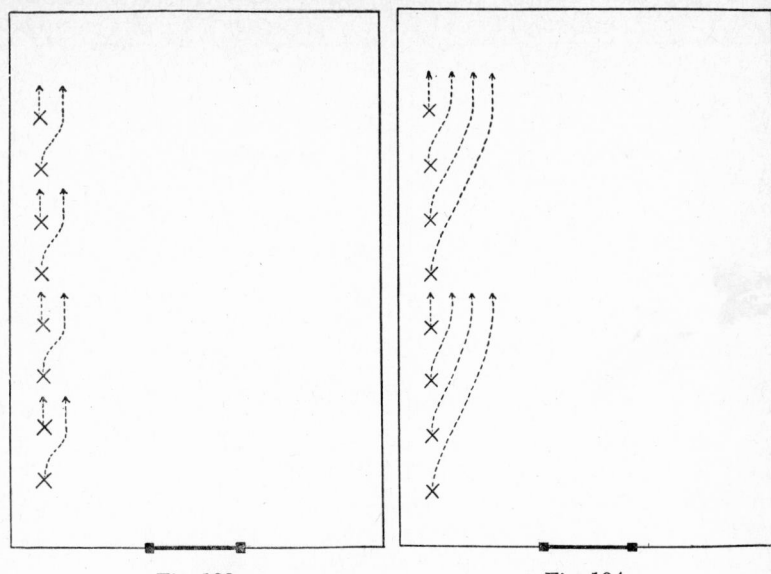

Fig. 103.   Fig. 104.

Fig. 103. Formation of two's to the right.
Fig. 104. Formation of four's to the right from single file.

quickly. The confidence and determination of the timid rider are greatly aided. Her mind is taken off the horse because she is so busy getting him to the correct place at the proper time. All students who have not developed the desired control make much more effort to control and direct their horses properly when riding in a drill. No one wishes to have her horse the only one in the ring not in the right place, so she becomes more determined when applying her aids. Lack of determination on the part of a rider is one of the major causes of poor control.

The speed at which a drill is ridden depends upon the ability of the class. A class of poor riders drills at a jog, and when an increase in pace is needed, it is at a trot, just fast enough to post comfortably. Better riders drill at a brisk trot and canter to increase the speed.

Figures used in class work are ones that do not require lengthy explanations to make clear the direction in which the horses are to be moved. When a new figure is taught, the riders walk their horses through it the first time to be sure all understand the direction in which they are to move.

Following are a few simple figures for class work:

1. FORM TWO'S TO THE RIGHT OR LEFT. The riders are in single file. The class numbers off "one, two" down the line. On the command,

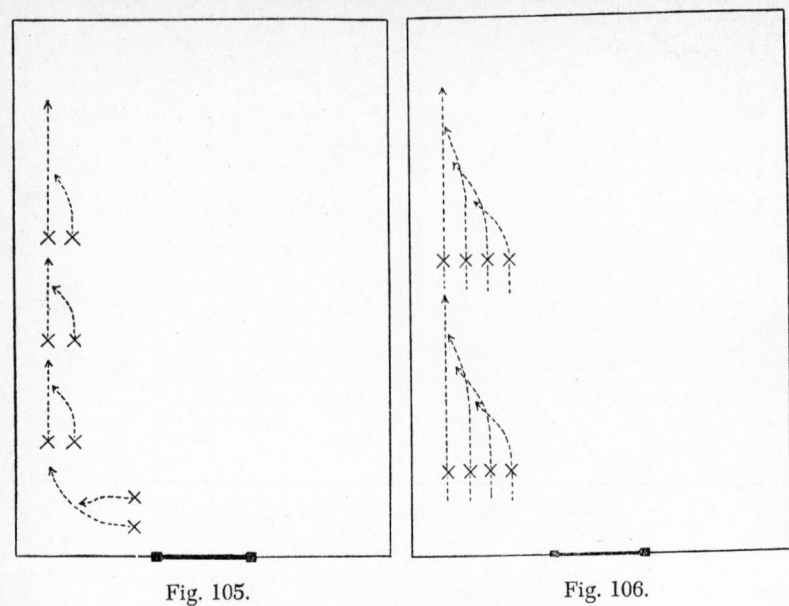

Fig. 105. Fig. 106.

Fig. 105. Single file from the left.
Fig. 106. Single file from the left from four's.

"Form two's to the right—go!" Number 2 rides up to the right side of the Number 1 that is ahead of her. Number 1 must prevent her horse from increasing the pace. Number 2 increases her pace to join Number 1 but brings her horse back to the original speed as soon as she reaches Number 1. The space that is left by the two's moving out of the line is not closed up by the pairs. Whether the command "right" or "left" is given depends upon the direction in which the horses are moving around the ring. Number 2 always comes up to Number 1 on the side toward the center of the ring. *1, 2, 3.* (Fig. 103.) This may also be used to form four's either from double or single file. *2, 3.* (Fig. 104.)

2. SINGLE FILE FROM THE RIGHT OR LEFT. The riders are in a file of two's. At the command, "Single file from the left—go" the rider on the left side of the pair increases her speed and moves into single file ahead of her partner. As soon as she is ahead, her partner increases her speed to keep a horse's length between the horses. When the class is all in single file and has traveled the length of the ring at the faster speed, the command, "Slow!" is given. All the horses then return gradually to the original pace. Quickness of execution is accomplished by a marked increase of speed on the part of the rider who moves out

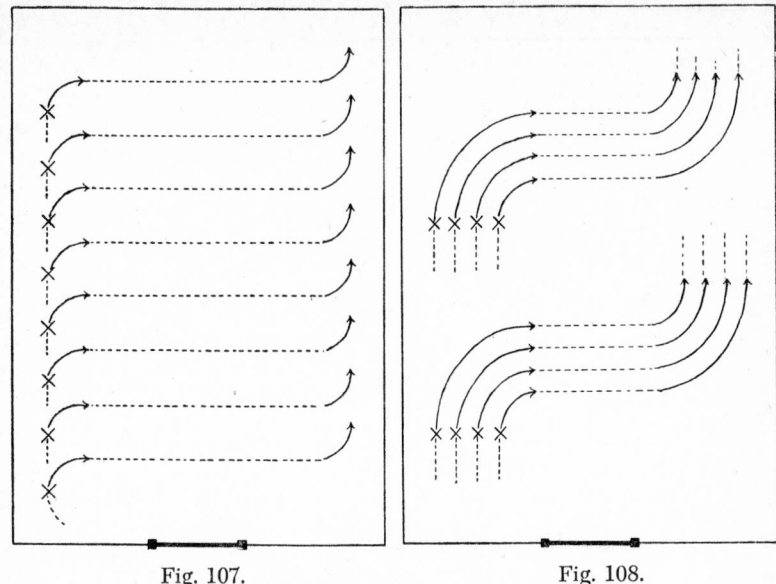

Fig. 107.   Fig. 108.

Fig. 107. Right flank.
Fig. 108. Right flank in fours.

first into single file. *1, 2, 3.* (Fig. 105.) This may be performed from three's or four's. *2, 3.* (Fig. 106.)

3. RIGHT OR LEFT FLANK. A right flank is done when the class is moving clockwise around the ring. A left flank is performed when the direction is reversed. The riders are in single file. The command is "Right flank—go!" Everyone makes a quarter turn to the right and rides straight across the ring. At a horse's length from the fence everyone makes a quarter turn to the left. The class is again in single file moving in the opposite direction around the ring. As the horses come across the ring they are side by side and all their heads are kept even by guiding toward whichever end of the line the leader is. *1, 2, 3.* (Fig. 107.) When the class is in two's, three's, or four's this same figure may be executed. *2, 3.* (Fig. 108.)

4. WALK, TROT, AND CANTER IN TWO'S, THREE'S AND FOUR'S. To keep even the horse next to the fence is used as the guide. The riders nearer the center of the ring must slow down just before each corner so that they do not get ahead of their group on the turn. They must, however, increase the speed in time to be moving at the original pace just as the corner is turned or they will drop behind the outer horses. The outside horses maintain a steady pace around the corner at a trot. At a canter it is necessary to slightly increase the speed for the turn; but at the

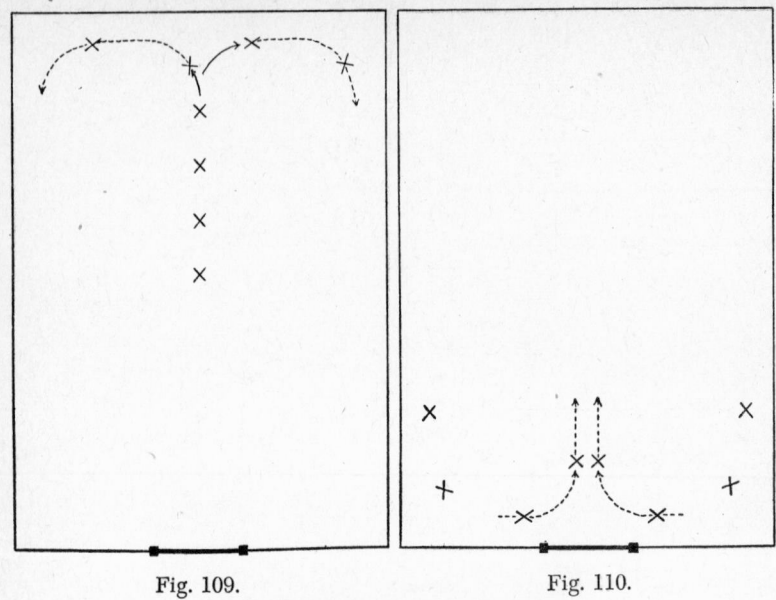

Fig. 109.   Fig. 110.

Fig. 109. Alternate horses right and left.
Fig. 110. Form two's from two single files.

completion of that turn, the outside horses must again be moving at the original pace. *1* (walk and trot in two's), *2, 3*.

5. ALTERNATE HORSES RIGHT AND LEFT. The horses come down the center of the ring in single file. When they reach the opposite end of the ring, the first horse goes to the right and the second to the left, and so forth. When coming down the center of the ring, each rider, before she reaches the place to turn, gently warns her horse that she is not turning in the same direction as the horse ahead of her by lightly applying her aids for the turn. *1, 2, 3*. (Fig. 109.)

Now the horses are in two single files on either side of the ring. To keep the horses even, the riders guide by the horses on the opposite side.

6. FORM TWO'S FROM TWO SINGLE FILES. From the above formation, each rider forms a two with the person with whom she has been keeping even. The two's are formed as the riders meet the opposite line. They ride down the center of the ring in a file of two's (Fig. 110). At the opposite end of the ring they may:

1. Divide again into two single files.
2. Alternate two's to the right and left.
3. All two's to the right or left, *1, 2, 3*.

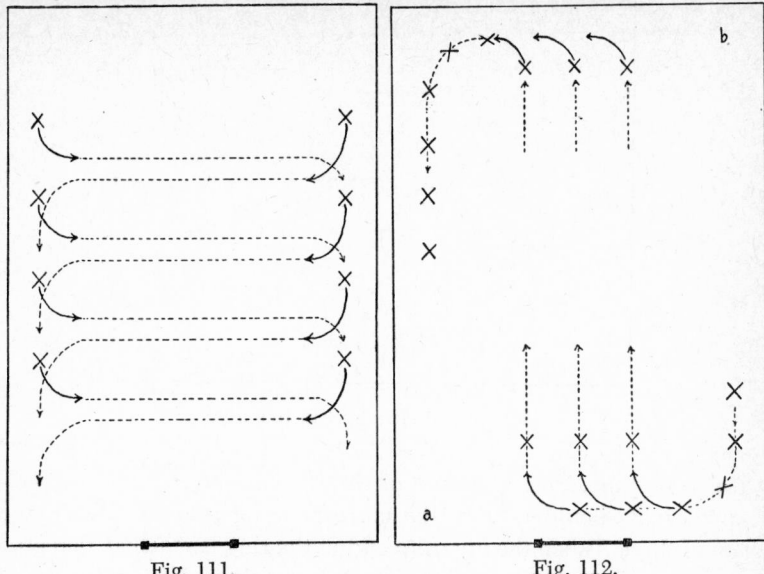

Fig. 111.   Fig. 112.

Fig. 111. Right and left flanks from two single files.
Fig. 112. Formation of three's and the return to single file.

7. RIGHT AND LEFT FLANK FROM TWO SINGLE FILES. There are two single files, one on either side of the ring. Both are moving toward the gate end of the ring. At the command, "Right and left flank—go!," each line makes a quarter turn so the two lines are facing each other. The two lines pass through each other by passing right shoulders with the person with whom they have been keeping even while on opposite sides of the ring. When the other side of the ring is reached, each rider makes a quarter turn toward the gate end of the ring. When the gate is reached, two's are formed as described in 6. 2, 3. (Fig. 111.)

8. FORM THREE'S AT THE GATE. The riders are in a single file moving clockwise around the ring. Number off by three's. Just before each Number 2 comes to the gate she calls "Turn!" On the command, each rider of the three makes a quarter turn to the right and rides toward the opposite end of the ring (Fig. 112, a). While moving down the center of the ring, the riders are in three's with a wide space between each horse in the group of three. At the opposite end of the ring, Number 2 again says, "Turn," and each rider of the three makes a quarter turn to the left so that they are in single file again in their original order and moving in the opposite direction around the ring (Fig. 112, b).

This formation may be started from the opposite ends of the ring

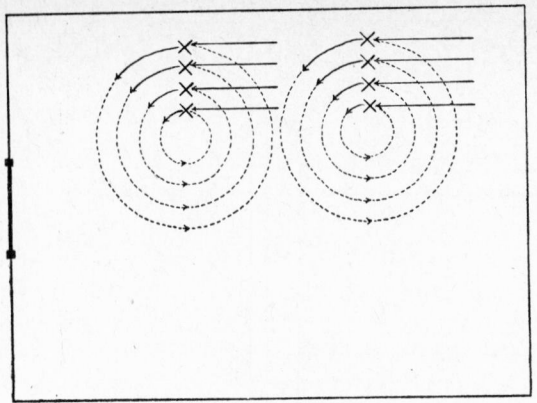

Fig. 113. Left wheel in four's.

at the same time. Then the lines of three's pass through each other by passing right shoulders with the corresponding rider in the opposite group of three. When the opposite end of the ring is reached, one group turns left into single file and the other turns right. Now the two lines are moving toward each other. When they meet they may either form two's or go into single file from alternate lines. 2, 3.

9. WHEELS RIGHT OR LEFT IN THREE'S OR FOUR'S. The class rides in three's or four's around the ring. The wheel is always made toward the center of the ring. On the command "Wheel," each group rides around a complete circle keeping the horses' heads in each group even, and the horses' bodies close together. The rider on the outside increases her speed on the command. It is essential that she ride a perfect circle to keep her horse close to the others and not cause any crowding. The inside or pivot rider decreases her pace. All guide by the outside horse. 3. (Fig. 113.)

10. THE ADVANCED CLASSES WORK IN SIXES, EIGHT'S, AND TWELVE'S. They practice the formation of them, keeping even while riding around the ring, wheels, and galloping out into single file. 3.

(B) *Working Individually.* To require the student to work individually with her horse is a most effective means of developing precision and gentleness in applying the aids. Other values of individual work are: (1) the instructor is made more aware of the specific weaknesses of each individual student; (2) the student is helped to recognize her own weaknesses and the need for further improvement.

Following are a few suggestions which may be used for individual work:

1. MAKING A FIGURE EIGHT. When a student first attempts to guide

her horse through a figure eight, she should be required to utilize the entire ring. As her skill improves the size of the figure should be reduced.

It is advisable to have the rider first trot through the figure, telling the instructor which lead she should be on if she were cantering. Next the student should canter around the loop at either end of the eight but should continue to trot diagonally across the ring. As the rider becomes more capable the length of the trot should be gradually reduced until the rider is changing her lead at the center of the eight.

2. USING THE LENGTH OF THE RING. Students should spend some-time working up and down the center of the ring. The instructor may request the rider to do such things as: walk four steps, halt, back three steps, trot half way down the ring on one diagonal and then change to the other, reverse at the end of the ring and canter back changing leads at the center of the ring.

3. PERFORMING A DEFINITE ROUTINE. Numbers or letters should be painted on the ring enclosure. These are used to designate the spots at which certain maneuvers are to begin or end.

An illustration of a routine which an advanced rider might be asked to perform is:

1. Walk from 1 to 2.
2. At 2 a collected trot.
3. At 5 circle.
4. At 7 an extended trot; continue two times around the ring.
5. At 7 a collected trot.
6. At 1 walk.
7. At 2 two track to the right.
8. At 3 two track to the left.
9. At 5 canter on the right lead.
10. At 2 make a figure eight, using only half of the ring.
11. At 3 walk.
12. Reverse at 4.
13. Canter at 3 on the left lead; continue once around the ring.
14. Walk at 3.
15. Halt at 2.

(C) *Tandem.** Tandem can be used as a device to accomplish better control of the horse. Unfamiliar to many horsewomen, tandem originated in the European cavalry officer training and has been used in this country because of the equitation value as well as the enjoyment and challenge it affords.

---

* This section was written by Jean Campbell, Physical Education Department, Smith College.

1. EXPLANATION OF TANDEM AND TANDEM TACK.

(*a*) Tandem involves the control of two horses by one rider and consists of riding one horse, termed the wheel horse, while driving a horse directly in front, the lead horse. The wheel horse consequently must be controlled by the rider's seat, legs, and balance, while the lead horse is driven by reins, whip, and voice as any horse in harness is. The lead horse must be kept up on the bit at all times.

(*b*) A white buckskin or webbing tack may be used which makes tandem more spectacular, but any light driving harness with a snaffle or curb bit, a check rein, surcingle and tail crop will suffice. Similar white bridle, breastplate, and girth may be used on the wheel horse. With whatever tack used, loops, which may be made of cord, should be fastened on the cheek straps, between the nose band and brow band of the wheel horse's bridle, through which the driving reins are threaded to prevent injury to the eyes of the wheel horse and to keep the driving reins in place.

2. EQUITATION VALUES OF TANDEM.

(*a*) The foremost value of tandem is the accomplishment of control of the wheel horse through the use of seat, legs, and balance. The rider's seat and body develop a sensitivity to the horse which is attained subconsciously at first. As more difficult horses are used the development of seat and use of balance are increased so that the rider eventually becomes hypersensitive to the horse. The rider's hands are occupied in driving and therefore involved only very slightly with the control of the wheel horse.

(*b*) The accomplishment of controlling two horses builds up confidence in the rider's own ability. After the first few confusing minutes, the rider sees that it becomes relatively simple to manage the team. Even though elementary ring figures are executed, their performance creates the impression of difficulty.

(*c*) Another value is obtained subconsciously. Particularly, a rider who normally tries too hard at her own form and control is so occupied with two horses, numerous reins, and the whip that she unconsciously relaxes, thereby losing the tension in her body and making her riding easier and more effortless.

(*d*) Horses are gregarious by nature and therefore submit willingly to following the leader. This lessens the task of the rider with the wheel horse and accomplishes the aforementioned values more easily.

3. INTRODUCTION OF TANDEM TO THE RIDER. The rider who seems to reach a plateau can be encouraged greatly by driving tandem. A lead horse well schooled and responsive to driving and a wheel horse easily manageable allow the rider's first attempts to be successful. Because

of the psychology of the horse, tandem is more easily done at a trot (rider sitting trot), since the horses are occupied and have less time to think up ways to cause trouble and to set themselves to balk or play. When first learning, the rider may forgo the whip and urge the horse forward with voice and rein. The half-school, circle, and diagonal change give the rider a chance to work on control with a minimum of resistance.

4. TANDEM FOR THE EXPERIENCED. This opens many possibilities for improvement of control and for performance purposes. Any of the following have audience appeal as well as equitation value:

(a) The individual performer may accomplish any advanced ring figure, as mentioned in the section on individual control, such as figure eight at trot and canter, half-halts, circles, two tracking, side stepping, etc.

(b) The rider who can jump may have a thrill at jumping a tandem team. This should be done with horses well schooled for jumping.

(c) Probably the greatest satisfaction for the advanced tandem driver is to school the horse to drive. Work on the lunge line to accustom the horse to voice and whip comes first. Then the long lines are used, driving the horse with voice and whip, while the rider walks behind on the ground. Eventually the horse is driven with the rider mounted behind. Naturally a horse who is a habitual kicker would be a bad choice. Common sense, patience, and carrots make the horse submissive to this and make tandem an enjoyable experience for him.

(d) The advanced rider may attempt "trandem," driving two horses and riding one. The two may be hitched side by side or one in front of the other. This is naturally more difficult, but it is an excellent means of improving advanced control.

(e) Advanced riders may then combine their skill and execute drills as suggested heretofore. Drills may be done with two, four, six, or eight teams, depending upon the horses and the available space. This demands precision control and anticipation on the part of all riders.

Tandem is fun but very tiring physically because the rider must be extremely alert at all times and ready for split-second decisions. The benefits derived from tandem seem to justify its inclusion in a riding program.

TEACHING PROGRESSION OF THE GAITS AND JUMPING

The teaching progression of the various gaits is very closely allied to the development of the rider's body control and the control of her horse. As control of body and horse increases, the student's ability to ride the gaits properly will improve. In the following teaching progression there are several items listed which a rider could not do until she had reached a certain level of ability. For these reasons "The Teaching Progression of the Gaits and Jumping" follows rather than precedes "Methods to Improve Riding."

In all the progressions that follow, the work starts with less difficult things and proceeds to the more advanced.

I. The Walk

(A) Correction of the fundamental position at a stand.

(B) Before the horse moves the student is told how to stop the horse so she will have more confidence.

(C) Walk and stop. Correction of the position is made each time the horse stops, and the student tries to maintain the position while the horse walks.

(D) Walk, watching the horse's head and attempting to follow that movement with the hands so contact with horse's mouth is maintained.

(E) Walk, trying to get a feeling of looseness through the waist so the buttocks are free to move with the motion of the horse.

(F) Practice (A)–(E) without stirrups.

(G) Turn horses at a walk.

(H) When the riders know how to "sit down," then incline the upper body very slightly forward as the horse walks.

II. The Trot

(A) Sit a slow jog with and without stirrups.

(B) At a Stand: Place both hands on the withers of the horse and rise straight up in the stirrups. Remain standing a few seconds and then return to the saddle. This gives confidence to rise from the saddle.

(C) At a Walk: Rise and sit in continuous rhythm. The movement is forward and up. The instructor counts 1–2–3–4 to the movement of one of the horse's front legs for the student. Each count is an up and a down.

(D) Sit a jog for seven or eight steps and then attempt to post, allowing the horse to increase its speed slightly for the posting. At first the student should think only of the rhythm. The length of time spent posting is increased as the class's ability improves. Posting is very exhausting for the beginner and great care must be taken at first not to tire the student by keeping her posting too long.

(E) Turn the horse at a jog.

(F) Perfect position of the rider's body, legs, and hands and correct height of posting after the rhythm has become automatic.

(G) Turn the horse while posting.

(H) Posting without reins.

(I) Post the trot and at the command "Up" place the hands on the withers of the horse and remain out of saddle until the command "Post" is given. While out of the saddle the upper body is forward and up and the thighs have contact with the saddle.

(J) Change diagonals by sitting an extra beat.

(K) Change diagonals by staying up an extra beat.

(L) Post without stirrups.

(M) Post without reins or stirrups.

(N) Post four counts, sit four counts, post four counts, stay up four counts.

III. The Canter

(A) (At a Walk.) The motion that the horse's walk gives to the seat is exaggerated by making the waist as relaxed as possible. Attention is called to the motion of the hands so that contact with the horse's mouth is maintained.

(B) The motion of the rider's seat and hands during the canter is explained and demonstrated. The demonstration includes an exhibition of the results of stiffening and pushing down on the stirrups.

(C) It is explained that to make a horse canter, one causes a "disturbance" by creating in the horse a desire to go, but not permitting him to do so immediately. He is held in until he canters and then the rider gives way with her hands. If the person releases the extra tension on the reins before the horse starts to canter, he goes into a trot. If the rider does not lessen the added pressure on the reins as the horse starts to canter, he will stop cantering.

(D) All of the riders are in single file walking around the ring with three or four horses which have a slow, easy canter and go into it easily at the end of the line. All the horses trot. The riders are told that the speed of the trot must decrease slightly when they are told to canter and that they must keep their places in the line. Then the riders on the last three or four horses are told to canter. The riders think of keeping the weight on the seat and the body, especially the spine, flexible.

(E) The riders change horses and the above is repeated so that the remaining students have an opportunity to canter.

(F) All the horses trot. On the command "Canter!" everyone draws her reins tight enough to decrease the speed of the trot. While maintaining that degree of snugness, the rider uses her legs and lifts the horse with her hands.

(G) The position of the rider and the movement of the hands and body with the horse are worked on. The rider must be able to "polish the saddle with the seat of her breeches" before she is permitted to incline her upper body forward.

(H) The ability to maintain a slow canter by giving and taking on the horse's mouth and increasing the weight on the buttocks is taught. To check the horse's speed, the student is told to bring her hands a little closer to her body than they are when just following the horse's head and to draw the buttocks under her a little more. Thus the horse's head is brought in a little more than is its normal position and additional weight is on the buttocks. Then the hands release the added tension on the reins and follow the horse's head as they did before, and the pulling under of the hips is no longer exaggerated.

(I) Canter from a walk by drawing the reins snug and using the legs to create forward motion. "Lift" the horse into a canter with the hands and legs. (See page 240.)

(J) Canter from a walk, putting the horse on the correct lead.

(K) Canter from a walk on the correct lead without stirrups.

(L) Canter faster by using the body as well as the legs to drive the horse forward. Then bring the horse to the slowest possible canter using the driving force of the seat, the application of the legs, and the maintaining of collection with the hands to prevent the horse from breaking into a trot.

(M) Canter bareback.

(N) Canter through a figure eight.

(O) Canter in and out between a line of upright posts changing leads.

IV. Jumping

(A) Walk, trot, and canter in jumping position.

(B) With a pole lying on the ground, the rider takes the jumping position as the horse walks over the pole. The rider rises as the horse starts to step over the pole with one front leg and comes back to the saddle when the last hind leg is brought over the pole. As the horse is stepping over the pole the rider does not interfere in any way with the horse's mouth. As the student returns to the saddle she gently applies the necessary contact to keep the horse walking.

(C) Same as (B) but at a trot.

(D) Same as (B) but at a canter.

(E) With a pole lying on the ground, the rider guides the horse toward it in a very slow canter. When the horse is about three strides from the pole, the rider increases the horse's speed. Then the rider gets into jumping position as the horse goes over the bar. As the horse lands on the ground on the other side of the pole the rider gradually and gently reduces the pace to the original slow canter.

(F) When the rider is able to control her horse coming toward the jump, increase the speed just before it, get up into jumping position at the correct time, cause no interference with the horse's mouth while he is jumping, return to the saddle at the proper time and reduce the horse's speed correctly with the bar on the ground, then the bar is raised 6 inches from the ground. Only when the rider performs well at a given height is the bar raised.

THE DIVISION OF CLASSES

The riders should be placed in classes according to their ability. The pace of a class has to be set so that the poorest rider in it will be safe. If the students are of varying abilities, the better horsewomen are held back, and, too, they generally get less attention from the instructor than the poorer pupils, no matter how hard the teacher tries to give everyone an equal share of attention. Besides, the weaker rider may become discouraged by seeing others able to do things that she is incapable of doing. It is a happier and more pleasant situation for both pupils and instructor, and much more can be accomplished, when classes are divided according to the ability of the riders.

A useful division of riders is to have sections for beginners, low intermediates, high intermediates, and advanced. If it is not possible for the instructor to see the students ride before they are put into their sections, any student who has either underrated or overestimated her ability should be changed to a section which suits her stage of advancement.

The maximum number in each class should be: beginners five, low intermediates eight, high intermediates ten, and advanced fourteen. By limiting the numbers in each division, it is possible to give more individual attention to each student.

The beginners should remain in the ring until they have learned enough to be considered safe on the road. With the other sections, assuming that they ride two hours a week, a workable plan is to have them spend one hour in the ring and one on the road. If the class wishes to spend its second hour in the ring, it should be allowed to do so. To achieve the desired advancement, at least half of the class hours should be spent in the ring.

How many terms of riding are offered during the year depends on whether the physical education program is on a semester basis or divided into three terms of fall, winter, and spring. In either case, a student who has improved sufficiently should be advanced to the next division. If, however, her degree of improvement does not warrant promotion, she should remain in the same class.

Following is an outline of the work covered in the different sections. This is based on a nine weeks' term with the class meeting for two one hour periods each week.

(A) Beginners

1. Approach horse.
2. Hold horse.
3. Lead horse.
4. Check girth.
5. Tighten girth from the ground and mounted.
6. Adjust stirrups from the ground.
7. Mount.
8. Dismount.
9. Fundamental position in the saddle.
10. Hold reins.
11. Shorten reins.
12. Lengthen reins.
13. Stop horse.
14. Start horse.
15. Walk and stop.
16. Turn horse at a walk.
17. Sit a slow trot with stirrups.
18. Walk and jog without stirrups.
19. Post a trot.
20. Turn horse sitting a jog with and without stirrups.
21. Turn horse while posting a trot.
22. Change reins from two hands to one and back to two hands.
23. Ride in two's.
24. Road-riding.
25. Canter (concentrating on rider's body and hand movement).
26. Simple drill figures.

(B) Low Intermediates

1. All the work covered in the beginners' section.
2. Adjust stirrups while mounted at a stand, walk, and jog.
3. Change of diagonals.
4. Back horse.
5. Canter with correct leads.
6. Bareback at a walk and jog.

7. Simple drills.
8. Individual work.

(C) High Intermediates

1. All of the work covered in the low intermediates' section.
2. Canter without stirrups.
3. More difficult drill work.
4. All gaits bareback on quiet horses.
5. Turn horses at a canter.
6. Figure eights at a canter.
7. More difficult individual work.
8. Ride more sensitive and spirited horses.

(D) Advanced

1. All the work covered in high intermediate classes but on more sensitive horses.
2. Bareback drilling and cantering.
3. Figure eights at a canter without stirrups.
4. Advanced individual work.
5. Tandem.
6. Jumping.

Next are given lesson plans for the nine-week term. These are based on the assumption that a class makes a normal rate of improvement. Consideration should always be given to the progress of each class and lesson plans altered to meet the needs of a particular class.

Improvement and perfection of a student's horsemanship, with the exception of items 1–8, page 256, under Beginners, are accomplished by the various exercises given in the section on the Methods of Improving Riding, pages 224-251. For the teaching progression of the various gaits and jumping, refer to pages 251-255. An explanation of the fundamental position is found on pages 222-224.

LESSON PLANS

(A) Beginners

LESSON 1. Give a brief talk to introduce the horse to the rider. Describe and practice items 1–6, page 256. Demonstrate stopping a horse. Teach items 7 and 8, page 256. Fix the reins correctly in the students' hands. Describe and practice shortening and lengthening the reins. Have the students sit forward in the saddles, keep their heels away from the horses' sides and the hands low. (This is all that is said about the correct position in the first lesson.) Demonstrate and practice walking and stopping, moving the horse slightly to the right and left, maintaining contact with the horse's mouth; and walking without stirrups.

LESSON 2. Teach the riders to pick up their own reins. Review lesson 1. Demonstrate and practice jogging with stirrups. Give an exercise for the control of the lower leg. Describe and practice the fundamental position at a stand and walk. Practice jogging without stirrups. Teach an exercise for flexibility of the hips and spine.

LESSON 3. Review lesson 2. Continue working on the control of the lower leg. Explain and practice the use of the weight. Teach an exercise in preparation for posting.

LESSON 4. Review lessons 2 and 3. Demonstrate and practice posting.

LESSON 5. Teach an exercise to improve the firmness of the seat. Practice posting. Explain and practice the use of the legs to urge the horse forward. Practice maintaining contact with horse's mouth. Give an exercise to develop the flexibility of the rider.

LESSON 6. Teach exercises for firmness of seat, control of the lower leg, maintaining contact with the horse's mouth and use of the legs to urge the horse forward. Demonstrate and practice turning the horse at a walk. Practice posting.

LESSON 7. Review lessons 1–6 as needed. Practice turning a horse at a jog. Ride in two's.

LESSON 8. Ride on the road at a walk and trot only.

LESSON 9. Work on firmness of seat, control of the lower leg, flexibility of the rider and use of the hands. Correct the position of the rider at a walk and trot. Practice turning a horse at a trot.

LESSON 10. Ride on the road at a walk and trot only.

LESSON 11. Review and practice the use of the legs, the use of the weight and the correct position of the rider in a walk and trot. Demonstrate and practice cantering.

LESSON 12. Review lessons 7, 9, and 11 as needed. Practice cantering.

LESSON 13. Teach changing the reins from two hands to one. Practice cantering. Give simple drill figures to develop control.

LESSON 14. Ride on the road.

LESSON 15. Ride on the road.

LESSON 16. Teach exercises for firmness of seat, maintaining contact with the horse's mouth, control of the lower leg and use of the weight. Practice simple drill figures and cantering.

LESSONS 17 AND 18. Ride on the road.

(B) Low Intermediates

LESSON 1. Demonstrate and practice items 1–6, page 256. Teach an exercise for firmness of the seat. Correct the position of the rider at a stand and walk.

LESSON 2. Review lesson 1 as needed. Teach exercises for control of the lower leg, flexibility of the rider, maintaining contact with the horse's mouth and use of the weight. Demonstrate and practice posting.

LESSON 3. Ride on the road at a walk and trot.

LESSON 4. Practice exercises for the use of the weight and the use of the hands. Describe and practice the use of the legs to urge the horse forward. Correct the rider's faults at a walk and trot. Demonstrate and practice backing the horse.

LESSON 5. Ride on the road at a walk and trot.

LESSON 6. Review lessons 1, 2, and 4 as needed. Explain and practice the use of the hands and legs to turn a horse. Demonstrate and practice cantering.

LESSON 7. Ride on the road at a walk and trot.

LESSON 8. Demonstrate and practice adjusting the stirrups while mounted. Work on firmness of the seat, flexibility of the rider, lightness of the hands, use of the hands and legs to keep the horse in a given path, correct the rider's faults in a trot and canter.

LESSON 9. Ride on the road.

LESSON 10. Review and practice use of the weight. Describe and practice changing diagonals. Practice cantering. Practice simple drill figures.

LESSON 11. Ride on the road.

LESSON 12. Test riders by having each student perform a definite routine. (Everything that has been covered in class should be included in the routine.)

LESSON 13. Ride on the road.

LESSON 14. Work individually or drill for the first half of the period. Ride bareback at a walk or jog for the remainder of the lesson.

LESSON 15. Ride on the road.

LESSON 16. Correct the rider's faults in a walk, trot and canter. Ride bareback the rest of the period.

LESSON 17. Ride on the road.

LESSON 18. Work individually. Drill the remainder of the period.

(C) High Intermediates

LESSON 1. Review items 1–6, page 256. Practice the mount and dismount. Practice adjusting the stirrups while mounted. Review the fundamental position. Teach exercises for firmness of seat and control of the lower leg. Correct the rider's faults at a walk, trot, and canter.

LESSON 2. Ride on the road.

LESSON 3. Review lesson 1 as needed. Teach exercises for flexibility of the rider and lightness of the hands. Practice cantering without stirrups.

LESSON 4. Ride on the road.

LESSON 5. Work individually. Ride bareback at all gaits.

LESSON 6. Ride on the road.

LESSON 7. Practice exercises for lightness of the hands, use of the legs to urge the horse forward, use of the weight and use of the hands and legs to turn a horse.

LESSON 8. Ride on the road.

LESSON 9. Review lessons 1, 3, and 7 as needed. Practice turning a horse at a canter. Drill the remainder of the period.

LESSON 10. Ride on the road.

LESSON 11. Practice figure eights at a canter. Ride bareback at all gaits.

LESSON 12. Ride on the road.

LESSON 13. Practice changing diagonals and turning a horse at a canter. Teach exercises for the use of the weight and lightness of the hands. Correct the rider's faults at a walk, trot and canter.

LESSON 14. Ride on the road.

LESSON 15. Work on the lightness of the hands. Practice turns at all gaits. Work individually.

LESSON 16. Ride on the road.

LESSON 17. Practice figure eights. Drill at all gaits.

LESSON 18. Ride on the road.

(D) Advanced

LESSON 1. Review items 1–6, page 256. Practice the mount and dismount. Review adjusting the stirrups while mounted and the fundamental position. Teach exercises for the firmness of the seat, control of the lower leg and use of the weight. Correct the rider's faults at a walk, trot, and canter.

LESSON 2. Ride on the road.

LESSON 3. Perfect the rider's performance at a walk, trot, and canter. Teach exercises for the use of the legs and preparation for jumping.

LESSON 4. Ride on the road.

LESSON 5. Review exercises leading up to jumping. Practice exercises for lightness of the hands and the use of the legs and hands to turn a horse. Practice jumping.

LESSON 6. Ride on the road.

LESSON 7. Demonstrate and practice a pivot on the fore-hand. Work individually. Practice jumping.

LESSON 8. Ride on the road.

LESSON 9. Practice an exercise for lightness of the hands. Review figure eights. Practice drilling.

LESSON 10. Ride on the road.

LESSON 11. Drill bareback. Use horses with saddles and jump the remainder of the period.

LESSON 12. Ride on the road.

LESSON 13. Demonstrate and practice two tracking. Teach tandem Work individually.

LESSON 14. Ride on the road.

LESSON 15. Correct the rider's faults at a walk, trot, and canter. Practice tandem. Practice jumping. Work on major needs of class.

LESSON 16. Ride on the road.

LESSON 17. Work individually or drill. Practice jumping.

LESSON 18. Ride on the road.

MEANS OF CREATING INTEREST IN RIDING

The most important means of creating interest in riding is for the instructor to teach interesting and instructive lessons and for her to feel and show a vital interest in the progress of her students. Three additional ways of arousing enthusiasm for the sport and interest in improvement are the riding club, recreational riding, and competitive riding.

I. Riding Club

The formation of a riding club is a good way to create not only interest in riding for enjoyment, but also interest in the perfection of one's ability. The organization and functions of the club will, of course, have to vary with different schools and colleges to suit the individual situation. A plan in which the club serves the entire student body is of more value both to the school and the club members than one in which its activities are limited just to club members.

(A) *Possible Organization.* The club should be composed of not more than thirty members. To be eligible to join the organization, a student must have taken part in at least two club events during the year. In the spring and fall of each year, tryouts may be held for all students who are eligible for membership in the club. The students are tested and judged by the club members. To become a member, a person must ride well enough to be able to manage and safely control a group on the road.

At the first meeting, after new members have been taken into the club, safety precautions may be discussed. These include such things as: never cantering on the way home, keeping the group together, setting the pace according to the ability of the group, and so forth. A new member should not be allowed to take a group on the road until she has had charge of a group under the supervision of an old member and proved her ability.

The officers of the club may be chairman or president, secretary-treasurer, and publicity manager. These students may be elected by the club to hold office for a year.

If there is an athletic association in which the different sports are represented, riding may be represented by the chairman.

The club needs to have business meetings once a month to plan a program of activities, to appoint people to take charge of them, and to discuss any problems or other business.

(B) *Possible Functions.* Besides the regular monthly business meetings, five or six meetings a year may be held to which any student interested may come. At these open meetings a program of interest to horsewomen may be offered. Lectures on such subjects as "Common Sense in Riding," "The Forward Seat," and "Buying and Caring for a Horse" may be given. A "Question Bee Evening" can be held. At this the students are divided into teams. Questions about horses and horsemanship are asked. Whenever a team cannot answer a question, a point is scored against it and the same question is asked the next team. The team with the lowest score wins. Movies that are related to riding are another suggestion for an interesting evening.

The club may also organize a riding clinic. A well known horseman may be invited to instruct at the clinic. Students from other schools and colleges in the area may be invited to participate in the program.

A gymkhana open to the entire school can be sponsored, organized, and managed by the club. If a horse show is held, the members, besides participating in it, can appoint or elect a horse show committee to publicize, organize, and manage the show.

Recreational riding which will be described next offers an excellent opportunity for the club to serve the entire student body. The members may furnish the necessary publicity and perform whatever organization is essential for a particular ride. As far as is safely possible they can be given the responsibility of managing the group during these rides.

II. Recreational Riding

Throughout the seasons of the year when the weather is good, various types of rides which are open to the entire college or school can be organized. How often these rides are held is dependent upon the number of students who ride. If the number is large enough to warrant it, they should be held once a week. These rides offer an excellent opportunity to foster co-recreation either by having the students invite men guests to attend the rides or by inviting clubs from nearby boys' schools to participate. Following is a list and description of the various types of rides which can be organized:

(A) *Breakfast, Luncheon, Supper, and Moonlight Rides.*[2]

(B) *Treasure Hunt.* The riders are divided into two teams. The clues have been put out the day before. They are placed so that one team moves in one direction around a loop and the other team in the opposite direction. The team that gets back to the stable first with all its clues wins.

(C) *Scavenger Hunt.* The riders are divided into groups of four to six. Each group is given a similar list of articles which it should bring back to the stable within three hours. For every five minutes that a group is late, an article is taken away from it. The group with the largest number of articles wins.

(D) *Coffee Ride.* The riders are divided into groups of four to six. A trail is marked by spots of white paint or small cardboard squares nailed to trees. The groups are told that if they follow the trail correctly they will find coffee and sandwiches being served somewhere along the way. Those that lose the trail must return to the stable hungry.

(E) *Hare and Hounds.* The hares (half of the group) start out fifteen minutes ahead of the hounds. They may not go faster than a trot. They have a bag of torn up newspaper fastened to one of the saddles. Some of this paper must be dropped every 100 yards. They may lay a false trail by dropping paper at both forks of a road. Every half hour a paper circle is made. At this spot the horses must be walked for five minutes. The hares attempt to reach the stable before they are overtaken by the hounds. The hounds must follow the marked trail but may ride at canter. The hares are considered caught if the hounds get within calling distance.

III. Competitive Riding

(A) *Class Riding Teams.* A workable plan for class competition

---

[2] Possible to combine with outing club group, to have them go ahead and prepare the food for first three types of rides.

follows. This can be easily altered to fit any situation in which it might be used.

Any student who is a member of the riding classes may be eligible for a team. Interest as well as ability should be considered. Teams can be picked from each of the school classes. These may compete against each other and at the end of the season an all-college or school riding team may be selected from the upper classes. The all-college or school team may not exceed a class team in number and may be composed of the best riders from the upper class teams.

These teams may compete in drilling, jumping, and games. Four riders from each team can drill, two jump, and four play games. The team winning first place in each event may be awarded five points, and the one winning second place can receive three points. The team with the highest score should be the winner of the class competition.

In the drilling all the teams may walk, trot, and canter by four's on both hands. Each team may also ride an original drill.

In the jumping the same four horses may be used for all the teams. The two students from each class who are jumping can each jump two of the horses. Each jump may be scored on a basis of ten. The scores of the two riders from each team can be added together to determine the team score.

In the games two points can be awarded for the winning of each game and one point for placing second. These points may be added together to determine which classes are first and second in the event. Games that can be played in teams should be used.

(B) *Horse Show.* Since class teams are limited to members of the riding classes and it is team and not individual competition, there is also room in the year for a show open to the entire college or school in which the competition is individual. The two forms of competition can be held during different seasons of the year, so one does not conflict with the other.

Following is a typical program which might be used:

1. Exhibition drill.[3]
2. Horsemanship class.
3. Pair class.
4. Jumping.
5. Musical chairs.
6. Bareback class.
7. Balloon game.
8. Bareback jumping.

The number of awards given in each class should be dependent upon the number of entries. If there is a large number as many as six ribbons may be given, while if the class is small only three may be awarded.

[3] This may be done by a picked team or riding club group.

CONCLUSION

Students should be taught that some horses have certain peculiarities; if the rider adjusts her riding to these, both she and her mount will have a more enjoyable ride. For example, some horses go more quietly and pull less when the reins are carried longer than is theoretically correct, so when a student rides that type of horse, she should carry her reins the length that affords them both the most pleasant ride. This adjustment to the individual horse can be acquired only by riding different types of horses. Again the necessity of having this variety of mounts in a riding school is stressed. An instructor should feel that her students know how to handle "pullers," the stubborn horse, the playful horse, and so forth as well as the perfectly schooled horse on which all theory works correctly.

An instructor should seize every opportunity that arises, whether in class, during competition, or on a recreational ride, to make the students realize that a horse is a living animal with feelings, and not a machine. She should develop in the students the feeling of kindness, consideration, understanding, and fondness for their mounts. This understanding of and feeling for the horse, combined with the ability to ride any type of mount well, constitute the true horsewoman.

For the thoughtful teacher there is even more to these various classes, the riding club, types of competition and recreation than the actual skill in riding. There goes with this the training of the individual student—the chance for individual responsibility, working with other people, and the feeling of belonging to or being a part of a group; for example, the feeling of mutual interest and responsibility as brought out by having the members of the riding club sponsor activities for the whole college and not being merely concerned with their own good times. For at the same time that an instructor is developing a true horsewoman, she need not lose sight of the opportunities to further the personal development of the student.

REFERENCES

Anderson, C. W.: *Heads Up, Heels Down*. New York, The Macmillan Co., 1944.
Chamberlain, Col. Harry D.: *Riding and Schooling Horses*. Washington, D. C., Armored Cavalry Journal, 1934. Revised 1947.
DeSouza, Baretta: *Advanced Equitation*. New York, E. P. Dutton & Co., 1926.
DeSouza, Baretta: *Principles of Equitation*. New York, E. P. Dutton & Co., 1922.
Disston, Harry: *Equestionnaire*. New York, Harper & Bros., 1936.
FitzGerald, Brian Vesey (editor): *The Book of the Horse*. London, Nicholson and Watson, 1946.
Fort Riley Manuals. Fort Riley, Kansas, Cavalry School, 1950.
Lewis, Benjamin: *Riding*. New York, Garden City Publishing Co., 1938.

Littauer, Capt. V. S.: *Common Sense Horsemanship*. New York, D. Van Nostrand Co., 1951.

Littauer, Capt. V. S.: *More about Riding Forward*. Syosset, N. Y., V. S. Littauer, 1938.

Littauer, Capt. V. S.: *Riding Forward*. New York, William Morrow & Co., 1934.

Official Sports Library for Women: *Official Individual Sports Guide*. Washington, D. C., American Association for Health, Physical Education and Recreation, 1950-52, 1952-54.

Self, Margaret Cabell: *Fun on Horseback*. New York, A. S. Barnes & Co., 1945.

Self, Margaret Cabell: *Horses, Their Selection, Care and Handling*. New York, A. S. Barnes & Co., 1943.

Self, Margaret Cabell: *The Horseman's Encyclopedia*. New York, A. S. Barnes & Co., 1946.

Self, Margaret Cabell: *Horsemastership*. New York, A. S. Barnes & Co., 1952.

Films

Refer to: Official Sports Library for Women: *Official Individual Sports Guide*, 1950-52, p. 159.

7 • SWIMMING • BY *Gertrude Goss*

In all swimming there are two factors which must be recognized from the beginning through the more advanced stages. These two factors are *breathing* and *relaxation*. They are of the utmost importance, because until the swimmer has accomplished both, she will never be "at home in the water." No great distance in the water can be covered, and a considerable tiredness will be the result. Often the swimmer herself doesn't know why it is difficult for her to swim with comfort. An experienced teacher can point out the reason and soon have the swimmer at ease in the water. One of the best aids in teaching swimming is music. No matter at what level—beginning, intermediate, or advanced—through the use of music the swimmer becomes more relaxed and therefore can swim more easily and farther. Music helps the beginner overcome her fear of the water. Intermediate and advanced swimmers can increase their endurance and power by swimming longer distances under the relaxing influence of music. This aid has been successfully used at Smith College since 1925. Most of the phonograph records used, particularly for beginning classes, are in 3/4 or 4/4 time because they provide a regular, even beat. Later on, uneven rhythms can be introduced and swimming strokes adapted to them.

Today many people learn to swim when they are very young. This is as it should be because then no fears have been built up to hamper the learning process. However, some who do not have access to the water receive their first instruction in school or college. It is they who make up the beginners' classes.

THE TEACHING OF STROKES AND DIVING

I. Beginners in School and College Classes

Usually a fear of the water has been built up by students who have reached adolescence without knowing how to swim because of lack of experience in the water or because they have heard of frightening accidents in the water. Along with this, co-ordination is usually lacking. The only uses they have had for water have been for bathing and drinking. They have always shut their eyes and held their breath whenever the water covered their faces. The water has never been deep enough for them to get the feeling of having the water support them, or else the water has been so deep and cold that a nonswimmer has had no desire even to try to swim.

Suddenly they are thrust into a new experience; they *can* open their eyes under water; they *can* breathe out under water; their arms and legs *can* be controlled while in the water.

Before anything else can be learned the potential swimmer must stand in water waist high and feel the water move around the body. The water must be splashed over the whole body while she moves up and down. In other words, she must get used to the *feel* of the water, standing and jumping up and down in it, while splashing the water over the chest and face.

When this has been accomplished, the next step is to have the potential swimmer float *on top of* the water and let the water support her.

(A) *Back Float.* The back float comes first because the swimmer doesn't have to put her face in the water. For this she merely drops back with the arms stretched sideways and lets the water hold her up. This should be practiced by two's, with one standing at the head of or beside the floater to give her support *if she needs it.* The floater must keep her eyes open and be relaxed while floating.

The *stand* from a back float must be learned next. The arms are extended out from the sides for the back float. In standing the arms are pulled in toward the body, then forward, as the legs are drawn upwards by bending the knees, and straightened toward the bottom (Fig. 114). This movement is done forcibly as the head is drawn forward to the chest. When this can be done, the individual can work alone without the help of another person.

If the water is shallow enough, a still easier way of letting the water

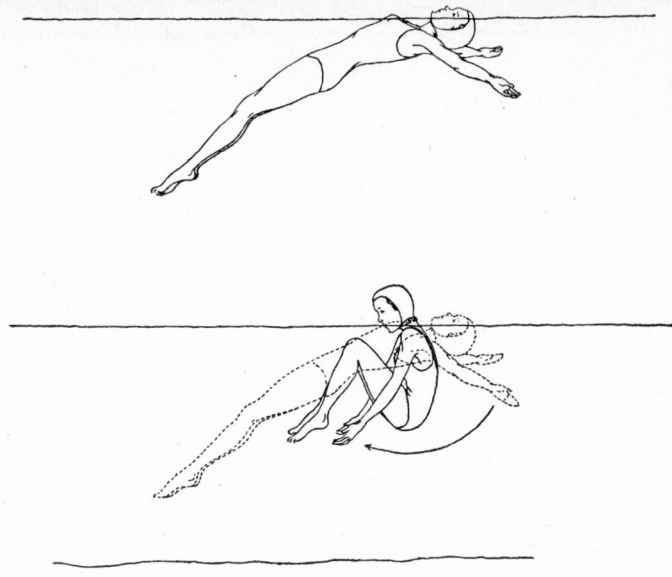

Fig. 114. Standing from a back float.

lift the body is having the beginner sit in the water, put her hands on the bottom behind her and move the upper body backward. As the upper body and head are moved backward the feet will rise and the whole body will be lifted by the water. When this has been accomplished, the beginner can move out into deeper water and, with a partner, drop back and float. The next step is to stand from a float, and finally to float and stand alone.

(B) *Breathing.* Before going on to the face float, practice in breathing should be given to the beginner. Breath-holding comes first. The beginner should stand in water about waist high, breathe in *through the mouth,* close the mouth, and submerge holding the breath. This should be done several times. Each time the face is put in the water the breath should be held for a longer time. The face should be put flat into the water with the beginner looking at the bottom of the pool.

Next continuous breathing should be practiced. This can be tried on land first. In swimming all breathing in is done *through the mouth.* Have the beginner take a breath through the mouth as the head is turned to one side. Turn the head forward and breathe *out* through the mouth and nose, or the mouth alone. This should be done continuously so that the breath is not held at any point. Now have the beginner stand in water waist deep with the body bent forward from the waist. Breathing should be practiced in and out, putting the face in the water for the exhalation, and turning the face to the side for the inhalation. This must be done until the beginner feels perfectly comfortable and does not get out of breath.

Opening the eyes under water can be practiced at the same time as practice in breathing.

(C) *Face Float.* The second float to be learned is the face or prone float. Once the beginner has learned to exhale under water, she can learn this float.

If the water is shallow enough so that the beginner can sit down in it, this depth is the easiest for the first trials. The beginner should roll over on to the stomach, with the legs extended directly behind and her weight supported on the hands. In this position a breath should be taken, and then the face moved forward into the water. At the same time the arms should be extended forward, slowly, over the head. When this is done the body will rise toward the surface. Sometimes a push with the feet will help.

If the water is too deep to sit in, the beginners can work by two's. Standing in the water, facing each other, one beginner can bend forward at the waist, take a breath, and give a slight pushoff from the bottom, extend the arms and legs, and go forward with the face in the water toward the other person, who gives assistance if needed in helping the floater to stand.

Both the floats and stands from floats should be practiced until the beginner is perfectly balanced and relaxed in the water.

The *face float* and *stand* must be learned before the beginner can be left to work alone.

(D) *Glide on Face and Back.* The beginner has now learned that the water will give support to the body, particularly if the body is *relaxed*. Movement across the water involves nothing more than a push with the feet, either from a wall or from the bottom. The aim in the glide should be to streamline the body so that it moves easily *across* the water and to give the beginner the feeling of having the water support her as she moves. If she tends to roll from side to side have her spread arms and legs apart. A greater distance can be aimed at with each glide.

(E) *Change in Body Positions.* Confidence and control are learned through the ability to change from face floating to back floating and vice versa.

1. TO TURN FROM FACE TO BACK. In the face float both arms are extended over the head. To turn on to the back, one arm remains ex-

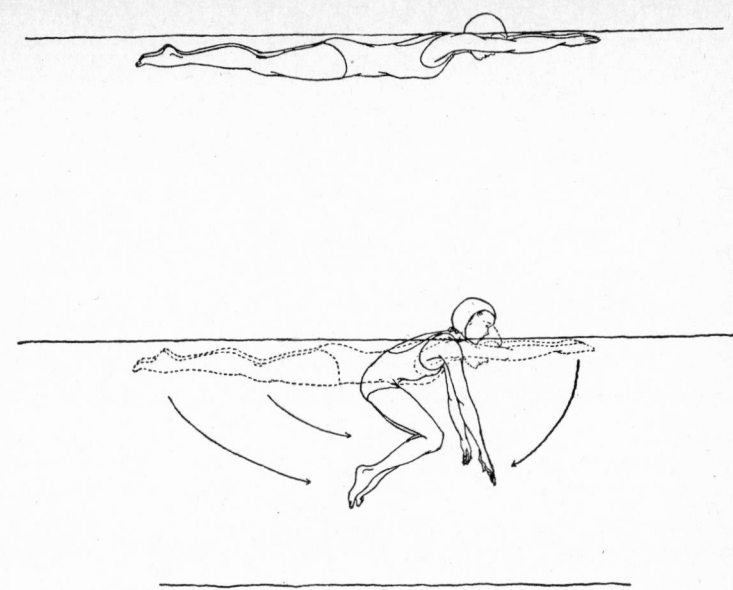

Fig. 115. Standing from a face float.

tended, while the other arm comes down and across the body and is extended to the other side. The head is turned to the side toward which the turn is made. Both arms finish in the side horizontal position.

2. TO TURN FROM BACK TO FACE. In back floating the arms are extended sideways from the body. To turn on to the face to the left, the right arm is swung across the body as the right leg is crossed over to the left. The arms move from a side horizontal position to an extended position over the head.

(F) *Floats Combined with Kicks.*

1. FACE FLOAT WITH KICK. Having accomplished the above, the beginner now adds a kick to the float and glide. At this stage the movements of the legs are very elementary. In most floats the legs tend to sink, and an easy kicking motion will bring them nearer to the surface. The start for the face float with kick is the same as for the glide. From the pushoff the legs are extended and an up and down thrashing movement from the hips is used. The emphasis is on the *up* kick. On the up motion only the heels should break the surface of the water. The knees and ankles should be relaxed. This kick can be practiced with hands supported on the bottom or with the hands bracketed on the wall, before it is used with the glide.

2. BACK FLOAT WITH KICK. The back float with kick is slightly differ-

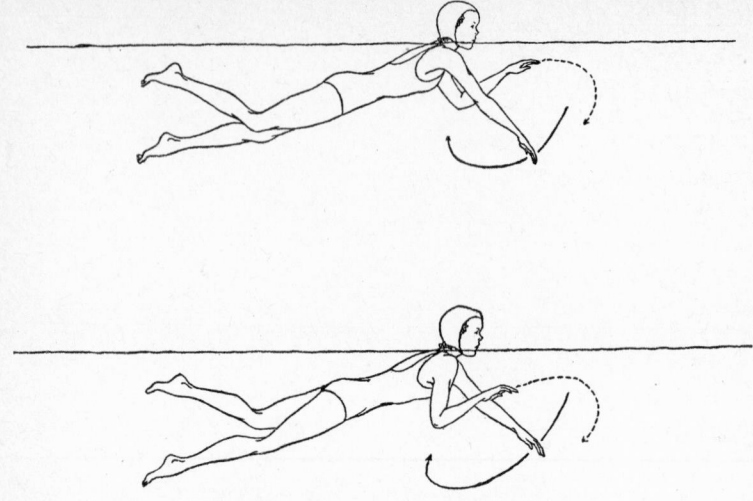

Fig. 116. The human stroke or the dog paddle.

ent, since a bicycling or pedal motion is used. Practice in this kick can first be done with the hands bracketed at the side of the pool. When the kick is used on a glide, the arms should be close to the sides of the body, and the back of the head should be in the water, the chin tucked forward.

(G) *Floats Combined with Arm Movements.*

1. ARM MOVEMENTS IN FACE FLOAT. The most natural movement of the arms when first used in the face float position is the "dog paddle," or "human stroke." In this movement first one arm is extended forward and pulled down and back toward the body, then the other. One arm is sliding forward as the other arm is pulling. The head is held high above the water, and there may be an easy kick of the legs while practicing. The arm motion may be practiced standing on the bottom, and then in the glide position. (Fig. 116.)

2. ARM MOVEMENTS IN THE BACK FLOAT. The movement of the arms used at this point is called "finning." The hands start close to the sides of the body, then there is a short draw of the arms toward the shoulders, with the fingers pointing toward the feet, up the sides of the body, followed by the palms of the hands being lifted and a thrust of the hands toward the feet. In the entire movement the arms are kept close to the body and beneath the surface of the water.

3. COMBINED ARM AND LEG MOVEMENTS. The beginner can now practice both arm and leg movements in the face float and back float positions.

When these movements have been accomplished, the beginner has a basis for some of the strokes which are to follow.

(H) *What the Beginner Has Learned.* Practice in the preceding phases of swimming should have proved to the beginner:

1. That the body is buoyant.
2. The importance of breathing in swimming.
3. That the eyes can be kept open under water.
4. That it is easy to float on both the back and face.
5. That with easy movements of the arms and legs she can move across the water.
6. That she can turn from her back on to her face and from her face on to her back.
7. How to bring her feet up from the bottom.
8. That she should have no fear of the water.

Having accomplished these things, the beginner is now ready to learn the strokes in swimming.

II. The Crawl

The crawl is the fastest of all swimming strokes. The body lies streamlined and flat on the water. The arms pull one at a time, and alternately. The legs move up and down from the hips, alternately. The head is in line with the body throughout the stroke. In order to *breathe in,* the head is turned to the side. For efficiency there should be a minimum of body roll when the head is turned.

(A) *Legs.*

1. FUNDAMENTALS IN USE OF THE LEGS.

(a) The legs are straight but relaxed; the toes pointed so that the flat of the foot will be against the water on the up beat.

(b) As one leg is lifted, the other is dropped in the water.

(c) The emphasis is on the *up* kick with very little splash, only the heels coming out of the water.

(d) The kick is from 12 to 18 inches in depth.

(e) The rhythm is even; when used with the arms, the six beat seems to be the best for most swimmers who use a deep drive, about 18 inches in depth. That means three beats to each arm stroke.

2. WAYS TO PRACTICE LEG MOVEMENTS ALONE.

(a) On land lying down with legs over the edge of the pool.

(b) On land lying on a stool or bench.

(c) Bracketed to side of pool or dock. (Practice first with emphasis on the kick only, then add breathing.)

(d) From face float kick across pool using the legs alone, first holding the breath, then with breathing turning the head to side.

(*e*) With flutter boards held in extended arms using the legs alone. In this practice the distance covered should be increased as the beginner progresses.

3. FAULTS OF THE LEGS.

(*a*) Too much bend at the knees and ankles.

(*b*) *Lifting* the legs out of water. Only the heels should break the surface.

(*c*) Pressing down with the legs. This will stop the progress forward and, in extreme cases, unless the toes are pointed the swimmer will move backward.

(*d*) Rigidly lifting and lowering the legs.

(B) *Arms.* Continue from the dog paddle. On the recovery the arms are now lifted out of water instead of moving forward under water as in the dog paddle. There is no one way in which the arms should be recovered, as the individual should be allowed to use her own best way so long as she does not impede her own progress forward. However, there are some basic principles from which all must start.

1. SOME OF THE FUNDAMENTALS IN THE USE OF THE ARMS (Fig. 117).

(*a*) The hand enters the water beyond the head with the elbow slightly higher than the hand. The hand is dropped forward from the wrist and cupped.

(*b*) The arm is extended forward over the water until at full reach.

(*c*) The pull down begins with the reach forward, the swimmer riding slightly on each separate arm.

(*d*) On the pull down the arm is bent slightly.

(*e*) The pull continues until the arm is almost under the hip on the same side.

(*f*) On the recovery the elbow is lifted out of the water first, the movement starting at the shoulder. The forearm is thrown forward to the point of entry beyond the head.

(*g*) The hand in front of the head does not start down until the other arm has started forward.

2. WAYS OF PRACTICING ARM MOVEMENTS ALONE ON LAND.

(*a*) The arm movements should be explained and demonstrated.

(*b*) As flexible shoulders are important in the crawl, the shoulder motion can be practiced first. To practice this stand with the upper body bent forward, letting the arms hang. Lift and rotate first one shoulder and then the other. As one shoulder is raised the other is lowered. At first use just the shoulders, letting the arms continue to hang. Then gradually lift the shoulder *and arm* with the forearm loose, until the elbow is high and there is no body rotation. The forearm and

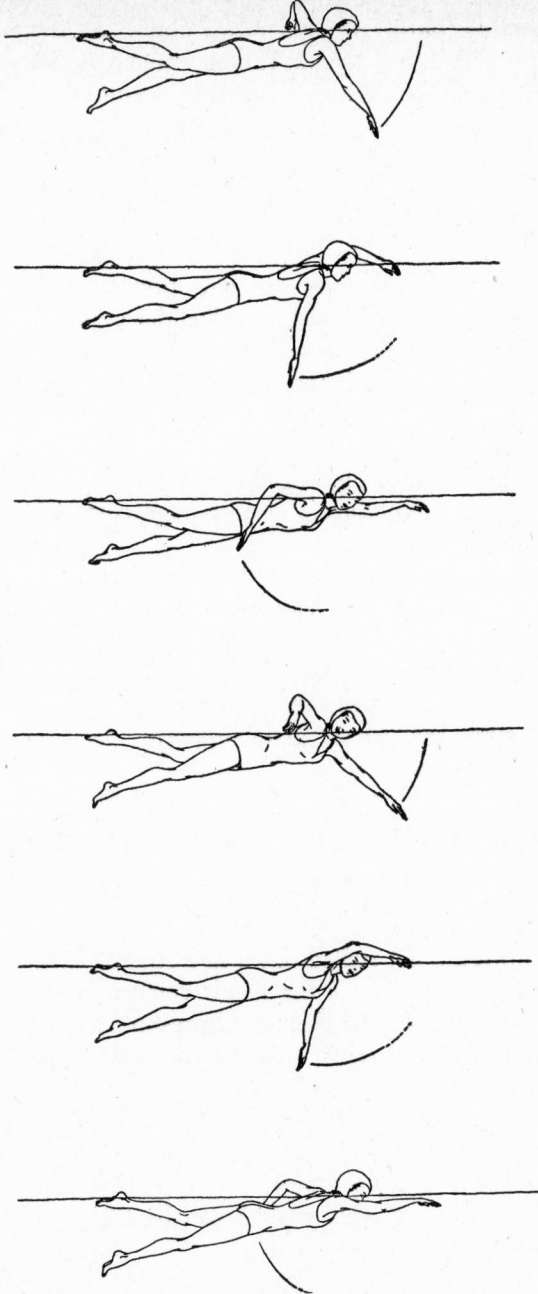

Fig. 117. Action of the arms and legs in the crawl stroke.

hand are then moved forward until the arm reaches straight forward. The hand is then pulled straight down under the shoulder, and the arm is ready to be lifted again. This movement is practiced on land until a certain amount of rhythm has been acquired.

(*c*) Still on land, breathing can be practiced having the swimmer turn the head to whichever side seems more natural for inhalation. The breath is taken in as the arm on the breathing side is lifted from the water. As the same arm moves forward the face is turned forward, and the swimmer breathes out.

3. IN WATER. The swimmer can now practice the movements of the arms in water between waist and shoulder depth.

(*a*) Lean forward from the waist with the arms extended in front of the body. *Continue* with the *breathing*, practicing with the arms alone. This practice may be done standing still or walking forward as the arms pull down.

(*b*) Same arm practice letting the feet come up from the bottom and flutter at will. Emphasize and encourage correct breathing at all times.

(*c*) With the feet bracketed at the side of the pool or dock, the arms and breathing practice can be done. If there is no place for bracketing the feet, the swimmer's feet may be held, low in the water, by the instructor, for arm practice. For group practice, divide the class in two's, having every other swimmer practice the arm movements alone while the partner gives support.

4. FAULTS OF THE ARMS.

(*a*) There is very little power in the pull if the wrist is turned up instead of dropping forward. The pull should start with the fingertips, fingers always closed.

(*b*) The arm is not pulled down far enough under the body, or the arm is pulled too far back.

(*c*) The arms are not pulled down in a straight line.

(*d*) In entering the water the hands come across in front of the head; this stops the progress ahead and prevents a straight pull down.

(*e*) The arms zigzag down through the water instead of pulling straight toward the hips.

(C) *The Whole Stroke.* Having practiced the leg and arm movements and breathing separately, the swimmer is ready to go on to all three together. The body assumes a better balanced position when a pushoff is used to start. This pushoff can be taken from the bottom or from a wall.

Music in waltz time may be profitably used at this point.

The swimmer should be encourged to breathe once every complete arm stroke.

(D) *Body Position in the Crawl.* The swimmer should be as flat in the water as possible, her head in line with her spine. This position tends to streamline the body so that it moves through the water with the least possible resistance.

(E) *Breathing.* The head should be *turned* for breathing and not lifted; a lifting of the head tends to change the body position and lower the legs.

III. The Elementary Backstroke

Along with the crawl it is helpful to practice a backstroke. The swimmer has learned to float both on the face and the back and should now learn strokes in both these positions. The elementary backstroke is a resting stroke, and allows the swimmer to move while in a resting position. In this stroke the back is flat on the water with the head in line with the spine and the chin tucked slightly forward. The arms and legs move entirely under water.

(A) *Legs Alone.* The legs start straight out and together with the toes pointed. *On count one* the legs remain in this position. *On count two* the legs are drawn up toward the body with the knees spread and either the heels or the soles of the feet together. *On count three* the legs are moved sideways and together. The power of the kick is in bringing the legs forcibly together at the end of count three. *On count four* the legs remain straight and together.

(B) *Arms Alone.* At the start of the stroke the arms are along the sides of the body. *Count one:* The hands are moved up along the sides of the body with the elbows back and the hands close to the body, the fingers pointing toward the feet until the hands reach the shoulders where the fingers point diagonally upward and outward. *Count two:* The arms are moved diagonally outward, half way between the horizontal and the straight upward position. *Count three:* The arms are pulled forcibly back to the sides of the body. *Count four:* The arms are held at the sides.

The pull with the arms and the drive together of the legs come at the same time.

(C) *Movements of the Whole Stroke* (Fig. 118).

Count one: The legs remain straight and together. The hands are moved up along the sides of the body to shoulder level. *Count two:* The legs are drawn up with the knees spread. The arms move diagonally outward. *Count three:* The legs are spread sideways and whipped

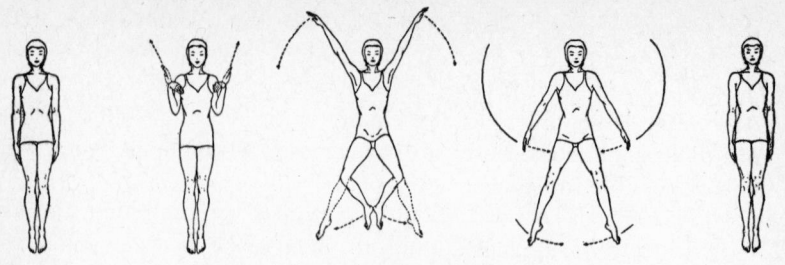

Fig. 118. The elementary back stroke.

together. The arms pull to the body, back to the starting position. *Count four:* Legs and arms are held for the glide.

(D) *Breathing.* Regular breathing is important in the backstroke even though the face is out of the water during the entire stroke.

The breath should be taken in through the mouth during the recovery of the stroke, and let out through the mouth and nose during the pull and glide.

(E) *Practicing the Leg Movements Alone.*

1. Sitting on land, lean the upper body back and rest on hands or elbows.

2. In water, lying on back holding on to the side of the pool or dock.

3. Assume the floating position on the back, hold the arms straight at the sides or place the hands on the hips.

(F) *Practicing the Arm Movements Alone.*

1. Standing on land.

2. In the water, by two's having one assume the back floating position. Number two supports number one's ankles.

(G) *Arms and Legs.*

1. Standing on land practice both arms and one leg. Use first one leg and then the other for this practice.

2. In water push off on back with the arms starting at the sides and the legs straight and together; practice the whole stroke.

(H) *Faults.*

1. OF BODY POSITION.

(*a*) Bringing the head too far forward causing the legs to sink.

(*b*) Bending forward at the waist in a near sitting position causing too much resistance against the water.

2. OF THE LEGS.

(*a*) Bringing the knees up too high on the draw causing the swimmer to curl forward.

(*b*) Moving the legs with a jerk and *kicking out* instead of moving them out slowly.

(*c*) Letting the legs float together instead of using a whip.

(*d*) Not holding the legs straight and together at the end of the whip.

3. OF THE ARMS.

(*a*) Not keeping the arms close to the body when the hands move up to the shoulders.

(*b*) Not making the movement continuous until back at the starting position.

(*c*) Not getting an even pull with both arms.

(*d*) Bringing the arms up across the body.

(*e*) Not pushing against the water with force on the pull to the sides.

(*f*) Not holding for the glide at the end of the pull.

(*g*) Breaking the surface of the water at any time.

IV. The Breast Stroke

This stroke has gone through so many changes, and so much is being done to it today that no mention of it can be made at this time without a review to bring us up to date. We have it in its oldest form (IV) as far as the movements are concerned. Originally the head was held high out of water as it still is today in life saving. This position, however, is poor for racing because it makes the body ride the water at too much of an angle, causing resistance. Therefore, the head was lifted *forward* during the pull of the arms, just high enough so that a breath could be taken in through the mouth, and lowered during the recovery and glide of the arms for speed. At first the "frog" kick of the legs was used.

Gradually since the frog kick days, the arm pull and the leg drive have dropped from the horizontal plane, with the knees well spread on the draw, into a plane between the horizontal and the vertical. The arms pull obliquely *downward* and *back,* and the knees *drop* (still slightly separated) so that the greatest amount of power comes from the circumduction of the leg and not from the old "frog" kick action with the knees wide spread and closed together.

Then using a *pull through* of the arms, *under-water* swimming of the breast stroke became very popular. This introduced the long arm pull, which gave added power to the stroke.

The real change came with the bringing of both arms out of water on the recovery part of the stroke, and the butterfly breast stroke (V) was introduced. This enabled the swimmer on top of the water to get a full pull through as in under-water swimming, which of course gave more power. This stroke was used by many men and some women in the Berlin Olympics (1936). All this time the leg kick remained the same except for a slight lowering of the knees as mentioned before. In this new arm stroke the Breast Stroke rules were obeyed as they state only that there must be a "simultaneous action of the arms."

Many swimming authorities have felt that it wasn't fair to allow the butterfly breast stroke to be used in the same race against the orthodox breast stroke because of the advantage gained. A swimmer was allowed to swim either method during a race, or to change from one to the other. In 1946 F.I.N.A. made a distinction between the orthodox (including the under-water style) and the latest stroke by ruling that the swimmer, on coming to the surface, must complete the race using the type he did on his first surface stroke. In the London Olympics nearly everyone chose to swim the butterfly breast stroke, and at Helsinki all were using this stroke.

We shall examine first the orthodox breast stroke.

(A) *Legs Alone.* At the start of the stroke the legs are straight and together, with the toes pointed. *Count one:* The legs are held in the starting position. *Count two:* The knees are drawn up and separated, the legs moving slightly apart. *Count three:* The legs move apart until straight, when they are "whipped" back to the starting position. *Count four:* Hold and glide.

(B) *Arms Alone.* Start with the arms extended forward, the hands just below the surface of the water and flat. The face is in the water. *Count one:* The palms turn outward and both arms are pulled slightly downward and sideward, almost to the side horizontal position. A breath is taken during this movement as the head is lifted forward. *Count two:* The elbows are bent and the arms are brought in together under the chest, the palms down, the elbows close to the sides, the index fingers meeting. The breath is let out on counts two, three, four, and the face is lowered in the water. *Count three:* The arms slide easily forward below the surface with the palms down, to starting position. *Count four:* Hold and glide.

(C) *Movements of the Whole Stroke.* The starting position is with the arms and legs extended, and straight. (Fig. 119.) *Count one:* The legs remain still. The arms pull to a position just in front of the shoulders. *Count two:* The legs are drawn up. The arms are brought in under the chest. *Count three:* The legs are moved outward, then together. The arms slide forward to the starting position. *Count four:* The legs and arms are held together.

(D) *Breathing.* The head is lifted forward on count one, as the swimmer breathes in through the mouth. On count two the head is

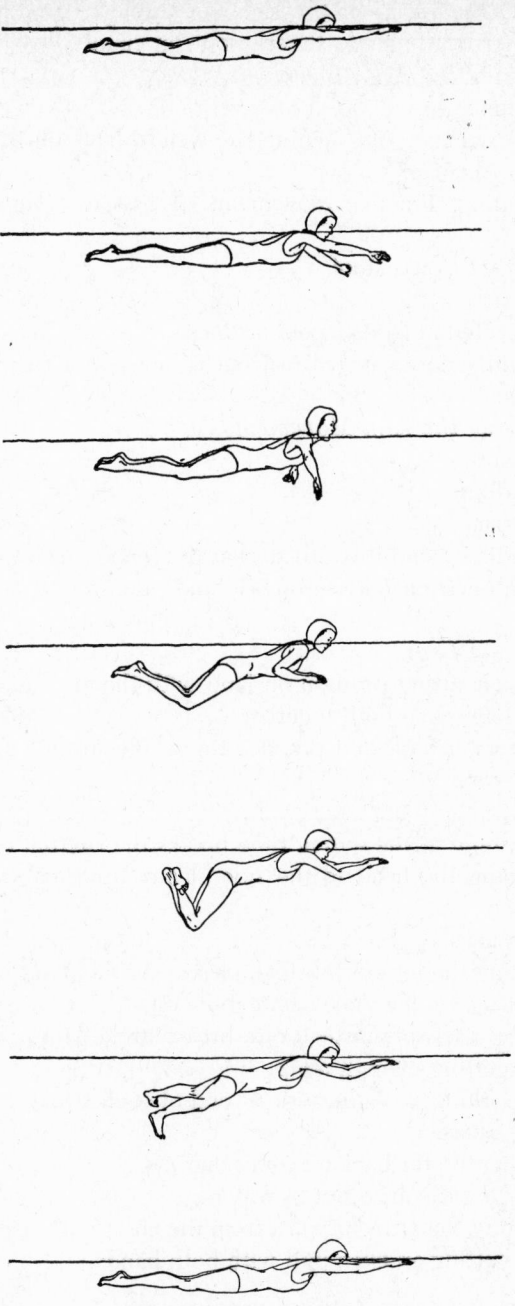

Fig. 119. The breast stroke.

lowered and the swimmer breathes out through the mouth and nose. The swimmer continues to breathe out on counts three and four.

(E) *Practicing the Leg Movements Alone.*

1. ON LAND.

(a) The swimmer sits, leaning the weight back on the hands, practice movements of legs alone.

(b) Standing. Practice movements of first one leg and then the other.

(c) Lying flat on a stool.

2. IN WATER.

(a) Bracketed at side of pool or dock.

(b) Holding flutter board in front of body, practice the leg movements alone.

(F) *Practicing the Arm Movements Alone.*

1. ON LAND.

(a) Standing.

2. IN WATER.

(a) Standing, bend forward so that the shoulders are submerged.

(b) Push off from bottom or side and practice the arm movements alone.

(G) *Arms and Legs.*

1. Assume a sitting position on land with the arms and legs in front of the body. Practice both together.

2. In water push off and practice the whole stroke.

(H) *Faults.*

1. BREATHING AND BODY BALANCE.

(a) Breathing at the wrong time breaks the rhythm of the stroke.

(b) Turning the head to the side at any time makes for incorrect body balance.

2. OF THE LEGS.

(a) Kicking the legs *out* instead of moving them out easily.

(b) Starting the leg movements too soon.

(c) Using a scissors instead of a breast stroke kick.

(d) Not getting enough *whip*.

(e) Not holding a slight glide at end of each stroke.

3. OF THE ARMS.

(a) Pulling too far back on count one.

(b) Bringing the arms out of water.

(c) Pushing the arms forward from the chest with a jerk.

(d) Not getting an even pull with both hands.

V. The Butterfly Breast Stroke

The first change in the breast stroke as a racing stroke came with bringing both arms out of the water on the recovery. The variation was called the butterfly breast stroke.

(A) *The Legs.* The kick is the same as in the breast stroke (see page 280), except that the knees are dropped a little more underneath the body, and there is not such a wide spread.

(B) *The Arms.* On the recovery, the arms are thrown outward and forward over the surface of the water. The elbows should be a little higher than the arms and the arms should be relaxed. The palms are turned down. The arms are moved to a forward point beyond the head. When the hands come in contact with the water, they start a downward pull. Since the pull is straight down, it gives the body a lift forward over the water.

(C) *Whole Stroke.* Starting with the body straight, arms and legs extended, the arms pull down, then the knees are dropped, and the legs move out and are driven together as the arms are lifted from the water and move back to the starting position. (Fig. 120.)

(D) *Breathing.* As the arms are pulled down, the breath is taken *in.* For some swimmers, it is best to breathe once every other stroke while practicing at first. When racing it is essential not to breathe so frequently.

VI. The Butterfly Stroke

The latest development is the *separation* of the *orthodox breast stroke* and the *butterfly breast stroke* into two separate strokes and events by F.I.N.A. and A.A.U.—which means they will be swum as such in the 1956 Olympics in Australia.

N.S.G.W.S. have not sanctioned this change in their rules, to this time, but it is a change which cannot be overlooked. Separating these strokes means that we will have *four racing strokes* instead of three, and that the *individual medley* and the *medley relays* will consist of four strokes. At present the F.I.N.A. and A.A.U. rules for the new *butterfly stroke* read:

When the swimmer is on the surface:

(a) Both arms must be brought forward together over the water and brought backward simultaneously.

(b) The body must be kept perfectly on the breast, and both shoulders in line with the surface of the water.

(c) All movements of the legs and feet must be executed in a simultaneous manner. *Simultaneous up and down* movements of the

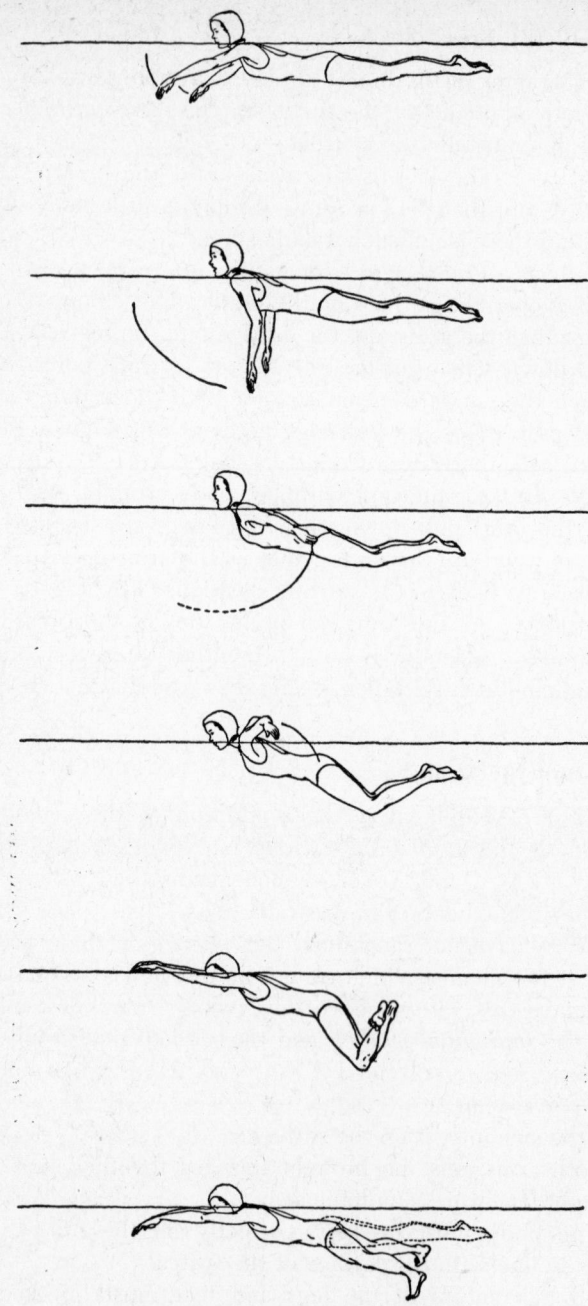

Fig. 120. The butterfly breast stroke.

legs and feet in a vertical plane are permitted. *Scissors* and *flutter kicks* are prohibited.

(d) When touching at the turn or on finishing a race, the touch shall be made simultaneously, with shoulders in the horizontal position.

(e) Any competitor introducing a side-stroke movement shall be disqualified.

Now that the *butterfly stroke* has come into being and the rules read "Simultaneous up and down movements of the legs and feet in a vertical plane are permitted," a different kick is being used called the *dolphin* or *fishtail*. This kick has been experimented with since 1930. It is most simply described as a *double flutter crawl kick*. It is easier to learn if the swimmer has swum only the crawl and not the breast stroke before.

(A) *Dolphin* or *Fishtail Kick*. The kick involves not just the legs alone, but a movement of the whole body in a fishlike action, with particular emphasis in the lower back region.

From a trailing position of the legs, the hips are lifted to start the upward movement of the legs. The knees begin to bend and spread a little as they pass through the line of body progression. When the feet are just below the water, the knees are quickly straightened and the legs brought forcibly down. Like the crawl kick, the feet are relaxed and the toes are turned in. In using this fishlike motion there is much less resistance to the water than when using the froglike kick with its recovery against the water. It can be practiced as follows:

1. First hold on to the side of the pool, legs together.

2. Go under water and do the dolphin kick with the arms at the sides of the body.

3. When the body or hip movement is felt, then the bend of the knees and drive at the end of the up and down strokes can be worked on.

4. After getting the above motions, stress the action of the ankles so that the feet press against the water on both up and down beats of the legs.

5. This kick can be practiced with a kick board.

(B) *The action of the arms is the same as described for the butterfly breast stroke.* The glide can be lengthened or shortened according to the distance to be covered.

(C) *The Timing of the Arms and Legs.* The most satisfactory rhythm to be used to date is two leg beats to one cycle of the arms. The legs being the controlling part of this stroke, it will be analyzed according to their action.

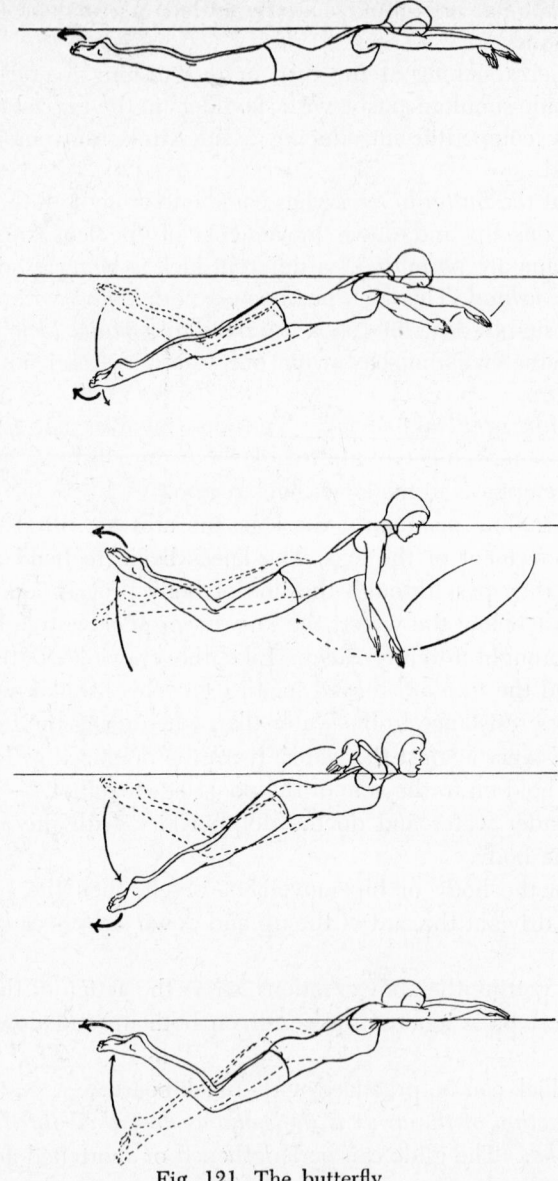

Fig. 121. The butterfly.

The legs start straight except for a slight bend at the knees. The arms extended begin the stroke.

The hands take hold of the water in the pull, the hips start upward, and the legs finish the down beat. The legs drive up while the arms are pulling. Then the legs begin the second down beat as the arms go back to the extended position.

(D) *Timing the Breathing with the Arms.* In this stroke, the head is highest out of water when the arms are out to the sides from the shoulders. Therefore, the breath should be taken in at this point. The legs are kicking down which enables both arms and head to be out of the water.

VII. The Side Stroke

The side stroke is *not* a racing stroke and most speed swimmers stay away from it believing it to be harmful. However, there are many swimmers who do not desire speed and who find this stroke very restful and powerful. It is also very important in life saving. With a knowledge of the side stroke, the single overarm and trudgeon can be learned. The side stroke may be executed on either side. The following description is for a swimmer who swims on the right side.

(A) *Side Balance and Glide.* Before going into a discussion of the movements used in the side stroke, it is necessary for the swimmer to learn the side pushoff and balance. This position requires more control than either the face or back floats which have already been learned.

1. Standing in shallow water, turn so that the left side is toward the edge of pool or dock.

2. Grasp the rail with the left hand and place both feet against the side of the pool, with the knees bent. The right arm is extended out across the water, the head resting on the right shoulder and turned so that the swimmer is looking *back* toward her feet.

3. Taking in a breath, push off with both feet letting the body lie on the side. Slowly exhale and straighten the body. *Hold the body balance on the side for as long as possible.*

4. The left arm should rest on top of the left thigh, the right arm extended beyond the head. The legs should be together with the left leg on top of the right.

(B) *Leg Movements Alone.* Start on right side—legs extended, together, and the toes pointed. *Count one:* Draw the knees slightly upward keeping the legs together. *Count two:* Separate the legs, moving the top leg forward as the under leg moves backward. *Count three:* Drive the legs together back to the starting position. The drive is with the sole of the left foot and the instep of the right foot. *Count four:* Hold the legs together at the end of the drive.

(C) *Arms Alone.* On right side. *Count one:* The right arm pulls down in the water. Just after the start of the right arm pull, the left arm is carried across in front of the body, with the hand leading.

Counts two and three: The right arm is drawn up toward the right shoulder and extended forward beneath the surface, to the starting position, as the left arm pulls down close to the body, back to the top of the left thigh. *Count four:* Hold and glide at the end of the stroke. (D) *Breathing.* A breath may be taken in during the glide, and let out slowly, during the stroke itself.

(E) *The Whole Stroke. Count one:* Pull the right arm down three-fourths of the way to the body. Just after the right arm pull starts, the left arm is brought across the body, beyond the right shoulder. At the same time the knees are drawn slightly upward. *Counts two and three:* The right hand is moved up toward the right shoulder and slides forward to the starting position as the left arm pulls back to the top of the left thigh. At the same time the legs are separated and drive together. *Count four:* Hold and glide.

(F) *Practicing the Leg Movements Alone.*

1. ON LAND.

(*a*) Lying across bench or stool.

(*b*) Lying on edge of pool or dock, with the legs extended over edge.

2. IN WATER.

(*a*) Bracketed at the side of the pool or dock.

(*b*) With flutter board push off from the bottom or the side, and practice the kick alone.

(*c*) Without flutter board push off maintaining the side balance, and practice the leg movements alone.

(G) *Practicing the Arm Movements Alone.*

1. ON LAND. Standing.

2. IN WATER.

(*a*) Stand in shallow water, with the water covering the shoulders, the body leaning to the right.

(*b*) Same as above, moving to the right letting the arm movement move the body. Feet may be dragged along the bottom for this practice.

(*c*) Push off using only the arm movements.

(H) *Practicing the Whole Stroke.* From pushoff, practice both arm and leg movements trying to decrease the number of strokes each time. (Fig. 122.)

(I) *Faults.* Not remaining on the side throughout the stroke.

1. OF THE LEGS.

(*a*) Using force on the separation of the legs instead of moving them easily apart.

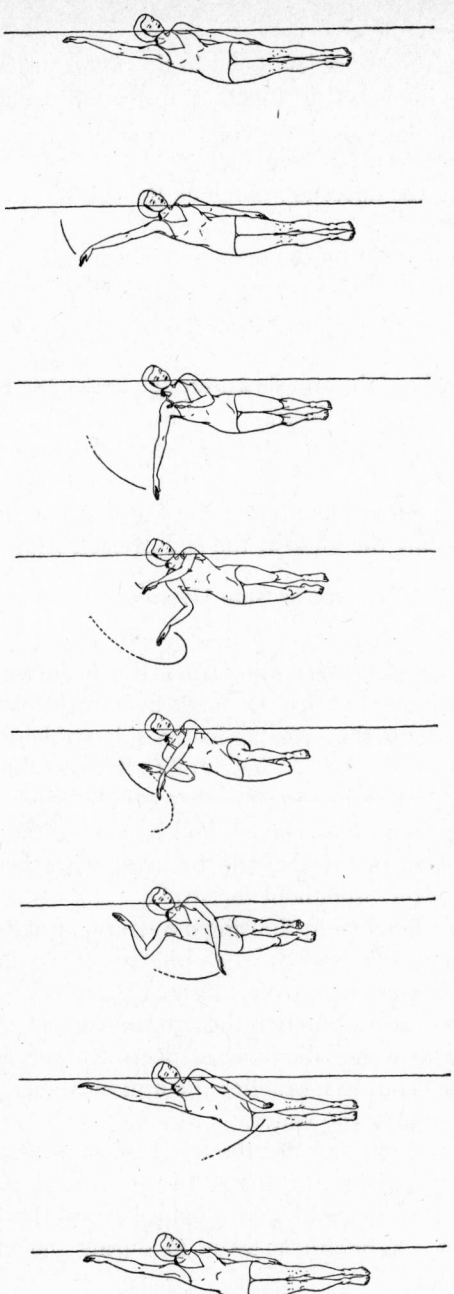

Fig. 122. The side stroke.

(*b*) Moving the upper leg *up* toward the surface of the water instead of forward.

(*c*) Moving the under leg down in the water instead of back.

(*d*) Letting the legs drift together, instead of using a drive.

(*e*) Crossing the legs at the end of the drive.

(*f*) Using a reverse scissors kick.

(*g*) Bending the knees too much on the draw.

2. OF THE ARMS.

(*a*) Using force during the recovery movements.

(*b*) Swinging the left arm out, away from the body.

(*c*) Letting the left arm go back beyond the thigh at the end of the pull.

(*d*) Pulling the right arm down too far under the body, causing the swimmer to bob up and down.

(*e*) Pushing the right arm forcibly forward from the shoulder on the recovery.

(*f*) Bringing either hand out of the water at any time.

(*g*) Not holding the glide at the end of each stroke.

VIII. The Single Overarm or Side Overarm

(A) *Single Overarm without a Roll.*

1. TECHNIQUE. After the side stroke has been learned, it is fairly easy for the swimmer to learn the single overarm stroke. For this stroke, the body position is the same as in the side stroke and the legs continue to do the scissors kick. The arms alternate their pulls, but the top arm instead of recovering under water is lifted out of the water with the elbow bent and relaxed, and is extended to a point beyond the forehead. A clean entry should be made with the hand. The body remains on the side throughout the stroke.

2. PRACTICE. Practice in the single overarm stroke may be done by simply continuing the side stroke and having the swimmer lift the top arm out of the water on recovery. (Fig. 123.)

It is possible also to practice the arm movement standing on land. Then standing in water about waist deep, leaning to the right side, submerging the shoulders, practice the arm movements alone, recovering the top arm out of the water.

When practiced in the water the left arm, as it lifts out of the water and reaches forward leaving the water, is *relaxed,* until it enters the water with the fingers leading, at a point beyond the head.

3. BREATHING. A breath is taken in during the glide and let out during the stroke.

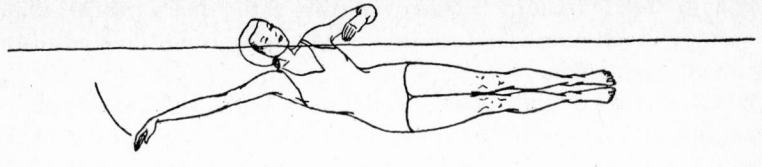

Fig. 123. The side overarm or single overarm stroke.

4. FAULTS. The faults of the under arm and legs are the same as in the side stroke. The top arm faults will be:

(*a*) Bringing the arm too high out of water, which tends to submerge the body.

(*b*) Not lifting the arm high enough so that it drags through the water, causing resistance against the water.

(*c*) Reaching too far forward with the arm, causing the body to roll onto the face, instead of staying on the side.

(*d*) Circling the arm around the head, instead of reaching straight forward.

(*e*) Letting the arm drop into the water on the entry instead of entering with the fingers first, and the arm following.

(*f*) Throwing the arm forcibly forward, making the stroke jerky.

(B) *Single Overarm with a Quarter Turn.* This is not a stroke, but sometimes is an easy progression in going from the single overarm to the double overarm or trudgeon stroke. In it the reach of the top arm is well beyond the head so that in reaching forward the body is rolled over on the face, and as the arm pulls down, the body rolls back to the side. The action of the under arm and the legs is the same as in the side stroke and the single overarm.

The quarter turn can be learned more easily without a land drill, by going directly from the single overarm into the quarter turn, adding the longer reach ahead and the roll of the body from the side to the front and back again.

1. MOVEMENTS OF THE ARMS. *Count one:* As the right arm is pulled down the left lifts out of the water and is moved as far in front of the head as possible. As the arm is reached forward, the body rolls on to the face, putting face in the water. *Counts two and three:* The right hand comes up to the right shoulder and moves forward under the water as in the side stroke. The left arm is pulled down to the left side and the body rolls back to the side. *Count four:* There is a *very short* hold or glide when the stroke is finished and while the body is on the side.

2. MOVEMENTS OF THE LEGS. The leg action is the same as in the side stroke except that the separation of the legs is somewhat narrower. The kick is made while the body is on the side and the legs are held together while the body is on the face.

3. FAULTS.

(*a*) Pulling the arms down away from the body instead of straight down. The right arm tends to do this more than the left.

(*b*) Dragging the left arm through the water on the recovery instead of lifting it out of the water.

(*c*) Bringing the left arm too high out of the water.

(*d*) Circling the left arm around the head on the recovery instead of reaching forward.

(*e*) Starting the leg kick when the body is on the face, instead of on the side.

IX. The Trudgeon or Double Overarm

The trudgeon is a hand-over-hand stroke plus a scissors kick with the legs. It is an excellent distance stroke and when once learned and coordinated it can be used indefinitely with very little effort. There is more roll in the trudgeon than the crawl due to the scissors kick. Having learned the scissors for the side stroke and the single overarm a good start has been made toward the trudgeon. The trudgeon can also be learned with the crawl for its background.

(A) *Leg Movements (for the person who does the side stroke on right side).* Grasp the side of the pool with the left hand high and the right hand low against the wall. In this manner, hold the body floating on the right side with the legs extended straight behind. *Count one:* Do the scissors kick while the body is in a semi-side position. Breathe in. *Counts two and three:* Complete the leg drive as the body rolls onto the face and hold the legs together after the drive. Breathe out.

(B) *Arm Movements.* Standing in shallow water, bend forward submerging the shoulders. The right arm should be extended straight forward, and the left arm straight back. *Count one:* The left arm recovers forward, over the water, as the right arm is pulled down. The body roll onto the face starts as the left arm is moved from back forward. *Counts two and three:* The body rolls back to a semi-side position with the pull of the left arm down, and the recovery of the right arm forward over the water.

(C) *Coordination of the Whole Stroke. Count one:* From a side pushoff, with the right arm extended forward and the left arm back, the legs together, breathe in. As the right arm is pulled down, the left arm recovers out of the water reaching well forward. The legs do the scissors kick while on the side, the body rolling onto the face as the leg drive is finished, and exhale. *Counts two and three:* The legs are held together. The body is on the face as the left arm is pulled down and the right arm recovers out of the water and the body rolls back to a semi-side position. There is a *very slight* pause each time the body rolls back to a semi-side position.

(D) *Faults.*

1. Incorrect coordination.
2. Kicking when the legs should be holding.
3. Not making the rhythm slightly uneven.
4. Not lifting the arms high enough to clear the surface.
5. Having an unequal pull with the arms.

(E) *Teaching.* The trudgeon can be learned from two approaches. The approach used depends on the strokes already learned by the swimmer.

1. THE FIRST APPROACH IS FROM THE SIDE STROKE. For this no land drills are necessary.

(a) Practice the single overarm.

(b) Practice the single overarm with quarter turn.

(c) Go directly from the single overarm into the trudgeon.

2. THE SECOND APPROACH IS FROM THE CRAWL.

(a) Practice the flutter kick alone; then add a major scissors kick and a slight body roll.

(b) Practice the scissors kick at the side of the pool or dock.

(c) Push off on face, roll the body to the left at the last half of the left arm pull. Let the legs drag, merely practicing the arm movements and body roll.

(*d*) After practicing the roll and arm movements, add a major scissors kick to the flutter kick as soon as the roll is back to the side.

X. The Trudgeon Crawl

For the swimmer who has learned the trudgeon or the crawl, the trudgeon crawl is a fairly simple stroke to learn. As a matter of fact many crawl swimmers are actually doing a trudgeon crawl unknowingly by employing a major scissors beat between flutters.

When learned from the trudgeon, the swimmer adds three or four flutters after the scissors kick in place of holding the legs still after the scissors.

When learned from the crawl, the swimmer rolls slightly to the breathing side and makes a narrow scissors, then rolls back on to the face continuing the flutter kick.

XI. The Backstroke

There are many variations in the backstroke, but in many ways it is the crawl turned over on the back. It is one of the four racing strokes, and is the fastest stroke on the back.

(A) *Legs.*

1. TECHNIQUE.

(*a*) The swing is from the hips with the legs relaxed. The toes are pointed and the pressure is on the up beat.

(*b*) The legs are bent slightly at the knees and ankles.

(*c*) The kick is an up and down motion about 10 to 12 inches in depth.

(*d*) The six beat rhythm seems best for most swimmers—that is, three beats to each complete arm cycle.

2. PRACTICE OF THE LEG MOVEMENTS ALONE.

(*a*) Sitting on land, leaning back on hands for support.

(*b*) Bracketed to side of pool or dock.

(*c*) From back pushoff practice kick alone with arms extended straight overhead.

(*d*) From back pushoff with arms along the body and "finning" or "sculling" with the arms.

(B) *Arms.*

1. TECHNIQUE.

(*a*) The arms work alternately. As one arm pulls, the other arm is recovering.

(*b*) The lift of the arms out of the water starts with the finger tips.

(*c*) The arm is thrown out away from the body so that no water splashes the face. The arm is straight.

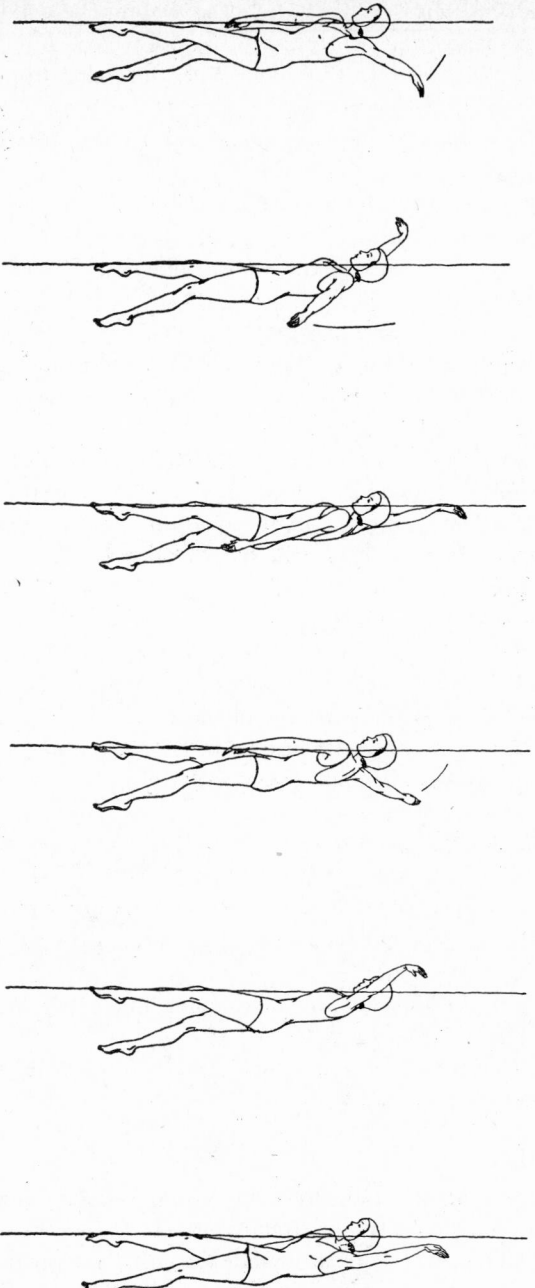

Fig. 124. The backstroke.

(*d*) The hand, cupped, goes into the water when the arm is *well above* shoulder height.

(*e*) The hand goes into the water with the palm dropped forward. The arm drops about 6 to 8 inches below the surface of the water. The pull starts with the finger tips. The motion is a pull, followed by a squeeze into the sides of the body.

2. PRACTICE OF THE ARM MOVEMENTS ALONE.

(*a*) On land standing.

(*b*) Lying on the back in the water with the legs held by another person.

(*c*) From back pushoff, practice the arm movements alone.

(C) *The Whole Stroke.* Push off on back in water and practice both arm and leg movements, making three leg kicks to each complete arm cycle. (Fig. 124.)

(D) *Body Position.* The body should be well back in the water, to make as little resistance against the water as possible. The head should be well back, with the chin tucked in just enough so the swimmer is looking toward her feet, the head in line with the body.

(E) *Breathing.* The breath should be taken in once every complete arm cycle.

(F) *Faults.*

1. OF LEGS.

(*a*) The entire motion is rigid (not relaxed).

(*b*) Kicking from the knees instead of from the hips.

(*c*) The toes turned up and the ankles rigid.

(*d*) Too shallow a kick.

(*e*) A downward pressure of the legs.

2. OF ARMS.

(*a*) Recovery is too rigid—the arms being brought too close to the face. The recovery should be a fling of the arms to the above-shoulder entrance.

(*b*) Letting the elbows drag and enter the water first instead of having the finger tips enter first.

(*c*) Completing one complete arm cycle before the other arm starts, breaking rhythm.

XII. Diving

Along with learning how to swim, there is considerable value in having the swimmer also learn how to enter the water head first. Courage and more and more confidence are developed as the individual goes through the learning stages and into more difficult dives.

An added skill is accomplished along with freedom of movement and grace. Diving also has value as an exercise.

Having the swimmer learn how to dive should not be left until the later stages of swimming. Instead, diving should be started early and while the swimmer is still a beginner. Even before the dive is done from the side, the beginner can *stand in shallow water,* with the arms extended over the head and the thumbs locked together, take a breath, bend forward from the hips, and, giving a push from the bottom, dive forward under the water.

It is always a good idea to have a demonstration and explanation. The swimmer must be shown:

1. How to come to the surface by lifting the head and turning the hands upward.

2. Breath control. Take a breath first, then *hold* the breath until back to a standing position.

3. Form. Keep the arms in front of the head with the thumbs locked together. Have the hands enter the water first and the feet last.

When this has been accomplished standing in the water, the beginner is ready to try the *Sitting Dive.*

(A) *Sitting Dive.* In teaching a beginner to dive, it is best to have her start from a point as close to the water as possible. In most cases, the first dive is the sitting dive. At first, the diver simply falls into the water, glides, and comes to the surface. The start is made with the arms extended over the head, the beginner bending forward until the finger tips are in the water. Keeping the head down, the beginner drops into the water. If the dive is done from the side of a pool, the heels rest in the gutter, and *knees are spread.* At first, the diver may stand at the end of the dive if done in shallow water, but soon she should be encouraged to swim across the pool from the dive before standing. Breathing is important, and the diver must be reminded to take a breath, then *hold the breath* until coming to the surface.

Assistance may be given by the instructor holding the diver's head low and giving her an easy push as she drops forward.

A sitting dive with the *knees together* is the next step.

(B) *Kneeling Dive.* Kneeling on one knee with the toes of the other foot over the edge of the pool or dock, fall forward into the water. In doing this dive, kneel alternately first on one knee and then the other. Keep the head between the arms.

(C) *Dive from One Leg.* Standing, with the toes of one foot over the edge of the pool or dock, with the knee bent, the other leg reaches well back, the arms are locked together over the head. The upper body

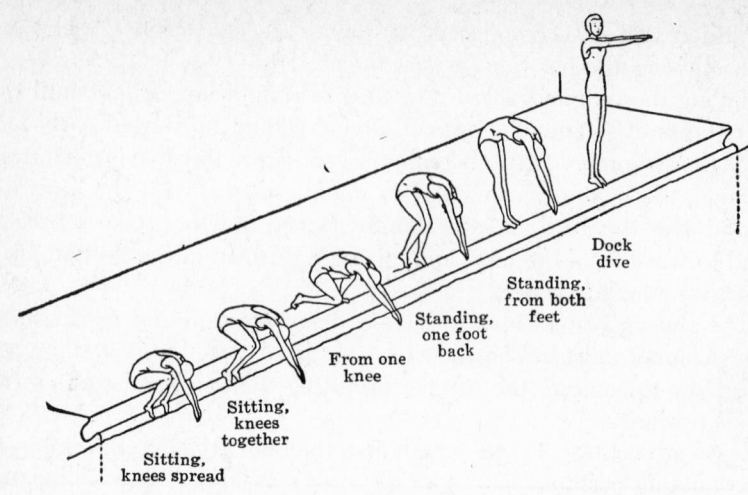

Fig. 125. Diving progression for a beginner.

bends forward over the water and the rear leg is lifted straight up. The balance is lost forward and both legs are lifted. In doing this dive stand alternately first on one foot and then on the other.

(D) *Falling Forward from Both Feet.* Stand with the arms up over the head, the thumbs locked together. Bending forward from the waist, reach for the water and drop in.

(E) *Standing or Dock Dive.* The diver should stand *erect* at the edge of the pool, with the legs together and the toes over the edge. The arms are extended forward at shoulder height.

Bend the knees slightly as the heels are lifted, push *up,* straightening the knees, then bow forward to the water, lowering the arms and head, with the finger tips reaching for the water.

After this dive has been practiced the diver may start with the arms at the sides and move them forward and upward over the head, as the push up is taken from the side.

1. WAYS OF PRACTICING.

(*a*) Standing back from the edge, practice an easy spring jump in place. The emphasis should be on the *push up* with an easy ankle and knee action. This practice may be done first without the use of the arms; then have the arms move forward and upward over the head as the ankles push up.

(*b*) Practice in the spring jump can also be done by placing the hands at shoulder height on a wall and jumping up in place.

2. GENERAL FAULTS IN DIVING.

(*a*) The Tendency to Overthrow the Legs. This is caused by a push back of the feet from the take-off, by putting the head down too soon or by pulling the arms down too soon and with too much force.

Corrections.

(1) Be sure to get an upward push, keeping the legs straight, and do not relax them on leaving the take-off.

(2) Keep the arms extended over the head and do not pull them down under the body on the entry into the water.

(b) Landing Too Flat and Too Far Out. This is caused by leaning forward on the take-off and pushing out instead of up.

Corrections.

(1) Continue to practice the spring jump with the emphasis on pushing up with the top of the head leading.

(2) Practice by two's, having one kneel down facing the diver. In this position, extend one arm out over the water in front of and just below the knees of the diver. The diver pushes *up*, going over the arm from the take-off.

(3) Practice the one-legged dive. Standing with all the weight on one foot with the knee bent, the other leg is lifted straight behind. As the upper body is bent forward over the water, the rear leg is lifted straight up. Giving a slight push from the take-off with one foot, both feet should meet well up in the air and enter the water together and straight, in line with the body.

3. REMEMBER.

(a) Push *up* from the take-off and do not lean forward.

(b) The position of the body on entry into the water should be perpendicular.

(c) Go *straight down* toward the bottom before starting up.

(d) The position of the head governs the line of flight.

(F) *Springboard Diving*. So far, the diving has been done from a stationary take-off. Having accomplished this, the diver is ready to go on and learn how to dive from a springboard which will "give" as the diver leaves it. When used correctly, the board will aid the diver greatly in getting height. It is therefore very important for the diver to learn *how* to use the board. *Height* and *balance* are essential.

1. STANDING DIVE PROGRESSION.

(a) Standing on the board and about 4 inches from the diving end, the feet apart, jump up and down getting the final push from the balls of both feet. On the upward life move the arms forward and upward. The arm lift must co-ordinate with the push from the feet. The arms aid greatly the body balance. When first practicing this jump, it is not necessary to strive for height. Balance must be maintained and then the diver can work for height.

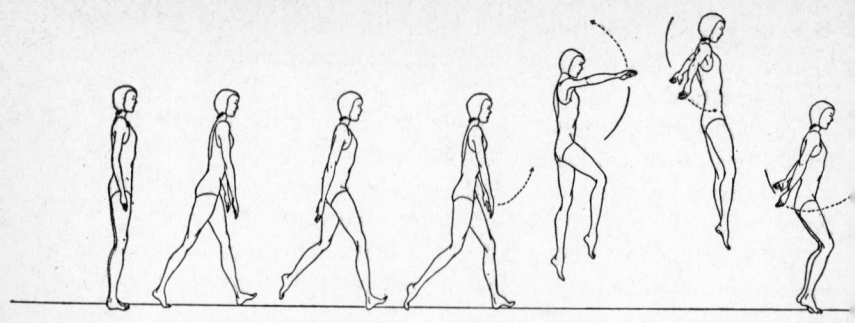

Fig. 126. The approach for running dives.

(*b*) After getting balance and a certain amount of height, the diver can use the same start as above, and on the lift, go straight up and enter the water feet first.

(*c*) From the same take-off, go up and enter the water head first. This practice should continue until the diver has control, balance, and a certain amount of height—in other words, has the "feel of the board." The diver must stay with the board and leave the board only as the board lifts.

2. THE RUNNING FRONT DIVE. In all running dives the required approach is at least three steps and a jump or hurdle. The diver should pace back from the end of the board the desired number of steps and hurdle to find where each dive should be started and then always start from the same place, and with the same foot. Practice in the approach can be done first away from the board, walking out the desired steps using both arms and legs. Having practiced this, she is ready for the dive.

(*a*) Position on the Board. Step up on the board. Assume an easy, good posture. Stand with arms at the sides, head up, and chin in.

(*b*) Approach and Take-off. At least three steps and a hurdle are required on the approach. The steps should be taken naturally and gracefully with the arms at the sides. In taking the hurdle, the knees should be lifted high and both feet should come down together on the end of the board. *As the board comes up*, the arms are lifted vigorously forward and upward, and the final push is from the balls of the feet. The lift of the arms should start at the shoulders. (Fig. 126.)

(*c*) Position in the Air. Good form in the air is what divers strive for. The body should be stretched at full reach, the balance controlled. The head should be in line with the body, the legs together and straight, toes pointed, the back slightly arched.

(*d*) Entrance into the Water. The tips of the fingers should enter the water first, the rest of the body following in a *straight line*. The entrance should be as nearly perpendicular to the water as possible. The legs should be straight and together, toes pointed.

(*e*) Practice.

(*1*) Practice the approach and use of arms first, when not on the diving board, then on the board.

(*2*) Work to get a *high hurdle*, bringing the knees well up in front, and at the same time lift the arms.

(*3*) In order to get the feel of the board, practice jumping going up *with the board*.

(*f*) Faults.

(*1*) Jacking on the dive. (Having a bend at the hips on a straight dive.)

(*2*) Going too far out and thus not entering the water in a vertical line. This is caused by leaning forward on the take-off or leaving the board too soon.

(*3*) Not lifting the arms well up on the take-off. This will cut down height and send the diver too far out.

(*4*) Over-throwing the legs. This is caused by pushing the legs back on the take-off or by relaxing the knees while in the air or by throwing the head forward from the board.

3. THE SWAN DIVE. This dive is quite similar to the running front dive and in competition the running front and swan dives are done as the same dive. The difference is the movement of the arms to a right-angle position while in the air. The take-off and entrance into the water are the same as in the running front dive. The feeling of the movement of the arms will come with practice.

(*a*) On Land. Lying flat on the floor with arms extended over head, move the arms to the side horizontal position with palms turned up or kept flat as desired. At the same time the back should be arched, the head raised, the legs should be held together in a straight line and the toes pointed, as the legs are lifted from the floor.

(*b*) Standing. Practice the position described above, with a jump upward and forward.

(*c*) From the Board. Standing at the end of the board with the arms extended and together over the head, swing the body forward from the ankles moving the arms to the side horizontal position. This position should be held until just before entering the water when the arms are moved back together over the head. As the body balance is lost the back should be arched and the head lifted. As the diver enters the water, the back is unarched or flattened and the head moved forward. (Fig. 127.)

Fig. 127. The swan dive.

(*d*) With the Approach. The approach is the same as in the running front dive. The body should go straight up from the board. On reaching the height of the dive, the arms move to the side horizontal position, the lower back is arched, and the head is lifted forward. This position should be held until just before entering the water, when the arms are brought together and the head is moved slightly forward.

(*e*) Entrance. The entrance is perpendicular to the water as in the running front dive.

(*f*) Faults in the Swan Dive.

(*1*) Same as in the running front dive.

(*2*) Taking the swan position too soon (from the board) thus cutting down the height.

(3) Holding the swan position too long.

(4) Failing to arch the body after the lift.

4. THE FRONT JACKKNIFE DIVE (RUNNING). Another type of running dive is the front jackknife. Instead of remaining straight throughout the dive, the body is jacked at the hips at the height of the dive. This position is held until just before entering the water when the body is straightened and a straight entry is made.

(a) Land Practice. Standing erect with the knees straight, bend the upper body forward and reach down with the hands until they touch the instep. The head should be held up. Practice this until it can be done easily.

To get the idea of the lift from the hips, stand erect, bend forward from the hips and swing the right leg forward, touching the instep with both hands. Return to standing position. Practice this, using first one leg and then the other.

(b) The Dive from the Board. The approach is the same as the running front or swan dive. From the take-off, the body should go straight up from the board. At the height of the lift, the jackknife position is taken. To assume this position, the hips are lifted, the body is bent at the hips, and the hands and insteps are brought together. The head is forward, the knees are straight. (Fig. 128.)

Just before entering the water, the body is straightened by raising the legs from the hips and the head is between the arms.

In learning this dive, the beginner may not at first reach the instep with the hands, but with practice, the hands will reach lower and lower. At all times it must be remembered to keep the *knees straight*.

(c) Faults in the Jackknife.

(1) Going out too far from the board. This is caused by going into the jackknife position too soon which takes away from the height of the dive.

(2) Holding the jackknife position too long which causes a poor entry into the water.

(3) Having an over-throw of the legs. This is caused by dropping the arms and ducking the head instead of bringing the feet up to meet the hands.

(4) Bending the knees. Rather than bend the knees, do not go so far down with the hands unless the *knees are straight*.

5. THE BACK DIVE. This is generally the first dive a diver learns with the back to the water.

(a) Beginning.

(1) The diver stands at the end of the diving board, back to the

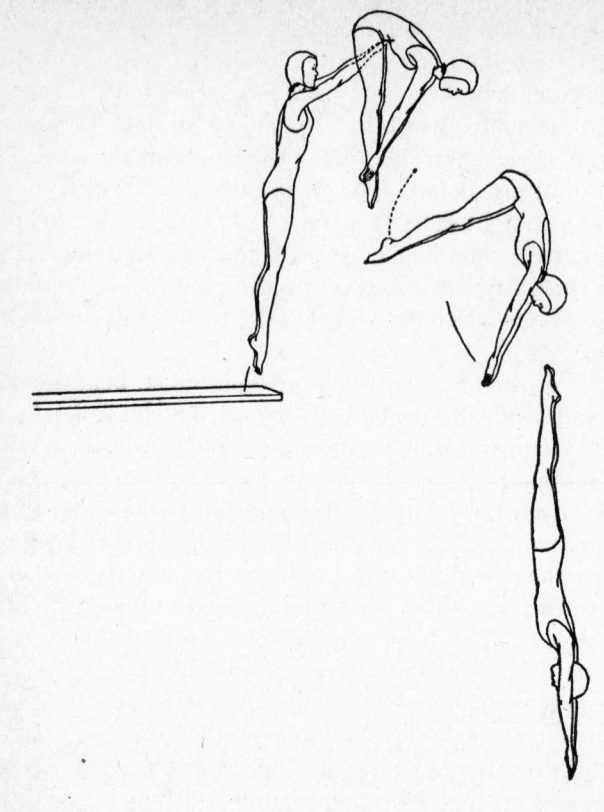

Fig. 128. The running front jackknife dive.

water and facing the board, with the feet parallel to the diving board. The arms are lifted straight over the head, the thumbs locked together. The diver is supported at the hips. Keeping the head well back, the diver bends backward over the water. When the upper body is pointing downward, the support is released and the diver drops into the water.

(2) Without support the diver bends backward over the water and drops in.

(b) With Spring. First the diver goes to the end of the board and turning away from the end practices the lift as for the running front dive, by jumping the board.

(1) Position: The diver stands at the end of the board, with the arms raised in front to shoulder level. The heels are slightly over the end of the board with the weight on the balls of the feet. To maintain

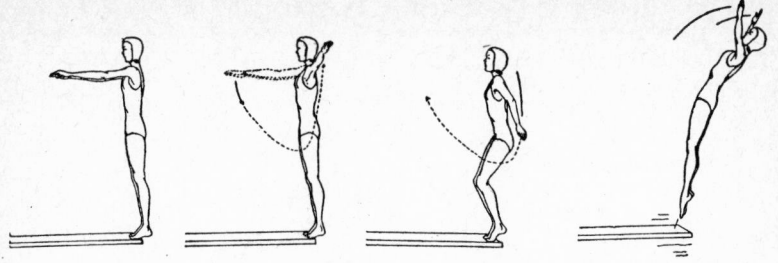

Fig. 129. The take-off on the board for the back dive.

balance a high eye mark is helpful. That is, the diver focuses her eyes on a spot on the wall in front of her. The legs should be straight and the body erect.

(2) The Lift: Holding the above position, the arms are lowered to the sides and raised to the side horizontal position (slowly and in one movement). As the arms are lowered, the heels are lowered, then as the arms move forcibly upward, the heels are lifted and the feet extended so that on leaving the board the movement of the *arms and legs together* lifts the body into the air. (Fig. 129.)

(3) In the Air: The lift is taken *with the board* and the body goes straight upward over the board; the arms are over the head and in line with the body. At the height of the dive, the head moves back, and the back is arched. The arms can be held over the head or move sideward to the swan position as the body drops backward to the water. But on the entrance the arms must be together. (Fig. 130.)

(4) Entrance into the Water: The finger tips enter the water first, the body is straight, legs together, and toes pointed.

(5) Faults:

(a) An over-throw of the legs. Caused by leaning backward from the board and not getting the push up through the whole body. Relaxing the legs.

(b) Going out too far from the board and too parallel to the top of the water.

(c) Turning in the dive. Caused by an uneven pushoff, or by trying to see the water.

6. THE BACK SOMERSAULT. The back somersault is done in any of three positions: in a tuck, pike, or layout (straight) position. For the tuck position, the knees are drawn close up to the body, and the front of the legs grasped by the arms. From a low board, this is the easiest

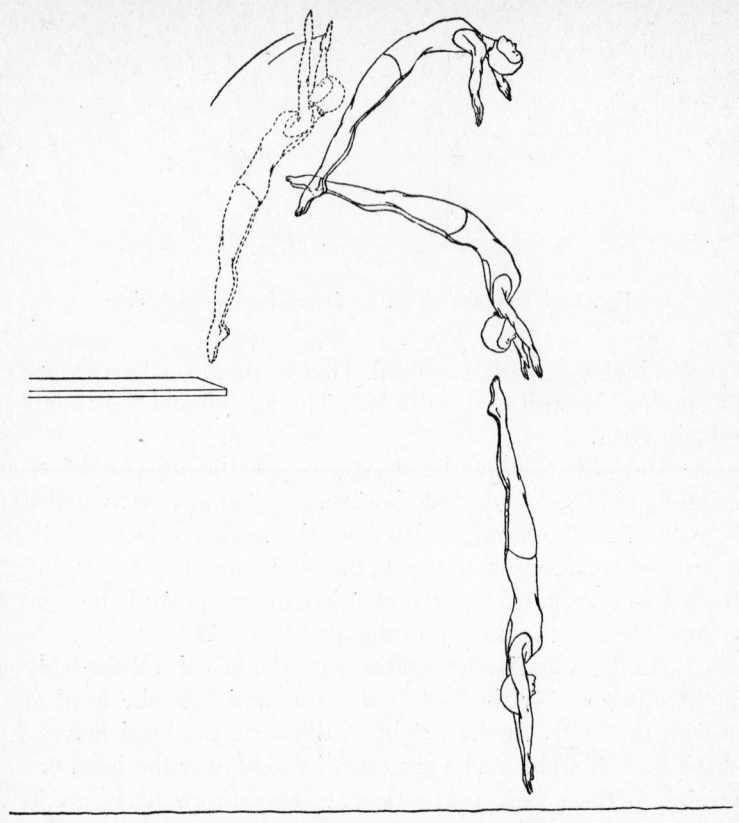

Fig. 130. The back dive.

position. In the pike position, the body is bent at the hips, legs straight, the same as in the jackknife dives. In the layout position, the body remains straight throughout the dive.

Back Somersault with a Tuck.

(a) Land Practice: As the somersault dives are a form of tumbling they are learned easiest first on a mat. The diver should assume a *squat position,* grasping the front of the legs and, sitting back, pull the knees up to the chin and roll over backwards. The next step is for the diver to *stand* and as the upper body is thrown backward, bring first one knee and then the other up to the tuck position.

(b) From the Board: The diver should take the same starting position as for the back dive. From this position the arms are thrown *forcibly* backward, the head moves backward, the knees are drawn close up to the body and grasped by the arms as the body moves back-

Fig. 131. The backward somersault in a tuck position.

ward. The legs are straightened for the entry and the feet enter the water first, the arms being at the side. (Fig. 131.)

The dive is then done in pike and layout positions.

In the beginning the diver does not try for height but rather to turn before entering the water, and to clear the diving board. Later on, height should be attained before the entry.

In all feet-first entries, the arms are close to the sides on the entrance into the water.

(c) Faults:

(1) Not entering the water in a vertical line with the arms at the sides and the body straight.

(2) Not springing up from the board before starting backwards.

(3) Twisting on the dive.

7. BACK JACKKNIFE. The start for this dive is the same as for the back

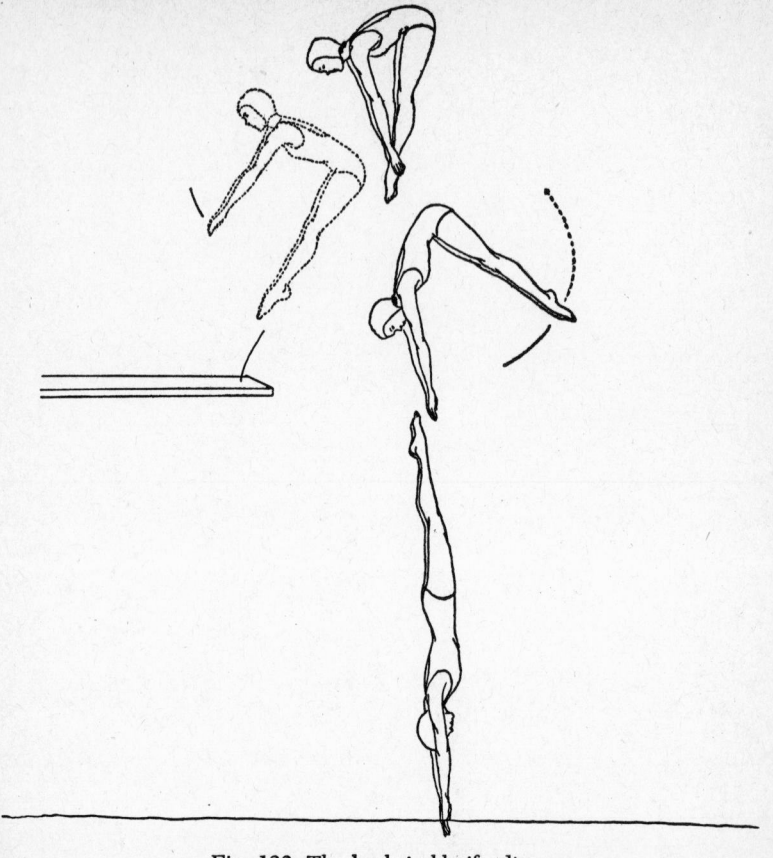

Fig. 132. The back jackknife dive.

dive. Before trying the dive from a board, a little land practice is helpful.

(*a*) Land Practice.   The same land practice can be given as in the front jackknife, remembering there must not be a backward lean on this dive, or on any dive.

(*b*) From the Board.

(*1*) Standing erect at the end of the board as for the back dive, jump *up* and *back*, entering the water feet first.

(*2*) Taking the same starting position jump up and back, lift the hips and bring the hands in front of the insteps in the pike position. The diver heads down toward the water and the legs are lifted back and up, the diver entering the water head first. (Fig. 132.)

This practice continues with the diver getting more and more lift from the board, and a better held pike position before opening. A shoulder lift on the take-off will aid in getting height.

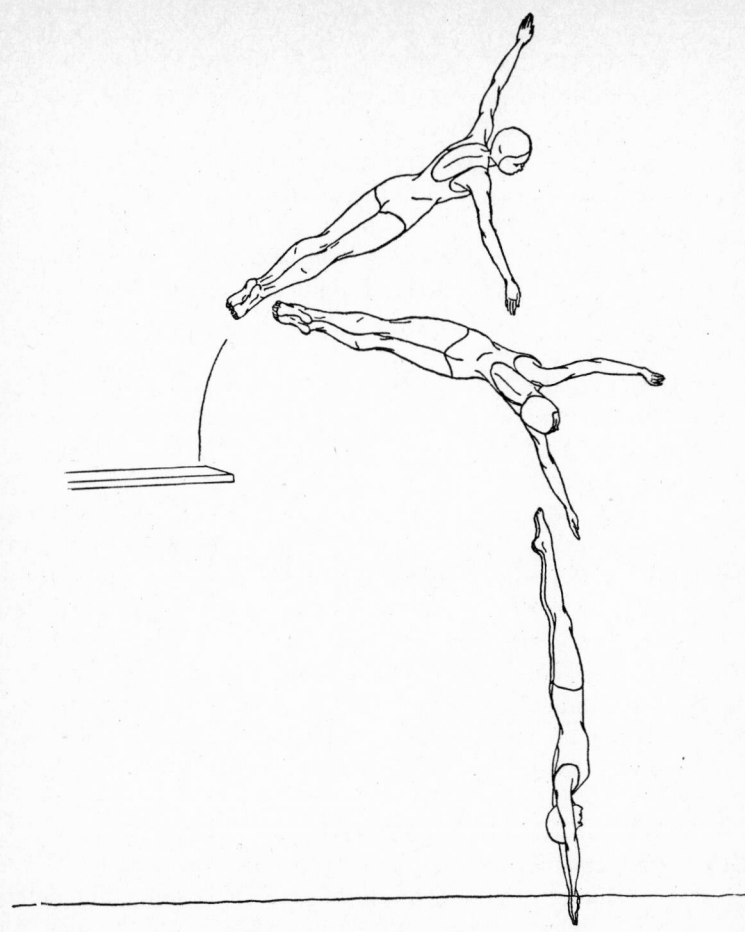

Fig. 133. The half twist dive.

(*c*) Faults.

(*1*) Twisting on the backward jump.

(*2*) Not jumping backward far enough to clear the board with the head.

(*3*) Bending the knees to get into the pike position.

8. RUNNING FRONT DIVE WITH A HALF TWIST. When a twist is used in diving, a turn of the entire body is made. The twist may be used in combination with jackknife dives and somersaults to make more difficult dives. The twist which is learned first is the running front dive with a half twist.

(*a*) Land Practice. Merely to get the movement of the arms and the upper trunk, stand with the arms extended over the head. To twist to the right, lower the right arm and turn the head to the right. Some prefer a *turn* of the body to the desired side, without lowering the arm. In this case the turn starts with the shoulders and a turn of the head.

(*b*) From the Board. The approach, take-off, and the start upward from the board are the same as in the running front dive. As the height is reached the arm to the side of the turn is lowered and the head is turned to the same side. The twist is made by the entire body. The entrance is made with the body straight and facing away from the board. (Fig. 133.)

(*c*) Faults.

(*1*) Lowering the head to the side instead of turning it throws the body over to the side.

(*2*) Starting the twist too soon takes away from the height and causes poor entry.

(*3*) Folding the body up for the turn instead of keeping it straight.

9. RUNNING FRONT DIVE WITH A FULL TWIST. In order to make a full twist, when the diver is at the height of the dive one arm is thrown across the chest, forcibly, and then is extended parallel to the other arm over the head. The head is turned forcibly in the same direction as the arm. If enough force is put into the turn, the body goes completely around and enters the water as in a front dive.

10. JACKKNIFE DIVE WITH TWISTS. The diver can now combine jack-knife dives with twists. In doing this, the diver must be sure to go into the jackknife position before starting the twist. Either the running front jackknife or the back jackknife can precede the twist.

11. THE FORWARD SOMERSAULT. The forward somersault is done in one of three diving positions, the tuck, pike, or layout. (For description, see back somersault, page 305.) From a low board the somersault in the tuck position is the easiest. It can be likened to the forward roll, which practically everyone has done in a gymnastics class or on the lawn, as a small child.

(*a*) Land Practice. On a mat, take a squat position, grasp the front of the legs with the arms, bring the chin well in and the head forward. Holding the position, roll over forward.

(*b*) At Side of Pool or Dock. Taking a squat position with the knees well up in front, grasp the knees with the arms, and roll over forward into the water. Hold this position and try to land in the water as far around as possible.

(*c*) From the Board. From a running approach push *up* from the board, tuck the chin well in, turn over once, and enter the water feet first, with the body straight and with the arms at the sides.

Fig. 134. The running forward somersault in pike position.

After learning the somersault in the tuck position, the diver can go on to the pike (Fig. 134), and then the layout positions. The last two should not be attempted unless the diver has unlimited skill.

12. THE HALF GAINER. The half gainer is one of the most beautiful dives to watch, and when it is well done, it appears very simple to execute. However, this is not the case as the dive involves leaving the board forward, and turning back toward the board for the entry. This makes the preliminary practice very important in order to avoid injury to the diver.

(*a*) Land Practice. A one foot take-off is sometimes easiest to learn. Therefore starting with the weight on one foot, swing the other leg forward and upward with straight knee and at the same time bend backward from the hips and move the arms up and backward over the head. Alternate the use of the legs remembering the dive is to be done from *both feet*.

(*b*) From the Board. Standing with the weight on one foot, jump

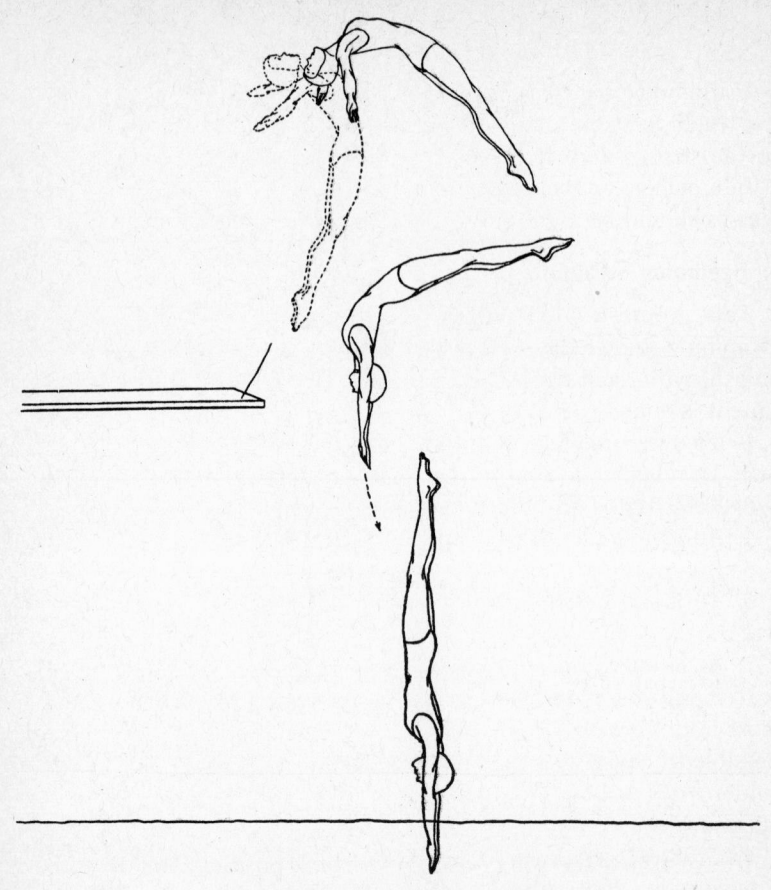

Fig. 135. The half gainer dive.

out over the water and at the same time swing the other leg forward and upward bending back from the hips and swinging the arms up and back over the head; enter the water head first.

After the one foot take-off has been accomplished, the diver goes on to the two foot take-off. (Fig. 135.)

(*c*) General Hints.

(*1*) At first get well out from the board to avoid hitting the board, then work to *get up*.

(*2*) Move the arms and upper body back, as the legs come forward and upward.

(*3*) The feet should be lifted well up from the board.

(*4*) The thrust forward of the feet from the board must be done with force and vigor.

OUTLINE OF TEACHING PROCEDURE

In this chapter there has been no attempt to give a definite order for teaching strokes and diving. Merely a description has been given of the strokes and dives, and some of the ways they may be taught.

In a college or school program where group teaching must be done, classes should be set up according to the students' abilities if possible.

I. Beginning Swimming

This group would contain those students who have little or no swimming knowledge. A term of swimming is generally ten weeks in length, with each class meeting twice a week for 30 minutes. In this time it is hoped that they can learn:

1. To overcome fear of the water.
2. To relax while floating on the back, face, and side.
3. To change body positions, while in the water.
4. An elementary crawl and elementary backstroke.
5. Breathing.
6. To jump and dive into water of shoulder depth, then into deep water.
7. As much of the side stroke as possible.

It should be stated that before attempting to teach beginners, it is most important that *the water be warm,* at least 80 degrees. It is impossible to have swimmers relaxed and comfortable if the water is any colder. Also, a beginning swimming class should not have more than 12 members.

The following is a possible outline of work for beginners:

LESSON 1.   10 minutes—Getting used to the water by means of simple water games.

Ball Tag.   The players are scattered around the shallow end of the pool. One is "It" and has a ball. The one with the ball throws it, trying to hit one of the other players. When hit by the ball that player is "It."

Walking Race.   Line all players along one side of the pool in shallow water. On a signal, they all get to the other side of the pool as fast as they can. The one getting there first is the winner.

10 minutes—Work on breathing. Start having the students put their faces in the water and hold the breath. Then have them breathe in through mouth, put faces in the water, and breathe out through the mouth, or mouth and nose.

10 minutes—Work on back float and stand.

LESSON 2.   10 minutes—Another game—putting their faces in the water this time if they are up to it.

Cap Tag. Players scattered in shallow end of pool. One or more persons "It." In order not to be tagged, the entire cap must be under the water.

10 minutes—Review and continue work on breathing. Review back float and stand.

10 minutes—Work on face float and stand.

LESSON 3. 10 minutes—Review as needed.

10 minutes—Work on change of body positions.

10 minutes—From a pushoff, do the face float and stand. From a pushoff, do the back float and stand.

LESSON 4. 10 minutes—Review as needed.

15 minutes—Use a land drill first, then in the water, practice the elementary backstroke.

5 minutes—End with a water game.

LESSON 5. 10 minutes—Practice jumping in from the side of the pool at the shallow end.

10 minutes—Review breathing and back and face floats.

10 minutes—Continue work on the elementary backstroke.

LESSON 6. 20 minutes—Demonstrate and have practice of the elementary crawl or the "human stroke" on land, then in the water.

5 minutes—Jumping in shallow water. On coming to the surface, swim to the opposite side either on the back or the face.

5 minutes—Continue work on breathing.

LESSON 7. 25 minutes—Review lesson 6. Start with the "human stroke" and go on to the overarm crawl.

5 minutes—Play a water game.

LESSON 8. 15 minutes—Jump in deep water. Swim to side of pool.

15 minutes—Review as needed.

LESSON 9. 15 minutes—Work on parts of the crawl or the whole stroke.

15 minutes—Work on "sitting" and "kneeling" dives from the edge of the pool.

LESSON 10. 20 minutes—Work on the crawl covering a longer distance, with correct breathing.

10 minutes—Review "sitting" and "kneeling" dive.

LESSON 11. 15 minutes—Dive from the standing position.

15 minutes—Work on the crawl.

LESSON 12. 10 minutes—Work on treading water and sculling.

15 minutes—The scissors kick for the side stroke. On land, bracketed at side of pool, and with kick board.

5 minutes—Continue diving from the standing position.

LESSON 13. 5 minutes—Demonstrate the side stroke for the class.

20 minutes—Drill on land for the arms alone. Drill standing in shallow water. Do side pushoff from wall for side balance. From the pushoff, try movement of the arms alone. Add the leg kick to the arms.

5 minutes—Work on diving.

LESSONS 14 THROUGH 20. Continue work on the side stroke. Continue work on the crawl and diving. Some will naturally learn faster than others and they should be allowed to go ahead.

II. Low Intermediate

For those who are beyond the beginning stage. This group will learn:
1. The crawl, continued from the elementary one.
2. The side stroke.
3. The single overarm stroke.
4. The trudgeon or double overarm.
5. Diving.
6. Simple water stunts and games.

We assume that anyone in low intermediate swimming has overcome all fear of the water, has learned an elementary crawl, and has started working on a side stroke.

LESSON 1. In order to find out the ability of the students, have them demonstrate the material given in beginning swimming.

LESSON 2. Continue work on the crawl and the side stroke.

LESSON 3. Repeat lesson 2 and add more work on diving.

LESSON 4. Start the single overarm. Diving and stunts.

LESSON 5. Repeat 4.

LESSON 6. Continue work on the single overarm. Review and continue work on the crawl. Diving and stunts.

LESSON 7. Work on the single overarm with quarter turn in preparation for the trudgeon. Continue the crawl.

LESSONS 8, 9, 10. Work on the trudgeon mostly, but give some part of each lesson to the crawl and diving.

LESSONS 11 THROUGH 20. Have the students work on being able to swim the crawl, side stroke, and trudgeon for greater distances, emphasizing relaxation, rhythm and power. Give them additional work on diving and stunts.

III. High Intermediate

1. Continue work on the crawl.
2. The backstroke.
3. The breast stroke.
4. The butterfly breast stroke.
5. A review of strokes already learned.

6. Diving.

7. Free style starts and turns. Backstroke starts and turns. Breast stroke turns.

8. Stunts.

In order to be classified as a high intermediate swimmer, the student should have a fair crawl, a side stroke, single overarm, and trudgeon.

LESSON 1. A demonstration by the class of the strokes they already know how to swim, and the dives they can do.

LESSON 2. Continued practice of the crawl. Demonstration of the breast stroke to show the class the complete stroke. Land drill for the breast stroke kick. Practice of the leg movements alone bracketed at the side of the pool. Using the kick boards, practice kick across the pool.

LESSON 3. Demonstrate the backstroke. Practice leg kick alone on land. Practice leg kick alone in the water, bracketed. Practice leg kick across the pool, scull with the hands, or have them extended over the head. Practice the arm movements alone on land. Practice the arm movements alone with legs bracketed in gutter or held by another student. Practice the arm movements alone across the pool. Try the whole stroke.

LESSON 4. Review practice of the leg movements alone for the breast stroke, as needed. Land drill for the arm movements. Water drill for the arm movements standing in shallow end of pool. Co-ordination of the whole stroke on land. Co-ordination of the whole stroke from pushoff in the water.

LESSON 5. Review 3 and spend half the period on diving.

LESSON 6. Demonstrate and work on the arm movements of the butterfly breast stroke. Practice the following ways: (a) on land, standing; (b) in shallow water, standing; (c) from a pushoff with the legs trailing.

LESSON 7. Work on the whole stroke (butterfly breast). Swim lengths to music using any desired stroke.

LESSONS 8, 9, 10. Work on the back and breast strokes. Diving and stunts.

LESSON 11. Demonstrate free style start and turn. Practice the start. Practice the turn. Practice the start and turn across the pool.

LESSON 12. Review lesson 11 and the crawl.

LESSON 13. Demonstrate the backstroke start and spin turn. Practice the start. Practice the turn. Practice the start and turn across pool. Diving and stunts.

LESSON 14. Review lesson 13 and work on the backstroke as needed.

LESSON 15. Demonstrate the breast stroke and the butterfly breast stroke start and turn. Practice the start. Practice the turn. Practice start and turn across the pool.

LESSON 16. Review lesson 15 and work on the breast stroke.

LESSON 17. Practice any of the strokes, starts, and turns. Swim the crawl in pairs to music.

LESSON 18. With music swim the crawl, backstroke, breast and side strokes in pairs.

LESSON 19. Work on diving the entire period.

LESSON 20. Review lesson 18 and add swimming by four's.

IV. Advanced

For those who wish to make a swimming team. They are already good swimmers or divers and are given work on conditioning and endurance as well as starts and turns for all racing strokes. The divers learn additional springboard dives.

V. Competition

This is a great stimulus. Swimming meets between the groups and classes are an added feature.

VI. The Red Cross Life Saving and Instructors' Courses

These should be made available in every well-rounded swimming program, to all those who can qualify for them.

USES OF TECHNIQUE

The material presented in this chapter on swimming can be taught to an individual or to a group of swimmers. In school and college teaching most of the work is given to a group. If it is possible, the beginners' classes should not have more than twelve students at any one time. The intermediate and advanced classes can have as many as thirty in one section. In order to have the swimmers in the proper groups, a swimming test should be given each student. If such a test cannot be given the teacher will find that she has sections with a wide variety of abilities, which will make her job much more difficult, and there will be less progress for each student. In some instances it is impossible for tests to be given and the teacher must have a mixed group at all times. Therefore, there are two possibilities for the teacher: (1) Groups which have been given tests for classification. (2) Groups with differing abilities where there is no classification.

For classified students a possible outline of work has been given and the teacher can keep the group working on more or less the same strokes, dives, and stunts. In each class period part of the lesson should be given over to games and stunts. To make the lesson more interesting, it is suggested that the teacher should change the order of work given to each class, and not always use the same set outline. This can be done by starting the lessons one day with games and stunts, followed by strokes and diving and starting the next day with diving, followed by strokes and stunts, and so forth.

In each class there will always be a number of "excused" swimmers. These girls can be given a reading assignment on some phase of swimming, or better still they can be brought down around the pool and be given some teaching to do. It has been found that having the students do a certain amount of work helping each other enhances their interest in swimming in general and makes them more intelligent concerning their own problems.

When the teacher has groups which have not been classified as to abilities she will have to make her own classification within the group. In this way she might have, in a group of thirty, possibly five or six working on the very beginning phases, another group of six or eight working on the side stroke, still others on the crawl, and another group on the backstroke. These groups must each be given a certain section of the pool in which to work and the teacher must distribute her time among the groups. As a safety measure, and to help in the teaching, one of the "excused" swimmers can be put in charge of each group. As well as getting work on strokes the swimmers must be given a part of each lesson to work on diving and stunts, or games. Motion pictures will also be of assistance in teaching all grades of students.

The dolphin stroke has purposely not been mentioned in the lesson plans. The kick (dolphin) is so different from the breast stroke kick that one would hesitate to advocate that it be taught following the breast stroke or the butterfly breast stroke. There is one theory that it is so similar to the crawl kick that it would be easier for swimmers of the crawl stroke to learn. The stroke as a whole will stand a lot of experimentation on the part of both swimmers and instructors.

I. Competition

It is human nature to want to measure one's abilities against another's. It is also necessary to organize competition, and to set up definite rules. The organized competition may be within a school or college, or it may be inter-school or inter-college, inter-club, or merely such competition as can be held in the regular sections in swimming. Another popular form of competition between schools and colleges is telegraphic meets. Certainly some form of competition is a great stimulus to the swimmer, and every swimming program should be planned with this fact in mind. It is important to have rules for all competition. Swimming rules for women are drawn up by a committee of the National Section of Girls' and Women's Sports. The guide book is obtainable from A. S. Barnes and Company; it would be repetitious for the rules to be restated here.

II. Water Safety

It is important for everyone to learn how to swim, but as the swimmer's ability increases it is equally important that her knowledge and practice in safety skills also develop and grow. It is therefore an essential of every well-rounded swimming program to include instruction in life saving and water safety. The American Red Cross, and Mr. Carroll Bryant in particular, have set up outlines of instruction and practice which should be followed and taught in every school and college program. Information regarding these courses can be secured through your local Red Cross Chapter or by writing to headquarters in Washington.

III. Recreational Swimming

This is a type of swimming which is not new, but in the last few years much greater emphasis has been placed upon it. This type of swimming includes all sorts of stunt swimming and diving, special formations en masse, and games, all of which are done "for fun." The stunts are first learned and played by the individual for the pure joy of the activity, and to see how many different water tricks she can learn. Then the individual can compare her skill with another's, and thus competition is introduced. In swimming meets stunt events can be run in between the more formal events, to entertain the participants as well as the spectators.

Today, in some sections of the country, stunts *are* put on a competitive basis, and teams of stunt swimmers compete against each other. In making stunts competitive it is a great mistake to forget they are primarily done for fun. The addition of stunts and formations has already done a great deal to make meets more interesting and educational. Spectators are generally inspired to try some of the stunts themselves. Through stunts the swimmer learns to handle the body in unusual positions in the water, and gains an added control and grace, which cannot be gained through just swimming strokes alone. There are stunts and skills for all types of swimmers, and these sculling and balancing movements should be taught in every swimming class.

IV. Swimming Clubs

Swimming is a sport which appeals to a great number of students because they wish to be able to swim at home and in the summer months. Not all wish to do more than be able to feel at ease in the water, yet in every school or college there is a group of students who are particularly interested in swimming. These girls can be organized into a swimming club which will have its special name, appropriate for the school and the sport. The members of the group should meet at least once a week and work out particular stunts and formations as well as increase their skill in swimming. Demonstrations by this group will arouse great interest and enthusiasm for the sport. This same group may have the special responsibility of assisting in the life-guard duty at the pool. They can assist in classes and be of great value when a class is large and of varied ability.

V. Coeducational Recreation

Another aspect of swimming is the part it can play in coeducational recreation. "Mixed swimming" is popular in many schools and colleges. If dressing rooms and other arrangements can be adapted to this plan, "splash parties" for boys and girls are popular and a valuable part of the program.

But basic is the careful progression in the teaching of swimming which makes possible the enjoyment and values of competitive and recreational swimming. Each step in the progression must be followed carefully, and in the end the girl who works and who has ability will improve to the point where her swimming is of the greatest pleasure to her.

REFERENCES

American Public Health Association: *Swimming Pools and Other Public Bathing Places.*

American Red Cross: *Swimming and Diving.*

Armbruster, David: *Competitive Swimming and Diving,* second edition. St. Louis, C. V. Mosby Co., 1950.

Beach and Pool: Hoffman-Harris, Inc., 123 Market Place, Baltimore, Maryland. A monthly magazine.

Brown, Richard: *Teaching Progressions for the Swimming Instructor.* New York, A. S. Barnes & Co., 1948.

Chicago Park District: *Diving.* Chicago, Illinois.

Collins, Earl K.: *Swimming Pool Data and Reference Annual.* 425 Fourth Avenue, New York.

Curtis, Katherine W.: *Rhythmic Swimming.* Minneapolis, Burgess Publishing Co., 1942.

Davies, Grace: *Swimming.* Philadelphia, Lea and Febiger, 1932.

Forsythe, Steve: *Better Swimming,* Allen J. Hull Co., 1935.

Gibson, Winifred: *To Start You Crawling*. New York, Pitman Publishing Co.
Goss, Gertrude: *Swimming Analyzed*. Third printing. Boston, Spaulding-Moss Co., 1954.
Goss, Gertrude: *Water Ballet Charts*. Medford, Mass., Jackson College.
Greenwood, Frances: *A Bibliography of Swimming*. New York, H. Wilson Co., 1939.
Hobden, F. W.: *Springboard Diving*. London, William Clowes and Sons, Ltd.
Jarvis, Margaret: *Swimming, for Teachers and Youth Leaders*. London, Faber and Faber.
Kiphuth, Robert J. H.: *Swimming*. New York, A. S. Barnes & Co., 1942.
Lipovetz, Ferd J.: *The Teaching and Coaching of Swimming, Diving and Winter Sports*. Minneapolis, Burgess Publishing Co., 1945.
Luehring, Frederick W.: *Swimming Pool Standards*. New York, A. S. Barnes & Co., 1939.
Lukens, Paul W.: *Teaching Swimming*. Minneapolis, Burgess Publishing Co., 1948.
Mann, Matt, and Fries, Charles: *Swimming*. New York, Prentice-Hall, Inc., 1940.
McCormick, Olive: *Water Pageants, Games and Stunts*. New York, A. S. Barnes & Co., 1933.
Official Aquatics Guide. New York, A. S. Barnes & Co.
Reichert, Natalie, and Brauns, Jeanette: *Swimming Work Book*. New York, A. S. Barnes & Co., 1937.
Spears, Betty: *Beginning Synchronized Swimming*. Minneapolis, Burgess Publishing Co.
Seller, Peggy: *Manual of Canadian Synchronized Swimming*. Montreal, 19 Bayview Ave.
The Swimming Times. Capt. B. W. Cummins, 4 Waddon Park Road, Croydon, England. A monthly magazine.
Torney, John A. J.: *Swimming*. New York, McGraw-Hill Book Co., 1950.
Ulen and Larcom: *The Complete Swimmer*. New York, The Macmillan Co., 1939.

Films

Oars and Paddles. American Red Cross.
Heads Up. American Red Cross.
Springboard Diving. Bell and Howell Co., 1801-1815 Larchmont Avenue, Chicago.
Swimming, Elementary, Advanced and Fundamentals of Diving. Directed by Fred Cady, Division of Audio-Visual Education, Los Angeles County Schools, 808 North Spring Street, Los Angeles, California.
Matt Mann and His Swimming Techniques. Coronet Productions, Glenview, Illinois.
Learn to Swim (Olympic Champions at Silver Springs). Castle Films, R.C.A. Building, Rockefeller Center, New York.
Springboard Techniques. Mike Peppe. Coronet Instructional Films, 65E. South Water, Chicago, Illinois.
Swimming: The Front Crawl. Bell and Howell, 1801-1815 Larchmont Avenue, Chicago, Illinois.
Swim and Live. Photographed by Army Air Forces at Miami Beach.
Fundamentals of Diving. Norman Sper, 1943 North Cherokee, Hollywood, California.

8 • TENNIS • BY *Gertrude Goss*

Granted that individual instruction in tennis is the ideal method, it is sometimes necessary to do group teaching. In the school and college field, this is almost always the case. Large numbers of students of varying abilities wish to be given instruction during the tennis season, and they can be taken care of only in groups.

As tennis is an individual sport, great care must be taken to treat it as such in group teaching. The teacher must allot a certain amount of time in each class period to each student, making allowances for individual build and temperament. Good form must be insisted upon at all times. But good form will be different for each player. These facts should always be taken into consideration while teaching. One has only to watch the champions play to see that each has his own particular style.

The essentials which each must have are ease of movement, which includes rhythm and balance; strength of stroke; and the ability to put the ball where it should go at the proper time, which requires footwork. Practice and unlimited patience are necessary. The player who is satisfied to push the ball back over the net with no regard for the essentials will never make a good tennis player.

In teaching it must be remembered that enjoyment of the game is important. At the end of each class period, the student should feel that something has been learned. This will help produce enjoyment of the game and give the necessary stimulation. If the student continues practice outside of the class period, it generally means that class instruction has been enjoyed, that she has gained something from the instruction and that there is stimulation for further practice.

HISTORY

The origin of the name is quite obscure, but it would seem to come from the French "tenez," meaning "take it," "play," "ready." In a poem written by Froissart the striker calls "Recipi" (take it) after each stroke. Good authorities find an ancient derivation of the game in

Egypt, Persia, and Arabia before Charlemagne. In A.D. 1300, it was known as La Baude. It was played in a crude form in the moats of castles where Charles VIII used to watch the game. Later Henri IV and Louis XIV (who kept a regular staff to look after his court) were patrons and players of tennis.

The sixteenth and seventeenth centuries were the heyday of the game both in France and England. Henry VII played and revoked the edicts that forbade it. There was a court at Windsor Castle in his time, and it was still in existence in 1607. Henry VIII built the court at Hampton Court Palace in 1529–30, and this court is in use today. A picture of James II as a boy shows him standing on a tennis court holding a short-handled racquet strung diagonally. Before a racquet was used, the players used gloves for protection; then, for greater protection, cords were wrapped around the gloves. Finally, in order to obtain a longer reach, a racquet was made from a combination of paddle and cords. The first balls were leather and filled with hair.

Scoring was difficult in the beginning. The points were called "chases" and were scored 1, 2, 3, 4, etc. Fifteen "chases" gave a player one point, and each game consisted of four or five points; thus came the use of "fifteen," "thirty," etc., in scoring. The term "love," which means "no score," came from "for love," which means "for nothing" or "without stakes." And so the player who has no score is said to be "love."

After the rules were simplified, tennis became more popular than ever and spread from England and France to Bermuda. It was brought to the United States in the 1870's by Miss Mary Outerbridge.

In 1881 the United States Lawn Tennis Association was formed in Boston and New York. All the official tournaments are sponsored by the U.S.L.T.A., whether on cement, asphalt, or clay. Few tournaments in this country are played on grass; however, the National Doubles Tournament at Longwood Cricket Club in Brookline, Massachusetts, is on grass, as is the National Singles Tournament at Forest Hills.

At first all sorts of local tournaments were played on different court surfaces. Then in 1900 international competition, namely, the Davis Cup Matches, began. These matches are for men only and the cup has been won by England, France, the United States, and Australia. Women have the Wightman Cup matches which are between England and the United States. These matches were started by Hazel Hotchkiss Wightman and are played alternately each year in England and over here. From 1939 until 1946, these matches were not played. City, state, sectional, and national tournaments on all surfaces are now being continued and tennis is back to its own.

CLASSIFICATION OF STUDENTS

The general classification of students for group instruction is as follows: (1) Beginners. (2) Intermediates. (3) Advanced.

I. Beginners

Those who have never played tennis at all join this group.

II. Intermediates

Those who have played tennis but have not had much instruction and have had no tournament experience. This is the most difficult group to teach since, in most cases, they have acquired bad habits. They are the students who have been playing "push" tennis and have no idea of footwork.

As the intermediate group is the largest and the most varied in skills, it is a great help to have two divisions here: low intermediates and high intermediates.

The *low intermediate group* are those who are little better than beginners and therefore need to be drilled on the work given to beginners. Their faults must be corrected, and when they are permitted to play tennis, they must continually be encouraged to use good form.

The *high intermediate group* are not quite up to the advanced group. They will need drill on footwork and anticipation. They should be given as much "playing" as possible and something very definite to work on during each lesson to better their playing ability.

III. Advanced

If possible it is a good idea to have tryouts for this group. The instructor should accept only those who have good rhythm, balance, footwork, and power. General play and court practice can be taught to them.

If a large number of courts are available and enough instructors, instruction can be given to each group throughout the day and the students can be put where they belong according to their ability. Remember, it is the individual need which is important.

The students should be encouraged to play on the courts at any time, and during the tennis season all the courts should be in use. On rainy days all the available backboard space can be kept busy. Advanced players, as well as beginners, need backboard practice. Experience has shown that footwork and stroke perfection sometimes can be improved more quickly by backboard practice than on a tennis court.

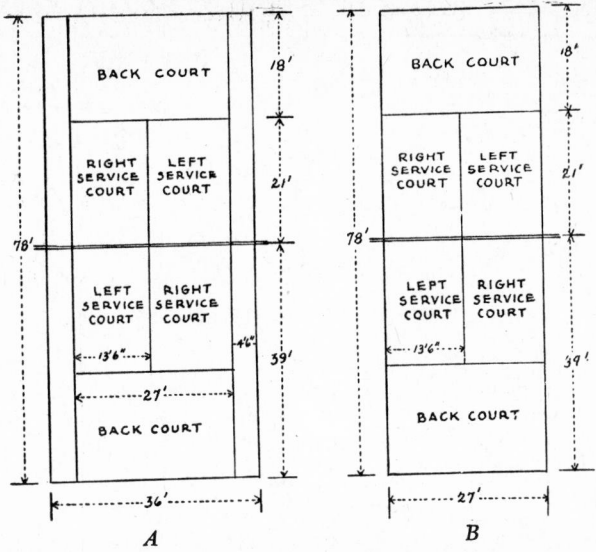

Fig. 136. *A*, diagram of a doubles court. *B*, diagram of a singles court.

TENNIS EQUIPMENT

Each potential tennis player should consider the matter of proper equipment for the game before going on to the courts.

I. Racquet

The player should choose her own racquet. In doing so there are several considerations. First of all, the racquet must "feel" right to the individual. The handle of the racquet should be small enough so that the thumb comes over the middle finger by a joint when using the Eastern forehand grip. The 4½ or 4¾ grip is right for most women. The racquet should be of light to medium weight, 12½ to 13¾ ounces for a woman. The balance should be even—or slightly heavier in the head—according to personal preference. In choosing a racquet the player should swing many different racquets (weights and grips) in order to find the right one. It is not always important to buy the most expensive racquet.

Care of the Racquet. A racquet should be kept in a press and cover when not in use. It should also be kept in a dry place. If your racquet becomes wet, dry it immediately with a cloth.

II. Balls

Only those balls which are approved by the United States Lawn Tennis Association should be used. Colored balls should never be used.

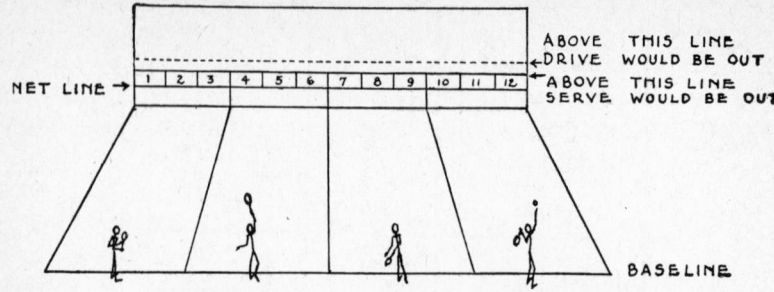

Fig. 137. Diagram showing backboard practice.

III. Tennis Clothes

White is the accepted color for tennis clothes. Either a dress or shorts may be worn and the clothing should allow for plenty of freedom of movement. Low white tennis shoes or sneakers should be worn and white socks, either of wool, which will absorb perspiration and help prevent blisters, or of cotton. A visor or tennis cap is very useful when playing against a bright sun. Dark glasses should never be worn while playing.

IV. Backboards

Backboards made of beaverboard are the most satisfactory to work on, as the rebound of the ball is not so fast as from wood or cement and it is more accurate. A line the height of the net should be drawn across the backboard. On the floor a line should be drawn parallel to the net line and at the distance from the net to the base line. Above the net line squares can be marked off and numbered. For accuracy the more advanced students can practice hitting certain numbers in front of them. This is very good for practice of the serve as well as the drives. (Fig. 137.)

One and one-half feet above the service boxes, a line can be drawn to designate the point above which balls hit would go out of court.

FOOTWORK

Footwork should be practiced before the strokes of tennis, as it is important, first of all, to have the body and feet in the right position. The player must learn that the feet should never rest flat on the ground. The weight should always be forward whether standing still or moving. The knees should be relaxed or slightly bent. Even while waiting for the ball, the feet are constantly in motion. Some players skip, others hop or slide, and still others rock back and forth from one foot to the other. The object of all this movement is to keep the body in motion so that when the ball comes, it can be driven to the desired place with the impact of the whole body.

To beginners various ways can be presented for improving their footwork. This practice can be given indoors at a backboard or outdoors around the tennis court.

I. Running

Run with the weight on the balls of the feet. The push should come from the ankles as each step is taken. The knees should be relaxed. Forward steps can be taken with slide steps at the end of a short run. Slides forward can be taken turning one shoulder or the other toward the net for forehands or backhands. These movements should first be demonstrated by the teacher with an explanation of why they are important.

II. Use of Jump Ropes

The use of jump ropes has been found to be excellent practice in starting and in getting the push from the balls of the feet.

1. Practice jumping from both feet, getting the push from the balls of the feet.

2. Jump first from one foot, then the other, getting the same push.

3. Jump starting from an erect position, go down to a squat position, then slowly back to a straight position.

To show how to get from "waiting position" with body square to net into a position to return a drive with the side to the net, have the students:

1. Stand square to net, feet apart, and weight on the balls of the feet. With a hop off both feet turn the body a one-quarter turn so that the left shoulder is toward the net. Do same hop turning the right shoulder toward the net.

2. Take a few running steps straight forward, hop, turning left shoulder toward the net. Shift the body weight from the rear foot to the forward foot.

3. As in Number 2, take steps straight forward, hop, turn right shoulder toward the net.

4. Take running steps, or slide steps, in crablike fashion diagonally forward; turn left shoulder toward net.

5. Take same slide or running steps forward, turn right shoulder toward net.

This practice may be given indoors or outdoors as desired or accord-

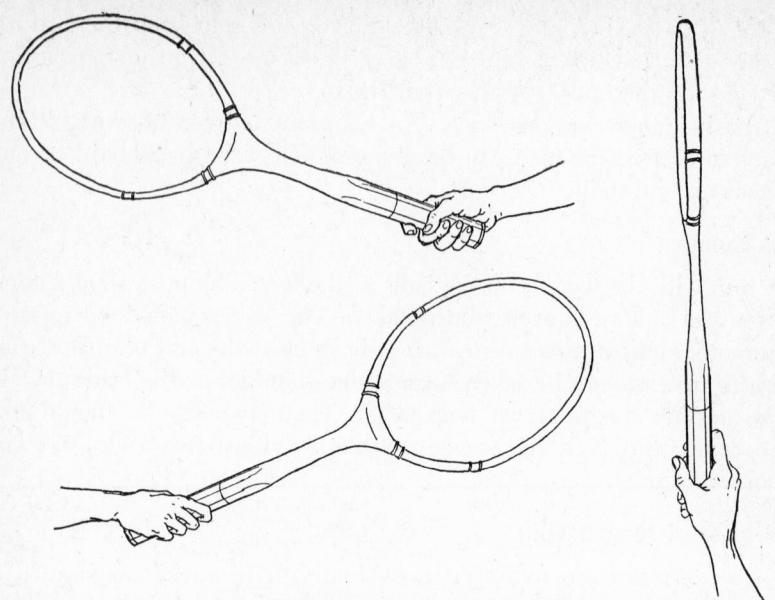

Fig. 138. The Eastern forehand grip.

ing to the weather. Practice in moving is first given without a racquet. With the exception of the rope jumping exercise, do the same practice with the racquet in hand.

STROKES

I. The Forehand Drive

It is essential that a player should have sound ground strokes before attempting any other. Therefore, the forehand and backhand drives should be learned first. The forehand drive is the stroke used to return balls which have hit the court in front and to the right of a right-handed player. This is the most important ground stroke in tennis, because more than one-half of the shots in tennis are made from the forehand. In returning such a drive, balls hit from just below waist height are the easiest. The object of the drive is to send the ball low over the net and deep to the opponent's base line.

(A) *The Forehand Grip.* The grip used most generally is the "Eastern" or hand-shaking grip. This grip has the strength of the hand *behind* the racquet. (Fig. 138.)

(B) *Ways of Finding the Forehand Grip.*

1. Hold the racquet by the throat, with the left hand. Have the butt end toward the body. Grasp the end of the racquet with the right

Fig. 139. The forehand drive.

hand as though "shaking hands" with it. When looking along the racquet, there should be a V between the thumb and first finger. When holding the racquet away from the body, the head of the racquet should be slightly higher than the wrist. The fingers and thumb should be well around the racquet and should slant toward the head of the racquet.

2. Hold the racquet by the handle. Place the head of the racquet on the ground in front of you with the narrow edge of the frame facing upward. In this position looking down at the racquet, there should be a V between the thumb and first finger. The fingers are spread and slanting toward the racquet head. Pick the racquet up, holding the head slightly higher than the wrist.

The grip should be accommodated to the individual and, therefore, will vary slightly with each player. At the moment of impact with the ball, the grip must be firm.

(C) *Body Position and Feet.* In stroking a forehand drive, the body must be at right angles to the net. For right-handed players, this means the left foot and shoulder must be forward. At the start of the swing, the weight is over the rear or right foot. The weight should be on the whole foot and the knees slightly bent. As the ball is met, the weight moves forward and over the ball of the forward foot so that the entire body is moving toward the net and in a line with where the ball is to go. (Fig. 139.)

(D) *Backswing.* Roughly speaking, there are two kinds of backswings: 1. circular, 2. straight or horizontal. Both of these backswings are accepted depending on which is better for the individual. Leading players and coaches are advocates of each type.

The circular backswing has more freedom and rhythm. However, with beginners there is sometimes a tendency to meet the ball from underneath. This causes the player to lift the ball too high in the air. To prevent this, the racquet should be lined up *behind* the ball, and the drive made in a line parallel to the ground.

For many players the straight backswing is easier in that in bringing the racquet straight back it is easier to swing forward and meet the ball from *behind*. After players have learned the straight backswing, they may change to the circular and more rhythmical backswing. The straight backswing is more efficient and more modern.

The backswing should be started before the ball bounces (that is as it leaves the opponent's racquet) so as to give the player plenty of time. Some players start the backswing as the ball crosses the net toward them. When an early backswing is used there is a slight pause at the end of the backswing before the player moves the racquet forward to meet the ball. As the arm is brought back, there is a slight rotation of the body away from the net.

(E) *The Impact with the Ball*. Watching the ball closely, the player moves the body and racquet forward, aiming to meet the ball with the middle of the racquet strings. Some players meet the ball *after* it has started to drop from the bounce. To speed up one's game it is faster to meet the ball before the peak of the bounce. The ball should be carried forward on the racquet, rather than jabbed at and let go from the racquet. On the follow-through the player should reach as far forward as possible, letting the racquet head do the work. There is a slight body rotation forward with the right shoulder coming forward and well around. The ball should be met slightly ahead of the forward (left) foot.

(F) *Essential Points on Making a Forehand Drive*.

1. Watch the ball until it comes off your racquet.

2. Have the body at right angles to the net.

3. Move forward into the stroke, not only with the racquet, but with the body weight.

4. Start the backswing as the ball crosses the net coming toward you, or as the ball leaves your opponent's racquet.

5. Keep well back from where the ball strikes the ground to avoid rushing your shot and crowding the ball.

6. In the beginning wait for the ball to come to you. The beginner's tendency is to be on top of the ball. This causes jabbing at the ball with a cramped elbow.

7. Meet the ball from behind in order to send a low, deep drive over the net. A 6-inch net clearance is the safest.

8. When meeting a low bounding ball, bend the knees to get down to it rather than drop the racquet head.

9. Carry the ball forward on the strings of the racquet rather than push the ball away from you.

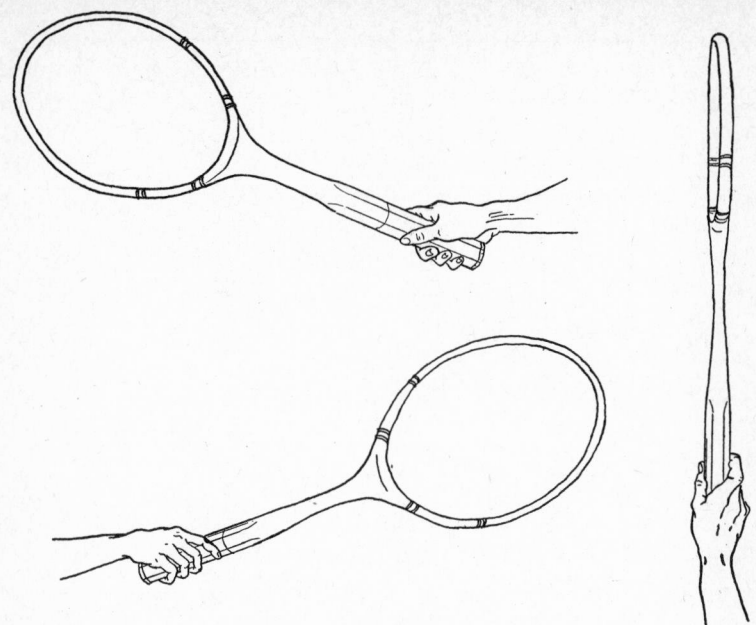

Fig. 140. The backhand grip.

10. Follow through as far as you can reach in the direction you want the ball to go.

II. The Backhand Drive

The backhand drive is used to return balls which come to the left and in front of a right-handed player. Many coaches teach the backhand drive along with the forehand as they have many points in common. The backhand should be just as easy to learn as the forehand for that reason. Unfortunately, it is the weaker stroke with most players. This often is due solely to lack of practice. It is just as important a stroke as the forehand, and woe be to the player who has a definite weakness on this side.

(A) *Grip.* Most women players and many men use the grip having the thumb up the back of the racquet. This grip gives added support and, therefore, added control to the stroke. The straightness of the thumb will vary. But part of the thumb should be *behind the racquet.* To find this grip it is necessary to shift the position of the hand on the racquet. This is done most easily while the player is in the waiting position. (Fig. 140.)

(B) *Body Position.* The body position will still be at right angles

Fig. 141. The backhand drive.

to the net. Right-handed players will have the right foot forward instead of the left. As in the forehand stroke, the body moves from the rear (left) foot to the forward (right) foot. The foot position is reversed. The arm must swing across the body instead of to the side of the body. The shoulder does not get behind the drive as in the forehand, but is used more at the time of impact with the ball, and on the follow-through. As in the forehand stroke the racquet *head* should carry the ball forward. (Fig. 141.)

(C) *Backswing.* The body weight moves back over the left or rear foot. At the same time the racquet is drawn well back across the body, with the arm not held rigidly, but with the hand grip firm. As the arm moves back, there is a slight body pivot to the left. The racquet face should be brought back on a line with the ball.

As in the forehand drive, the racquet should be brought back as the ball crosses the net, or when the ball leaves the opponent's racquet.

(D) *Meeting the Ball and the Follow-through.* The ball should be met about 1 foot in front of the right or forward foot, with the body weight moving forward from the rear foot. The knees should be bent. The swing forward starts with a pivot from the hips. The arm moves forward with the racquet well away from the body to avoid crowding the ball, which would result in a cramped, jerky stroke. On the start of the swing, the arm is slightly bent, but it straightens out as the ball is met and for the follow-through. The arm swing should not stop when the racquet meets the ball but should be carried forward in the direction of the flight of the ball. The racquet head should be held up throughout the stroke.

(E) *Essential Points in Making a Backhand Drive.*

1. Watch the ball at all times.

2. Be sure to meet the ball with shoulder toward the net.

3. Get in position to meet the ball as soon as it leaves your opponent's racquet.

4. Don't crowd the ball.

5. Have the proper grip (the best one suited to you, but be sure part of the thumb is behind the racquet).

6. Let your racquet head carry the ball forward.

7. Follow through after hitting the ball.

8. Keep the racquet well away from the body with the head held up.

9. Don't run around your backhand.

III. The Serve

The opening stroke of every point and game is the service. This should be the opening for the attack. The importance of having a

Fig. 142. The flat serve.

good serve, therefore, cannot be overestimated. A good serve must have two features, speed and direction. The ball should be placed where the receiver will have a difficult time in returning it. In order to obtain speed, the ball should be "hit down" from a high point with the whole body weight in the swing. A tall player has an advantage over a short player in that she can hit down on the ball from a higher point. The short player can concentrate on direction, which can be just as advantageous as speed.

As the object of the serve is to make it difficult for the opponent to return the ball, a change in the direction of the serve can be as effective as speed. The ball should be placed in serving so that the receiver cannot come immediately to the net. As it is tiring as well as unnecessary always to hit the ball hard, advantage can be gained through placement.

(A) *Grip.*   In learning the straight flat service there are two grips which may be used. The first and simplest for most players is achieved by placing the racquet on the ground and picking it up by the handle. (Fig. 143.) The second grip used is the same as the Eastern forehand.

(B) *Body Position.*   Standing sideways to the net, the left foot is 2 or 3 inches behind the base line, the right foot is almost a foot and a half behind the left. The shoulders are turned in the direction

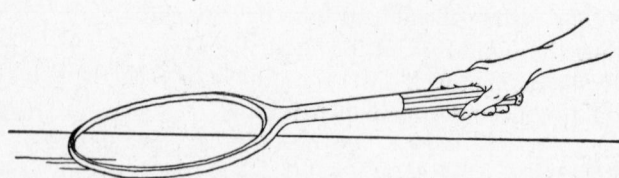

Fig. 143. The easiest way to find the grip for the flat serve: picking the racquet up from the ground.

the ball is to be sent. The balls and racquet are held in front of the body. The weight should be evenly balanced on both feet.

(C) *Backswing.* From this position the racquet is swung *down,* the head of the racquet pointing toward the ground, and *back* and *up* to a bent arm position behind the shoulder. At the same time the body weight is brought back over the right foot and the body rotates slightly away from the net. The motion is much the same as used in throwing a ball.

(D) *Meeting the Ball and the Follow-through.* From behind the shoulder the racquet is swung well *up* over the head. The ball should be met with a straight arm reach. At the height of the reach, the wrist is dropped forward; the racquet head, therefore, drops slightly and leads on to the follow-through forward and across the body. The force of the body goes along with the arm swing and the weight is brought well forward on the follow-through. (Fig. 142.)

This movement may or may not be continuous from start to finish. The continuity depends on the toss of the ball.

(E) *Toss of the Ball.* The ball toss is one of the most important factors in the serve. The toss should be as high or higher than a reach with a fully extended arm, as the ideal is to meet the ball well up in the air. If the toss is too high, it necessitates a break in the arm swing and a pause behind the shoulder. This causes a loss in momentum from the beginning of the swing and a loss of rhythm.

If the toss is too low, it makes for a hurried swing and generally the ball is met too low and is netted. At least the swing is cramped by a low toss, and the body action is taken out of the stroke.

If the toss is wide and to one side, it causes the server to swing out to the side of the body and the forward motion is lost.

The ideal toss is straight up with the proper height, a little to the right, the ball being met with a fully extended arm.

The toss demands practice by each individual to find and maintain the desired height.

(F) *Essential Points in the Service.*

1. A free, well-coordinated backswing.
2. Meet the ball well overhead with a fully extended arm.
3. Practice the toss until the desired height and direction are consistently maintained.
4. Follow through forward with the racquet after meeting the ball.
5. The body weight must move *with* the arm swing.

IV. The Volley

In addition to having a good drive, it is important to know how to

Fig. 144. The forehand volley.

volley. The drives are used mostly from the base line, while the volley is used closer to the net. In using the drive, the ball first comes off the ground. In the volley, the ball is met *before* it touches the ground. To be able to go to the net and volley often means the end of a long rally with the point going to the better volleyer. If your volley is deep or well-angled, your opponent has little chance to return it. In the drives the pace is put on the ball by the person driving, while in the volley the pace has been put on the ball by your opponent. In the volley there is very little, if any, backswing.

(A) *Grip.* The grip for the volley may be the same as used in the forehand drive. For some players it is advisable to shorten the grip. It is best not to change the grip for the backhand volley. The racquet head should be raised at a more decided angle than for the drives, probably around 45 degrees. If the racquet head is allowed to drop, the power goes out of the stroke. The grip must be firm.

(B) *Backswing and Action.* There is generally a very short back-swing in volleying. While waiting to volley, stand squarely facing the net and about half way between the service line and the net. As the ball comes start the backswing. For a forehand volley step forward on the left foot and, at the same time, turn the body slightly to the side in order to move the body weight into the stroke. The ball should be met well in front of the body. Volleys that are taken shoulder high are the easiest. The movement of the swing is forward and slightly downward, according to the height of the ball and the distance from the net. When volleys are taken lower than net high, it is important to get down to them by bending the knees. At the same time the face of the racquet must be opened (tilted back) in order to clear the net with the ball. (Fig. 144.)

V. The Backhand Volley

The action in hitting a backhand volley is much the same as that in the forehand volley. The ball is taken on the opposite side of the player; therefore, the step is taken on the right foot instead of the left. The grip on the racquet may or may not be changed. The grip must be firm, the backswing short, and the side of the player should

Fig. 145. The backhand volley.

be turned slightly to the net in order to put weight into the shot. (Fig. 145.)

In volleying remember to angle the shot, or send the ball deep to your opponent's base line. When played correctly, it should be a point for the one who employs it. It is an invaluable stroke in doubles especially, and, as tennis is played today, it is becoming more and more important to singles players.

VI. The Lob

The lob is a ball hit high into the air. Its use is to drive your opponent back from the net in order to get to the net yourself or, perhaps, to give yourself a short rest after being run around the court.

(A) *There Are Two Kinds of Lobs.*

1. The deep lob drops just inside your opponent's base line.

2. The shorter lob is just high enough to clear your opponent's reach.

These lobs are both fairly deep, but the shorter lob gives your opponent less time in returning. The best place to send a lob is into your opponent's backhand corner. (Fig. 146.)

(B) *How and When to Lob.* In the lob there is less of an impact against the ball than in the drive. Instead of there being a straight follow-through there is a definite lift of the racquet. The backswing is slowed down and shortened. The ball is hit from underneath and is lifted into the air. (Fig. 147.)

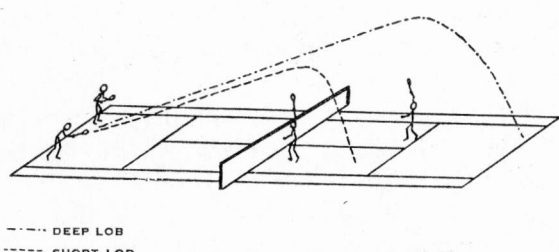

—·—·· DEEP LOB
----- SHORT LOB

Fig. 146. The deep or long lob and the short lob.

Fig. 147. The lob.

In doubles play the lob is one of the most effective strokes. It should be used when your opponents have come up close to the net. Remembering that points are generally won by the players who are at the net, using the lob against such players is a successful way to send them back, and to give the users the important attacking position. It is invaluable against players who are good at volleying.

The lob is not used as much in singles as in doubles, perhaps because most players do not come to the net as often in singles as in doubles, and it is a useless shot against base line players. In tennis, today, in order to be a ranking singles player one must be able to go to the net. It should be used more as a surprise to your opponent as she comes to the net. It is safest to use the lob against a player whose smash is weak, or one who is weak at returning high balls.

(C) *The Lob as an Attack.* The lob used to be thought of as a purely defensive stroke and a sign of weakness on the user's part. As tennis has developed, however, variety in strokes has become more and more necessary. Now the lob, when used correctly, can be an attacking weapon. Accuracy and timing are of the utmost importance in its use. It can be used against players who have come to the net, to drive them back, and give the users the opportunity to gain the net and the attacking position.

VII. The Chop

To add to the variety of strokes, a player can use the chop to good advantage. A chop alone should not be relied upon. It should be interspersed with the drive. The change in spin and speed of the ball will often throw an opponent off balance and break up her rhythm.

(A) *Grip.* The best grip to use is with the racquet held half way between the Eastern forehand and the backhand. This grip can be used for both the forehand and backhand chops.

(B) *Action.* In the chop the action is actually that of "chopping" the ball. Some say to meet the ball as though one were slicing off its back cover. The swing is short in the back and forward-downward in

Fig. 148. The chop or slice stroke.

movement. This motion cuts down the bounce of the ball making it shorter and lower. The right shoulder leans into the ball and the body weight moves from the rear foot to the forward foot. The player faces the net more squarely than in the drive. The racquet head is held above the wrist. (Fig. 148.)

(C) *Use.* The chop is used chiefly to break up the game of a player who has a stronger drive. The player who uses a chop can slow down the pace of a faster player. It should never take the place of the drive, but when used in conjunction with it can be very dangerous to an opponent. By itself it is seldom a winning stroke, as it is more a defensive than an offensive stroke.

VIII. The Drop Shot

Another stroke which has become very popular in the last few years is the drop shot. This stroke calls for a much lighter touch than the chop and has a shorter follow-through. However, it is hit in much the same manner as the chop. The object in using the drop shot is to drop the ball just over the net and catch your opponent at the base line. Therefore, it is used as a change of pace, as a surprise stroke, and is particularly effective when your opponent's drives are going well and she can cover the base line from side to side.

(A) *Grip.* The grip is the same as for the chop; namely, half way between the Eastern forehand and backhand.

(B) *Action.* The body should face the net more squarely than for

Fig. 149. The smash.

the drive. There is very little backswing and a light touch on the ball. The follow-through is shorter than in the chop. The face of the racquet is dropped back to give back spin to the ball. The "chopping" movement is the same as for the chop.

(C) *Use.* The drop shot is even more useful than the chop in breaking up the movement of an opponent from side to side along the base line. This is true because the drop shot should actually just "drop" over the net, and chop strokes often drop deeper on the court. It should, of course, be interspersed with drives and lobs.

IX. The Overhead Smash

This stroke is useful against a player who uses the lob. When used correctly it should mean a winning point. It is hit in the same way as the serve. The smash can be used from any position on the court. There are times, particularly when the player is forced to move backward to take a lob, when the lob should hit the ground before "smashing." Usually, however, this stroke is used in the middle of the court. Of course, to hit a smash, the ball must first have been lofted in the air by the opponents.

(A) *Grip.* The same grip as for the serve should be used.

(B) *Action.* As the ball is dropping, the player about to use the smash stands behind where the ball would strike the ground in the same relation to the ball as when catching a high fly ball. The racquet is swung back as in the serve, and the ball is met well over the head, as high as possible in the air, the player often leaving the ground to reach the ball. The racquet is brought forward and downward after meeting the ball. The body weight comes forward with the swing.

(Fig. 149.) If the ball is allowed to drop too low before being hit, it will be netted.

TEACHING METHODS

This concludes a brief description of the strokes most generally used in tennis. The problem now is to describe the teaching of these strokes to groups of students. It is most desirable, if possible, to teach each individual separately. However, in school and college situations where most of the student body wishes to learn tennis, the lessons must be given in groups.

First of all, footwork is of the utmost importance. Several minutes at the beginning of each lesson should be devoted to footwork, with and without racquets. For this practice be sure to have enough jump ropes for all the students. Encourage these students to take ballet lessons. Aside from giving exercises in footwork, it is sometimes helpful to show moving pictures of the leading players in action. Students are great imitators and seeing how they should move is one of the most helpful ways of starting them. The teacher should be able to demonstrate the strokes she wishes to teach. Students should be encouraged to see as much good tennis as possible. Early in a season this is not always possible, but the showing of moving pictures has a very good effect, and the teacher can point out the things she is emphasizing in the class periods.

I. Backboard Practice

In the beginning, students make more progress and advance faster with stroke practice at a backboard than if all their work is given on a tennis court. Footwork improves and the ball will always come back to them from the board. This is important in group practice, as the teacher cannot be with every student every minute. If they are left on the courts to do stroke practice among themselves, they are unable to give each other the desired practice. The boards may be outside near the tennis courts, or in the gymnasium. The most desirable place for them is at the courts. In this case, the group can be divided, some working at the boards while others go on to practice over the nets. There is also an advantage in having a place for indoor practice, so that when the weather is rainy or cold classes can be held as usual. See Fig. 137.

(A) *Forehand at Backboard.* The teacher should demonstrate the forehand grip and swing, first without hitting a ball, then hitting a ball at the backboard. Have the students practice the forehand swing.

For practice hitting against a backboard, have the students number off to use the available space. This space should not be crowded, and each student should be given ample time to get the feel of what she is doing.

It may be desirable in the beginning to have the class work by two's.

1. Number one stands with her side toward the net or board. Number two drops the ball in the proper place for number one. Number one drives the ball at the backboard, but does *not* return it from the board. Numbers one and two alternate in practicing.

2. Each girl tosses and hits her own ball, number one driving and number two retrieving the balls. At first, hit the ball without returning it. As soon as possible go on to the drive and the *return*, working on footwork and getting into the proper position for the return. Insist on the students moving and returning the ball after one bounce.

3. To add the element of a game, have two players drive the ball alternately at the backboard. First one player drives, then the other must return the drive, and so forth. This is similar to handball. Points can be scored as in tennis. Encourage the players to rally the ball for as long as possible. Be sure that they watch the ball the entire time and have the side position to the net line when meeting the ball.

(B) *Backhand at Backboard.* The teacher first demonstrates the grip and the swing. As in the forehand have the students then practice the backhand grip and swing. Pay particular attention to the shift in grip from the forehand to the backhand grip. Explain and demonstrate why the thumb is used in the backhand.

For practice again number the players and line up at the backboard with plenty of space for each.

1. Practice by two's. Number one stands with side to the net or board. Number two tosses the ball in the proper place for number one. Players practice the backhand drive without returning the ball. Players alternate practice.

2. Number one tosses and hits own balls. Number two retrieves the balls. Alternate practice. At first do not return ball from the board. As soon as possible return the ball taking it either forehand or backhand as it comes off the board.

3. Players rally with selves off the backboard seeing how many returns they can make.

4. Players play the same game as with the forehand. Alternate taking balls, returning whichever balls come to their backhands.

(C) *Combine Forehand and Backhand Drives.*

1. Rally with oneself seeing how long a rally can be kept going. Return balls on either side as they come off the board. Allow only one bounce. In a given time, count the number of good drives made.

2. Play a game using tennis scoring taking the balls on either side.

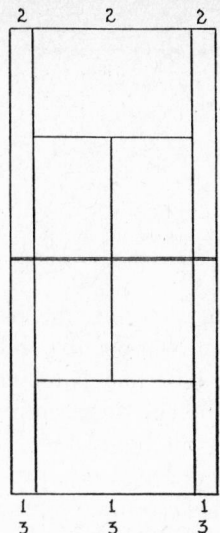

Fig. 150. Practice over the net.

Have two players each taking turns in driving. Start with a forehand drive by one of the players; the other player must make the return, and so forth.

(D) *Serve at the Backboard.*   A demonstration of the serve by the teacher. Describe and point out the value of having a good serve. Compare with motion used in throwing a ball. Practice throwing balls at the backboard.

Players practice the grip and swing, without a ball. For practice with a ball:

1. Players working by two's. Number one stands behind the base line. Practice serving without returning the ball. Number two retrieves. Alternate practice. Endeavor to have the ball hit the board above the net line and below the top box line. When fairly accurate, count the number of good serves in five minutes' time. Change with partner.

2. Practice serve and follow up ball for a return after the service.

3. Serve and follow up for return and continue keeping ball going.

4. Play a game with partner. Start with service and take alternate balls on return. Score as in tennis. Have each player serve through one game.

II. Practice over the Net

(A) *Forehand over the Net.*

1. A demonstration of the forehand drive over the net by the teacher.

2. Students practice the drive from a self toss, or hit a ball tossed

 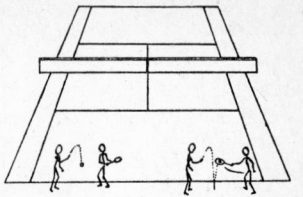

Fig. 151. Diagram showing two students working together—one tossing the ball, the other stroking.

by another player. Number one hits the ball trying to drive it deep to number two's base line. Number two collects the balls and drives them back to the opposite base line. Number three then tries the same drive. All take turns practicing. No attempt is made at first to return the drives. Out of a given number of tries, see how many good drives can be made. (Fig. 150.)

3. To practice hitting a ball coming from a toss or a throw: Number two tosses or throws the ball to number one's forehand. Number one hits the ball trying to send a long, low drive over the net to number three's base line. All take turns with this practice giving each the same length of time to practice the drive. (Fig. 152.)

At first the throws should be to the ideal place for a return. They then should be changed so that the hitter must move forward or to the right for the forehand drive.

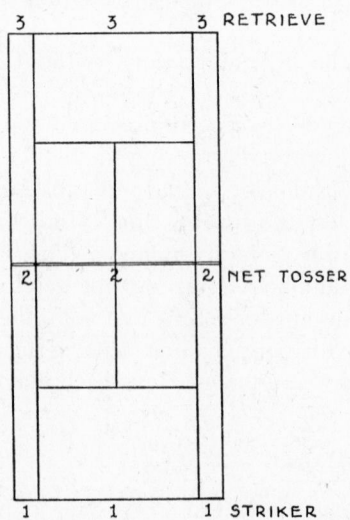

Fig. 152. Showing nine on one court practicing strokes (forehand and backhand): 1, stroking; 2, tossing; 3, retrieving.

(B) *The Backhand over the Net.* The same formations for practice as used for the forehand can be used for backhand practice in the following order:

1. Drive from self-tossed ball.
2. Drive from toss or throw by another person.
3. Backhand drive making striker move by use of variety in throw.
4. Have the thrower mix the throws between forehand and backhand until the striker can hit from both sides. Making the striker move is the most practical as tennis is a game of continual movement, and very few shots are taken while the players are standing still. The players must move, getting to the proper place to return the ball, and then stroke it back over the net. Also, the player must learn to take balls on both sides equally well, and so the toss to both sides is important.

III. Rally by Two's

When the players become fairly accurate at returning the ball from throws, they should be encouraged to rally over the net. The teacher should if possible take each member of the class separately and rally with her. Then the student must go on practicing with someone of the same, or better, ability.

One of the most difficult problems in teaching a group of beginners is to give each member of the class practice with someone who is a better player than the beginner. The teacher cannot play with each member of the group all the time, but must give each student an equal amount of her time. This being the case, it is sometimes necessary to have the group work for a longer time hitting thrown balls, rather than have them work together rallying and not getting anywhere with the practice. The teacher must see this situation and be alert for any needed changes. The students can be asked to practice between class lessons with players who are *better* than they are, and who will give them the practice they need.

IV. The Service over the Net

It is possible to have twelve players practice the serve over the net on one court. Number ones can serve first, serving straight over instead of into the service courts on a diagonal line. Number twos retrieve the balls and serve them back to number threes, who retrieve and serve to number fours, who in turn serve. In some cases the students not serving can correct the serves of those who are serving. This often helps the students who are not serving, for, in watching others, they

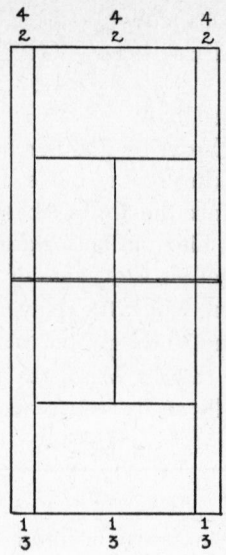

Fig. 153. Practicing the straight service over the net with six or twelve on one court.

see what they should and should not do when it is their turn to serve. (Fig. 153.)

If there are backboards by the tennis courts, the players can take turns serving at the boards, and serving over the net. This is an ideal situation.

If there are enough courts for the group, have them practice with four on a court and serve into the proper service court. (Fig. 154.)

To the serve, practice in the return of service can be added. Number ones serve first. Number twos return. Number twos serve. This practice can go on until the players are ready to play a game.

At this point the players would work on the three-stroke game—the serve, forehand drive, and the backhand drive. The emphasis should be on driving the ball correctly and keeping the rallies going. The ball must be hit properly, and bad form must be stopped in the beginning.

Having learned the drives and service, the next stroke for a player to know is the volley. Tennis has developed rapidly in the last few years, and it is necessary for players to be able to go to the net as often as possible. To do this, one must learn to volley. A player who can volley well need not have long, tiring rallies with an opponent, as the volley is often the finishing stroke which will "put the point away."

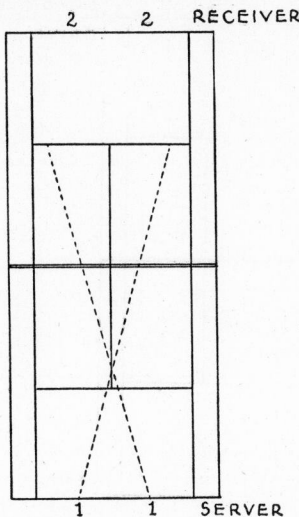

Fig. 154. Practicing the serve into the proper service court.

V. The Volley

The teacher demonstrates the volley, showing body position, foot-work, and stroking. Both forehand and backhand volleys should be

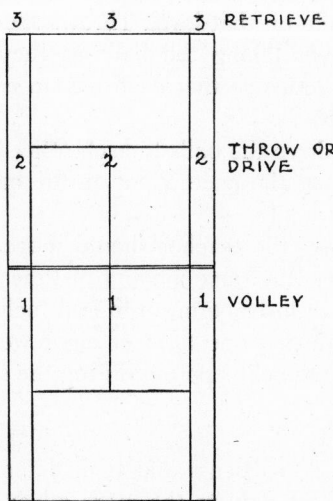

Fig. 155. Practicing the volley with nine on one court: 1, volleys; 2, throws or drives ball; 3, retrieves.

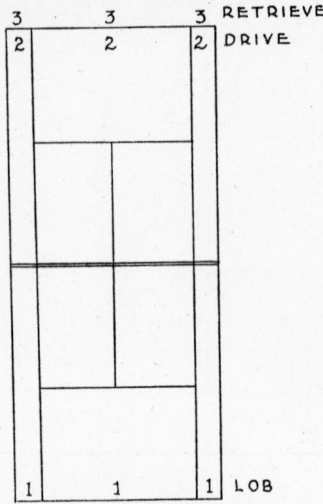

Fig. 156. Practicing the lob with nine players on one court: 1, lobs; 2, drives; 3, retrieves.

shown. Then the group, without a ball, should go through the motions used in volleying.

Nine players can then be put on a court to practice the volley. Number ones volley, number twos throw, and number threes retrieve. Shoulder-high balls are the easiest to volley. In the beginning, the throws should be made on that level. Throws should be made to both sides with the volleyer taking the balls as they come. The players rotate during this practice so that each has an equal amount of time to practice. (Fig. 155.)

If the players can drive the balls to each other for this practice, it is better than throwing as the pace is put on the ball by the thrower or driver.

During this practice, the teacher should move around the class so that each member gets the same amount of time taking her drives.

It is possible to give instruction up to and including the volley to a group of beginners during one term of eight weeks. But the players must practice outside the class period during the season.

VI. The Lob

The teacher must first discuss and then demonstrate the lob. The stroke should be taught only to the more advanced groups, as there are other strokes which should be learned first, and to be able to lob

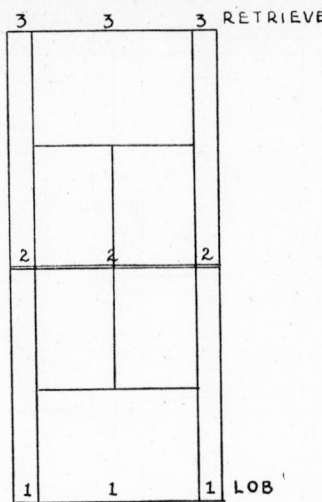

Fig. 157. Practicing the short and deep lobs over head of player at net.

really well requires a great deal of skill. After the demonstration by the teacher, the players can practice the lob with nine players on one court. Number twos drive the balls to number ones who lob the balls back to the opposite base line. Number threes retrieve the balls. The players must rotate so that each has an equal practice time. (Fig. 156.)

In some cases in the beginning, number ones will need to practice lobbing self-tossed balls, and then go on to lobbing balls which are coming toward them from other players.

To practice the short lob, number twos move up to the net while number ones practice the lob, sending the balls just above the reach of the number twos and not deep to the base line. The threes retrieve the balls. Again the players must rotate so that each has an equal practice time. (Fig. 157.)

VII. The Chop

The teacher first demonstrates the chop. The players can practice the stroke by three's having nine players on one court. Number twos hit the balls to number ones. The ones in returning the balls use the chop. The threes retrieve the balls. In some cases ones and twos rally with each other, both players using the chop. Number threes change in for practice, while number ones retrieve, and so forth. (Fig. 158.)

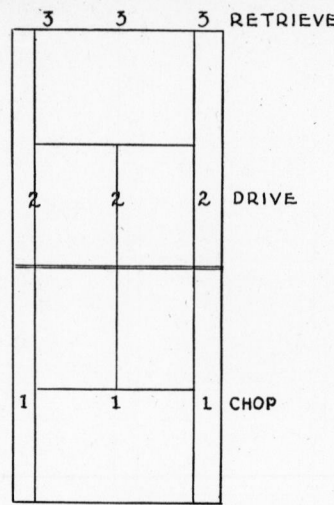

Fig. 158. Practicing the chop. Nine on one court: 1, chops; 2, drives ball to No. 1; 3, retrieves.

VIII. The Drop Shot

The same type of practice formation can be used to practice the drop shot.

IX. The Overhead Smash

This stroke is the same as the overhead service. Instead of tossing the ball herself, the player hits a ball which has been lifted into the air toward her.

1. Number twos practice this smash, number ones having thrown the ball well up for twos to hit.

2. Number ones lob the ball while the twos use the overhead smash in returning it.

3. Number threes change in for equal time in practice. (Fig. 159.)

Along with the practice of strokes taken up separately, the players must be given time to apply the strokes while playing in a game. The players must be encouraged to think for themselves. Stroke practice alone will not let them do this. Therefore, in each class period time must be given over to playing. Good form in strokes must be insisted upon at all times but not a set type of play to which all must conform. So long as a player is moving easily and has strength of stroke and accuracy, she may be said to have good form.

Many players having a foundation of good strokes are beaten because they fail to think. A player must have the "will to win" or she

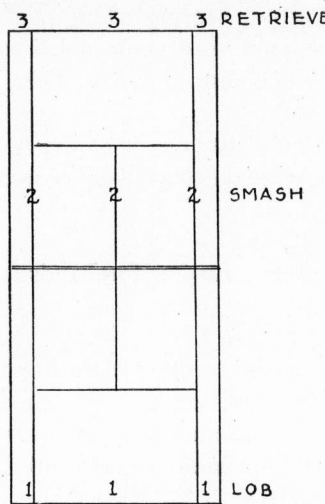

Fig. 159. Practicing the smash from a short lob: 1, lobs to No. 2; 2, overhead smash; 3, retrieves.

will find herself beaten by inferior players whose strokes are poor, but who have the power of concentration and have learned to think quickly and put their thoughts into action.

LESSON PLANS

The following is a suggested outline of lessons for:

I. Beginners

LESSON 1. Discuss importance of footwork. Give group exercises in moving. Rope jumping exercises. Running short slides sideward and forward. Discuss and demonstrate forehand grip and body movement. Practice.

LESSON 2. Review lesson 1. Add hitting forehands at backboard.

LESSON 3. Review 1 and 2. Discuss and demonstrate backhands. Practice.

LESSON 4. Practice hitting forehands and backhands at backboard.

LESSON 5. Continue forehand and backhand practice. Emphasize footwork. Keep rally going off backboard.

LESSON 6. Forehands and backhands over the net. First just driving balls without return. Then from throws by three's.

LESSON 7. Review lesson 6. Add rally.

LESSON 8. Review parts of 6 and 7 as needed.

LESSON 9. Rally taking balls forehand or backhand as they come.

Discuss scoring. Demonstrate scoring taking one court. Use forehand for serve. Have students score. Instructor makes corrections.

LESSON 10. Serve by demonstration first. Then have group practice at backboards or back stops.

LESSON 11. Review 9 and 10.

LESSON 12. Practice serve on court over the net. Combine serve and return practice.

LESSON 13. Review 12.

LESSON 14. Practice serve. Review forehands and backhands, rallying. Play.

LESSON 15. Play.

Many beginners will not be ready to learn to volley at this point. If not, the time is best spent devoting part of each period to *practice* on the serve, forehands and backhands, and the latter half of the period to playing the "three stroke" game. Lessons 16 through 20 could be based on this kind of practice.

LESSON 16. Demonstrate volley. Discuss its use. Practice volleys by three's using throw.

LESSON 17. Continue practicing volley from throws or drives.

LESSON 18. Individual review as needed.

LESSON 19. Individual review as needed.

LESSON 20. Individual review as needed.

During each lesson the instructor *must* give time to each individual separately, in order to correct mistakes before they become fixed habits and to give as much encouragement as possible.

II. The Intermediate Group

In teaching college classes in tennis, we have found that most of the players should be classified in what we call the intermediate group. As this group contains a wide range of ability, it seems best for teaching purposes to divide it into two groups, namely, *low intermediate* and *high intermediate*. The low intermediates are those who are just beyond the very beginners and who need some work on the beginners' level before going on. The high intermediate players are those who have played a weak sort of tennis with a limited variety of strokes and need considerable instruction in more strokes and practice before they can be called advanced.

The teacher must remember that at all times the student must *enjoy* playing. The learning should never become drudgery. Accomplishment gives one great satisfaction. Lessons should be planned so that the student gets the feeling of enjoyment and accomplishment. A good test of this is when at the end of a class period students want to stay on for more practice, or you find that they are playing extra hours outside of class. Encourage them to see as much good tennis as possible, as this is a great stimulus.

A possible outline of teaching for low intermediates:

LESSON 1. Review exercises to develop footwork—rope jumping, etc. Discuss forehand and backhand grips. Practice change from forehand to backhand. Practice hitting forehands by three's over the net.

LESSON 2. Review lesson 1 as needed. Practice forehands by three's with emphasis on moving before hitting the ball.

LESSON 3. Repeat discussion of backhands. Practice backhands by three's.

LESSON 4. Review 2 and 3. Practice mixing forehands and backhands. Start from the waiting position each time.

LESSON 5. Review parts of lessons 2, 3, 4 as needed.

LESSON 6. Discuss and practice the serve at backboards.

LESSON 7. Practice the serve over the net, first without the opponent returning the serve, then with return of service.

LESSON 8. Review scoring. Then have all play "three strokes" game.

LESSON 9. Repeat lesson 8.

LESSON 10. Practice the serve. Continue playing, trying for deep base line drives.

LESSON 11. Discuss and practice the volley.

LESSON 12. Practice the volley.

LESSON 13. Discuss singles tactics. Play, working for a forcing shot in order to go to the net and finish off the point with a volley.

LESSON 14. Review lesson 13.

LESSON 15. Review lesson 13.

LESSON 16. Review practice of strokes as needed.

LESSON 17. Repeat lesson 16.

LESSON 18. Discuss doubles. Play doubles.

LESSON 19. Play doubles.

LESSON 20. Play doubles.

A possible outline for high intermediates:

LESSON 1. Give exercises for footwork, including rope jumping. Have students choose opponents and play. Instructor goes to each court and makes necessary suggestions.

LESSON 2. Discuss general play with the entire group. Have them continue to play.

LESSON 3. Have them all rally, working for depth of drive. Practice the serve.

LESSON 4. Repeat lesson 3.

LESSON 5. Work on volleys the first half. Play the last half, trying for forcing shots.

LESSON 6. Repeat lesson 5.

LESSON 7. Discuss the lob. Practice the chop and short lobs.

LESSON 8. Repeat 5 and 7. Play the last half of the period, trying to use these two strokes at the right times.

LESSON 9. Continue playing.

LESSON 10. Continue playing.

LESSON 11. Discuss the drop shot. Practice the drop.

LESSON 12. Repeat lesson 11. Play the last half of the period.

LESSON 13. Discuss and play doubles.

LESSON 14. Play doubles.

LESSON 15. Play doubles.

LESSON 16. Play round robin doubles tournament of one set each within the group.

LESSON 17. Continue round robin.

LESSON 18. Continue round robin.

LESSON 19. Play singles round robin of one set.

LESSON 20. Play singles round robin of one set.

III. The Advanced Group

The advanced group can be a selected group. Tryouts can be held, and only those players accepted who have good footwork, rhythm, and power. They are generally found to need more playing time with emphasis on court tactics in both singles and doubles, and additional strokes to add variety to their game. They are found to have good forehand and backhand drives, fairly good serves, and possibly a "volley" they can count on.

A possible outline for teaching this group for one season would include:

LESSON 1. Have a discussion of tennis, emphasizing the importance of footwork. Spend five to ten minutes jumping rope. Have the players rally with each other watching stroking and footwork.

LESSON 2. The players choose opponents and play singles.

LESSON 3. Teach the volley to the group. Demonstrate and have students practice.

LESSON 4. Singles play with emphasis on getting to the net to volley.

LESSON 5. A discussion of singles play. Continue practice as needed.

LESSON 6. Demonstrate the chop, discussing its value. Practice the chop.

LESSON 7. Review practice of the chop. Play.

LESSON 8. Demonstrate the drop shot. Practice the chop and the drop shots.

LESSON 9. Play, using as much variety of strokes as possible.

LESSON 10. Discuss doubles play. Play doubles.

LESSON 11. Continue playing doubles.

LESSON 12. Demonstrate the overhead smash. Practice the smash.

LESSON 13. Review lesson 12. Doubles play.

LESSON 14. Review of strokes as needed by class individually.

LESSON 15. Continue the review of stroke practice. Play.

LESSON 16. Demonstrate and discuss the lob. Practice.

LESSON 17. Review lesson 10. Practice other strokes as needed.

LESSON 18. Practice or play as needed.

LESSONS 19 AND 20. Practice or play as needed.

It is most important that students should play outside the lesson period as much as possible. No one can learn to play tennis without continued practice. The above outline seems like a lot to teach a group, but the most that can be done for many students is to show them the different strokes. Those who *want* to learn will practice and apply the strokes they need to their game.

TACTICS

I. The Singles Game

The first thing which any tennis player must learn is that there are only two sections of the court in which to stay for any length of time: namely, the forecourt, well inside the service line, for an attacking game, and behind the base line for a defensive game. The ground in between is called "no man's land" and should be passed through as quickly as possible. If a player is caught in this "no man's land," her opponent will either drive deep beyond her so that she cannot get back for returns, or will drive the ball at her feet, which is an almost impossible shot to return. Therefore, learn in the beginning either to stay behind the base line or get well up to the net. When playing against a steady base line player, do not hesitate to go to the net—and keep going to the net.

(A) *The Serve.* The ideal serve, of course, is one which is hit so hard and is so well placed that your opponent cannot reach it. As this cannot always be done, you must at least place your serve so that your opponent is only able to hit back a weak return. This will enable the server to go up to the net and so be the attacker. The serve should be varied, from side to side, short and deep, and straight at the receiver, so that she is unable to anticipate it. If your opponent has a weak backhand, do not always play to it, or she will move to be in a position to make the return. To keep her in the back court, have the serve drop back as deep as possible. Try to make your opponent move to meet the ball. Have a change of pace as well as a change of direction. The main point in serving is to keep the opponent wondering where the ball is coming and to gain an attacking position for the server.

(B) *The Return of Service.* The receiver will want to place herself where she can get the ball back and place her return so that her opponent will have difficulty in returning it. The server momentarily is the attacker and what the receiver does with the ball determines whether or not the attacking position can be won by her. If the serve pulls the receiver well over to one side off the court, the server should come to the net for a volley. The receiver should hit the ball hard, straight down the side line, or if the server is well up to the net, on her serve, the receiver should lift a lob well over her head or pass her down either side line. If the server is slow in coming up, a drive right at her feet is an effective shot. If the service comes to the receiver's backhand in the left service court, a cross court drive on the return is a good one. These returns are good if the server comes to the net to volley. They are for the most part "passing shots." If the server insists on staying at the base line, the problem is not how to pass her, but how to vary your returns so that she not only must run from side to side but must come up. The shot to use in this case is a chop or drop shot, as this will break up a hard hitting-driving type of game on which a person who plays on the base line depends. Find out her weak points and play through her strength to them as much as possible and have a variety of shots for yourself which you can use and depend on.

(C) *General Positions during Rallies.* First of all remember to keep out of "no man's land." Then if you find yourself playing against a hard hitting-driving game from the back court, stand 4 or 5 feet *behind* and in the middle of the base line. If your opponent is not a hard hitter, stand a little *inside* the base line. Then be sure to move your weight forward into your drive and do not be caught moving backward. On your return either follow your drive directly to the net or get back quickly behind your base line. If you are a good volleyer, you should endeavor to get to the net, as points can be scored more quickly for you there than by prolonged base line rallies which in the end, particularly in a long even match, may simply tire you out. Another point to remember is that if your plan of attack is not working, be quick to change to another plan. Never play the kind of game your opponent likes. There are certain fundamentals a player must never lose sight of:

1. ALWAYS BE ON THE ALERT. Weight must be forward. Keep the heels off the ground. Always keep moving. Be in position to move *forward*. Don't be caught moving backward.

2. WATCH THE BALL. Follow it right *on to* the *middle of your racquet* and off the racquet. Also keep an eye on your opponent to see *where* she is on the court and the *type* of stroke she is using on her return to you.

3. ANTICIPATE. When watching good players you will note that they never seem to be moving. On further observation, you realize that they have anticipated the shot to them and are already in the proper position to make their return.

II. The Doubles Game

Today in doubles it is important to have speed and be able to *get to the net*. The doubles team which can get to the net first and has the ability to volley well is in a position to win more points than its opponents. The secret of good doubles play is to have good teamwork with your partner. It is important to give information to each other such as "mine," "yours," and "out." The partners should be equal in playing ability. A strong and weak combination will often be beaten by two players who are beneath them in general playing ability but have learned to play well together. Good singles players do not always make good doubles players, as doubles is a team game and the first principle is to play well *with* your partner. It is often true that to be a good doubles team the players must also be good friends. So, in choosing a doubles partner, it is a good plan to choose someone from whom you will receive encouragement and support rather than a person you know to be a better player, but one with whom you are uncongenial.

(A) *Position on the Court.* The best court formation is to keep as nearly parallel as possible. Either both players should be well up together or both should be back. In playing on a parallel line and when both are up, you must watch for returns which come right between you. It is a good idea to have an understanding between you as to which one is going to take these shots. If you are at the net, your opponents will try to pass you by sending a ball right between you, or one just inside the side lines, or they will put up a lob. For the passing strokes you must be alert, have good footwork and skill in volleying. For the lob you must both get back and have an understanding as to which one is to take it. Then if you can, both get to the net again. The Australian formation is a very successful one to use. This means that the receivers have one player at the net as well as the side which is serving. To avoid trouble for your partner, the return of serve must be out of reach of the opposing net player.

(B) *Service in Doubles.* The service in doubles is probably more important than the service in singles. If your service is weak and you cannot get to the net on it, your partner will have to come back with you, and your opponents in the meantime can come to the net and so gain the attacking position. A serve which is down the middle of the service court is a difficult one for the receivers to hit to the side lines and should be tried on the serve as often as possible. The server must remember that her job is to get to the net on her serve, or else she will put her side immediately on the defensive. In doubles the serve must be won by the server.

(C) *Receiving in Doubles.* One of your opponents is already at the net and should be able to handle any shot which comes to her. The exceptions are if she has been drawn to the center of the court, in which case a drive down her alley is a good return, or a well-placed lob over her head. The server is often the best one to attack. If she is slow in coming up to the net, a drive at her feet is a good one. If she comes in fast, a diagonal lob will often work out well for you and confuse your opponents. Another shot which will bother her is a slow angled drop shot.

Some important things to remember in doubles are:

1. Doubles is a *team game.*
2. Have a thorough understanding with your partner.
3. Always be in a parallel position with each other.
4. Both should be able to get to the net, but should also know when to get back to the base line.
5. The serve, volley, and overhead smash are of greatest importance.
6. Most points are made by the team which is at the net.
7. The lob is used in doubles to send your opponents away from the net.
8. Decide who is to get the center ball.
9. Give information to each other such as "mine," "yours," and "out."

USES OF TOURNAMENTS

I. Competition

In tennis many types and kinds of tournaments are of value. These are discussed elsewhere, but there is also opportunity here for class, school or college, and inter-house or dormitory tournaments. The number of tournaments depends upon length of season and number of courts available. Ideally, there should be some competition for groups on all levels of ability—particularly for intermediate as well as advanced groups. But this takes time, and the shortness of the season limits the number of tournaments it is possible to run off. At least an all-school tournament and class competition can be arranged.

II. Tennis Clubs

In some institutions there is a tennis club which has special hours for practice and special competition. These students can help coach less experienced players, give demonstrations, and help officiate and act as linesmen and ball boys in important matches.

It is a great stimulus to the sport to bring in some excellent players, amateur and professional, to show the students the best in the sport. Matches in the vicinity can also be brought to the attention of the students.

III. Play for Boys and Girls

Tennis, like badminton, is a very popular sport for boys and girls together, and courts should be made available for them. This as a rule needs no planning as it is a natural weekend sport. Students are, moreover, glad to have instruction to improve their game for playing with friends both at home and at school.

MATCH ADMINISTRATION

I. Setting up the Court for a Match

One of the chief problems in running off a tennis tournament is having enough able officials on hand. The United States Lawn Tennis Association holds clinics to train school and college students in umpiring and lining. This instruction has been received very enthusiastically by players and non-players alike. After the clinic the students are given practice in umpiring and lining and those who qualify are given rating cards and may be called upon for tournament matches.

There follows a diagram of a tennis court set up with the proper officials. (Fig. 160.)

(A) *Duties of the Umpire.*[1]

1. MUST HAVE ABSOLUTE KNOWLEDGE OF THE PLAYING RULES, TOURNAMENT REGULATIONS, AND THEIR CORRECT ENFORCEMENT.

[1] The material on officiating at a tennis match was obtained from Mr. Winslow Blanchard through an Umpires Clinic held at Smith College. Further material on officiating may be secured from The United States Lawn Tennis Association, 120 Broadway, New York City.

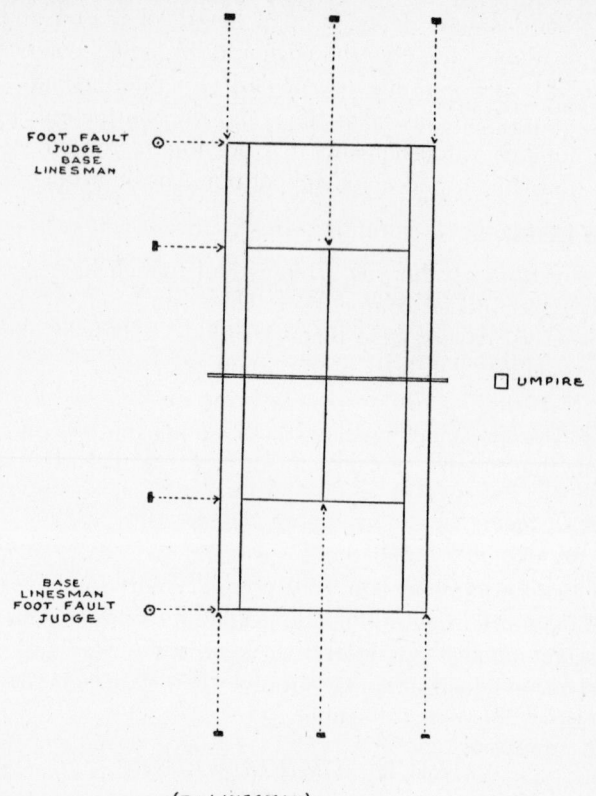

FOOT FAULT
JUDGE
BASE
LINESMAN

□ UMPIRE

BASE
LINESMAN
FOOT FAULT
JUDGE

(■ = LINESMAN)

Fig. 160. Diagram showing the position of linesmen, foot fault judge, and umpire in a doubles match.

2. BEFORE THE MATCH STARTS. Have score card and pencils. Write down names of players and know how to pronounce them. Measure height of net. Supervise players' toss for serve or court. See that other officials are in their places. When players have finished warming up, announce the match and start the play with "Linesmen ready? Play."

3. DURING THE MATCH.

(a) Keep entire attention on the match.

(b) After each point mark the score first—then announce it. Announce the score clearly and correctly.

(c) Repeat the decision of the linesman and foot fault judge, so the players and audience can hear.

(d) If the score has been given incorrectly, say "Correction" and give the right score.

(*e*) Call "Not up" if a player does not reach the ball on the first bounce.

(*f*) See that the gallery does not disturb the players. If it does, stop the play, and ask for the cooperation of the spectators. If necessary call a "let" and have the disturbed point played over.

(*g*) See that the players change courts at the end of odd games.

(*h*) In announcing the score, give the server's score first. *Announce advantage* by saying, "Advantage Miss Smith"—never say, "advantage striker or receiver." *Announce the game score* by saying, "Game Miss Smith; games are three to one, Miss White leading, first set." *Announce the set score* by saying, "Game and second set Miss Smith, 6–5; sets are one all." At the end of the match say, "Game, set, and match Miss Smith, score 2–6, 6–4, 6–4."

(B) *Duties of Linesman.*

1. Know that ball falling on any part of the line is good.

2. Only call "out" or "fault," *never* call "good."

3. Must sit *facing* the line she is to call. Must not leave without the umpire's permission or until another linesman has taken her place. During play must not smoke or move about. Should not catch or return balls for the players. This is the ball boy's job; if there are no ball boys let the players get their own balls.

4. Give decisions instantly, loudly, and decisively. On close decisions it is permissible to wait an instant. Never call "out" until the ball has struck the ground outside the court.

5. If the linesman does not see whether the ball is good or out, she should put her hands over her eyes as a signal to the umpire that she failed to see the play. The umpire makes the decision or calls on another linesman to do so. In case no one can decide, the umpire has the point replayed.

6. If a player is standing between a linesman and the line for which she is responsible, the linesman should stand so that she is able to make a decision on her line.

7. A linesman may change her decision if she is sure she has been wrong. The umpire must then decide whether or not a "let" shall be given.

(C) *Foot Fault Judge.*

1. A foot fault judge must know the foot fault ruling and when to enforce it. She should do this with a clear, definite voice.

2. The foot fault judge should sit directly opposite the base line and should not converse with the base linesman.

3. It is customary to warn a player first before penalizing her, although there is nothing in the rules requiring this procedure.

TENNIS TERMS

I. THE RACQUET

Racquet Face. The hitting surface.
Open Face. When the hitting surface is facing upward.
Closed Face. When the hitting surface is facing downward.
Flat Face. When the racquet frame is at right angles to the ground.
Handle of Racquet. The wooden shaft.
Throat of Racquet. The part between the head and the handle.
Head of Racquet. End farthest away from where racquet is held.

II. THE COURT

The Base Line. The back line at either end of the court.
Side Line. The line at either side of the court marking the outside edge of the playing surface.
Service Line. The line 21 feet from the net on either side which bounds the back of the service courts.
Center Service Line. The line which divides the service courts in half and separates the right and the left service courts.
The Alley. The space between the side lines used in doubles.
Net. Netting across middle of court—3 feet at the center.
Post. One of the metal or wooden uprights supporting the net.
Band. The strip of canvas at the top of the net.

III. THE GAME

Server. The player who serves.
Receiver. The player who receives the service.
Fault. A ball served which does not enter the proper service court, or is incorrectly served.
Ground Strokes. Strokes made after the ball has struck the ground, or playing surface.
Drive. A ground stroke, taken either on the forehand or backhand, in which the racquet is swung parallel to the ground.
To Volley. To make a return by hitting the ball before it has hit the ground, except when serving.
To Lob. To hit a ball high into the air, over the head of an opponent who has come to the net.
Smash (Overhead). A ball hit forward, and down, from the highest point possible over the head.
To Chop. To hit a ball from above, downward, so as to give back spin to the ball.
To Drop Shot. To hit the ball in such a way that it barely clears the top of the net and drops close to the net.
Let. A ball on the service which touches the net and falls into the proper service court. Any stroke which does not count and may be played over.

REFERENCES

Agutter, George: *Lessons in Tennis.* New York, A. S. Barnes & Co., 1939.
Anderson, Lou Eastwood: *Tennis for Women.* New York, A. S. Barnes & Co., 1926.
Browne, Mary K.: *Streamline Tennis.* New York, American Sports Publishing Co., 1940.
Bruce and Bruce: *Tennis Fundamentals and Timing.* New York, Prentice-Hall, Inc., 1940.
Budge, Donald: *Budge on Tennis.* New York, Prentice-Hall, Inc., 1939.

Budge, Lloyd: *Lawn Tennis.* London, Nicholas Kaye.
Connolly, Maureen: *Strong Tennis.* New York, A. S. Barnes & Co.
Cooke, Sarah Palfrey: *Winning Tennis.* Garden City, New York, Doubleday and Co., 1946.
Driver, Helen: *Tennis for Teachers and Tennis Fundamental Chart.* Forest Woods, Madison 4, Wisconsin.
Hillas, Marjorie, and Randle, Dorothy D.: *Tennis Organized.* New York, A. S. Barnes & Co., 1932.
Jacobs, Helen Hull: *Beyond the Game.* Philadelphia, J. B. Lippincott Co., 1936.
Jacobs, Helen Hull: *Modern Tennis.* New York, Bobbs-Merrill Co., 1933.
Jacobs, Helen Hull: *Tennis.* New York, A. S. Barnes & Co., 1941.
Kramer, Jack: *How to Win at Tennis.* New York, Ziff-Davis Publishing Co., 1949.
Noel, Susan: *Tennis Without Tears.* London, Hutchinson's Library of Sports.
Ollif, John: *Ollif on Tennis.* London, Eyre and Spottiswoode, 1949.
Ollif, John: *Romance of Wimbledon.* New York, Hutchinson and Co.
Patterson, Norman: *Lawn Tennis Courtcraft.* London, Adam and Charles Black.
Riggs, Bobby: *Tennis Is My Racket.* London, Stanley Paul and Co., Ltd.
Tennis-Badminton Guide. N.S.G.W.S., 1201 16th St. N.W., Washington, D. C.
Tilden, William T.: *Art of Lawn Tennis.* New York, Doran and Co., 1926.
Tilden, William T.: *Match Play and Spin of the Ball.* New York, American Lawn Tennis, Inc., 1924.
Wills, Helen: *Fifteen-Thirty.* New York, Charles Scribner's Sons, 1937.
World Tennis. Gardnar Mulloy, Box 3, Gracie Station, New York, N. Y. (Monthly magazine.)

Films

Fundamentals of Tennis: Donald Budge, Transfilm, Inc., 35 West 45th Street, New York.
Technique of Tennis: Lloyd Budge, Bell and Howell Co., 1801-1815 Larchmont Avenue, Chicago.

· Index ·